The Process of
Rural Transformation

Pergamon Policy Studies on Socio-Economic Development

Related Titles

PERGAMON
POLICY
STUDIES

ON SOCIO-ECONOMIC
DEVELOPMENT

The Process of Rural Transformation

Eastern Europe, Latin America and Australia

Edited by
Ivan Volgyes
Richard E. Lonsdale
William P. Avery

Comparative Rural Transformation Series

Pergamon Press

NEW YORK • OXFORD • TORONTO • SYDNEY • FRANKFURT • PARIS

Pergamon Press Offices:

U.S.A   Pergamon Press Inc., Maxwell House, Fairview Park, Elmsford, New York 10523, U.S.A.

U.K.   Pergamon Press Ltd., Headington Hill Hall, Oxford OX3 0BW, England

CANADA   Pergamon of Canada Ltd., 150 Consumers Road, Willowdale, Ontario M2J 1P9, Canada

AUSTRALIA   Pergamon Press (Aust) Pty. Ltd., P.O. Box 544, Potts Point, NSW 2011, Australia

FRANCE   Pergamon Press SARL, 24 rue des Ecoles, 75240 Paris, Cedex 05, France

FEDERAL REPUBLIC   Pergamon Press GmbH, 6242 Kronberg/Taunus,
OF GERMANY   Pferdstrasse 1, Federal Republic of Germany

Library of Congress Cataloging In Publication Data

Main entry under title:

The Process of rural transformation.

   (Pergamon policy studies)
   Bibliograpy: p.
   Includes index.
   1. Rural development—Europe, Eastern—
Addresses, essays, lectures. 2. Rural develop-
ment—Latin America—Addresses, essays, lectures.
3. Rural development—Australia—Addresses,
essays, lectures. 4. Europe, Eastern—Rural
conditions—Addresses, essays, lectures. 5. Latin
America—Rural conditions—Addresses, essays,
lectures. 6. Australia—Rural conditions—
Addresses, essays, lectures. I. Volgyes, Ivan,
1936-   II. Lonsdale, Richard E.
III. Avery, William, 1942-
HD1917.P74 1979   330.9'173'4   79-10190
ISBN 0-08-023110-1

Printed in the United States of America

Contents

Preface

This volume is the third in the Pergamon Series on Comparative Rural Transformation and in a sense the most intriguing to date. Unlike the previous two which were concerned with the roots of rural transformation and were largely restricted to the Eastern European region, this third volume attempts to compare the experiences of three quite diverse geographical regions of the world, Eastern Europe, Latin America and Australia.

The choice of these areas for comparative and contrastive purposes is the result of the fortuitous combination of interests on the part of the editors, each of whom has been fascinated for many years by the multiplicity of processes that have affected the rural scene in their own geographical specializations. These interests in the changes affecting the countryside came to light during 1975-1976 as the editors began to pool their resources in studying the process we have labeled "comparative rural transformation." Aided by a generous two-year grant from the Division of International Education of the United States Office of Education, Department of Health, Education and Welfare, a graduate program on comparative rural transformation was established during the academic year 1976-1977 at the University of Nebraska-Lincoln, under the leadership of the three editors.

The core of the program was a seminar in which 36 graduate and advanced undergraduate students grappled with the concepts and problems of comparing the process of rural transformation. Arguments over vocabulary and definitions tended originally to obscure the larger picture of how in each geographical area the processes of transformation had altered the countryside. Rates of change that applied to one area were often regarded as inapplicable to the other, methods and processes that had worked in one culture area were found inadequate or inapplicable in others, and even the bases of philosophies that affect the process of rural change were viewed with suspicion as problematical in their application in other cultures. And yet, throughout the two years of the seminar, there appeared certain basic structures and processes that broadly characterize the field of comparative rural transformation.

These structures and processes form the basis of this volume. In shortened form, the authors suggest that the countryside is altered by purposive changes as a result of policies that have their origin largely in the urban centers. The changes affect the geographical, economic, and sociopolitical spheres; in combination, these changes then alter the life and processes of existence in the countryside. Our conviction from these studies, however, should not be viewed as implying that the people of the countryside do not play a role in the transformation process. Rather, we believe that they play a very significant role and are the crucial variable according to which successes and failures of these processes can be measured. At the same time, all our studies seem to indicate that the rural people are not the originators of the change, nor are they definers of the direction the change may take. They set the limits with their sporadic jaqueries, their stubborn reluctance, or their willingness to support the policies; but the policies deciding their future generally originate elsewhere.

The guest speakers invited to address our students in the first year of the seminar were as follows:

George W. Hoffman,
   University of Texas-Austin
Jan F. Triska,
   Stanford University
Tom L. McKnight,
   University of California-Los Angeles
John Duncan Powell,
   Tufts University
Gregory Grossman,
   University of California-Berkeley
William C. Thiesenhusen,
   University of Wisconsin-Madison
Henry A. Landsberger,
   University of North Carolina-Chapel Hill
Joel Martin Halpern,
   University of Massachusetts-Amherst
Robert H. T. Smith,
   University of British Columbia
Alan Reed,
   University of New Mexico

John P. Augelli,
        University of Kansas
John Greenway,
        University of Colorado

These scholars have been the mainstays of our experience, our
resource persons when it comes to dealing with specific areas
of change. Their dedication, assistance, support and intellectual contributions were of enormous benefit to us and to our
students. The volume that follows is based upon their contributions to our seminars and edited for the purposes of this
volume. Papers of two of the students of the seminar, Jean
Williams Ferrill and Nancy Volgyes, are also included in this
volume.
        This volume is organized into five parts. In the intro-
ductory part we attempt to provide the reader with a comprehensive overview of comparative rural transformation, setting
its limits and boundaries as a field of study. The second part
examines broadly the interrelations of space with the process
of change. The third part deals extensively with the economic
aspects of rural transformation, while the fourth part of the
volume examines the alteration in political and social patterns
as the process of transformation affects the rural sphere.
Finally, we attempt to pull together in the last part of the
book the diverse processes and draw some very tentative
conclusions that can hopefully be the bases of further
explorations by us and by other scholars interested in the
field.
        Our search for a better understanding of the problems of
rural transformation has extended beyond the Fall 1976
seminar. Two conferences have been held in Lincoln,
Nebraska, devoted to the topic of rural transformation. The
Fall 1977 seminar theme was "Planning for Rural Change: The
Comparative Experiences of Eastern Europe, Latin America,
and Australia." Further volumes based on this seminar and on
the papers presented at the April 1978 meeting held in Lincoln
are being planned.

I
Introduction

1 Rural Transformation: A Field for Comparative Study
Ivan Volgyes

INTRODUCTION

The modernization of any rural society is associated with a process of change that alters the traditional bases of the polity and tranforms that society.(1)   A more industrial basis of operation replaces the prevalent agrarian mode of production, and rural values are transformed into urban, cosmopolitan ones.   With the transformation, rural and, in some instances, predominantly "backward," "underdeveloped" members of the peasant society, adopt new, less traditional and hence, more open values toward life and society.   The process of modernization is common to the rural sector in every country, although its speed and direction is influenced by many variables.(2)

The concept of modernization, however, is far too broad to deal with adequately on a precise basis.   For that reason, generally speaking, scholars have been likely to concentrate their efforts on discussing segments of the process dealing with political, geographic, economic, social, and other aspects of modernization.(3)   To date, very few social scientists have attempted to deal with one aspect of the interrelated process of change that is a part and parcel of modernization, namely, with the component loosely defined as comparative rural transformation.

It is, perhaps, not surprising that the whole topic of rural transformation has been given relatively scant attention. After all, the indicators of modernity have always been associated with urban-oriented activities, such as urbanization, industrialization, the changing role of women, and the drop in birthrate.(4)   The changes in the countryside that have occurred either concomitantly or parallel with the changes that

were taking place in the cities have always been regarded as
contributing to the general level of development, but were
never really examined in a comprehensive manner as sui
generis processes. The purpose of this chapter is to delineate
the examination of the process of change that has taken place
in the rural sphere during the process of modernization.
Simply defined, the study of rural transformation is the examination of the changes that take place in all aspects of rural
life as the processes of modernization affect the entire polity.
Such changes as the development of better production
techniques, the decreasing importance of agrarian labor in
food production, the new attitudes among traditionally
rural populations, the changes in social regulations, the
location of new rural centers, the process of rural/small-town
industrialization, and a multitude of other subject matters
easily fall into this field.

RURALITY DEFINED

We should emphasize that the changes that take place in the
process of transformation take place in the rural environment
and affect rural people. Thus the delineation of the concept
of rurality is essential to the understanding of this field of
study. The constituent parts of the concept of rurality, of
course, are much harder to define. Generally, however,
rurality is characterized by four more or less clearly identifiable components, namely: 1) the existence of a landscape or
habitat commonly recognized by its visual elements as
"country" or "countryside"; 2) the presence of a relatively low
population density; 3) the predominance of labor-intensive,
usually agricultural, occupations; and 4) the possession of
traditional attitudes and a life-style easily identified as
"country" in character. The process of rural transformation
refers to changes that are taking place in any one of these
four components or in all of them simultaneously.
     Rural people are of a great variety. The peasants of
Europe, the inquilinos of Latin America, the farmers and
ranchers and rural community dwellers of North America and
Australia, the collective farmers of China and the landless
agricultural laborers of many lands are all parts of the world's
"rural living space." This is not the place to debate the
nature of peasants or landless laborers; this task has been
accomplished elsewhere by greater authorities than the present
author. What is common, however, to all the rural populations
is that they are almost always distinct and separated
from "urban" or "city-oriented" fellow citizens. The rural
populations of many lands have been regarded by historians as
backward and separate from a historical process that has been

viewed from the pro-urban bias of historians, politicians or
social scientists. Their rurality may have had advantages that
they perceived for themselves, but that advantage was rarely
perceived except by the few - Owens, Tolstoy or the idealistic
communally oriented hippies of the United States in the 1960s.
     Rural environments include the multitude of villages and
small towns which serve largely rural areas. It is difficult to
quantify the distinction between an urban place and a rural
small town and to do this would only confuse the issue. In
Australia, all places outside the larger cities are considered
"country" areas, even though they contain towns with
populations up to 25,000 or more people. In the United
States, the term "nonmetropolitan" serves rather well to
delineate those regions largely dependent on primary economic
activities, together with the smaller towns directly associated
with these activities.
     In addition to being viewed by others and by themselves
as "rural," their traditional occupational structure also defined
them in the same nonurban context. Until quite recently,
rural occupations were regarded almost solely as those
connected with agriculture. While it is true that there have
always been public officials, priests, teachers, some entre-
preneurs and landlords who lived in rural localities, rural
occupations were, by and large, agrarian occupations
connected with the growing, tilling, and harvesting of the
land. Even in the most modern farms, whether collective or
private, the main occupation has been connected with agrarian
activities. "Rurality," therefore, has been practically
synonymous with "agrarian" for most specialists. More
recently, with the expansion of recreation and tourism in rural
areas, the decentralization of industries, and the expansion of
service activities associated with the development of the
commercial economy, we have noticed a more pronounced
diversification of activities and a greater introduction of
nonagrarian tasks into the rural sphere. Although this
process has been ongoing in some localities for several
centuries through the utilization of cottage industries, its
general extension to the rural sphere has been a relatively
recent development.
     Rural life-styles and rural attitudes are closely bound to-
gether. Once again, they exist in contradistinction to urban
life-styles and urban attitudes. The prevalence in the rural
areas of many societies of one-story, single-family, or
communal dwellings located near the fields, the lack of comfort
and the lack of modern urban conveniences, the lack of
adequate transportation and communication networks, the lack
of high-quality educational and hygienic services are all parts
of the rurality of life. The exclusion of the rural population
from adequate participation and hence from an adequate share
of decision making is also noticeable in the rural sphere of

most societies. On the other hand, the positive benefits, tight kinship bonds, the close-knit communities, the communal activities of the rural society, the creation of a rural culture with its own distinctive specificities - special, separate designs in folk art, special dialects, etc. - must also be viewed as part and parcel of the concept of rural life-styles.

Out of these relationships there have developed attitudes that are rural in character. These attitudes have, of course, been characterized by the various analysts throughout the ages as distrustful and cunning, backward or nonmodern, "anticity" and "antiauthority," individualistic and conservative, tending to occasional jacqueries and hence nonstable. What is important, however, is that the rural attitudes of the population must not be viewed from the standpoint of condescending urban metropolitan observers alone. Rather, rural attitudes can only be viewed as important and deter-mining parts of the attitudes of the entire society. As the allocation of values becomes more favorable toward the rural localities, the attitudes of the people living in these localities also change drastically.

Consequently, what distinguishes the field of rural transformation from many other areas of the social sciences is primarily the fact that rural transformation is always concerned primarily with purposive man-made results in society. Thus, for example, climatic considerations, natural resources availabilities, or locational factors affect this field of study only insofar as they contribute to or condition the general process of rural change utilized by purposive action.

THE STUDY OF COMPARATIVE RURAL
TRANSFORMATION PROCESSES

Rural transformation is not a unique phenomenon restricted to certain cultures or civilizations. It takes place in practically every society where modernization occurs. In general, rural transformation on a global basis results in the modernization of the rural institutions, rural economy, and rural culture where traditional values are replaced with newer, more modern values.(5) Because of the complex nature of this process, however, such studies as have been conducted to date have largely neglected to study the commonalities of this transforma-tion on an international and comparative basis. Consequently, the aim of studying comparative aspects of rural transformation is to search for common themes of development. This study attempts to identify the similarities and dissimilarities of the process in search of common goals of development and common strategies created in order to solve problems peculiar to this process.(6)

Clearly, the concept of comparative rural transformation is incredibly broad, and it is this mandatory breadth that poses an immediate problem and challenge for researchers interested in this field. The fact remains that the process of rural transformation can only be studied on an interdisciplinary, international, and intercultural basis.(7) Let us illustrate this point. It is well known, for example, that population trends affect the socioeconomic development of the rural community. An increasingly older population that fails to adequately replenish its agrarian stock cannot meet the ever-increasing labor demands of a rapidly developing industrial society. Hence, the changes in the cultural values of agrarian populations that will result in decreasing population growth are of concern to cultural anthropologists, economic demographers, geographers, and ultimately to industrial planners as well. Similarly, "traditional" peasant reluctance to work on collective farms is of concern to economists, political scientists, and social psychologists alike. While no one can claim expertise in all these subjects, it is important to bring together all those individuals in the various disciplines who are concerned with the divergent aspects of this transformation process.

Needless to say, the process of comparative rural transformation cannot be adequately studied without taking into account the international nature of this process.(8) Such aspects as the commonalities between similar remnants of various feudal systems in Latin America and Eastern Europe and the international politics affecting the value of scarce food crops can only be studied on an international basis.(9) To be sure, one can learn a great deal from individual case studies such as the changes in the social and cultural values of a small Hungarian, Yugoslav, or Italian village.(10) Nonetheless, the most significant elements that our field of study should consider are the international bases of the process.

We cannot regard the field of comparative rural transformation as open to scientific inquiry if we neglect the intercultural nature of this discipline. After all, it is precisely the various culturally based attitudes that affect productive relations, social, economic or cultural value changes.(11) The attitude of a peasant toward the ownership of land is widely divergent from one culture to the next, as is the attitude of the rural society toward many similar subjects. For all these reasons, then, comparative rural transformation must be studied from an interdisciplinary, international and intercultural perspective.

8 THE PROCESS OF RURAL TRANSFORMATION

THE DELINEATION OF THE FIELD

As mentioned earlier, the most difficult task facing scholars involved in this field is the very breadth of the subject. Prior to undertaking our study, it is mandatory that we attempt to delineate the various facets of the field. Accordingly, and by no means can we say exhaustively, the process of rural transformation can be studied from six major perspectives. These six perspectives are: 1) historical descriptive studies; 2) analytical-prescriptive studies; 3) disciplinary studies; 4) regional studies; 5) ideologically oriented studies; and 6) subject matter studies.

The aim of descriptive studies is to describe historical processes in search of common patterns.(12) Thus, studies falling in this category may deal with the changes of feudal relationships among the peasantry in Latin America or Eastern Europe,(13) with the effect of introduction of the collective farm system in the Soviet Union, or with the manner in which individual rural localities have become suburban bedroom communities.(14) In each of these studies the importance of the research lies in the ability of the author to discern and describe the manner in which the process of modernization has brought historical changes to the life of a rural community.(15)

Prescriptive studies, on the other hand, attempt to prescribe special models of development. Their aim is to advocate certain methods, processes or models of development for the rural communities. Whether they are suggestive of the establishment of planned or unplanned, coercive or voluntary strategies of change, such studies generally tend to identify global values and processes and take a position for the adoption or rejection of certain models of rural development.(16) Analytical or prescriptive studies, by and large, are concerned with cost-benefit analysis, processes occurring in the rural sector as the modernization process begins to take hold. In this area there is an abundant collection of studies, often dealing with the rural development of one nation, but sometimes comparing development schemes and suggesting common models of change as well.

The process of rural transformation may be studied from a purely historical perspective. Whether analogical or chronological, such studies, as for example Cyril E. Black's The Dynamics of Modernization, give us excellent records of the process of change.(17) Historians tend to take segments of the process both by giving a broad sweep of the process and by examining the minutiae of certain past developments. An economic historian, E. A. J. Johnson, for example, has contributed an outstanding work on the spatial evolution of rural landscapes.(18)

Economists tend to view their area of rural transformation largely from the perspective of economic development. Ranging from such early studies as Frederic List's The Rational System of Political Economy,(19) to such modern economic analyses as W. W. Rostow's Stages of Economic Growth, (20) economists have attempted to study the process of rural transformation largely from the perspective of the contribution of the rural sector to the general process of modernization. The economists have been most clearly responsible for providing us with some extremely detailed analyses of economic changes such as the effect of various types of land ownership or production techniques. They attempt to analyze the effects of international trade or aid and offer us highly analytical studies on the specific effects of certain measures of economic development.

Demographers enjoy the uncommon advantage among social scientists of being able to deal with reasonably reliable, solid data bases that are the results of relatively bias-free demographic indicators.(21) Demographic studies of rural transformation, thus far, have been responsible for the identification of population growth and decrease trends pointing to the expected results of existing policies. Thus, for example, the projection of Hungarian demographers that indicated that the rural population of Hungary by the year 1990 would not be adequate to insure the population an abundant supply of foodstuffs was an important contribution to the adoption of pronatalist policies by the Hungarian government in the 1960s and 1970s.(22)

Geographers have contributed to the study of rural transformation through their concern with locational and spatial problems. Of note have been their spatial analyses of settlement systems, ranging from Christaller's classic work on central place theory,(23) to Hudson's modern theoretical work on rural settlements.(24) Other areas of interest to geographers have been regional development, rural industrialization, decentralization of people and industry, spatial diffusion and adaptation innovation(25) and the character of rural land use patterns.(26)

Sociologists have made immense contributions to the field of comparative rural transformation by undertaking the measurement of social changes that accompany this process. Rural sociology, of course, has been a far more important and accepted field of study for a considerably longer period of time than any of the other fields discussed heretofore. Starting in the 1930s, through the work of such giants as Pitrim Sorokin, sociologists have consistently dealt with the changes that affected rural society.(27) They have dealt with the effects of the introduction of new modern housing structures, the decreasing importance of the traditional family,(28) the concept of peasant workers and worker peasants, the structure of commuting or migrant workers' families, and a broad array of traditional subjects.(29)

Sociological analyses, of course, could hardly be distinguished from the tasks undertaken by such cultural anthropologists as Joel Halpern or Tamas Hofer.(30)   Detailing, through exhaustive case studies, the lives of small peasant communities, the cultural anthropologists have followed the same path, by and large, as was followed by the sociologists. But, unlike the sociologists, cultural anthropologists generally tended to study smaller communities; instead of generalizations on a broad scale, they tended to study the perseverance, survival and alteration of folk customs, mores, structures and traditions in the "little community."(31)

Specialists in literature also contributed to the understanding of the transformation of rural society.(32)   The most outstanding studies of the traditional society and the changes that took place in them frequently have been the contributions of great writers or poets, such as the Polish writer W. Reymont, whose work The Peasants must remain a part of the obligatory reading of any specialist on rural transformation.(33)   Similar works abound and are especially important in Eastern Europe, where the various regimes of a region rarely tolerated social science research but allowed the undertaking of literary, sociological reporting.(34)

Finally, the field of political science also began to contribute to the study of the rural transformation sphere.   Using such diverse bases as the study of community structures and local decision making in Eastern Europe and the study of the political ramifications of land reforms in Latin America, political scientists have attempted to analyze the political implications of rural change.(35)   They concentrated their efforts after a halting beginning on both the perspective of policy output - the development, administration and effects of public policies - and the process of affecting input - the attitudes, behavior and value change of the rural population - as part of the ongoing research in political science.(36)

Rural transformation, as a field of study, can also be examined from the perspective of area studies or regional studies specialization.(37)   Such studies attempt to understand the process of rural transformation from the perspective of the area studies scholar, who identified certain common regional cultures and attempted to study social, cultural, or geographic regions for perceived similarities.(38)   Needless to say, within this field, arguments about the meaning of "regions" and the meaning of "area" continue.   The bases of regional divisions are admittedly very loose. One may debate about the limit and extent of a region, quarrel with the classification utilized by one researcher versus another.   What is significant, however, is that certain commonalities can be identified and that these commonalities do provide us with a basis for area studies.

Characteristically, some broad regions can be delineated simply. Thus, we can identify the United States and Canada, Western Europe, Eastern Europe, the Soviet Union, China and Southeast Asia, Australia and New Zealand, northern Africa, sub-Saharan Africa and Latin America as broad areas where the process of rural transformation does take place in a relatively similar, comparable manner. Such regional delineation provides us with a "broad-brush" view only. In such regional studies, the search for commonalities far exceeds the need for local specificity. In the particular element of regional basis for the study of rural transformation, the differences in the pattern of development are subsumed by the similarities of the process of change.(39)

While not intending to criticize those scholars who are interested in pursuing the process of rural transformation on a regional basis, we would be remiss in our task if we did not point out that regional studies frequently are broken down into even smaller microscopic units. Thus, for example, a specialist who examines Eastern Europe, sooner or later must realize the enormity of this task and the great differences that exist between the rural transformation process in East Germany or Yugoslavia. By attempting to study a subregion, a regional scholar will look for similarities and may attempt to compare and contrast two Eastern European states where the system of land tenure is essentially the same - for example, East Germany, with its highly efficient and developed agriculture, and Romania, with the relative backwardness that characterizes its agrarian sphere. Or, he may study the similarities and differences between Poland and Yugoslavia, where the similarities of the land tenure system are obvious, but where the results of benefits accruing to the state are vastly different.(40)

And yet, a regional specialist will also be compelled to break down still further his unit of analysis. He may focus on just one of the countries involved and choose to study, let us say, Yugoslavia alone. But here, too, the scholar will be forced to conclude that he cannot adequately accomplish this task. After all, he would have to generalize concerning highly backward, practically illiterate rural communities in Macedonia and compare the rural transformation process there with the changes that take place in rural Slovenia, where the heads of the families work in the factories of Stuttgart and the women are engaged primarily in local cottage industries. Under such circumstances and handicaps, regional specialists must expect to identify mostly major areas of developmental strategies and suggest how certain patterns may or may not be applicable to the region as a whole.

Needless to say, the study of rural transformation can also be analyzed from the perspective of ideological biases. After all, ideology offers a model, a guide for action and attempts to prescribe certain goals and directions in which the process of change must proceed.(41) Whether such ideology favors speedy and coercive change in productive relations or encourages, through economic incentives, quantitative, voluntary and slow changes in the land tenure system, of course, depends largely on the ruling class, on the degree of acceptance or nonacceptance of the prevailing system of rule by the polity as a whole.(42) Generally speaking, there seem to be three basic models of rural transformation from the perspective of ideology. While there are great variations within each of these categories, generally we can identify the following models: 1) Western; 2) Asiatic; and 3) Marxist.

The Western model is characterized by the attitude that rural society will also become modernized and that the process of rural transformation will be dictated by the push and pull, supply and demand requirements of increasing modernization. This model allows a large amount of free play for economic and social forces of the market and its bias lies in the differentiated benefits that accrue from industrial urban structures.

The Asiatic model suggests a great deal of governmental interference in the life of the rural society.(43) This interference may be accomplished by a determined ruling minority in its own interest or by a semirevolutionary government that interferes in the lives of the people in the interest of a higher ideology.(44) In each case, however, forces of supply and demand are important only insofar as they affect the goals of the minority and little attention is paid to the opinions or intrinsic needs of the peasant society.

The Marxist model proceeds from the importance of the industrial sector and from the supremacy of the proletariat.(45) To Marx and his orthodox followers, rural transformation essentially meant the abolition of the peasantry as a class and the transformation of agriculture into miniature industrial units.(46) The Marxist bias against the peasantry and the strong pro-industrial bias toward modernization cum urbanization has, of course, resulted in the collectivized agriculture of many communist states.

Once again, however, we must emphasize that there are no pure models. Even in the "free market" United States, the government engages in the deliberate manipulation of rural life through such actions as the Rural Electrification Administration of the 1930s, the agricultural commodities price support system, or through the various hydroelectric projects. The lack of purity, however, and the greatest amount of "mixture" can be demonstrated best in the Marxist bias toward rural transformation. Thus, for example, we have witnessed such varieties of policies within the Soviet practice alone as the policies of War Communism (1917-1921), the New Economic Policy (1921-1929), the collectivization policy (1929 to date), and the abortive attempts at the creation of agro-gorods under

Khrushchev. Moreover, we have witnessed inordinately different policies toward rural transformation between the policies of Mao on the one hand, and the policies of Kadar, Gomulka and Gierek and Tito on the other. In spite of these variations, however, once again, the goal orientation, some of the methods and some of the processes are similar enough so that the study of rural transformation in communist states can and should be studied from comparative perspectives.

Finally, let us not be remiss in identifying perhaps one of the most significant bases from which comparative rural transformation can be studied, namely from the perspective of subject matter orientation. The basis of these studies lies in the topics the authors select to research. Hence, some specialists may study cross-national population trends, cross-cultural relationships to land and land tenure, the similarities in controlling the process of change, the general phenomenon of peasant urbanites or the general rise in education and hygiene levels that seem to be the concomitant of the extension of communication brought about by the rural transformation process.(47) Such specialized studies, dealing with similarities of subject matter, are of enormous interest in identifying common denominators and indices of change.

It is safe to conclude that the study of comparative rural transformation can be attacked from various perspectives but nonetheless, from whatever aspect these studies are carried out on the macrolevel, they are all aimed at studying the general process of rural transformation. The bases of similarity lie in our attempts to discern common patterns of rural change. As the development and modernization of society continues with ever-increasing fervor and speed, the study of comparative rural transformation can help in determining those policies and processes that are beneficial or harmful to the existence of rural life and to the quality of life existing in the rural environment.

NOTES

(1) D. Lerner, The Passing of Traditional Society (Glencoe, Ill.: Free Press, 1958), pp. 6-7.
(2) For a cogent statement on the varieties, the speed, and the direction of the modernization process, see Barrington Moore, Jr., Social Origins of Dictatorship and Democracy (Boston: Beacon Press, 1966), pp. 472-75. For the best definitions of modernity, see Alex Inkeles and David H. Smith, Becoming Modern (Cambridge, Mass.: Harvard University Press, 1974).
(3) Max F. Millikan and David Hapgood, No Easy Harvest (Boston: Little, Brown, 1967).

(4)   Albert O. Hirschman, The Strategy of Economic Development (New Haven, Conn.: Yale University Press, 1959); Myron Weiner, Modernization: The Dynamics of Growth (New York: Basic Books, 1966).

(5)   G. M. Foster, Traditional Cultures and the Impact of Technological Change (New York: Harper and Row, 1962).

(6)   For a nice statement on the search for common goals see Robert Redfield, The Village that Chose Progress (Chicago: University of Chicago Press, 1950).

(7)   Several studies have attempted to accomplish, at least partially, these tasks. For the most successful ones, see V. Erlich, Family in Transition (Princeton, N.J.: Princeton University Press, 1966); J. M. Potter, M. N. Diaz, and G. M. Foster, eds., Peasant Society (Boston: Little, Brown, 1967); J. G. Prestiany, ed., Honor and Shame: The Values of Mediterranean Society (London: Weidenfeld and Nikolson, 1965); and Robert Redfield, The Primitive World and Its Transformation (Ithaca, N.Y.: Cornell University Press, 1953).

(8)   Charles W. Anderson, Fred R. von der Mehden, and Crawford Young, Issues of Political Development (Englewood Cliffs, N.J.: Prentice-Hall, 1967), pp. 220-37.

(9)   Cristobal Kay, "Comparative Development of the European Manorial System and the Latin American Hacienda System," Journal of Peasant Studies 2 (1974-75): 69-98.

(10) Tamas Hofer and Edit Fel, Proper Peasants (Chicago: Aldine, 1969); Joel M. Halpern, A Serbian Village (New York: Columbia University Press, 1958); and E. C. Banfield, The Moral Basis of a Backward Society (Chicago: Free Press, 1958). Other such microlevel studies are: G. M. Foster, "The Dyadic Contract: A Model for the Social Structure of a Mexican Peasant Village," American Anthropologist 63 (1961): 1173-92; Margaret Mead, The Changing Culture of an Indian Tribe (New York: Columbia University Press, 1932); L. W. Moss and S. C. Capponari, "Patterns of Kinship, Comparaggio and Community in a South Italian Village," Anthropological Quarterly 33, (1960): 24-32; and Zdenek Salzmann and Vladimir Scheufler, Komarov (New York: Holt, Rinehart, and Winston, 1974).

(11) E. R. Wolf, The Peasants (Englewood Cliffs, N.J.: Prentice-Hall, 1966); and E. Goffman, The Presentation of Self in Everyday Life (New York: Doubleday, 1959).

(12) G. Childe, What Happened in History (Baltimore: Penguin Books, 1964).

(13) Kay, "Comparative Development."

(14) Maurice Hindus, The Kremlin's Human Dilemma (New York: Doubleday, 1967), especially pp. 113-95.

(15) Cyril E. Black, The Dynamics of Modernization (New
      York: Harper and Row, 1966); and S. H. Franklin,
      The European Peasantry: The Final Phase   (London:
      Methuen, 1969); and Childe, What Happened in History.
(16) See, for example, R. Dahl and C. E. Lindblohm,
      Politics, Economics and Welfare (New York: Harper and
      Row, 1953); or Lucian W. Pye, Aspects of Political Devel-
      opment (Boston: Little, Brown, 1966) among the many
      similar volumes.
(17) For additional examples of the process of change, see F.
      Dvornik's, The Slavs (Boston: American Academy of Arts
      and Sciences, 1966); Joel M. Halpern and M. D.
      Anderson, "The Zadruga," in Proceedings of the First
      International Balkan Conference, Sofia, 1966); Eric
      Kerridge, Agrarian Problems in the 16th Century
      and After (New York: Allen and Unwin, 1969); and Marc
      Bloch, Feudal Society, 2 vols. (Chicago: University of
      Chicago Press, 1961).
(18) E. A. J. Johnson, The Organization of Space in Devel-
      oping Countries (Cambridge, Mass.: Harvard University
      Press, 1970).
(19) Frederic List, The Rational System of Political Economy
      (Philadelphia: C. A. Matile, 1856).
(20) W. W. Rostow, Stages of Economic Growth (Cambridge:
      Cambridge University Press, 1961).
(21) Of course, we do not mean to imply that official statis-
      tics concerning demographic data are the most reliable
      sources for researchers. Indeed, most underdeveloped
      nations' statistical analyses suffer from lack of adequate
      sampling, reporting, and collection techniques and they
      are frequently used for the delivery of highly inflated
      figures intended to serve political goals. The demo-
      graphic figures published by a government, however, are
      less likely to be inflated than other figures dealing with,
      let us say, economic development.
(22) For an English-language source, see Projection of the
      Hungarian Population, 1966-2001 (Budapest: Statisztikai
      Kiado, 1965).
(23) Walter Christaller, Central Places in Southern Germany,
      trans. C. W. Baskin (Englewood Cliffs, N.J.: Prentice-
      Hall, 1966).
(24) John C. Hudson, "A Location Theory for Rural
      Settlement," Annals, Association of American Geographers
      59 (June 1969): 365-81.
(25) Julian Wolpert, "The Decision Process In Spatial
      Context," Annals, Association of American Geographers 54
      (December 1964): 537-58.
(26) Michael Chisholm, Rural Settlement and Land Use (Chi-
      cago: Aldine, 1970).

(27)   Pitrim A. Sorokin, C. C. Zimmerman, and C. J. Galpin, A Systematic Source Book in Rural Sociology (Minneapolis: University of Minnesota Press, 1931).

(28)   J. H. Jensen, "The Changing Balkan Family," National Archives of Ethnography, 1968, pp. 20-48, for example, deals with the alteration of traditional family structures under the impact of modernization. For similar studies, see, V. Erlich, Family in Transition; P. E. Mosley, "Adaptation for Survival: The Varzic Zadruga," Slavonic and East European Review 21 (1943): 147-73; and Robert Redfield, The Little Community (Chicago: University of Chicago Press, 1956).

(29)   Andrei Simic, The Peasant Urbanites (New York: Seminar Press, 1973); F. Bonilla, "Rio's favelas: The Rural Slum within a City," in W. Mangin, ed., Peasants in Cities (Boston: Houghton Mifflin, 1970); O. Buric, "Rural Migrants in Urban Family Life" (Paper presented at the Second World Congress on Rural Sociology" Amsterdam, 1968); D. Butterworth, and "A Study of the Urbanization Process among Mixtec Migrants from Tilaltongo to Mexico City," America Indigena 22 (1962): 257-74.

(30)   See Halpern, A Serbian Village, The Changing Village Community, and The Zadruga, as fine examples of cultural anthropological research as Hofer and Fel, Proper Peasants.

(31)   R. T. Anderson, Traditional Europe: A Study in Anthropology and History (Belmont, Cal.: Wadsworth, 1971); L. Baric, "Levels of Change in Yugoslav Kinship," in M. Freedman, ed., Social Organization (London: Cass & Co., 1967); Marriot McKim, ed., Village India: Studies in the Little Community (Chicago: University of Chicago Press, 1955); E. Friedl, "The Role of Kinship in the Transmission of National Culture to Rural Villages in Mainland Greece," American Anthropologist 61 (1959): 30-38.

(32)   See, for example, Carlo Levi, Christ Stopped at Eboli (New York: Farrar, Strauss, 1947); or Ignazio Silone, Fontamare (New York: Dell, 1961).

(33)   Wladislaw Reymont, The Peasants (New York: Knopf, 1924-25).

(34)   Rural sociology is the most free in Poland in the manner and choice of subjects in which sociologists can conduct research in the village environment. In other states, for example, in Hungary, historically, the regimes tolerated sociographer-journalists - called village explorers - who in the thirties and early forties were able to depict the backwardness and horrible social conditions of the Hungarian village through literary channels. Similarly, it was a poet, Peter Kuczka, who in 1953 first detailed the horrors resulting from the Stalinist collectivization drive.

(35) See for example, Rodolfo Stavenhagen, Agrarian Problems
      and Peasant Movements in Latin America   (Garden   City,
      N.Y.: Doubleday, 1970).
(36) David   Apter, The Gold Coast in Transition (Princeton,
      N.J.:   Princeton   University   Press,   1955);   Douglas
      Ashford, Political Change in Morocco (Princeton, N.J.:
      Princeton University Press, 1961); and L. B. Fallers,
      Bantu Bureaucracy (Cambridge: W.   Heffer & Sons,
      1956).
(37) Daniel Lerner, The Passing of Traditional Society (Middle
      East); Saul Rose, Socialism in Southern Asia (New York:
      Oxford University Press, 1959); William R. Bascom and
      Melville J. Herskovits, eds., Continuity and Change
      in African Cultures (Chicago: University of Chicago
      Press, 1958); and Franklin, The European Peasantry.
(38) See, for example, the continuing debate over the
      "Balkan peasantry" in P. K. Block, ed., Peasants in
      the Modern World (Albuquerque, N.M.: University of
      New Mexico Press, 1969), pp. 75-98; or the debate over
      regionalization in Ivan Volgyes, "The Relevance of an
      Area-Studies Approach to the Politics of Eastern Europe,"
      Rocky Mountain Social Science Journal 5 (October 1968):
      127-132.
(39) H. Growning, "Recent Trends in Latin American Ur-
      banization," in G. M. Foster, ed., Readings in Con-
      temporary Latin American Culture (New York: Associated
      Education Services Corporation, 1965).
(40) Generally speaking those specialists who study the rural
      scene in Eastern Europe tend to group the countries of
      the region into two distinct areas: the northern and
      southern tier. The first consists of East Germany, Hun-
      gary, Poland, Czechoslovakia; the second of Romania,
      Bulgaria with Yugoslavia and Albania either included or
      excluded by the author's choice.
(41) Once again it is up to the personal bias of the re-
      searcher, policy maker, or scholar to regard ideology as
      a "guide to action," like Lenin did, or as a generally
      loose value system as is recognized by Western prodemo-
      cratically biased thinkers.
(42) Samuel P. Huntington, and Clement H. Moore, "Author-
      itarianism, Democracy and One-Party Politics," in Samuel
      P. Huntington and Clement H. Moore, eds., Authoritarian
      Politics in Modern Society (New York: Basic Books,
      1970), pp. 509-50.
(43) Lyle Shannon, ed., Underdeveloped Areas (New York:
      Harper and Row, 1957).
(44) "The Peasant Question and Agricultural Development Are
      Basic to Socialist Construction Once the National Demo-
      cratic Revolution is Completed," in Harry G. Shaffer and

Jan S. Prybyla, eds., From Underdevelopment to Affluence (New York: Appleton-Century-Crofts, 1968), pp. 213-218.

(45) David Mitrany, Marx Against the Peasant (Chapel Hill, N.C.: University of North Carolina Press, 1951), is the most cogent statement of the Marxist view concerning peasant society.

(46) Karl Marx, Communist Manifesto, Part II. Point number 9 states the Marxist precepts quite clearly.

(47) Lucian W. Pye, ed., Communications and Political Development (Princeton, N.J.: Princeton University Press, 1963).

II
The Changing
Rural Environment

2 Rural Transformation in Eastern Europe Since World War II
George W. Hoffman

The rural transformation in the Eastern European countries(1)
has been a continuing, though not an even, process in the
area and is the result of a long-term historical evolution. The
transformation of the feudal estates, as well as important
changes in the direction of trade routes, left devastating results for many regions. Eastern European linkages played an
important role in trade with Asia, but with the occupation of
its southern part by the Osmanli Turks in the fourteenth and
fifteenth centuries, this trade was interrupted. Increased use
of ocean shipping also left its impact on agricultural production. With the establishment of the national states in the
nineteenth century and the abolishment of serfdom, the
existing social system based mostly on large-scale latifundia,
especially in Poland, East Germany, Czechoslovakia and
Hungary, underwent rapid changes, bringing about a great
increase in landless and seasonally unemployed peasants, as
well as a rapidly growing surplus agricultural population. The
landholdings in areas under Turkish administration - all of
Albania and Bulgaria and parts of Romania and Yugoslavia -
were largely of communal ownership, joint family units, or extended peasant family types.(2)
    Rural transformation was accelerated by the formation of
the new national states after World War I. Every one of these
newly organized states attempted one or more land reforms,
with varied impacts. All these reforms contributed to a continuing rise in subsistence farming and an even further increase in the surplus agrarian population. Croatia alone had
five land reforms between 1755 and 1953. Various feudal
relations were very slowly abolished and generally were
completed only by the agrarian reforms of the interwar period.
In Yugoslavia, the reform lasted over 100 years and is
best described in Jozo Tomasevich's detailed work about the

Yugoslav peasants and in Rudolf Bicanic's masterly analysis of
life in Croatia in the mid-1930s.(3)   These reforms gave some
peasants access to land and to some extent reduced large
landholdings, particularly of foreign owners.   But in
Yugoslavia, for example, roughly 2,100 large landowners (over
100 hectares) in 1931 owned more land than 710,000 small
peasants (less than 2 hectares).(4)   In Poland, at the end of
the interwar period, approximately 0.5 percent of the total
holdings still belonged to large estates owning 40 percent of all
land and 25 percent of the agricultural land, while small farms
(less than 5 hectares), representing nearly two-thirds of the
total holdings, occupied only 15 percent of the agricultural
land.   Nearly 750,000 peasant families had less than 2 hectares
each and about 600,000 were landless peasants.

There was also large-scale underemployment among agricultural workers in every one of the East European countries.
The total number greatly increased with the restrictions placed
on emigration to the United States in the early 1920s.   A
League of Nations study in 1945 estimated that over 50 percent
of the agricultural workers in Poland, Romania, Bulgaria,
Albania, and Yugoslavia were surplus to actual needs.(5)   The
situation in Hungary and eastern Czechoslovakia (Slovakia),
with 30 to 49 percent considered surplus, was little better.
Only in the German Democratic Republic and western
Czechoslovakia (Bohemia and Moravia) were manpower supplies
deemed not in surplus.

In the interwar period the problem of an effective rural
transformation had already become of concern to a number of
developing countries as part of their development strategy.
Though the measures taken by some of the East European
countries, such as the earlier mentioned land reforms, debt
forgiveness, as well as increased state-induced investments for
the building of a diversified economy with priorities given to
building industries related to military needs by participation in
the development of an infrastructure - a basic network of
railway lines, utilities, public education - and by encourage-
ment of agricultural exports, brought an increasing amount of
state involvement in the economy.   But it became clear that an
increasing number of people came to realize that basic structural changes in rural areas was a precondition for a successful process of economic advance.   The specific development
processes and strategy of the countries of Eastern Europe
obviously differed, though the achievement of basic structural
changes - the transition from a traditional agrarian economy to
a modern industrial or mixed economy - had been attempted
though not achieved by the outbreak of World War II.   A base
had been laid, however, from which to proceed after the
destruction caused by the war had been repaired.   The lack of
a balance between the rapidly increasing population and the
accumulation of capital, of vital importance in modernizing a

country, was not solved by 1939. Regional differences between the large underdeveloped regions were even sharpened, in part due to political conditions. Many of the problems of the countries of Eastern Europe must be related directly to the period of nation building in the preceding century and were mostly a legacy of the Ottoman Empire and the division of the national territory among one or more countries. This legacy of backwardness among the poverty-stricken peasantry created a serious problem of economic development and contributed, for example, to the great spatial differences and internal political problems, especially in today's multinational Yugoslavia.

The process of rural transformation for many regions of the world, including Eastern Europe, has been analyzed in publications too numerous to even attempt to mention in this chapter. This process has taken place as a result of both external and internal developments in the East European countries and has generally been the result of an erosion of the traditional societies at both the village and national levels.(6) While such a transformation has occurred in most countries of the world, the actual method, scope and direction differs widely from country to country.

The new elite group which gained effective central authority over the landscape in the countries of Eastern Europe, as one of its first measures, initiated a violent transformation of the traditional peasant societies.(7) There is perhaps no better illustration of Whittlesey's concept of "the impress of central authority on the landscape" than postwar Eastern Europe. With the adoption of the Marxist form of government by the eight countries of this area, a transformation process was set in motion, and nowhere has this transformation been more evident than in the rural areas of the region. Basic to the problem of rural transformation is increased attention to agricultural developments, especially the modernization process from subsistence to commercial farming, its development in close coordination with other sectors of the economy, as well as the reorganization of rural communities with their new social and economic functions. Inasmuch as rural transformation in the socialist countries resulted largely from a social, economic and political transformation, it is important that a close relationship be established between the newly organized large commercial farms (varying degrees of collectives and cooperatives) and the small family farm still existing in several of the socialist countries (Poland and Yugoslavia), or the small family-operated farming plot.

The objective of the following discussion is to outline the major characteristics of the rural transformation in Eastern Europe since 1945. Important trends within the whole area are analyzed, but specific examples are drawn primarily from the countries of southeastern Europe - countries in which rural transformation has been especially profound. As part of this transformation, important structural changes occurred in agricultural production as well as in the traditional rural functions. Inasmuch as the transformation was extremely rapid – within the life of a single generation – and was accompanied by important changes in society, in the relationships within the village and between the village and the urban centers, and changes in the organization of agricultural production, it occurred quite differently than the transformation in the Western industrialized countries a century earlier. To this empirical analysis will be added an assessment of major facets of success and failure as obtained by field observations stretching over many years, as well as from the existing literature, within the framework of the current economic and political restraints.

THE SOCIALIST PLAN OF TRANSFORMATION

Since World War II, few countries in the world have experienced such far-reaching basic structural changes in their cultural, economic and political life as the countries of Eastern Europe. To accomplish these aims, the whole development strategy of the postwar period emphasized rapid industrialization, which was to accomplish basic structural socioeconomic changes in the shortest possible time. Industrialization as the main vector of change was intended to absorb rural surplus labor in the increasing number of new industries and also to provide a rapidly growing number of secondary and tertiary employment opportunities. Industrialization also meant an increasing mechanization of agriculture that in turn would permit accelerated transfer of underemployed rural labor. Such a policy, it was hoped, would bring rapid changes to the rural landscape, including its social transformation. The basic premise of such a policy was intensification of agriculture and conversion to industrial methods. The main emphasis in the rural transformation of the socialist countries was on the restructuring of farming into a rural industrial organization and ultimately the development of vertical and horizontal cooperation among the various production units. Yugoslavia after 1952 launched what is called "socialist democracy," a new and different type of socialism. Its development was characterized by a slowly increasing degree of decentralization in all aspects of economic and social development. The Yugoslav doctrine emphasized decentralization and popular participation, using workers' management as the vehicle to counter the excesses of the Stalinist-type bureaucratic planning and management of the economy. The impact of its previous agricultural policies was an immediate one. Collectivization was discontinued, the private farmer, while being encouraged to cooperate with the remaining peasant cooperatives, had most of his land returned, including most of the equipment and animals he was forced earlier to turn over to the collectives. Slowly over the years a new policy evolved toward the private farmers, though the "socialization of the village" still remained an important objective.(8)

The theoretical basis for the planned restructuring of the rural landscape can be seen in the basically antipeasant attitude of the leadership which came to power at the end of World War II. Generally it can be said that all perceived economic change in the socialist countries must be viewed in the context of Marxist ideological belief with its common roots to be found in the writings of Marx, Engels, and Lenin. For example, their belief in the public ownership of the means of production - agricultural production included - set in motion the far-reaching transformation of rural Eastern Europe which is continuing to this day. In the Communist Manifesto (1848) Marx and Engels emphasized the need for the "gradual abolition of the distinction between town and country by more equable distribution of population over the country."(9) The notion of combining agriculture with manufacturing industries was also included in one of Marx's theses.

Following their ideological belief, it was clear that the main concern of the new leadership was rapid industrialization, and for that purpose it was essential to redistribute the population - a rapid move of people from agriculture to industry. Collectivization of agriculture was viewed as the main vector to accomplish this redistribution and it was used shortly after the enactment of the wide nationalization measures. The land reform started immediately at the end of the war marked the beginning of a series of important structural changes in the agrarian sector of the economy. All medium-size and large farm holdings were broken up and either distributed initially to the landless peasants or taken over by the state and administered as machine-tractor or peasant cooperative farms in preparation for subsequent collectivization. From the policies enacted between the end of the war and the first long-term plans in the late 1940s, it became clear that the example of the Soviet Union, as well as its historical experience, had become the model after which all socialist countries of Eastern Europe were patterning their socioeconomic transformation.

The effect of this transformation is discussed in the following pages under three broad headings: transformation of agricultural patterns, transformation of the settlement structure, and transformation of population characteristics.

Transformation Of Agricultural Patterns

By 1948 most of the socialist regimes had solidified their power base in the countries of Eastern Europe, and had begun to make plans for the economic and social transformation of their societies. These plans emphasized, above all, rapid industrialization. Industrialization in turn required two things of rural Eastern Europe: manpower and the maintenance of an agricultural surplus sufficient to meet growing internal needs and to retain foreign markets.(10)

The policy which has done most to alter the agricultural pattern of Eastern Europe is collectivization. All eight nations of the region embarked upon collectivization of agriculture during the latter 1940s and early 1950s. However, two states, Poland and Yugoslavia, abandoned forced collectivization in the 1950s. Today in Poland and Yugoslavia only about 15 percent of the land is in state farms, with 85 percent remaining in the hands of peasant farmers. Over 90 percent of the arable land in all other Eastern European nations is collectivized.

Collectivization has greatly transformed the rural landscape of Eastern Europe. Small farms and fragmented field patterns have given way to large cooperative and state farms with fields suitable to mechanized farming. Fences, hedgerows, and dispersed farmsteads have been virtually eliminated from the countryside in the collectivized areas.(11)

The drive for collectivization of all farmland went on intermittently all during the 1950s and was brought to a successful conclusion by 1962. (Table 2.1 shows the percentage distribution of agricultural land according to the type of holders for 1950, 1960, and 1975.) Together with this drive, great effort was made to modernize the various agricultural operations. The ultimate goal was never out of sight - transforming the erstwhile peasants into a rural proletariat while at the same time creating new productive structures by linking farm production directly to the factory, thus increasing productivity.(12) Gyorgy Enyedi stresses the increased economic activity within rural space and mentions several features of the economic transformation which are closely related to the drive for modernization. The most recent emphasis is on agrarian-industrial complexes, especially on large-scale vertical integration "within the framework of large-scale socialist farming units, which, at least partially, are themselves able to play an integrative role."(13) Such vertical associations exist in the Soviet Union and were introduced in Bulgaria some years ago. Reduction in farm holdings in Bulgaria started earlier, from 1.5 million to 854 cooperatives and 152 state farms between 1950 and 1972, with the average farm size during this period increasing from 8-10 acres to 10,000 acres. Since that time Bulgarian cooperatives and state farms have

Table 2.1. Percentage Distribution of Agricultural
Land According to the Type of Holders,
1950, 1960 and 1975
(Year Closest to That Listed)

Country	Year	State Farms	Collective Farms	Private Farms	Personal Plots
Bulgaria	1950	n.a.	41.5	n.a.	2.9
	1960	10.9	79.9	1.1	8.1
	1975	20.8	69.7	0.5	9.0
Czechoslovakia	1950	13.0	14.4	69.2	1.0
	1960	20.3	63.1	11.7	4.8
	1975	33.0	61.2	0.9	4.9
German Democratic Republic	1950	5.7	-	94.3^b	-
	1960	8.0	73.2	7.6^b	11.2
	1975	10.9	80.4	4.2^b	4.5
Hungary	1950	13.5	3.6	82.5	0.2
	1960	19.3	48.6	24.6	7.5
	1975	15.7	72.3	4.7	7.3
Poland	1950	13.5	3.6	82.5	0.2
	1960	19.3	48.6	24.6	7.5
	1975	13.5	0.9	84.9	0.1
Romania	1950	21.5	1.9	76.4	0.2
	1960	29.4	50.2	18.1	2.3
	1975	20.5	71.5	3.4	4.6
Yugoslavia	1951	- 22 -		- 78 -	
	1960	- 14 -		- 86 -	
	1970^a	- 30 -		- 70 -	

n.a. Not available

[a]Total agricultural land area in socialist sector.

[b]Including private plots cultivated by nonagricultural workers.

Sources: National Statistical Yearbooks, various years.

been reorganized into 170 agro-industrial complexes of up to 90,000 acres each.

In Hungary, the whole question of merging agricultural cooperatives and developing cooperatives of 30,000 to 40,000 hectares is now being considered.(14) The size of these cooperatives has slowly been increasing with the total number decreasing, between 1970 and 1975, from 2,441 to 1,598. During the same period the average area per cooperative increased from 1,988 to 3,374 hectares.

The drive for modernization in the various socialist countries has shown a variety of new relations and effects and was summarized by Enyedi: large-scale collective and state farms may establish relations with the commercial or processing network as equal partners; new industrial-like technologies, their diffusion and the related researches, were carried out mostly within the individual state farms; numerous new processes led to the decentralization of a series of previously urban functions to rural regions resulting in many people employed on the large farms actually performing industrial or service work; modern technology contributed to a constant reduction of the differences between urban and rural modes of living and as a result agricultural and industrial work became closer; the modernization of agriculture brought about a general decline in the demand for agrarian labor and at the same time opened up numerous new employment opportunities.(15)

The modernization process also affected settlement and population characteristics and these are discussed later in this chapter.

Other aspects of the transformation of agricultural patterns are evident in the types of farming activities currently carried on in most Eastern European countries. The old cereal monoculture of the area has given way to a more diversified land use pattern which lays greater stress on industrial crops (e.g., sunflowers and sugar beets), vegetables, fruits, vine products, and, above all, livestock raising. In Bulgaria, for example, production of industrial crops in 1974 was 300 percent of the 1952 figure; meat was 200 percent; milk, 200 percent; sugar, 300 percent; and orchard products, 400 percent. Conversely, the acreage allotted to wheat production dropped from 1.6 million hectares to 1.2 million hectares and by 1980 plans call for only about 800,000 hectares to be devoted to this crop. In most of the other Eastern European countries the trend of decreasing acreages devoted to cereals and increasing industrial crops and livestock production is also apparent.

Another major change in the farm scene in postwar Eastern Europe has been the ever-increasing use of mechanization in farm production. Before the war, an average of only 0.34 tractors were in use in Eastern Europe for every 1,010 hectares (or 0.88 tractors per 1,000 farm workers.) In 1973, the figure was 18 tractors per 1,010 hectares (or 69 tractors per 1,000 workers).(16)

Transformation Of Settlement Structure

Settlement structure varied widely among the eight nations prior to World War II and this legacy responds to transformation forces perhaps a little more slowly than other aspects of the rural environment. Still, definite transformation trends exist in rural settlement structure in terms of both the settlement hierarchy on the macroscale, and in the village structure on the microscale.

On the macroscale, in keeping with the Communist Manifesto exhortation by Marx and Engels to "eliminate differences between the town and the country," there has been a general effort on the part of most East European countries to bring urban-industrial characteristics to the countryside. Especially since the 1960s, regional centers in most agricultural areas have been given investment priorities to encourage their conversion into "growth poles" of urban industrialism. In the case of Bulgaria, industrialism has even reached the village level in the form of small factories designed to employ the agricultural labor force in periods of slack agricultural activity. During the 1971-75 five year plan, 20 percent of all new industrial investment in Bulgaria went directly to villages. According to Taaffe, "many of the central villages of Bulgarian agricultural complexes are often indistinguishable from small towns as far as general development and amenities are concerned."(17)

On the microscale, despite a wide variance in prewar settlement types in Eastern Europe (from the more ordered Strassendorf, Angerdorf and Rundlinge villages of the North European Plain to the dispersed farmsteads and irregular clustered villages of the Balkans) certain common characteristics of the post-1945 "socialist village" have emerged, especially among villages associated with collectivized agriculture. New housing units and sometimes even blocks of apartment buildings have been built using modern techniques and material, e.g., masonry blocks, pre-stressed concrete. A particularly blatant intrusion of modern housing into the rural setting is made by the large, ornate (often grotesque) homes built in the Yugoslavian countryside by peasants who have left their villages and worked in Western Europe as "guest workers."

Another transformation in the appearance of the East European village has resulted from the construction of government buildings. Most villages of consequence in Eastern Europe have at least a "house of culture" through which Party policy and propaganda is conveyed. Other government struc-

tures such as administration buildings, schools, libraries and
health facilities are also more abundant in rural areas now than
in previous periods. One of the largest outlays by the governments for buildings in the rural area, however, are the
many new structures associated with the transformation of
agricultural patterns. Buildings to support expanded livestock
production, increased use of mechanical power, and storage
and/or processing for the products of the large collectives are
prominent features of the socialist village. These buildings
are usually constructed in an area adjacent to, but distinctive
from, the orginal village.

Other features of rural transformation evolving since
World War II include expansion of electrical service, improvement of water and sewer facilities, and the upgrading of
roads and other transportation facilities.(18)

Transformation of Population Characteristics

The transformation of the population component in the rural
areas of Eastern Europe has been even more dramatic than in
other aspects of the landscape. The transformation of rural
population is characterized by the following major features:

1. The role of agriculture in the employment
    structure of the nations has rapidly decreased.
2. There has been large-scale relocation of popula-
    tions from rural to urban areas.
3. The median age of the rural population has
    become older due to the departure of the
    younger people to work in the new industries
    located in the urban centers.
4. The natural growth rates in rural areas have
    declined, especially vis-a-vis urban areas.
5. There is a greatly increased female population
    working on collectives and state farms, as well
    as on private farms in Poland and Yugoslavia.
6. The rural employment structure has broadened
    considerably due to the decentralization pro-
    cesses of industries.
7. There is an increase of worker-peasants in
    every one of the Eastern European countries;
    these village commuters largely form the base of
    the industrial labor force.

Perhaps the most significant feature of the spatial transformation of rural population in Eastern Europe has been the
decline of agriculture as an occupation. In 1956, 21.8 million
workers (45 percent of the labor force) in the region were
engaged in agriculture. By 1971, however, the number of

agricultural workers had dropped to 16.6 million (31 percent of the labor force). Table 2.2 shows the reduced percentage of population employed in agriculture in Eastern Europe for selected years.

Table 2.2. Percentage of People Employed in
Agriculture in Eastern Europe for Selected Years
(Nearest Year)

	1938	1950	1960	1970
Bulgaria	80	73	55	45
Czechoslovakia	28	39[b]	26	18
German Democratic Republic	27[a]	23	17	13
Hungary	51	51	38	26
Poland	65	57	44	36
Romania	78	74	66	49
Yugoslavia	79	67	56	44

[a]Estimated.

[b]Increase occurred as a result of transferred territories and the destruction of some industry during the war.

Sources: National Statistical Yearbooks, various years.

Closely associated with the shift in employment structure is a strong trend for rural-to-urban migration. In contrast to the 1945 situation, by 1974 only three countries in Eastern Europe (Romania, Yugoslavia, and Albania) had rural populations larger than their urban populations, and even in these nations the rural-to-urban migration trend is evident. In Bulgaria, the percentage of rural dwellers in the population decreased from 75 percent in 1946 to 43.5 percent in 1974. In absolute numbers, a rural Bulgarian population of 5.3 million in 1946 decreased to 3.2 million in 1973. In the 1971 census, 31 percent of the total Yugoslav population reported that they had resettled some time between 1945 and 1971 (and over

61 percent of the population were still classified us rural),
while in Bulgaria, 28 percent of the 1970 population had relocated some since 1957.   In Hungary, 35 percent of the 1970
population had relocated since 1950; 73 percent of the Yugoslav
relocations and 76 percent of the Bulgarian migrations were
from rural to urban areas.   Similar figures exist in the other
East European countries.   Table 2.3 shows the urban shift in
the countries of Eastern Europe since World War II.

Table 2.3.   Urban Population, 1939 and 1971-74
(in Percent)

	1939	1971-74
German Democratic Republic	72.2	75.3
Poland*	27.4	54.6
Czechoslovakia	33.2	62.3
Hungary	34.5	49.9
Albania	15.4	34.5
Yugoslavia	20.2	38.6
Bulgaria	24.6	56.5
Romania	23.4	47.7

*The changes in the Polish boundaries and the acquisition of
the urban Silesia and east Prussian areas accounts in part for
the radical transformation of the population structure.

Sources: National Statistical Yearbooks, various years.

     Economic development policies were the main factors which
influenced the large number of people in these countries to
move from their rural habitat to urban centers since World War
II.   Most of the migrants moved only short distances and a
sizable number of the migrants retain close ties to their rural-
agricultural villages.   They are known as "peasant-workers"
and number in the millions.   Because of housing shortages in
the urban areas, many rural dwellers who have changed their
primary employment continue to live in the villages but com-

mute to nonagricultural jobs in the urban centers. These
people are distinctive additions to the rural landscape of
Eastern Europe since World War II. In 1973, peasant-workers
comprised the following percentages of the nonagricultural
labor force in these Eastern European nations: Czechoslovakia,
40 percent; East Germany, 33 percent; Bulgaria, 25 percent;
Hungary, 30 percent; Poland, 20 percent; and Yugoslavia 30
percent.(19)

Many members of agricultural households today are
employed outside agriculture. In Hungary, for example, it is
estimated that the heads of 64 percent of the village households have their principal employment outside agriculture. If
actual work is counted, only 21 percent of those gainfully
employed work as farmers. In Yugoslavia roughly one-half of
the agricultural households (with over one-third of the arable
land) have members employed outside agriculture. Very often
it is the male member who works in a nearby urban center
while his wife continues the household chores, also working
the family plot, or working as an active member of the collective.(20) This is also reflected in the higher percentage of
female workers in the agricultural labor force of most East
European countries. The majority of those migrating to the
urban centers are under 40 years of age.

In 1973 the median age of the rural population of Bulgaria
was 40 years, compared with 28 years for urban dwellers.
Furthermore, even though 44 percent of the Bulgarian population was still classified as rural, only 25 percent of those
between the ages of 15 and 30 lived in rural areas. As a
consequence, the natural growth rate of the urban population
in Bulgaria in 1973 was over 11 times greater than that of the
rural population (11.3 per 1,000 versus 0.9 per 1,000).
Similar age imbalances exist in other Eastern European countries. In Poland, for example, a 1970 survey revealed that
67.5 percent of Polish farmers were over 45 years old, 33
percent over 60.(21)

Among those younger families left in rural areas, there is
an increasing tendency for the male to become a peasant-
worker employed outside agriculture, leaving the female to
work in the traditional rural occupation. In 1957, for example,
only 19.7 percent of the Bulgarian agricultural force was
female but by 1972, the percentage rose to 48.5. Similar
trends exist elsewhere. In 1973, 45 percent of the agricultural labor force of East Germany was female, as were 38
percent in Hungary, 51 percent in Czechoslovakia, and 47
percent in Yugoslavia.

One other phenomenon influencing rural transformation
must be mentioned briefly, though its immediate impact is
largely on Yugoslavia alone. These are the foreign workers,
called Gastarbeiter in the German Federal Republic, the largest
employer. Traditionally, surplus agricultural workers, includ-

ing landless peasants and those with farm holdings too small to
provide a living, have emigrated mostly overseas. When
overseas opportunities became greatly restricted after World
War I, these would-be emigrants swelled the army of those
unemployed at home. The radical social changes in the countries of Eastern Europe, including the great emphasis on
industrialization and collectivization in the postwar period,
gave some sort of employment to everyone. Only when the
Western European industrialized countries, chiefly West
Germany and France, were in need of additional workers did
emigrants again find an outlet for personal initiative and more
rapid improvement in their standard of living. Those who
could sought work in foreign countries and the Yugoslavs were
at the forefront of the move to foreign employment. A small
number of workers from other East European countries found
employment in countries of the socialist bloc.(22)

For Yugoslavs foreign employment reached its height in
1973 when about 4.7 percent of the total population found employment (largely temporary) in foreign countries. For every
100 persons employed within Yugoslavia, an additional 23.5
were employed abroad. The sizable unemployment in
Yugoslavia, the extent of which was only brought into the
open after the economic reform of the mid-1960s, the desire for
improving one's standard of living, and the differences in the
income levels between the country's developed and underdeveloped regions were the main impetus for this mass migration. Only when an economic slowdown forced a reduction
in the employment of foreign workers in the Western industrialized countries, did this migration diminish. Relatively few
were forced to return home, however, and those who did
return had accumulated sizable savings, a large part of which
was put into improving their dwellings and buying machines
for their private farm holdings. Socialist ideology did not
permit the establishment of individual enterprises and private
investment opportunities were greatly restricted. But in
Yugoslavia, with its large percentage of private farm holdings,
these returned foreign workers could make improvements in
their properties. However, rural transformation was still
dependent upon providing more jobs in industries and services
and some real structural changes.

There are obviously other ways in which the rural population has been transformed, and perhaps the most important
changes have been in village life. With the large number of
peasant-workers, the amenities of city life have been brought
to the villages in many regions, and the differences between
towns and villages have been rapidly diminishing. With the
changes in the occupational structure of the village inhabitants, including the increased rural functions which have been
enhanced by the decentralization of industrialization, farming
has become one of the less desirable jobs and this is especially

true for the younger people. Increased literacy has resulted
in better educational opportunities and higher educational
attainment levels. Greatly increased attention to health and
hygiene has made village life, away from the overcrowded
cities and their housing shortages and pollution, a more
desirable place to live. Perhaps this has been one of the
major accomplishments of the rural transformation in the postwar period.

CONCLUSION

The study of rural transformation, as has been pointed out by
Ivan Volgyes, can be undertaken from various viewpoints.
This analysis has emphasized the geographical and economic
dimensions, though it has referred to the social, and to a
lesser extent, the political aspects. Inasmuch as the socioeconomic transformation during the postwar period has been
made possible by a central political authority, invariably
usurping the traditional rural authority, all decisions have
been based on political-ideological dimensions, often overriding
basic socioeconomic demands.
    Rural transformation in Eastern Europe since 1945 has
been profound. Both visible and nonvisible aspects of the
rural environment have undergone, and are continuing to
undergo, radical alteration. The fragmented and unorganized
landscape of the peasant farmer has given way to the large-
scale, organized collective. Industry has virtually been
brought to the village level in many regions. The role of the
rural area as the home of most Eastern Europeans has vanished
with the migrations of the young to the cities. Agriculture
has increasingly become the occupation of technicians with most
of the labor force consisting of women and older men.
    In assessing the accomplishments and failures of rural
transformation in the socialist countries of Eastern Europe, it
must be noted that the changes thus far are perhaps easier
to observe in the landscape than in the actual fabric of
societal relationships, though obviously the latter has been
profoundly affected. Time has been too short to make a final
determination of its success or failure thus far, but it is
already clear that a profound change has occurred in every
aspect of rural life and in the broader national interrelationships. Perhaps it is of importance here to question the
original aim of rural transformation. Basically, it was to be
the Marxist model for modernizing the rural landscape, according to Enyedi, bringing about "the simultaneous alteration
of (a) the relationship between towns and villages, and (b)
the internal structure of the village. These spatial transformations are the result of the mutual interrelationships

between towns and villages."(23)   The often-expressed view
that the industrialization and growth of urban areas is the
main vector of change in rural areas, to my mind, omits the
vital role played by rural dynamism, of special importance in
the establishment of regional balances.

Among the still-unresolved problems are local labor
shortages on collectives and state farms due to the attraction
of industrial employment and the greater amenities of life
available in the urban centers.   While this problem is slowly
being counterbalanced by the introduction of more technology
and higher agricultural income, new problems have emerged in
the more developed countries such as Hungary.   A recent
article in the Hungarian weekly Elet es Irodalom listed such
problems as changing work attitudes, specialization-induced
diversity of interest, restrictive organizational relationships,
the shackling effects of the economic control system and a
shortage of middle-level technicians required by an industrialized agriculture.   There is also the problem of material incentives used in the agricultural sector with farm workers more
easily earning increased income from nonagricultural pursuits.
While increasing opportunities for farm workers to earn supplementary income from nonagricultural pursuits in their own villages, can be considered an indication of the success of the
policies of rural transformation, and the distinction between
villages and towns is being abolished.   The low priority given
to agricultural work in the past produced this problem and
finally created opportunities for the motivated peasant.(24)

The trend in some of the less urbanized Eastern European
countries toward an accelerated emphasis on increased urbanization is also slowly being recognized as encouraging a further
increase in the peasant-workers phenomenon due to an acute
housing shortage, as well as encouraging the indirect creation
of a new urban proletariat, not to mention the creation of
serious social problems.   The peasant-worker movements result
in split families, with the male members often commuting weekly
or at times even monthly between their new urban-based jobs
and their permanent home in the village.   (This development is
even more serious in Yugoslavia where foreign-employed
workers leave their families, or at least their children, at
home, under the watchful eyes of relatives, and generally
return twice a year at the most).   The sizable number of
peasant-workers in every Eastern European country is indeed
a serious postwar development (there was increase in Hungary,
for example, from 130,000 in 1931 to over a million in 1975)
which is now being slowly recognized.   Several of the East
European countries, and especially Bulgaria and Yugoslavia,
now follow a strict policy of dispersal of industry(25), and a
greater attention to the building of an infrastructure such as
road linkages to facilitate the movement of goods.   This is of
special importance in the less developed countries of the region

such as Romania and the underdeveloped regions of Yugoslavia. While the establishment of new towns to serve as
growth poles had a high priority until recently, efforts to
decentralize industrial production among the more advanta-
geously located villages serving as regional centers now have
high priority in the development strategy of several countries.

It has become obvious that in the more complex economic
relationships developing in the socialist countries of Eastern
Europe, with the state serving as the major source of investments (Yugoslavia being an exception), basic structural
changes, including decentralization of major economic decisions,
are imperative. With the increased sophistication of economic
activity, regional forces must play a more important role in
influencing both local and national policies, in addition to
simply improving the decision-making processes. The whole
problem of structural imbalances in the spatial distribution of
economic activities affecting the rural transformation demands a
variety of regional policies encouraging regional and sub-
regional initiatives.(26) Only then can the complex problems
of a rapidly changing, but thus far incomplete, rural transformation be solved.

NOTES

(1) The countries of East Europe with which this paper is
     concerned are Poland, the German Democratic Republic
     (East Germany), Czechoslovakia, Hungary, Romania,
     Bulgaria, Yugoslavia and Albania. Examples in this paper
     will be drawn from all these countries, though the major
     emphasis will be on the countries in Southeast Europe,
     Hungary, Romania, Bulgaria and Yugoslavia (with the
     exception of Albania).
(2) Rudolf Bicanic, "Occupational Heterogeneity of Peasant
     Families in the Period of Accelerated Industrialization,"
     Third World Congress of Sociology 4 (1956), book 2:
     88-90, discusses the characteristics of the "community
     family" with all family members giving all their income to
     the family in return for their entire keep. A peasant
     family according to Bicanic is a group of people related
     by blood or marriage, and mainly engaged in agricultural
     production on a family holding. They operate the family
     holding as one economic unit, and consume jointly a large
     part of its produce and the bulk of the earned income of
     the holding. Also many extra-economic services are
     supplied to a great extent as family services. For a
     classical study of the peasant family see Philip E. Mosely,
     "The Peasant Family: the Zadruga or Communal Joint-
     Family in the Balkans and Its Recent Evolution," in

The Cultural Approach to History, ed. Caroline F. Ware
(New York: Columbia University Press, 1940), pp.
95-108.

(3) Jozo Tomasevich, Peasants, Politics and Economic
Changes in Yugoslavia (Stanford, Cal.: Stanford University Press, 1955); and Rudolf Bicanic, "Kako Zivi
Narod, Zivot u pasivnim krajevima" [How people live life
in the passive regions], trans. Stephen Clisold, London
1941 (Zagreb, 1936).

(4) Branko Horvat, "The Postwar Evolution of Yugoslav
Agricultural Organization: Interaction of Ideology,
Practice, and Results," trans. Helen M. Kramer from
original Serbo-Croatian, IASP, Eastern Europe Economies
12 (1973-74): 3-93.

(5) Wilbert E. Moore, Economic Demography of Eastern and
Southern Europe (1945, Geneva: League of Nations; re-
print ed., New York: Arno Press, 1972), pp. 65-66.
See also the classical study dealing with the problem of
surplus agricultural population in the area by P. N.
Rosenstein-Rodan, "Problems of Industrialization of
Eastern and Southeast Europe," Economic Journal 53
(1943): 202-211.

(6) Jack M. Potter, "Implementation of Rural Development,"
in Rural Development in a Changing World, ed. Raanan
Weitz (Cambridge, Mass.: Massachusetts Institute of
Technology Press, 1971), pp. 353-63.

(7) For details of this concept see Derwent Whittlesey, "The
Impress of Effective Central Authority upon the Landscape," Annals, Association of American Geographers 25
(June 1935): 85-97. For the different interpretation by
geographers of the term "landscape," see the discussions
in Dean S. Rugg, "Aspects of Change in the Landscape
of East-Central and Southeast Europe," in Eastern Europe:
Essays in Geographical Problems, ed. George W. Hoffman
(London and New York: Methuen and Praeger, 1971),
pp. 83-122.

(8) For details see the discussions in George W. Hoffman and
Fred Warner Neal, Yugoslavia and the New Communism
(New York: Twentieth Century Fund, 1962), parts 3 and
4.

(9) Karl Marx and Friedrich Engels, "The Manifesto of the
Communist Party," The Essential Left (New York: Barnes
and Noble, 1961), p. 35.

(10) Gyorgy Enyedi, "The Changing Face of Agriculture in
Eastern Europe," Geographical Review 57 (1967): 361.

(11) Rugg, "Aspects of Change," 25:87.

(12 Gyorgy Enyedi, "Rural Transformation in Hungary," in
Rural Transformation in Hungary, ed. Gyorgy Enyedi
(Budapest: Academiai Kiado, 1976), pp. 9-26; Ronald A.
Francisco, "The Future of East German Agriculture: The

Feasibility of the 1976-1980 Plan," mimeographed (Paper presented at the Eighth National Convention of the AAASS, St. Louis, Mo., October, 1976).

(13) Enyedi, Rural Transformation, pp. 19-20; and idem, "Development of Agrarian-Industrial Complexes in Socialist Large-Scale Agriculture," in Agrarian-Industrial Complexes in Modern Agriculture, ed. Gyorgy Enyedi (Papers presented for Symposium K-23, Rural Planning and Development of the Twenty-third Institute of Geographers Congress, Odessa, July 1976) (Budapest: Research Institute of Geography, Hungarian Academy of Sciences, 1976), pp. 10-12.

(14) Radio Free Europe, Research, The Agricultural Cooperatives: Collaboration Preferred to Merging, Hungarian Situation Report/44, November 30, 1976.

(15) Enyedi, "Development of Agrarian-Industrial Complexes," pp. 11-12.

(16) Gregor Lazarcik, "Agricultural Output and Production in Eastern Europe and Some Comparisons with the USSR and USA," in Reorientation and Commercial Relations of the Economies of Eastern Europe (Washington: U.S. Government Printing Office, 1974), p. 237.

(17) Robert N. Taaffe, "The Impact of Rural-Urban Migration on the Development of Communist Bulgaria" (Paper presented at Conference on Demography and Urbanization in Eastern Europe, University of California at Los Angeles Center for Russian and East European Studies, February, 1976), p. 24.

(18) George W. Hoffman, "Transformation of Rural Settlement in Bulgaria," Geographical Review 54 (January 1964): 45-64.

(19) Radio Free Europe, Research, Urban Demography: Past Developments and Projections - Eastern Europe, Eastern Europe/3, June 6, 1974, p. 15.

(20) Gyorgy Konrad and Ivan Szelenyi, "Social Conflicts of Underurbanization," in Urban and Social Economics in Market and Planned Economies: Policy, Planning, and Development, vol. 1, ed. Alan A. Brown et al. (New York: Praeger, 1972) vol. 1, pp. 2,6-226; and Horvat, "Postwar Evolution," pp. 11-12.

(21) Taaffe, "Impact of Rural-Urban Migration," pp. 12-14; and Alexander Matejko, Social Change and Stratification in Eastern Europe (New York: Praeger, 1974), p. 76.

(22) See the discussions by George W. Hoffman, "Social and Economic Changes in Postwar Europe," in A Geography of Europe: Problems and Prospects ed. George W. Hoffman (New York: Ronald Press, John Wiley, 1977), pp. 91-96; and the specific discussions on the foreign workers in Yugoslavia, idem, "Currents in Yugoslavia: Migration and

Social Change," Problems of Communism 22 (November-
December 1973): 16-31. Also see Ivo Baucic, "Economic
Consequences of External Migration for Yugoslavia," in
International Migration in Its Relationship to Industrial and
Agricultural Adjustment Policies (Proceedings of the
Seminar organized by the OECD Development Center,
Vienna, May, 1974) (Paris: Development Center of the
OECD, 1974), pp. 95-108; and the various publications
of the Center for Migration Studies, Institute of Geo-
graphy, University of Zagreb, Yugoslavia, Ivo Baucic,
director.
(23) Enyedi, Rural Transformation in Hungary, p. 9.
(24) Harry Trend, "Some Problems Affecting Agriculture in
Eastern Europe," summarized and trans. from an article
by Istvan Lazar, in Elet es Irodalom July 10, 1976: 1, 4.
Radio Free Europe Research, RAD Background
Report/211, Eastern Europe, October 7, 1976.
(25) See the discussions in George W. Hoffman and Ronald L.
Hatchett, "The Impact of Regional Development Policy on
Population Distribution in Yugoslavia and Bulgaria," and
George J. Demko and Roland J. Fuchs, "Spatial Popu-
lation and Regional Development Policies in Eastern
Europe" (Papers presented at Conference on Demography
and Urbanization in Eastern Europe, University of
California at Los Angeles Center for Russian and East
European Studies, February 1976), in Population and
Migration Trends in Eastern Europe, ed. Huey Louis
Kostanick (Boulder, Colo.: Westview Press, 1977).
(26) Bohdan Gruchman, "Delimitation of Development Regions
in Centrally Planned Economies," in Development Regions
in the Soviet Union, Eastern Europe and Canada, ed.
Andrew Burghart (New York: Praeger, 1975), pp. 1-13;
George W. Hoffman, Regional Development Strategy in
Southeast Europe: A Comparative Analysis of Albania,
Bulgaria, Greece, Romania and Yugoslavia (New York:
Praeger, 1972); and Kosta Mihailovic, Regional Development - Experiences and Prospects in Eastern Europe, UN
Research Institute for Social Development, Geneva,
Regional Planning, vol. 4. (Paris, The Hague: Mouton,
1972). The literature discussing regional policies, including decentralization of important economic decisions is
sizable. Gruchman presented his ideas in a recently
published paper. Hoffman has attempted to discuss the
problems for the countries of Southeast Europe, including
a comparison with Greece and Mihailovic in his discussions
presented the experiences and prospects for all East
European countries, though he gave special attention to
those of Yugoslavia. While none of the authors focus on

rural transformation specifically, the problems of the villages were considered as part of the whole problem of overconcentration in the small number of expanding development poles.

3 Australia's Changing Rural Geography
Tom L. McKnight

Australia is a predominantly urban country whose international reputation is rural. Despite the fact that 86 percent of all Aussies reside in towns or cities, the image of the typical Australian is that of a sunburnt drover following sheep across a dusty, kangaroo-studded plain. From an areal standpoint, of course, the rural image is eminently correct. Australia is by far the least densely populated of the inhabited continents; well over two-thirds of its area contains less than one person per square mile, and most of the remainder has less than five people per square mile.

It is on this very expansive but very sparsely populated portion of Australia that this essay focuses. How has the geography of rural Australia changed in the last few years? Where, how, and why has rural transformation taken place, if indeed it has? In the limited space available here these questions can only be addressed in generalities, but an attempt will be made to describe and assess the patterns of change that seem relevant to the geography of rural Australia.

TRADITIONAL PATTERNS OF RURAL OCCUPANCY AND LAND USE

One of the attractions of studying rural Australia is the relative simplicity of its general geographical patterns. Its landforms, climate, flora, and to a lesser extent its soils are arranged on the landscape in such a fashion that they are not difficult to comprehend in their gross aspects. There was also considerable homogeneity in the diffusion of European settlement over the continent. In consequence, the patterns of human occupancy and land use that have evolved Down Under have been relatively uncomplex, and can be described more simply than is possible for any other inhabited continent. This is not to say that all generalizations will be without exception, but that they will be more broadly valid in Australia than is likely on other continents, or large portions of continents.

With the passage of time, of course, the simplicity has diminished. As population increases, society becomes more cosmopolitan, technology is enhanced and new and diverse elements are introduced into the traditional milieu. This chapter will proceed from the traditional to the contemporary. The former will be sketched in broad strokes prior to a somewhat more detailed consideration of recent and ongoing changes in the geography of "country Australia."

The word "country," applied as an adjective in the areal sense, is widely but imprecisely used Down Under to refer to that part of the continent that is beyond the larger cities. It is not really synonymous with either "rural Australia" or "the Outback." There are no objective standards for defining these three terms, nor is there any general agreement on a subjective definition for them. In general it can be presumed that "country Australia" encompasses the entire continent except for the environs of the ten or twelve largest cities. "Rural Australia" is somewhat less expansive, and would exclude, in addition to the above, another one or two dozen medium-sized urban places and their vicinities. "The Outback" is a still more restrictive term - although it includes more than four-fifths of the continental area - and further excludes some areas of closer agricultural settlement and their associated country towns.

Land Tenure

In striking contrast to the rural scene in the United States, land tenure in Australia is typically leasehold. About seven-eighths of the national land area is still in public ownership. Such a statistic, however, is somewhat misleading, as approximately one-third of the continent is virtually uninhabited.

Altogether there are some 250,000 rural landholdings in the agricultural/pastoral sector.(1) As many as 200,000 of those may be freehold, but nearly all of them are small. More meaningful is the fact that only about 12 percent of the national area is in freeholding or in the process of becoming so; this amounts to some 18 percent of the occupied area of the country. Only in the more closely settled districts is there a high proportion of freehold land. For example, 60 percent of the area of Victoria is in freehold, and more than 40 percent of Tasmania; by contrast, only eight percent of Western Australia and seven percent of South Australia are freehold land.

It is important to note, however, that the distinction between freehold and leasehold in Australia is less meaningful than in almost any other part of the world, because leasehold tenure there is very secure. Most leases are for very long terms (often lifetime) at relatively low rentals. In part as a result of this security of tenure, subsistence farming has been inconsequential. There has never been a peasant class, or even a tenant class, although "sharefarming" agreements are common, particularly in wheat, vegetables, and tobacco.

A very high proportion of all agricultural/pastoral endeavors are family operations. There are some corporate holdings, to be sure, and they are usually large and sometimes spectacular, but they comprise a small minority of all holdings.

Individual Settlements

Farming, then, is still essentially a family function. Most farms are family owned and family operated, and most labor is provided by the family members. Moreover, there is no indication of a reduction in the proportion of family farms.

The universal settlement pattern is one of dispersed individual homesteads. There is very little agglomeration, except on a few large pastoral holdings where there may be a number of employees domiciled around the homestead. The relative isolation of a homestead from its neighbors is worth emphasizing. The subhumid-to-arid climate of most of agricultural/pastoral Australia causes the individual landholdings to be generally large and extensive. In better-watered coastal fringes or irrigated districts there is a closer spacing of homesteads, but in most of the rural areas it is a long distance from one homestead to the next.

Country Towns

As with homesteads, country towns were often sited, particularly in drier areas, where water was available, which usually meant near or along natural watercourses. In many areas, then, there is a lineation of towns along drainage lines.(2) Country towns normally developed in response to the usual inducements to urban growth, such as transportation crossroads, watering places along stock routes, river crossings, and mineral deposits. Almost always, however, water availability was an important factor.

A fairly normal hierarchical pattern of urban places has developed in much of rural Australia, with the state capitals dominating most urban functions, and most other levels in the urban hierarchy showing clearly but less importantly (see table 3.1). The two principal exceptions are these:

Table 3.1.   Population of Urban Places, 1971

Grouping	Number	Total Population	Proportion of National Pop.
Urban centers over 100,000	10	8,226,775	64.5%
Urban centers, 25,000 to 100,000	17	730,021	5.7%
Urban centers, 10,000 to 25,000	46	714,245	5.6%
Urban centers, 5,000 to 10,000	66	467,184	3.7%
Urban centers, 1,000 to 5,000	342	752,586	5.9%

Note: Almost all urban places with a population of less than 25,000, and a few of those with a population exceeding 25,000, would be considered as "country" towns.

Source: Commonwealth Bureau of Census and Statistics, Official Year Book of the Commonwealth of Australia, 1974 (Canberra: 1975), p. 142.

1.   The great dominance of state capitals has generally inhibited development of second- and third-order centers.
2.   There are vast expanses of arid Australia that are essentially without towns.

A few of the larger country towns are growing modestly, but the great majority of them, especially the small communities, are stagnating or dying. Their marketplace function is inadequate to sustain them, and there is little nonagricultural activity other than small-scale manufacturing directly concerned with local raw materials or local markets.

Land Use Pattern

The agricultural/pastoral land use pattern has been long established and is relatively simple to comprehend. Its basic ingredients are several concentric zones extending outward from the major cities and inward from the coast (see fig. 3.1). The pattern becomes more irregular interiorward and northward. The major elements of the pattern include the following:

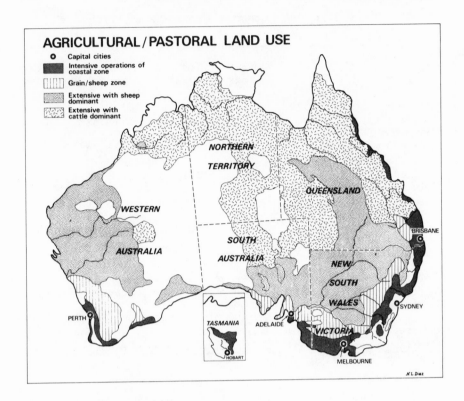

Fig. 3.1.   Agricultural/Pastoral Land Use.

Source: Generalized   from   <u>Atlas of Australian Resources</u>,
Dept. of Minerals and Energy, Canberra, 1973.

1.   An urban fringe dominated by market gardening
      and dairying around the state capitals and a
      few other major cities;

2.   The better-watered coastal margins of the
      eastern, southeastern, and extreme south-
      western coasts, with intensive pastoral opera-
      tions (especially fat lamb raising and dairying)
      and specialty crops (of which the most
      prominent is sugar cane along the Queensland
      coast);

3.   A broad crescent in southeastern Australia,
      reiterated in the southwest, of mixed grain
      farming and sheep raising, punctuated by
      occasional ribbons of irrigated farming;

4.   An immense extensive pastoral zone, dominated
       by sheep in the southern half of the continent,
       but almost exclusively by beef cattle in the
       north and center; and
5.   The vast unoccupied deserts of the interior and
       west.

There are, of course, numerous variations on this theme. In
general it is in the more productive regions that the mixture of
land uses is most complex and also the most variable from year
to year, while the least productive districts tend to be the
simplest and least changeable.

By and large, the rural scene is dominated by simple
unimproved grazing land. Only one acre in thirty of all rural
holdings is cropped, and only one acre in twenty consists of
sown pasture.(3)   Even where the land is irrigated, more than
half the acreage is in pasture.

Rural Population

In addition to the continuing modest decline in the rural population, there are several other notable demographic characteristics.(4)   Although rural families tend to be larger than the
national average, in aggregate they have imbalanced age/sex
ratios.   There is a scarcity of females of marriageable age, a
relatively high proportion of single males, a general absence of
teenagers (many of whom are sent off to boarding schools for
their secondary education), and fewer than average older
people (who often retire to the city).

Farming, however, has increasingly become an older man's
activity.   This trend reflects mechanization, the desire of
many young men for urban amenities, and the cost/price
squeeze that afflicts the farming sector.   On most properties
it is now difficult to support more than one adult male.

Aborigines comprise only a small proportion of the total
agricultural/pastoral population of Australia.   However, they
are very prominent in certain situations, particularly the
extensive cattle industry of the northern and interior parts of
the country, where aboriginal jackeroos (cowboys) are often in
the majority.   Their contribution to this industry is difficult to
overstate.

Aborigines also constitute a sizable minority of the population of many Outback towns.   They nearly always occupy the
lowest economic and social strata, and are frequently only
shadowy fringe-dwellers in the life of the town.   Their story
is an important one, but their impact on the geography of
rural Australia is limited, and will not be further discussed
here.

Farming/pastoralism is generally looked upon as a way of life rather than as simply a business. This outlook reflects the dominance of family landholdings, and makes most farmers/graziers occupationally immobile.

Many Australian ruralites do not belong to any farm organizations, and there is a great fragmentation in the organizations that do represent rural interests. More than 300 farm organizations are registered. They have generally differed from analogous organizations in most other countries in being commodity, rather than vocationally, oriented. Most Australian farm organizations reflect the special interests of producers of a single commodity, or at most a closely related group of commodities, with the notable exception of the state grazier organizations which represent principally the larger and wealthier wool growers and cattlemen. Most such organizations are administered by older men with vested interests; like the farms themselves, the farm organizations are the domain of older men.

The farmer/grazier class still has considerable political muscle throughout Australia with more than proportionate representation at both state and federal government levels. At the local level, however, government is relatively weak. Authorities of many local governments (called "shires" in most states) administer vast areas but very few people. Moreover, they have little money with which to work. Often their main concern is simply to keep the principal roads trafficable, and this expense exhausts their finances. The prevailing roadway infrastructure is generally adequate to accommodate a much denser population, but is still necessary for the sparse population that exists.

There has been a widely publicized effort to provide two important necessities - medical service and education - to the man-on-the-land, with particular emphasis on serving the remote areas of the Outback. These services are made possible in part by the availability of two-way radio communication to every rural homestead that is remote enough to need it.

Well-organized radio networks make daily medical consultation available through a dozen widely scattered radio centers (see fig. 3.2). Homesteads have government-subsidized medicine chests for minor ailments, and flying doctor and ambulance service is available for more serious situations.

The basics of a formal education are also made available to rural children in an effort to counteract the condition that country folk are less well educated than their urban counterparts. At present about half the rural work force has not attended school past the primary level, and only one percent has had any college education. One-room primary schools, usually taught by a teacher with special training in multilevel

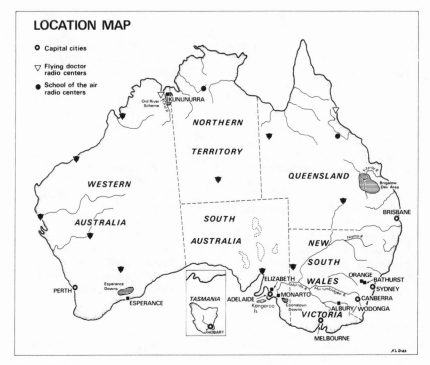

Fig. 3.2.   Location Map.

teaching, are widely scattered in rural districts, and comprise
about one-fourth of Australia's government schools.   Also,
correspondence schools operate from every state capital, with
more than 20,000 primary and secondary students enrolled.
An additional dimension of expanded and personalized teaching
is provided by the Schools of the Air, which share the "flying
doctor" radio network to give direct student/teacher contact at
primary levels.

Mining

Australia is self-sufficient in all but a very few minerals
of economic value, and has become a major exporter of many.
However, prior to the early 1960s the exploitation of mineral
wealth had been limited mostly to the mining of those elements
that were needed for domestic markets (see fig. 3.3).   The
federal government and several state governments had enacted
restrictive regulations to minimize the export of raw ores and
concentrates.   Thus the map of mining activities as of about
1960 shows a few outstanding mining districts - notably Broken

Established prior to 1960:	Established since 1959:
Broken Hill - lead, zinc, silver	Barrow Island - oil/gas
Ipswich - coal	Bowen Basin - coal
Kalgoorlie - gold	Cobar - copper
Latrobe Valley - coal	Frances Creek - iron
Leigh Creek - coal	Gidgealpa/Moomba - gas
Mary Kathleen - uranium	Gippsland Basin - oil/gas
Middleback Ranges - iron	Gove - bauxite
Mount Isa - copper, lead, zinc, silver	Groote Eylandt - manganese
Mount Lyell - copper	Jarrahdale - bauxite
Mount Morgan - copper, gold	Kambalda - nickel
Northern Fields - coal	Koolyanobbing - iron
Radium Hill (now defunct) - uranium	Moonie - oil
Rosebery - lead, zinc, silver	Nabarlek/Ranger - uranium
Rum Jungle - uranium	Pilbara - iron
Southern Fields - coal	Roma - oil/gas
Tennant Creek - gold, copper	Savage River - iron
Western Fields - coal	Weipa - bauxite
Yampi Sound - iron	

Fig.   3.3.   Major   mining   operations.

Hill, Mt. Isa, Kalgoorlie, Mt. Lyell, the Middleback Ranges, the Latrobe Valley, Leigh Creek, and the New South Wales coalfields - and a limited number of less expansive operations (see fig. 3.4). Mining was clearly a well-established aspect of the rural economy, but the notable developments had occurred in the past. This situation was to change dramatically.

THE CHANGING RURAL SCENE

The occupancy and land utilization patterns of rural Australia have been well established for decades. In contrast to the urban/industrial sector, in which change has occurred rapidly, change has come for the most part only slowly and sporadically to the rural scene. The rest of this chapter will focus on the nature and extent of changes in the geography of rural Australia during the last few years.

Errata for: Volgyes, Lonsdale, Avery: THE PROCESS OF RURAL TRANSFORMATION

p. 178

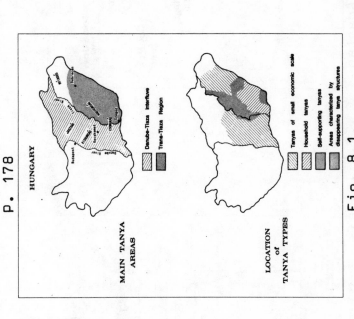

Fig. 8.1.
Source: Derived from Pal Romany
A tanya rendszer ma, Budapest:
Kossuth, 1973.

P. 69

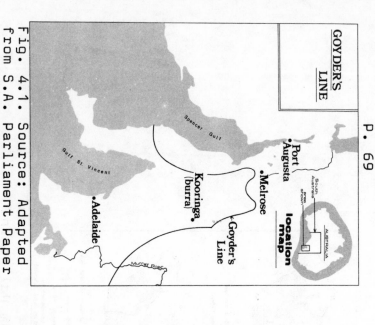

Fig. 4.1. Source: Adapted from S.A. Parliament Paper 154, 1865-66, map.

P. 164

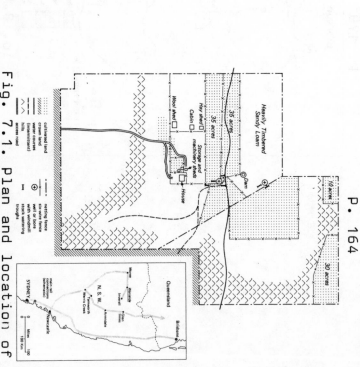

Fig. 7.1. Plan and location of case-study family farm near Warialda, New South Wales.

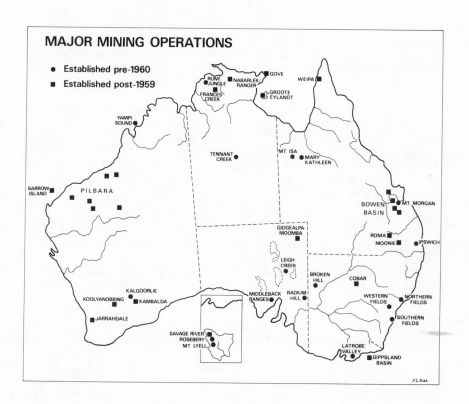

Fig. 3.4. Major mining operations (map). Source: Compiled by author from various sources.

Population Redistribution

Like most other developed countries, Australia has for some time experienced a general drift of people from rural to urban areas. This trend is by no means new, but it is current. It has been evident in all recent census counts, and generally applies to the whole country, although there are several clear-cut areas of local exception.

This countryside-to-city movement has been less conspicuous in Australia than in many countries because it has been disguised by "the concurrent opening-up of new areas of settlement and the intensification of land use in certain other areas."(5) Nevertheless, all recent studies have documented the continuance of the trend - general population decrease and net out-migration from the nonmetropolitan portions of the nation, and especially from the rural areas.(6)

During the most recent intercensal period for which statistics are available - 1966-1971 - the following data are pertinent to this theme: Of the 58 country(7) statistical divisions in Australia, 40 recorded a total population increase and 46 showed a growth in the "urban" component, but only 11 recorded an increase in the "rural" component of their population.

Concomitant with decrease in rural population, the full-time rural work force also continues to decline. It reached a record low of less than 300,000 in the mid-1970s, and nearly four-fifths of that total consisted of property owners or managers. Permanent rural employees, apart from owners/managers, are few except on large extensive pastoral properties. There is still considerable seasonal employment (but the number of seasonal workers is also declining, although at a slower rate than that of the total rural work force), especially in shearing and harvesting. Also, contract labor is used for much dam building, fencing, land clearing, and application of fertilizers, pesticides, and seeds.

The contemporary distribution of Australian population, based on the latest published census data, is shown in figure 3.5.

Country Towns: The Struggle to Survive

The small cities, towns, and villages of Australia have fared variably over the past few years, in contrast to the rapidly growing major urban areas. The proportion of Australia's population that resides in towns and smaller cities has remained virtually stable (at about 25 percent) over the last two decades, an aggregate statistic that masks considerable variation from place to place. Most of the larger country urban centers (those with populations between about 15,000 and 100,000) have maintained a growth rate commensurate with, or greater than, that of the national population. Urban places below about 15,000 in population, however, have, with a number of exceptions, tended to stagnate or decline.

There are hundreds of smaller urban centers in Australia that were functional for the kind of farming, services, transportation, and distribution systems that prevailed 50 or 100 years ago. However, the shrinking rural population, its greater mobility, and a modernized infrastructure for transportation, communication, and distribution leave these towns with a greatly diminished functional significance. In effect, they a·e easily bypassed. In a process that appears to be "irreversible and accelerating," there seems to be "little practical reason...for many of the country's small towns to survive."(8) The towns that are declining are mostly general service centers (i.e., market towns), and mining towns whose ore has been exhausted.(9)

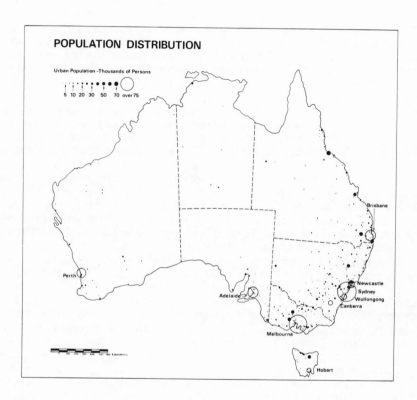

POPULATION DISTRIBUTION

Fig. 3.5. Population Distribution. Source: Compiled by author from 1972 census data.

In some cases it can be recognized that small towns which are the seat of local government derive an added benefit from this administrative function by virtue of shire council expenditures (for payrolls, construction, etc.) in or near the town, thereby partially offsetting their normal decline.(10) Other towns benefit from specialized situations in their hinterlands, which permit them to prosper in direct opposition to the trend. The most notable examples of this are in areas of recent mining activity, like the Pilbara iron country, Mt. Isa, and some of the Queensland coal mining districts, but there are also less conspicuous instances that reflect more intensified agricultural/pastoral development, such as the upper Murray Valley or Queensland's Fitzroy Basin.

Decentralization: Who Needs It?

Decentralization has often been considered as an eventual panacea for all of Australia's real or imagined economic and social ills. If only the population and urban-based economic activity could be deconcentrated away from the major cities, the argument goes, prosperity and happiness would naturally be multiplied. Despite this laudable expectation, however, little actual decentralization has occurred; indeed, metropolitan concentration of population and economic activity was higher at the time of the latest census than at any date in history. The reasons for public disinterest in deconcentration are clear enough.(11) It is evident that a metropolitan location has all sorts of advantages over a country location in most economic contexts. Spate's apt phrase that "decentralization is good for one's competitors"(12) encapsulates the idea that the theoretical advantages that are to be gained by moving away from the city are more than outweighed by the economic benefits of remaining close to where the action is.

Australia's massive postwar immigration program was implemented partially with the goal of expanding the rural population, but it has been relatively ineffective in this endeavor. Indeed, the foreign-born population is more highly centralized than the total population. Most migrants have chosen to settle in the major cities; significant exceptions have been Italians, many of whom have been attracted to irrigated farming districts; and Dutch and Greeks, some of whom have gravitated to country towns.

One ballyhooed effort at decentralization took place in South Australia in the late 1950s. The state government successfully created the new town of Elizabeth, primarily by providing significant financial incentives to industries and low-cost housing for workers.(13) Elizabeth, however, was only 17 miles from Adelaide, and has since been officially included in the Adelaide urban area - hardly a significant deconcentration effort in a state of 380,000 square miles!

More recently the federal government designated three extra-metropolitan "growth centers," and committed considerable financial support to their development. The first of these, Albury-Wodonga, on the New South Wales-Victoria border, grew significantly under the aegis of federal patrimony. The others, Bathurst-Orange, New South Wales, and Monarto, South Australia, were scheduled for similar treatment in the near future. However, the "growth center" program was substantially, de-emphasized following the return of Liberal Party rule in late 1975.

Aids To Rural Development

Federal and state governments have been active sporadically in establishing new farming/grazing areas, partly by subdivision of existing properties and partly by other forms of development. Most agricultural enhancement projects require federal-state cooperation because legal powers are vested in the states but the financial resources are mostly under federal control. Some developments have also involved government cooperation with commodity marketing boards, private corporations, and individuals.

The most notable of these projects has been the initiation or expansion of irrigation schemes along the Murray and Murrumbidgee rivers, the Namoi River in New South Wales, various small river drainages in Queensland, and the ambitious Ord River project in Western Australia. In most cases the irrigation expansion has been generated by government investment in dams and major water diversion facilities.

Some drainage schemes have also been completed, particularly in the southeast of South Australia. Scrub clearing has been done to encourage agricultural development, especially in central Queensland, south-central Western Australia, and South Australia. Another major recent enterprise is the Beef Roads Scheme, in which the federal government financed the construction of roads to facilitate cattle transport to market in the Kimberleys, the Northern Territory, and portions of northern and central Queensland.

Landholding: Fewer but Larger

Three factors have combined to determine recent trends in the number and size of rural holdings:

1. There has been a general administrative initiative to subdivide larger properties, thus proliferating the number of units of tenure.(14) This has by no means been a universal approach; rather, it has been applied very selectively. The most notable result has been the breaking up of some of the largest leasehold properties in Australia.

2. Partially offsetting the above trend has been the steady and widespread dissolution of properties, usually small, because of farm abandonment, economic difficulties, urban sprawl, and a general retreat from rural industry by marginal producers. This dissolution has resulted in fewer landholders and larger holdings.

3.   The opening of new lands to farming or the intensification of agricultural operations in older districts has provided opportunities for an increase in the number of operating units.

The result of these three processes has been a slow but steady decrease in the number of holdings and a corresponding increase in the average size of holdings. This has been a general phenomenon in most of rural Australia, although it does not apply in several areas, particularly those in which new land is being developed. In five of the six states there has been a distinct decrease in the number of holdings and an accompanying increase in the total area of rural holdings, each changing by an average of about 0.5 percent per year during the past decade. Only South Australia and the Northern Territory have run counter to this trend. In the former there has been essentially no change in the number of rural land-holdings in the past ten years; in the latter there has been a significant proportional increase in the number of holdings, reflecting the subdivision of larger properties and the opening of some new areas for settlement, although the total number of individual holdings in the Territory is still less than 500.

Both rural population and employment on rural holdings continue to decline, the former at a rate of about 0.5 percent per year and the latter at about two percent annually. Some sampling has indicated that, at least in Victoria, the one-man farm is declining, and more farms are becoming large and complex enough to employ permanent labor(15); gross statistics, however, do not yet confirm this trend.

The Australian media, and some politicians, have devoted much attention to the matter of foreign investment in and ownership/management of rural landholdings. Actually, this is nothing new; agricultural and particularly pastoral properties have long been a favored locale for British investment. In recent years, however, there have been conspicuous - in some cases, flamboyant - instances of the infusion of American capital and ownership/management, especially for large cattle properties. Investors from a scattering of other countries, particularly Japan, are also represented in recent activities.

Changes In Land Use

The long-established pattern of Australia's agricultural/pastoral land use is still, in its gross characteristics, much the same as it has been in the past. However, in detail it is becoming much more complex and variable. The changes involve expansion of cropland, different cropping patterns, pasture improvements, a trend toward more intensive station management, and some new livestock patterns.

Expansion of Cropland

Until the late 1950s the total area devoted to cropping had remained virtually the same over a long period. However, beginning in 1958 the cropped acreage increased significantly, essentially doubling between 1958 and 1968. This increment largely reflects expanded wheat acreage in the drier lands of New South Wales and Western Australia, and the expansion of wheat and other grains in South Australia. It was predicated on technological improvements, good seasons, and especially the market advantages of wheat vis-a-vis wool. Wheat acreage has declined irregularly since the 1968 peak, but has remained well above its pre-1960 levels.

Increasing irrigation has also played a notable and continuing role in the expansion of cropland. During the 1967-77 period there was an increase in irrigated cropland of about 90,000 acres per year. Not all of this growth involved bringing land under the plow for the first time, for much of the acreage had been in nonirrigated cropping, but indications are that a large share of the "new" irrigated acreage had not previously been cropped.

Diversification of Crops

With the important exception of hay and green fodder, cereal grains are overwhelmingly dominant in the Australian crop landscape. The grains occupy about three-fourths of all cropped land. However, the components of the grain group have experienced varying emphases in recent years. Wheat acreage fluctuates significantly from year to year, depending partly on seasonal conditions, but particularly on relative markets for grain and wool. The greatest increase among the grains in recent years has been in barley, which burgeoned to a peak acreage nearly forty percent as great as that of wheat in 1971-72 (although it has since decreased), with particular expansion in Western Australia; grain sorghums, the acreage of which increased almost tenfold from the mid-1950s to the early 1970s, mostly in southeastern Queensland; and rice, the acreage of which tripled in the same period, with nearly all production in New South Wales' Riverina irrigation areas.

Hay and green fodder crops, comprising mostly grass, clover, lucerne (alfalfa), and oats, have doubled in acreage since the mid-1950s.

Among industrial crops, the major gainers have been cotton and various oilseeds. Cotton acreage has expanded prodigiously, and its production evolved from a small-scale dryland operation to a big business based on large-scale irrigated enterprises in northern New South Wales and various parts of eastern Queensland. Oilseed acreage continued to increase rapidly into the mid-1970s, paced particularly by linseed, safflower, and sunflower seed, mostly in southeastern Queensland and parts of New South Wales.

There has been little expansion in fruit and vegetable acreage in recent years, except for oranges in New South Wales and green peas in Tasmania. A minor but apparently continuing trend is for some vegetable production to be shifted away from city-fringe market gardening locations to slightly more distant but better-suited land.

The Livestock Mix

Sheep are still the favored livestock species in most parts of the country, but their numbers fluctuate widely in response to weather and markets. Generally speaking, the number of sheep in Australia in the early 1970s was the lowest in two decades.

Beef cattle, on the other hand, have increased markedly. Their numbers grew by 50 percent from the mid-1950s to the mid-1960s, and by another 75 percent from the mid-1960s to the mid-1970s. Much of the increase resulted from adding cattle to sheep properties and wheat farms. More than 80 percent of wheat farmers have always raised sheep as well; now more than 30 percent of all wheat farmers also keep beef cattle.(16) The dominant beef breeds in Australia for more than a century have been Shorthorn and Hereford; these are still by far the most numerous, but there has been a continuing and increasing addition of such non-British breeds as Brahmans, Santa Gertrudis, Droughtmasters, and Africanders.

The number of dairy cattle has been on a decline for two decades, although output of milk products has been slowly rising due to increased average productivity per cow. Long plagued by economic difficulties, the industry experienced a decline of almost 50 percent in the number of active dairy farms between 1970 and 1976, to a total below 33,000(17), yet it is predicted that even this record low number needs to be reduced by about one-fourth in order to bring supply closer in line with demand.

The number of pigs doubled between the mid-1950s and the mid-1960s, and burgeoned by another 75 percent from the mid-1960s to the mid-1970s. In the past most swine were raised in conjunction with dairy farms, where they were fed skim milk; now, however, they are increasingly kept on grain farms or as an intensive specialty operation, with much greater reliance on grain for feed.

Poultry has increased even more spectacularly; the number of chickens has tripled in the past decade. Similar proportional increases also occurred for turkeys and ducks, although the volume was much smaller. Poultry husbandry has changed rapidly from a small-scale adjunct to general farming to a large-scale "factory" enterprise that specialize in roasters, broilers, fryers, or eggs.

Pasture Improvement

In areal extent, the most notable change in the Australian rural landscape in recent years has been the expansion of pasture improvement. This development has mostly involved clearing of scrub or removal of trees, planting of grass or other pasture vegetation, and fertilization. The full extent of pasture improvement is unrecorded, but its magnitude is indicated by the area under sown grasses and clovers; in the last decade this figure has grown by about four million acres per year.

A great variety of exotic legumes and grasses has been introduced as the keystone to most pasture improvement programs. They often possess the multiple virtues of producing large amounts of fodder, surviving under difficult conditions, such as heat and drought, and improving soil fertility. Most widespread of these exotics are subterranean clover (Trifolium subterraneum) in the subhumid portions of southern Australia, various of the medics (Medicago) in the semi-arid portions of southern Australia, and Townsville stylo (Stylosanthes humilis) in northern Australia.(18)

The great upsurge in pasture improvement resulted from the realization, confirmed by experimentation, that it was possible for "two blades of grass to grow where one grew previously."(19) The larger grazing capacity does not necessarily spur an increase in sheep numbers, but it almost invariably raises wool production. The average weight of fleeces shorn has been on a continuing upward trend. This increase is due to a variety of factors, including better breeding and control of diseases and parasites, but pasture improvement is thought to be the main cause.

More Intensive Property Management

A trend that became conspicuous shortly after World War II and has been continuing is the technological improvement of farming/pastoral operations and efforts at more intensive management. This involves more and better farm machinery, attention to breeding for both crops and livestock, and technical improvements in equipment and many farming techniques.

On pastoral properties it includes tighter control over grazing by subdivision of paddocks and provision of more watering points, expanded pest control, and more effective action against animal diseases and parasites. Now becoming conspicuous in the landscape of some pastoral holdings are artificial feeding stations where the livestock are provided with hay, grain, and dietary supplements. This is a major departure from past Australian practice, where cattle and sheep were expected to fend for themselves in the matter of feeding.

Related to this development is the beginning of intensive
feedlot operations in some of the better-watered portions of
southeastern Australia.(20)   Feedlotting is still in its infancy
but is likely to become very significant in the near future.

A Sampling of Major Rural Development Schemes

In recent years there have been several major rural development schemes in various parts of Australia.   Some have been
essentially governmental projects, others were undertaken by
private enterprise, and most have been a combination of the
two.   The procedure here will be to examine several of the
more conspicuous schemes and try to evaluate their results in
terms of "rural transformation."   No field work has been
undertaken by the writer, so any evaluation is likely to be
superficial and tentative.

Kangaroo Island Land Development

The scheme.   In 1948 the South Australia Department of
Lands, with federal financial support, embarked on a project
to develop 150,000 acres of previously unoccupied land, with
the idea of opening up about 200 new leasehold properties.(21)
The scrub was cleared and burned, the land was plowed and
seeded with clover and perennial grasses, and various structural improvements - houses, sheds and fences - were added.
The blocks were then granted in perpetual leasehold to
returned servicemen from World War II.

Tentative evaluation.   In this clear-cut case of new land
being opened for settlement, based on a heavy infusion of
development capital, the results appear to have been relatively
modest.   Pasture apparently has become well established over
most of the development area, and there are viable enterprises
raising sheep, beef cattle, and dairy cattle, as well as a little
farming.   Kangaroo Island's population more than tripled
between the 1947 and 1954 censuses, from 788 to 2,522, but
was 2,285 at the 1961 census, remaining at approximately that
level since.   It is probable that most of the early growth was
due directly to the land development scheme.

Coonalpyn Downs

The scheme.   A large Australian insurance company began an
extensive land development program in 1949 in the so-called
"Ninety Mile Desert" of South Australia, and later extended
the effort into the "Big Desert" just across the state border in
Victoria.(22)   The company obtained large blocks of unimproved land by purchasing existing leases or by Crown allot-

ment. The scrub was cleared, the land was plowed, improved pasture species were planted, and superphosphate and trace element - copper, zinc and molybdenum - fertilizers were added. More than 420,000 acres of land have been settled by company employees or sold to the public in the South Australian section, which is now called the Coonalpyn Downs, and a further 100,000 acres is under development in the Victorian portion, now known as Telopea Downs.

Tentative evaluation.   Vast areas of almost valueless scrub have been converted to expanses of verdant pasture, and stocking with sheep and cattle has manifolded. There are special problems in the area's soils, not all of which can be solved by the application of trace elements, but the overall transformation of the landscape has been spectacular. Population growth has been notable. Tatiara District Council, the South Australian local government unit within which most of the Coonalpyn Downs project is located, experienced an increase from 1,793 in 1947 to 4,977 in 1954 and 7,071 in the most recent census (1971) for which statistics are available.

Esperance Downs

The scheme.   The area east, west, and north of the port of Esperance, Western Australia, has had a complex and somewhat checkered land development history over the last few decades.(23) In brief, the government of the state has made land available for settlement, largely leasehold, at various times, much of it in contractual agreements with large land development or real estate companies. The early occupancy (1948-54) involved about 100 mostly smallholders. During the late 1950s several large investors, notably the Esperance Land Development Company, were involved. A lot of scrub clearance and pasture improvement has been carried out, with partially developed blocks being sold to settlers and investors. Several hundred properties have been thus distributed, with further development work by the new owners. The process continues.

Tentative evaluation.   In many ways this represents the most spectacular of all recent Australian rural development schemes. Many of the properties are show places, and there have been prodigious increases in cattle, sheep, grain, and oilseed output. Not all settlers have prospered, of course, and as recently as 1970 it was reported that, considering the vast expense of development, "none have made a take-away profit."(24) Nevertheless, the region's economy and landscape have been transformed on a gigantic scale. Population growth, while substantial, has been less spectacular. Esperance Shire, in which nearly all of the development has taken place, approximately doubled its population in every census from 1947 till 1966(25), although there has been essentially no further growth since then.

Ord River Scheme

The scheme. The most controversial of Australia's land development projects is underway in the remote East Kimberley District of Western Australia. The plan is to supply some 180,000 acres of the Ord River drainage with irrigation water for close farm settlement in the northwestern corner of Western Australia and an adjacent section of the Northern Territory.(26) A small first-stage dam was completed in 1963, and 30 farms (averaging 660 acres) were established. In addition, a completely new town, Kununurra, was built as the focal point· of the project, and, in a radical departure from other Australian rural occupancy, all the first-stage settlers live in the town and commute to their farms. The principal storage dam, further upstream, was dedicated in 1972; however, second-stage farm development has been inhibited by the total failure - at least temporarily - of cotton, the area's only previously viable crop, due to massive insect problems.

Tentative evaluation. Disregarding economic considerations, which are disastrous in the short run and dismal, at best, in the long run, it is unfair to evaluate the Ord River Scheme in its present very incomplete condition. By 1975 only 15 of the original 30 farmers were still farming(27), and, despite optimism, their future was unassured. Kununurra persists as the only "modern" town within an area of 300,000 square miles, and Lake Argyle, behind the storage dam, has become the principal tourist attraction of the entire Kimberleys Division. It will take another decade or two to determine whether the Ord River Scheme is a viable northern development project, an impressive but uneconomic status symbol, or merely a costly white elephant.

Queensland's Brigalow Development

The scheme. A very extensive portion of southeastern Queensland is covered with a scrubby natural vegetation association that is dominated by an acacia species called brigalow (Acacia harpophylla). It is land of reasonable natural fertility, and since the early 1950s there has been much large-scale clearing of the scrub. In the early 1960s the Queensland government, with federal financial assistance, embarked on a massive twelve-year program to clear some 12 million acres, almost entirely in the drainage basin of the Fitzroy River, of brigalow and develop the land for pastoral/agricultural usage.(28) At present the program is

virtually completed. In addition to this major project, there
has been considerable small-scale scrub clearance as well.

Tentative evaluation. The brigalow area in general and the
Fitzroy Basin in particular have substantially increased in
population, livestock, and crop output. There is greatly
expanded acreage in both improved pasturage and cropland.
Increased production of such winter grains as oats and barley
and summer crops such as sorghum are helping to provide a
basis for much sounder mixed farming in this cattle country.
The government is considering extending the clearing of scrub
into other brigalow areas, as well as into the drier gidgee
(Acacia cambagei) country just to the northwest.(29) Population growth in the two shires, Banana and Duaringa, containing most of the development has been steady and substantial, increasing from 10,296 in 1954 to 18,343 in 1971.

The Mining Boom

Since 1960 there has been mineral exploration and exploitation
on a scale previously unknown, with immense capital investments, detailed scientific prospecting, highly mechanized
extraction techniques, and extensive construction of associated
facilities (fig. 3.3). This abrupt acceleration of mineral-
related activity was stimulated by a coincidence of several
unrelated events, but by far the most dynamic catalyst was
the repeal, within a three-month period in 1960, of previously
existing bans on the export of iron ore by both the federal
government and the state of Western Australia. Almost overnight several dozen already discovered but not divulged ore
bodies were patented, and systematic exploration began in
earnest. Less than six months later Australia's first commercial petroleum field was discovered in southeastern Queensland, and other unrelated discoveries of economic deposits of
various minerals followed in short order.
     As a result of all this activity, the national value of
mineral production quintupled in a decade and a half. More
pertinent for our consideration here, however, is the effect on
the geography of rural Australia. In many local areas, of
course, the result was a complete transformation of landscape,
economy, and even demography. Barren desert or dusty
scrub became a bustling center of noisy machines and frantic
construction. It is inevitable that some of these developments
will be short-lived, leaving a residue of crumbling ghost towns
and ugly mine dumps. Others, however, will be long-lasting
and may attain the stability of a Broken Hill or a Mt. Isa.
     Indeed, in some areas the magnitude of the development
is almost too immense to comprehend. The outstanding example
is in the Pilbara country, where the enormous scale of ex-

ploitation and the staggering sums of money that are involved
augur well for relative permanence in the complex infrastructure of transportation, communication, and general urban
development.   The landscape of the Pilbara has been ir-
revocably metamorphosed: modern townships sprout among
barren ranges, deep-water ports appear where crumbling
jetties or unbroken mangrove swamps once stood, transportation and communication have been revolutionized, and
population has grown by ten- or twenty-fold within a few
months.   It is abundantly clear that the rapidly changing
geography of the northwestern shoulder of Western Australia
will be notably different in the foreseeable future from what it
was a brief decade or so ago.

SOME SUMMARY THOUGHTS

The term "rural transformation" has misleading implications
when applied to Australia.   Only in limited areas have there
been abrupt and conspicuous changes in the rural landscape,
economy, or demography in the past decade or so.   To be
sure,   the   transformation   has   been   remarkable   in   some
regions - newly irrigated sections such as the Namoi Valley, or
areas of massive scrub clearance and land development such as
the Coonalpyn Downs, or districts of intensive mining activity
such as the Pilbara country.   But for the most part the
geography of rural Australia in the mid-1970s differs little
from the geography of rural Australia in the 1950s - indeed,
some might say from the 1930s.   Many of the country areas
have not changed at all, and in most of the rest of the land
changes have been very slow and gradual, and are related to
better roads, enhanced communications, and increased use of
such   agricultural/pastoral   improvements   as   fertilizers,
machinery, fencing, water development, and superior breeding
of crops and livestock.
    Many trends are evident - toward more beef cattle, fewer
dairy cattle, larger numbers of minor livestock such as swine
and poultry, crop diversification, pasture improvement, and
more intensive property management.   But these developments
are intermittent and uneven in their extent and magnitude.
    The principal changes have largely been brought about
by major investments, particularly in mining, irrigation, scrub
clearance, pasture improvement, and fertilization.   These are
the things that have the greatest impact on the rural work
force and hence on the total rural population.   Where efforts
have been large-scale and carefully planned, the rural scene
has been truly transformed.

NOTES

(1) Donald P. Whitaker et al., Area Handbook for Australia
     (Washington, D. C.: American University Press, 1974),
     p. 267.
(2) A prominent example of this lineation is documented in
     Adrian Allen, "Frontier Towns in Western Queensland:
     Their Growth and Present Tributary Areas," Australian
     Geographer 11 (September 1969): 137.
(3) Whitaker et al., Area Handbook, p. 267.
(4) The rural component of the population decreased from 18
     percent in 1971, to 17 percent in 1966, to 14 percent in
     1971.
(5) June A. Sheppard, "Rural Population Changes in New
     South Wales, 1921-1954," Australian Geographer 9 (March
     1964): 156.
(6) See, for example, A.C.B. Allen, "Marginal Settlement -
     A Case Study of the Channel Country of Southwest
     Queensland," Australian Geographical Studies 6 (April
     1968): 1-23; R. J. Johnston, "Components and Correlates
     of Victorian Rural Population Change, 1954-1961," Aus-
     tralian Geographical Studies 5 (October 1967): 165-81;
     Brian S. Marsden, "Types of Population Change in
     Queensland, 1961-6," Australian Geographer 6, (Septem-
     ber 1968): 525-27; Sheppard, "Rural Population Changes":
     156-63; P. J. Smailes and J. K. Molyneux, "The Evolution
     of an Australian Rural Settlement Pattern: Southern New
     England, N.S.W.," Transactions, Institute of British
     Geographers, no. 36 (June 1965): 31-54; John C. Steinke,
     Regional Trends in Australian Population Distribution,
     1947-1966 (Sydney: Department of Decentralization and
     Development, 1971); and D.B. Williams and T.G.
     Macaulay, "Changes in Rural Population and Work Force
     in Victoria, 1961-66," Australian Geographical Studies 9
     (October 1971): 161-71.
(7) "Country" statistical divisions are all those that do not
     contain a major urban area, i.e., all Australian statistical
     divisions except those containing Sydney, Melbourne,
     Brisbane, Adelaide, Perth, Newcastle, Canberra, Wol-
     longong, Hobart, and Geelong.
(8) Whitaker et al., Area Handbook, p. 295.
(9) R. J. Johnston, "The Australian Small Town in the
     Post-War Period," Australian Geographer 10 (March 1967):
     216.
(10) See, for example, Allen, "Frontier Towns," p. 129.
(11) Lack of success in decentralization has been analyzed in
     many studies, including "Australian Cities - How Big and
     Where?," Bank of New South Wales Review (July 1975):
     308; R.K. Hefford, "Decentralization in South Australia:

A Review," <u>Australian Geographical Studies</u> 3 (October 1965): 79-96; and Richard E. Lonsdale, "Manufacturing Decentralization: The Discouraging Record in Australia," <u>Land Economics</u> 48 (November 1972): 321-28.

(12) O.H.K. Spate, <u>Australia</u> (New York: Praeger, 1969), p. 108.

(13) For more details, see Tom L. McKnight, "Elizabeth, South Australia: An Approach to Decentralization," <u>Australian Geographical Studies</u> 3 (April 1965): 39-53.

(14) For specific examples, see R. L. Heathcote, "Changes in Pastoral Land Tenure and Ownership," <u>Australian Geographical Studies</u> 3 (April 1965): 1-16; P. J. Smailes and J. K. Molyneux, "Twentieth Century Developments in the Rural Settlement Pattern of the Southern New England Tablelands," in <u>New England Essays</u>, ed. R. F. Warner (Armidale, Australia: University of New England Press, 1963), pp. 85-95.

(15) D. B. Williams and T. G. Macaulay, <u>Rural Work Force and Population in Victoria</u> (Melbourne: School of Agriculture, University of Melbourne Press, 1970), p. 19.

(16) Whitaker et al., <u>Area Handbook</u>, p. 280.

(17) Harlan J. Dirks, "Cut Output, Raise Prices, Australia's Dairies Ask," <u>Foreign Agriculture</u> 19 (July 19, 1976): 8.

(18) See examples in Juergen Dahlke, "Evolution of the Wheat Belt in Western Australia: Thoughts on the Nature of Pioneering along the Dry Margin," <u>Australian Geographer</u> 13 (March 1975): 13; and C. R. Twidale and Derek L. Smith, "'A Perfect Desert' Transformed: The Agricultural Development of Northwestern Eyre Peninsula, South Australia," <u>Australian Geographer</u> 11 (March 1971): 449.

(19) E. W. Thorpe, J. H. Holmes, and P. Brownie, "Farm Size and Changing Farm Practices in Southern New England," in <u>New England Essays</u>, ed. Warner, p. 125.

(20) See "Lot Feeding in Australia," <u>ANZ Bank Quarterly Survey</u>, July 1973, pp. 14-16.

(21) For more details, see F. H. Bauer, "Government Land Development on Kangaroo Island, South Australia," <u>Proceedings, Royal Geographical Society of Australasia, South Australian Branch</u> 53 (December 1952): 1-17.

(22) For more details, see K. J. Collins and D. D. Harris, <u>A Regional Geography of Victoria</u> (Melbourne: Whitcombe & Tombes, 1965); D. D. Harris and D. A. M. Lea, <u>A Regional Geography of South Australia</u> (Melbourne: Whitcombe & Tombes, ca. 1960); and Ann Marshall, "'Desert' Becomes 'Downs': The Impact of a Scientific Discovery," <u>Australian Geographer</u> 12 (March 1972): 23-34.

(23) For more details, see Thomas P. Field, <u>Postwar Land Settlement in Western Australia</u> (Lexington: University of Kentucky Press, 1963).

(24) Duncan Graham, "The Agrimoguls of the West," <u>Bulletin</u> 92 (February 28, 1970): 77.

(25)   The population of Esperance Shire was 427 in 1947; 1,087 in 1954; 2,285 in 1961; and 4,854 in 1966.

(26)   For more details, see Malcolm Douglas and Dave Oldmeadow, "The Ord Dam: Friend or Foe?," Walkabout 40 (February 1974): 4-10; T. A. G. Hungerford, "Harnessing the Ord," Walkabout 29 (December 1963): 51-56; and Gavin McDonnell, "The Ord Debate and Public Decision-Making: A View from the Terrace," Australian Quarterly 38 (September 1966): 44-56.

(27)   Don Lipscombe, "The Ord Buries Its Problems," Bulletin 96 (November 30, 1974): 28.

(28)   For more details, see A. C. B. Allen, Interior Queensland (Sydney: Angus and Robertson, 1972), pp. 66-67; and Vic Worstead, "Queensland Tackles the Brigalow," Bulletin 89 (September 2, 1967), p. 63.

(29)   See, The Economics of Land Development in the Belyando-Suttor Rivers Region, Queensland (Canberra: Bureau of Agricultural Economics, 1968).

4 The Marginal Lands of Australia and the American West: Some Comparisons in Their Perceptions and Settlement

Jean Williams Ferrill

PERCEPTIONAL EXPERIENCES

The early environmental perception of an area often influences its later settlement. It has been suggested that differences in perceptions can be explained by cultural attitudes current in the societies that produce the observers.(1) If this is true, one might expect people with a common cultural heritage to share like images and reactions to similar environments, and subsequently similar settlement experiences, even though the environments are separated by an ocean and thousands of miles.

Comparisons of Australian and American perceptional experiences are facilitated by a number of circumstances shared in common. The cultural heritage and technological levels of the settlers were similar, being largely European, and predominantly English-speaking northern Europeans. Both countries experienced an expansion of agricultural settlement during the mid- to late 1800s, in each case in the direction of dryland areas. Thus, in each society, the pioneer settlers or "observers" faced an arid frontier. In the United States this frontier appeared on the Great Plains, roughly along the 100th meridian. In Australia settlers faced an arid frontier whenever they moved inland toward the dry continental interior. Of particular significance were the experiences of Australian wheat farmers in the state of South Australia, in the general area north of Adelaide and Goyder's Line (see figs. 4.1 and 4.2).

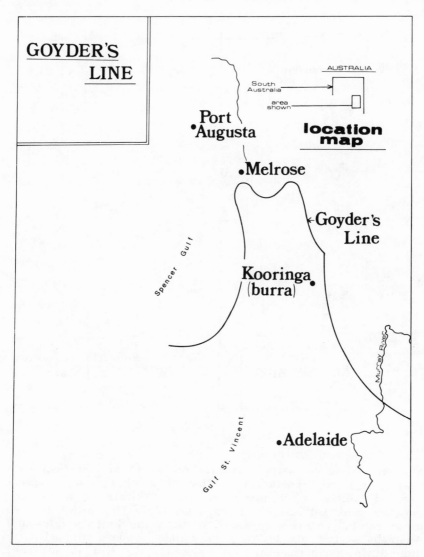

Fig. 4.1. Source: Adapted from S.A. Parliament Paper 154, 1865-66, map.

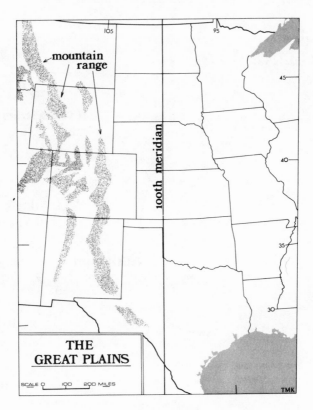

Fig. 4.2.

According to Ralph Brown, "no phase of historical geography is more important than that of weighing the effectiveness of beliefs as distinct from actual knowledge in the occupance and settlement of regions."(2) The belief in two major rainfall theories appeared in both the United States and Australia in the late 1800s. These theories were supported by individuals, governments, and railroads, and had an apparent influence on the pioneer settlements of the marginal lands in both countries. Comparing such beliefs in different yet similar areas of settlement should give a more complete picture of man's attempts at rural transformation, and lay the foundation for understanding the philosophies and policies of the present.

A Desert or a Garden?

Some early explorers in the United States such as Coronado, Pike, and Long saw the Great Plains as a "desert." Maps in Willard's Geography for Schools and others perpetuated this image. A desert was specified in scientific journals, such as the American Journal of Science and novels, including Washington Irving's Astoria. In 1865, D. F. Mackay, who traveled down Australia's Darling River valley with cattle, described the area as a "perfect desert." An explorer, Captain Sturt, spoke of the interior of this country as "a heartless desert."(3) Even today, central Australia is described by one writer as "the most inhospitable region in the habitable world."(4) Thus in both countries the early perception of the interior was a desert image. It is important to note here that the American perception was generally wrong, but the Australian one was quite correct. Regardless of reality, however, the images were remarkably similar.

These desert images were satisfactory in both countries until settlers began to push onto their fringes and population growth became linked to national development. The new settlers hoped to transform the desert into farms. For this to become a reality, they needed water. An increase in rainfall would have been ideal. Thus began the myths or theories of "rainfall follows the plow" and "trees as weather modifiers" to challenge the notion of aridity which the settlers faced. Proponents of the plow theory believed that once the prairie sod was broken, rainfall could be absorbed into the soil, eventually slowly evaporating back into the atmosphere and thus causing an increase in humidity and rainfall. In this way the desert would be transformed into a garden. Those who believed in trees as weather modifiers said the planting of trees would check the sweeping winds, reduce evaporation of moisture from the soil, and distribute rainfall more evenly. The most adamant exclaimed that the trees would also cause an increase in the rainfall.

THE PLOW THEORY

A few early explorers and writers of the Great Plains in America had suggested the possibility of altering those plains by cultivation. Josiah Gregg said, "Why may we not suppose that the general influence of civilization...that extensive cultivation of the earth...might contribute to the multiplication of showers...?"(5) Sir Richard Burton pointed to the efforts and results of the Morman settlements in Utah and attributed the change to cultivation and tree planting.(6) Articles were published in the United States Geological Reports and by the

Smithsonian Institution. One of the most vocal and widely recognized scientific supporters of the plow theory was Dr. Samuel Aughey, professor at the University of Nebraska. Professor Aughey wrote numerous articles, read papers to the Kansas and Nebraska state boards of agriculture, gave addresses to the Nebraska State Legislature, and published a book entitled, Sketches of the Physical Geography and Geology of Nebraska, where he explained:

> After the soil is broken, the rain as it falls is absorbed by the soil like a huge sponge. The soil gives this absorbed moisture slowly back to the atmosphere by evaporation. Thus year by year as cultivation of the soil is extended, more of the rain that falls is absorbed and retained to be given off by evaporation, or to produce springs. This, of course, must give increasing moisture and rainfall.(7)

Following in Dr. Aughey's footsteps was Charles Dana Wilber, who popularized the phrase, "rain follows the plow," in his book, The Great Valleys and Prairies of Nebraska and the Northwest. Wilber read papers to such organizations as the Nebraska State Horticultural Society. Thus when the United States Public Land Commission, acting upon Powell's famous Report on the Lands of the Arid Region in 1878 as well as the commission's own findings in 1879, declared the land west of the 100th meridian unfit for agriculture, officers of the Nebraska State Board of Agriculture wrote Wilber and Aughey for their views. These two proponents of the plow theory answered in a letter that was later published. They stated that the assumptions of the Public Land Commission were completely untrue and that "the present rate of increase in rainfall...will in a comparatively short time fit these regions for agriculture without the aid of irrigation."(8) Other individuals joining the plow theory in the United States in the late 1800s included H. R. Hilton, a Kansas farmer-agriculturist; Orange Judd, editor and publisher of the Prairie Farmer in Chicago; and Professor Frank H. Snow, later chancellor of the state university at Lawrence, Kansas.

The settlers in Australia were faced with an even more arid frontier. The Surveyor-General of South Australia, G. W. Goyder, in 1864 established a line of demarcation between those areas with adequate rainfall and those where drought had occurred in the previous twelve months. The line itself, however, did not stop the attempts to expand the South Australian agricultural frontier in the early 1870s. With excellent harvests to the south of Goyder's Line, the farmers soon looked upon the line as an obstacle and demanded that it be "shifted out of the colony."(9) They explained that the good harvests were a result of "rain follows the plow," and gave this theory as a further reason for expansion. A university professor in Australia at this time explained the situation thus:

> There is good reason to believe the old agri-
> cultural saw "rain follows the plough" to be a good
> one, and that whispering cane fields and billowy
> breadths of wheat or oats, well kept vineyards and
> orchards or even the humble potato-plot and melon
> ground are as effective agencies for tempering heat
> and precipitating moisture as the leafy jungle or the
> hill-top bristling with pines.(10)

The government, and particularly Goyder, had said the areas which now were producing good crops were too arid for agri-culture. Unless the government had always been wrong, there must be a reason for the increase in moisture. "Rainfall follows the plow" seemed a good explanation. This doctrine was supported by the rural press and by the minister of agri-culture, and it became a prominent ingredient in the optimism of the time. The overall objective of population dispersal and the fuller development of the continental interior could now be achieved.

Government Support

The state boards of agriculture in both Nebraska and Kansas supported the theory that rainfall followed the plow. Certainly enough articles appeared in their reports to give considerable emphasis to the idea, and it had enough support to influence Congress in the rejection of the report of the Public Land Commission. This report recommended withdrawing from home-stead entry, temporarily, the land west of the 100th meridian. The Homestead Act of 1862 was in operation as settlers reached this meridian on the Great Plains. The act gave up to 160 acres of "free" land to a settler for a ten dollar fee and five years of continuous cultivation. This was a reduction in quantity over previous acts, but an even greater reduction in price. It made land available to the small farmer. Until the Kincaid Act of 1904, Congress did nothing to revise the public land system as farmers settled beyond the 100th meridian. The Kincaid Act enlarged the homestead to 640 acres in western Nebraska and encouraged the farmers to venture further into the "arid frontier."

The land legislation during this period, offering acreage at low prices, resulted in more land being sold between 1862 and 1889 than in all the years before the Homestead Act. However, the largest proportion of this land went to specu-lators - 100,000,000 acres - whereas only 80,000,000 acres

were granted to homesteaders. An additional large amount was
given to railroads.(11) Most of this land was west of the
100th meridian. Settlers were demanding land beyond this line
and the United States government made it available.

The situation in Australia was quite similar in the sense
that the plow preceded the land laws. The government of
South Australia was pressured into supporting the plow
theory. Prior to 1872, the agricultural areas which were open
to future expansion were quite limited, but as the good rainfall
years produced bountiful harvests, pressures on the legislature resulted in a government policy to encourage settlement
in marginal lands. These districts were labeled "good agricultural land" by the government and restricted to not more
than 320 acres each.

The Strangeways Act of 1869, allowing the sale of land on
credit, was a major development and ushered in a period of
new settlement. In July 1872 a new act abolished the agricultural areas and opened the entire agricultural frontier of
South Australia to credit sales. Overall, the agricultural
frontier was pushed 150 miles north and nearly two million new
acres were brought under cultivation. The settled area of
South Australia more than doubled.(12)

The land laws of both the United States and South Australia were inadequate for the semi-arid environments beyond
the 100th meridian and Goyder's Line. English land laws to
which the settlers were accustomed were developed for humid
environments and could not be applied successfully without
significant modification in the more arid areas. The 160 acres
available under the Homestead Act were not sufficient to make
a living with the poor and unreliable rainfall which was encountered west of the 100th meridian. With the argument
among "authorities" about a possible increase in rainfall,
Congress was not quick to change the land policy. Powell
suggests that since "there was no store of experimentation to
guide the myriad decisions which had to be made at every
level," then each American settler "was left to discover his
own management techniques by trial and error at the expense
of his local environment."(13) Even the 320 acres available in
more arid South Australia certainly did not insure a successful
farm. With the abolishment of "agricultural areas" listed by
the South Australian government, settlers were left to judge
what land would produce and what would not. The results
were often disastrous.

Railroads and the Plow

There was a definite contrast in the railroad development on
the two frontiers of the Great Plains and South Australia.
The railroads in America were developed by private individuals

or corporations and preceded the settlement of the Great
Plains. In South Australia where the railroads were, and still
are, government owned and operated their expansion lagged
behind the settlement frontier.

Railroads were a big business in the United States during
the second half of the nineteenth century; thus their support
of "rainfall follows the plow" carried a great deal of influence.
Given an early emphasis for pushing onto the Great Plains by
the cattle industry as well as the push to reach the West
Coast, the railroads had already crossed the 100th meridian
before the mass of pioneers reached that point. With the
railroads preceding the population on the plains, their future
success depended upon the rapid development of the regions
they served. Towns often developed around railroad water
and wood stops and can still be traced in some areas by their
alphabetical name order. Certainly the railroads contributed
greatly to the expansion of the frontier in the United States.
They brought millions of settlers into the wilderness. It is
not surprising that to help make this frontier more attractive
to the settlers, the railroads quickly adopted and supported
the theories advocating an increase in rainfall on the "Great
American Desert" and used them in their promotional slogans
and other devices. For example, the Santa Fe Railroad
printed a pamphlet showing a Kansas farmer using a steel
plow. The pamphlet asks, "Who killed the Great American
Desert?" The sturdy yeoman answers, "I did with my team
and plow."(14) They also advertised, "The rainline has moved
steadily, year by year, at the rate of about 18 miles per
annum, keeping just ahead and propelled by the advancing
population."15) When Professor Aughey spoke, a stenographer
employed by the Burlington and Missouri River Railroad was
usually close at hand. Copies of these speeches were published, many finding their way to prospective emigrants in
Europe.(16)

As the Great Plains "opened up" the condition often
reversed and towns subsequently competed with each other to
attract the railroads. Ellis wrote that Nebraska towns spent
four million dollars and Kansas towns over eighteen million
between 1872 and 1890 to bring a railroad into town.(17)
Towns in the Great Plains came to believe that the railroad was
essential to their existence, just as the railroads knew that
settlement expansion was necessary for their own survival.

Settlement expansion preceded the railways in Australia.
The railroads were built by the individual state governments
and each state had its own system, including differing track
gauges. Even though the government had full control and
planned to build the railways in a preconceived pattern, the
design was soon modified in response to the demands of both
the settler and the frontier.

The South Australian railways seemed to follow the march of the plow, although several steps behind. A new government committee on railway construction was formed almost every year resulting in constantly changing proposals, especially after the removal of Goyder's Line as a limit to agricultural advance. However, Goyder was appointed chairman of the 1875 railway commission and exerted considerable influence in the new railway construction proposals. His ideas were based on long-term interests of the colony rather than immediate local demands of agriculturists, whom he was sure were doomed to failure for overextending themselves beyond his agriculture line.(18)   Greenway claims that the "Australian railroads have done very little to open the frontier."(19) They exerted practically no influence on the theory of rainfall following the plow, but rather seemed to be directed by those who stood behind the theory. There was also the presence of Goyder, with his warnings and conservatism on behalf of the government in South Australia, as opposed to the high speculation in hopes of quick gains by private individuals and corporations in America. One might well wonder if the situation would have been any different in Australia had the railways been privately developed.

TREES AS WEATHER MODIFIERS

A second theory for pushing back the arid frontier was tree planting. The idea of trees modifying the weather did not originate, however, on the Great Plains or in Australia. The European settlers on both continents brought with them certain plant-climate theories that can be traced back to ancient Greece, about 600 B.C.(20) The belief in trees having a tempering effect on dry lands or deserts became widespread in Europe by the time of Columbus or earlier. A publication in the mid-eighteenth century attributes much to a single forest:

> A single forest, however, in the midst of these parched deserts, would be sufficient to render them more temperate, to attract the waters from the atmosphere, to restore all the principles of fertility to the earth, and, of course, to make man, in these barren regions, enjoy all the sweets of a temperate climate.(21)

As settlers faced a new life on the arid frontiers of the two countries, they saw land lacking the humid-type vegetation to which they had been accustomed. Perhaps, they thought, the absence of this vegetation was the cause of the limited precipitation. If trees were planted, then rain might follow.

This was not a new idea, but merely the application of older principles to the needs of the new arid frontier.

Suggestions of trees tempering the climate of the Great Plains in the United States began to appear in limited numbers a decade or two before the farmer pushed out onto the "desert." Explorer Frederick Olmsted, traveling through Texas in the 1850s, noted increasing amounts of moisture, the appearance of new springs, and farming without irrigation in the vicinity of San Antonio. He attributed these changes to "an increased growth of trees and grasses upon the plains."(22) Ferdinand V. Hayden of the United States Geological Survey suggested in his report of 1867 that forests planted in proper quantities would bring rain to the very foot of the Rocky Mountains.(23)

It was during the twenty-year period of 1870-1890 that planting trees to change the climate on the Great Plains received its greatest support. Although many articles were written by laymen, the most influential supporters were members of the United States Forest Service. The first three chiefs of the newly created Division of Forestry all supplied official government support. One of them, Bernhard E. Fernow, held the theory that the whole world was a potential forest. Nature, if left to herself, would forest the entire world, with few exceptions. His other theory was that a forest to some extent creates its own existence, or, "Where a tree would perish a forest may persist."(24) Other "authoritative" support came from the Dean of the Industrial College at the University of Nebraska and state botanist, Charles Bessey, and Professor Harvey Culbertson of the Agricultural College faculty at the same university. Bessey told the Nebraska State Board of Agriculture, "The Plains are dry because they are treeless...."(25) Culbertson stated that climate is composed of three parts: rainfall, humidity, and temperature. He believed man was capable of changing all three conditions, primarily by planting trees.(26)

If a change in the climate was also necessary for Australia to extend her agriculture, the planting of trees became another logical means to increase the rainfall. The editor of the Port Augusta Dispatch in 1878 thought that trees would be more effective than the plow.(27) The Director of the Botanic Garden in Adelaide, Dr. Richard Schomburgk, was an advocate of this theory and was a major force in getting several forest preserves established. He further suggested giving rate reductions to landholders for planting trees.(28) Another eminent botanist, Dr. F. Von Mueller, wrote that, "fig-trees, like in Egypt, planted by the hundreds of thousands, to increase and to retain the rain will then also have ameliorated here the climate."(29) Even Goyder proposed planting trees, and he became chairman of a forest board in 1875. However, his views were more conservative in that while he believed

"tree cover could have a local ameliorating effect on climate,"
he did not believe it could increase the rainfall.(30)

John Ednie Brown was chosen as the new Conservator of
Forests for South Australia in 1878. According to Meinig,
"Brown elevated trees from a mere 'influence' into an almost
complete 'control' over climate, and explained the aridity of
interior Australia simply by the absence of trees."(31)   Although much support for this idea was voiced by the rural
press and persons of authority, it seemed to be largely
ignored by the Australian farmer. Meinig suggests that the
reason may have been that such a theory clearly pointed out
the unpleasant and unwanted idea that the country at present
was too dry, even though there was a cure.(32)   This could
also be said of the plow theory, however, since rainfall follows
the plow; yet the farmer seemed to heed this idea. Perhaps
the Australian farmer was too accustomed to clearing trees,
scrub, and stumps from the land to envision any good results
by adding trees.

Government Support of Tree Planting

As the South Australian state government followed the plow, it
also followed the farmer and his notions of tree removal. The
clearing of scrub and forest land was encouraged by the Scrub
Lands Act of 1877. The tree-clearing operations were widespread enough, however, that eventually several state governments recognized a need to arrest this waste of timber and
embark upon a tree conservation program. A forestry administrative branch was formed in South Australia with James
E. Brown at its head. He was the major force behind the
government support of tree planting and its influence on
rainfall. He launched programs in three separate states - New
South Wales, South Australia, and Western Australia - between
1870 and 1900.(33) Although the programs got off to a good
start, they again faltered when government support lagged.

The situation was different in the United States, where
the state governments early recognized the need to encourage
tree planting. Primarily this need developed because many of
them were on the "treeless prairie," but others on the edges
of the prairie found their forests being rapidly destroyed by
settlers and railroads. Another factor, competition among the
states in attracting immigrants, resulted in state bounties,
premiums, and tax exemptions for tree planting. In 1873, the
new Federal Timber Culture Act required that a settler plant
at least forty acres of a quarter section to trees and cultivate
them for eight years in order to secure patent to the land.
The law was amended in 1874, reducing the forty acres to ten.
Nebraska Senator Phineas W. Hitchcock defended his bill by
stating, "The object of this bill is to encourage the growth of

timber, not merely for the soil, not merely for the value of the timber itself, but for its influence upon the climate."(34)

Tree planting on the Great Plains continued to be supported by both the state and federal governments even after attitudes concerning the beneficial effects of trees became more realistic. While it became recognized that the impact of trees on precipitation was minimal or nonexistant, the beneficial qualities of windbreaks and shelterbelts has continued to be emphasized.

COMPARISONS IN PERCEPTIONS AND SETTLEMENT

Similarities in Perception

The early perceptional experiences of South Australia and the Great Plains region of the United States were apparently quite similar. When the first explorers and later settlers originally viewed the marginal lands in each country, they saw "deserts" which were unsuitable for settlement. When the farmer, railroad promoter or state "booster" looked over Goyder's Line in South Australia or the 100th meridian in the United States, many saw "gardens" waiting to be utilized and enriched by man's labors. The plow and/or the tree could transform the landscape. Hadn't this been proven in ages past as Europeans conquered the wilderness?

Similar regional descriptions and agricultural images were written in both countries in the mid- to late 1800s. Mention was often made of gardens and exceedingly healthy climates as the new myths were promoted. An apparent optimism and joyous anticipation of the wonders to be achieved on the new agricultural frontier were expressed in vivid adjectives and stimulating phrases. Many such descriptions were directed at prospective settlers and seemed to be staunch beliefs expressed by the composers. Apparently both continents produced similar images as the comparisons in table 4.1 illustrate.

Contrasts in Settlement

Although the perceptions were similar, there were important differences in the settlement processes of the marginal lands in South Australia and the United States. Both governments encouraged overextension into semi-arid lands by laws that were misused by speculators and large stock owners. The government in the United States, however, was strongly influenced by such commercial interests as the private railroads, which were active in promoting the new "garden" image and in encouraging settlement in the marginal lands. The South

Table 4.1.   A Comparison of Regional Descriptions

Period	Great Plains	Australia
1860s	"One mighty field of flowing grain."[a]	"Boundless pastures, bottomless depths of alluvial soil."[i]
1870s	"Italy of America."[b] "Paradise for invalids."[c]	"This glorious climate suits my nervous state to admiration."[j]
1880s	"Health resort."[d] "Garden."[e] "Corn patch of the world."[f] "Hub of the country."[g]	"Capable of producing within its boundaries everything that grows on the face of the earth."[k] "Turn the wilderness into a garden."[l]
1890s	"Fairest domain on earth."[h]	"Land of boundless possibilities."[m] "Exceedingly healthy."[n]

Sources: (a) Statement attributed to Cyrus Thomas in Charles Robert Kutzleb, "Rain Follows the Plow: The History of an Idea (Ph.D. diss., University of Colorado, 1968), p. 56. (b) Statement by Stephen Marcou from David M. Emmons, Garden in the Grasslands (Lincoln: University of Nebraska Press, 1971), p. 70. (c) Lawrence D. Burch, Nebraska As It Is (Chicago: C. S. Burch, 1878), p. 26. (d) Samuel Aughey, Sketches of the Physical Geography and Geology of Nebraska (Omaha: Daily Republican Book and Job Office, 1880), p. 150. (e) C. D. Wilber, The Great Valleys and Prairies of Nebraska and the Northwest (Omaha: Daily Republican Book and Job Office, 1881), p. 71. (f) Orange Judd, "Address of Mr. Orange Judd," Annual Report of the Nebraska State Board of Agriculture, 1885 (Lincoln: Nebraska State Journal, 1886), pp. 183-99. (g) Ibid. (h) From The Nebraska Farmer, April 3, 1890, as found in Emmons, Garden, p. 74. (i) Statement by John Woolley in Ian Turner, ed., The Australian Dream: A Collection of Anticipations about Australia from Captain Cook to the Present Day (Melbourne: Sun Books, 1968), p. 84. (j) Statement by James Bonwick from Turner, ed., Australian Dream, p. 82. (k) Statement by Henry Gyles Turner from Turner, ed., Australian Dream, p. 104. (l) Statement by Rev. James Jefferies from Turner, ed., Australian Dream, p. 112. (m) William Epps, Land Systems of Australia (London: Swan Sonnenschein, 1894), p. 1. (n) A. R. Wallace, Australasia, vol. I (London: Edward Stanford, 1893), p. 34.

Australian government was at first reluctant, but then pressured by the farmer, to expand the utilization of arid-type
lands. Yet Goyder, with his warnings of overextension onto
lands unsuitable for cultivation, always lent a note of moderation on behalf of the South Australian government that was not
present in the United States. Perhaps this moderation coupled
with less population pressure for new land development and
the various Australian state governments' policies of land
leases rather than individual ownership had their effect on the
settlement pattern. Would Australians have taken more
initiative in arid land settlement if the above factors were not
present? Because of these reasons, and others to be sure,
and in spite of a philosophy bent upon settling and developing
the continent, the marginal lands in South Australia, remained
sparsely populated or unpopulated. The defeats and retreats,
according to Powell, and the lessons learned from them, were
important contributions to the South Australian's awareness of
his environment. The development of more conservative agricultural practices, leasing systems, and land classification
systems produced a wheat belt that was the result of "a
peculiarly Australian agricultural revolution." (35)

The Impact of Drought

What was the effect of the droughts on both the myths of
"desert" and "garden" and on the settlement expansion? The
plow theory essentially ended in the United States after the
severe droughts of the 1890s. The belief in the benefits of
tree planting continue today on the Great Plains, with the
stress however on local modifications by the use of shelterbelts
or windbreaks. It is interesting to note that Meinig suggests
that the droughts of 1880-82 in Australia, despite their
severity, did not destroy the hope for climatic change by the
use of the plow or trees. He says:

> Although some members of parliament pointed
> out that quite evidently the rain had not followed
> the plough in South Australia, and contrary to all
> the talk about world-wide evidence in support of the
> theory it had not done so in similar areas such as
> California either, the proponents of the rainfall
> theories were not yet ready to admit defeat.(36)

The proponents suggested that the plowing had not been deep
enough, or that the devastation of forests had gone too far,
but with time, more cultivation and more trees, some relief
would be seen. It is also interesting that this period of the
1880s, when South Australia had experienced drought and
still clung to the rainfall theories, was the same time that

Dr. Aughey and others in the United States were so strongly advocating these same theories as solutions for the dry conditions on the Great Plains. Optimism remained high on both continents and more experiences with drought were necessary before those trying to conquer the arid frontier gave up their beliefs in the rainfall theories concerning plows and trees.

What was the effect of the droughts on settlement expansion? According to Heathcote, "It is doubtful whether any land has been permanently abandoned solely as a result of drought, though temporary abandonment was reported."(37) After the theories of an increase in rainfall were discarded, such things as irrigation, drought-resistant crops, and dryland farming techniques, have been tried and accepted or rejected. Advances and retreats, successes and failures have been the experiences on both continents.

HISTORICAL IMPRINT ON THE TWENTIETH CENTURY

Basic European concepts and traditions were the foundation of both Australia and the United States. Part of this tradition included a compelling urge to people the continents and to make the land productive. Thus population distribution became a concern quite early in each country's frontier expansion. The Australians were urged to "fill the empty spaces" and Americans were advised to "go west, young men." When the frontier moved onto the "marginal lands" of South Australia and the Great Plains, the perceptions of the environment and consequent settlement of it, in spite of the hazards, were still based on this deeply imbedded philosophy to settle and develop.

The Australian government supported the philosophy with policies of closer rural settlement, irrigation schemes, and a large number of subsidies and concessions to both rural residents and later rural industries. The American government encouraged population growth on the Great Plains with such programs as the Homestead and Kincaid acts, federal irrigation projects, and the planting of shelterbelts.

Today many of the land use limits are established, thus eliminating the advances and retreats of the agricultural frontier as was seen in the earlier trial-and-error phase of settlement. In South Australia, this limit closely follows Goyder's Line, which the farmers in the 1870s had demanded be "shifted out of the colony." In Nebraska, the "Kincaiders" have long abandoned their marginal small farms in the Sandhills, leaving the land to the cattle ranchers.

Yet the value patterns set early in the development of a country are difficult to change. The populations of rural areas remain important, both politically and economically to the rest of the United States and Australia. Public expenditures on rural support programs, intended to maintain or to increase rural population numbers, remain high, often at the expense of much-needed urban benefits. The myth of the yeoman farmer does not die easily.

Although the belief in the rainfall theories has disappeared more rapidly than the belief in the yeoman farmer, the underlying reason for those beliefs - to achieve maximum rural and regional development - has continued into the twentieth century. The American dream is also the Australian one. Such dreams, handed down through the history of a nation, are abandoned or redirected with great reluctance.

NOTES

(1) David M. Emmons, "The Influence of Ideology on Changing Environmental Images: The Case of Six Gazeteers," in Images of the Plains, ed. Brian W. Blouet and Merlin P. Lawson, (Lincoln: University of Nebraska Press, 1975), p. 125.

(2) Ralph H. Brown, Historical Geography of the United States (New York: Harcourt, Brace and World, 1948), p. iii.

(3) C. M. H. Clark, ed., Select Documents in Australian History, 1851-1900 (Sydney: Angus and Robertson, 1952), p. 188.

(4) John Greenway, Australia: The Last Frontier (New York: Dodd and Mead, 1972), p. 49.

(5) Josiah Gregg, Commerce of the Prairies, ed. Max L. Moorhead (Norman: University of Oklahoma Press, 1954), p. 362.

(6) Richard F. Burton, The City of the Saints and Across the Rocky Mountains to California (New York: Alfred A. Knopf, 1963), pp. 305-06.

(7) Samuel Aughey, Sketches of the Physical Geography and Geology of Nebraska (Omaha: Daily Republican Book and Job Office, 1880), pp. 44-45.

(8) Samuel Aughey and C. D. Wilber, Agriculture Beyond the 100th Meridian, or A Review of the U. S. Public Land Commission (Lincoln: Nebraska State Journal, 1880), p. 3.

(9) Michael Williams, "Delimiting the Spread of Settlement: An Examination of Evidence in South Australia," Economic Geography 42 (1962): 42.

(10) As quoted by R. L. Heathcote in Back of Bourke (Melbourne: Melbourne University Press, 1965), pp. 26-27.

(11) H. C. Allen, Bush and Backwoods (Sydney: Angus and Robertson; reprint ed., Michigan State University Press, 1959), p. 54.

84 THE PROCESS OF RURAL TRANSFORMATION

(12) D. W. Meinig, "Goyder's Line of Rainfall: The Role of a Geographic Concept in South Australian Land Policy and Agricultural Settlement," Agricultural History 35 (1961): 210.
(13) J. M. Powell, Environmental Management in Australia, 1788-1914 (Melbourne: Oxford University Press, 1976), p. 57.
(14) David M. Emmons, Garden in the Grasslands (Lincoln: University of Nebraska Press, 1971), p. 141.
(15) Ibid., p. 49.
(16) Robert Manley, "Samuel Aughey: Nebraska's Scientific Promoter," Journal of the West 25 (January 1967): 116.
(17) David M. Ellis, ed., The Frontier in American Development (Ithaca, New York: Cornell University Press, 1969), p. 367.
(18) D. W. Meinig, On the Margins of the Good Earth (Chicago: Rand McNally, 1962), pp. 131-40.
(19) Greenway, Australia, p. 178.
(20) For further discussion of these early theories, refer to Clarence J. Glacken, Traces on the Rhodian Shore (Berkeley: University of California Press, 1973).
(21) As quoted in W. M. Kollmorgen and Johanna Kollmorgen, "Landscape Meteorology in the Plains Area," Annals of the Association of American Geographers 43 (December 1973): 425.
(22) Fredrick Law Olmsted, A Journey Through Texas (New York: Dix Edwards, 1857), p. 447.
(23) Henry Nash Smith, "Rain Follows the Plow: The Notion of Increased Rainfall for the Great Plains, 1844-1880," Huntington Library Quarterly 10 (1970): 170.
(24) B. E. Fernow, "Forest Planting on the Plains," in Annual Report of the Nebraska State Board of Agriculture, 1890 (Lincoln: Nebraska State Journal, 1891), p. 140.
(25) Charles Bessey, "The Grasses and Forage Plants of Nebraska," in Annual Report of the Nebraska State Board of Agriculture, 1886 (Lincoln: Nebraska State Journal, 1887), pp. 208-09.
(26) Harvey Culbertson, "Meteorology," in Annual Report of the Nebraska State Horticultural Society, 1885 (Lincoln: Nebraska State Journal, 1887), pp. 29-44.
(27) Meinig, On the Margins, p. 70.
(28) Powell, Environmental Management, p. 66.
(29) Charles Robinson, New South Wales: The Oldest and Richest of the Australian Colonies (Sydney: Government Printer, 1873), p. 28.
(30) Alexander Rule, Forests of Australia (Sydney: Angus and Robertson, 1967), p. 63.
(31) Meinig, On the Margins, p. 71.
(32) Ibid.

(33) Rule, Forests of Australia, p. 61.
(34) C. Barron McIntosh, "Use and Abuse of the Timber
      Culture Act," in Annals of the Association of American
      Geographers 45 (September 1975): 349.
(35) Powell, Environmental Management, p. 109.
(36) Meinig, On the Margins, p. 87.
(37) R. L. Heathcote, "Drought in Australia: A Problem of
      Perception," Geographical Review 59 (April 1969): 184.

III
Economic Change in the Rural Sphere

5 Economic Aspects of Rural Transformation in Eastern Europe
Ivan Volgyes

Economic transformation is a major part of the modernization of rural life. This transformation is assisted by the simultaneous political, social and cultural changes that take place in every society in which modernization begins to alter the traditional bases of existence. In addition to its part in the general process of transformation, economic change plays a more crucial role in the general pattern of development than do the other aspects of change: economic transformation in general is the basis on which the general process of transformation becomes possible.

Economic transformation is the process that turns backward, subsistance peasant economies into modern, agriculturally productive units. Thus, the purpose of economic transformation is to modernize these economies by creating "farmers" from peasants and by transforming small-scale agrarian economies into modern agrarian units.(1) The general process of rural transformation in the economic sphere diminishes labor-intensive agrarian activities through the adaptation of modern agrarian techniques. This is accomplished through the infusion of modern machinery and cultivating techniques and through the modernization of the traditional basis of peasant economy.(2)

It must be noted, however, that our inquiry is restricted here to the peculiar condition of the Eastern European states and to the Eastern European peasantry. Consequently, our first efforts should be to delineate the meaning of the peasantry in the Eastern European context. While there is no place here to provide an exhaustive review of the enormously rich literature dealing with the term "peasantry," some attempts must be made to offer a definition that can serve as a useful basis for the generalizations that follow.(3)

The term "peasant" as used in the English language was originally used as a reference to persons who were living and working on the land in a non-English-speaking country. Etymologically, "peasant" was used in contradistinction to "noble" and since the seventeenth century it has become normal to refer to peasants in a pejorative sense, i.e., as uncultured individuals who do not know how to behave and act under "civilized" circumstances. In contrast to the practice of the English-speaking countries, historically the term "peasant" has been used elsewhere without pejoration; in fact, in the Slavic languages the term originally was used somewhat synonymously with the term narod, or liudi referring to the "folk" or "people." The term krestianin, the original term for Christians, had become a part of Russian usage by the thirteenth century in reference to the Russian peasants, thus differentiating them from the non-Christian nomads who occupied Russia and many of the Eastern European states.(4) While in English usage the differentiation between a farmer and a peasant continued to grow, this differentiation has not taken place in the usage of Eastern European states.

The most widely accepted definition of the peasantry has been offered by Norbeck in his study of peasant societies. According to him:

> A peasant society is a subsociety of a large stratified society which is either pre-industrial or only partly industrialized. It is further characterized by most or all of the following traits: rural residence; familial agriculture on self-owned small land holdings or other simple rural occupations providing a modest or subsistence livelihood; the family as the centrally important social unit; low social status; economic interdependence in varying degree with urban centers; simple culture; and attachment to the soil, the local community and tradition.(5)

Other attributes of the peasantry might be: a lack of literacy,(6) close ties with family (zadruga),(7) lack of modern hygienic standards or backward attitudes toward such standards,(8) an information isolation, missing institutional normative guides to action,(9) lack of equal access to government apparatus,(10) a nontribal society,(11) etc. Whatever definition of peasant society is employed, it is important to recall that peasant societies in Eastern Europe, while comparable to other peasant societies, generally exhibited some peculiar trends. These trends can best be identified as: 1) an isolation from rule; 2) a relative backwardness in all aspects of life in comparison to urban existence; 3) relatively close-knit ties within a village community or within various forms of kinship structure; 4) a largely agrarian form of employment; and 5) an independent existence as a nonmodern social stratum regarded by the urban polity as conservative, cunning and relatively stable, tending only to jacqueries when conditions have become absolutely intolerable.(12)

These societies in Eastern Europe possess, as most authorities describe clearly, a peculiarly peasant economy. The economic relationship of the peasant to the larger society is subsumptive and one-sided; the peasant economy exists as one "whose supluses are transferred to a dominant group of rulers that uses the surpluses both to underwrite its own standard of living and to distribute the remainder to [other] groups...that must be fed for specific goods and services in turn."(13) Thus, the peasant is regarded as an exploited entity, existing at the mercy of the ruling class. The three major types of economic activities of peasantry are: agricultural producers, landed proprietors, or subsistence cultivators.(14)

Once again, however, such a broad definition must be limited to the Eastern European sphere. For the peasant economy in Eastern Europe is sharply different from the neat typologies that are developed with a view of universal applicability. In the special context of the region, the peasant economies have ranged widely from nonmonetary or subsistence economies to modern agriculturally productive units.(15) Some aspects of the East European peasant life have begun very early with formal commodity exchanges through the market, while in many areas there has been no market integration and the use of money has been quite restricted.(16) In the peculiarly East European case of peasant economies, rates of exchange were frequently set by noneconomic factors and all of the above considerations relate to a political environment that defined a great deal of the economic limits within which such exchanges can take place.(17) In sum, the traditional peasant economies in Eastern Europe have involved agriculturally productive members of the society, landed or landless cultivators and, also, those agricultural workers and nonagrarian employed persons who were utilized by oppressive landowning classes.

The peculiarities of the peasant structures of Eastern Europe, of course, are the results of the general historical development of the region. Eastern Europe as a whole, in its historical development, has been specifically different from the Western European pattern and it is this difference to which we must call attention. The first major difference was the distinctiveness with which urban structures were separated from the rural environment very early in history. Urban, in the West, meant locations with certain rights such as the "right of defense, the right of coinage, the right of holding markets and the right of maintaining a court."(18) Urban

development in the West has followed or has been precipitated
by the advance of commerce, but at any rate, urban development in the West has always been a native development.(19)
Urban development in the West, whether an outgrowth of
Roman garrison towns or of any other growth patterns, nonetheless followed a pattern that reflected continuous national-
ethnic development and represented national-ethnic achieve-
ments.   The towns, which meant places that were clearly and
markedly different from the economic productivity of the
countryside possessed legal status and were associated with
containing people who had achieved certain liberties.   The
complexity of urban development, of course, does not permit
simple generalizations; nonetheless, all over Western Europe
certain basic similarities prevailed.(20)

Unlike Western Europe, in Eastern Europe the first
centers that can be called urban were those which were associated with the court that moved frequently and carried with
it the administrative-military functions of government.   The
court and the king resided in places where administrative
actions took place.   The court did not reside in market
locations; at best, it can be said that the market came to
them.   Krakow or Buda, for example were not commercial
centers originally but administrative seats.

The court in its original characteristics was also associated with the presence and active power of the church and
here we must call attention to the twin influences of Eastern
Orthodoxy and Catholicism.   On the one hand, the southern
tier of the region, including what is now Yugoslavia, Bulgaria
and Romania as well as Albania, developed since the fifth and
sixth centuries largely under the influence of the Byzantine
tradition.   This tradition strongly stressed the power of the
centralized authorities over those of the feudal forces sub-
ordinating the church to the state.   This development, however, also made the exercise of authority from a centralized
and distant place much more difficult than the exercise of
feudal authority that would have emanated from the immediate
vicinity.

In the northern tier the power of the central authorities
and their close association with the Catholic Church was established very early but began to fall apart in the thirteenth
century.   While there were further attempts at increasing the
power of the absolute ruler throughout the centuries, the
development that characterized the northern tier was that of
the enormously growing power of the nobility at the expense of
the centralized authority.   It gave the nobility far greater
power than that ceded to their counterparts in Western Europe
and allowed them to exercise far greater control over the
peasantry than was possible in Western Europe.   Unlike the
West, where the nobility remained checked by the power of the
absolute ruler on the one hand and by a rising commercial

class on the other, in Hungary and Poland specifically, the
power of the nobility kept growing at the expense of the
peasantry and at the expense of the central authorities. This
development was further enhanced by the changes in the
nature of the feudal institutions that began in the fourteenth
century.(21)

The development of feudalism also occurred in a peculiar
manner in Eastern Europe. The outside pressures and influences on the region have influenced the development of
specific types of feudalism and created specific economic, social
and political structures that, by and large, established a
peculiarly Eastern European pattern of economic relationships.(22)

Feudalism had at least three but possibly more phases in
Eastern Europe. It is highly likely that it was not introduced
by the Roman-German combination as it was in the West.
Possibly, Byzantine influences were at work in the Balkans,
through the taxation system of Diocletian-Constantine I, the
theme system, and various other schemes of the Byzantine
state intended to control the early Slavic populations of the
region. Christianity thus acted two ways in Eastern Europe;
the Orthodox version brought in the specific type of Byzantine
feudalism, while the Roman Catholic Church may have introduced the Western version during the ninth to eleventh
centuries.(23)

The Western type of feudalism was operative in the
northern parts of Eastern Europe, in East Prussia, Poland,
Hungary, Bohemia-Moravia. This type of feudalism was based
on the activities of the Grundsherren, whose operations included the recognition of mutual obligations between serfs and
lords. The consequence of this type of feudalism was that the
burden of the peasantry was fairly stable; the obligations (not
taxes) had usually been agreed upon and such agreements
lasted often for centuries. The Grundsherren dominated this
type of feudalism well into the end of the fourteenth century,
wherever Western-type feudalism existed.(24)

By the end of the fourteenth and beginning of the
fifteenth century, there emerged a new type of state whose
organization began to resemble the bureaucratic state of
modern times. With the arrival of the Turks in the Balkans,
necessitating the employment of huge armies, feudalism in
Eastern Europe began to change. There is much debate about
the cause of this change. Some orthodox Marxist historians
maintain that early feudalism had fulfilled its role and the
changing nature of the control over the means of production -
i.e., early capitalism - brought about the change. However it
may have been, most reputable historians do not accept such
clear-cut explanations. In any case, the major difference
appeared in the form of feudal rent. In the earlier case of
the Grundsherren, this was collected partly in the form of

produce, partly in cash. Manual labor played a minimum role in this type of feudalism, with the peasants usually required to spend less than twenty days a year on the lord's demesne. The main reason for this was that the lord did not concern himself with production; all he wanted was enough food for himself, his soldiers and his household, in order to enable him to concern himself with affairs of politics and war. Consequently, the lord's demesne in Eastern Europe was of minimal size, most of the land being distributed among peasant communities who tilled it according to their wishes. As long as they paid the rent agreed upon, the lord did not care one way or another what they did in their spare time; that was the concern of the church.(25)

During the transitional period of the fifteenth century, more and more landlords found it profitable to sell part of the produce which they collected from their serfs in the market-place. This was necessitated by the increasing demands made on them by the kings. As the great lords spent more and more time at the royal court, as their power increased through the increase of the size of their private armies, they needed additional income to maintain themselves. Since traditional peasant communities had little cash on hand, the lords found it more profitable to gather more lands within the demesne and sell the produce - produced by the serf's labor - to rural towns and cities. This resulted, by the early sixteenth century, in the emergence of a new type of landlord, whom we call Gutsherren.(26) These landlords increased the land holdings which they controlled in the demesne; instead of demanding produce in lieu of the land rent, they wanted labor from the peasants. Hence, the number of days the peasants were required to spend in the service of the lord drastically increased. Until the end of the fourteenth century, this number rarely exceeded twenty days a year per family (and an extended family paid the same amount as a nuclear one). During the fifteenth century the number was about fifty-two days a year, and by the sixteenth century it was not unusual for peasants to spend one hundred and seventy-five days a year working on the lord's demesne land.(27) At the same time, the lords usually demanded rent for the land, to be paid for in produce. No wonder then, that the great peasant revolts came in lands where this type of feudalism was established. In the case of Eastern Europe, this type of feudalism survived the longest. In Western Europe, feudalism as an economic system disappeared by the end of the seventeenth century, largely because of the tremendous inflation - about four percent annually - that was brought about by the influx of gold and silver from the New World through Spain and England; in Eastern Europe feudalism received a new lease on life. This so-called "second serfdom" developed for a variety of reasons, the most significant of which were: 1) the increasing importance of cereal export to the West,(28) 2) the greater cohesiveness and survival of a relatively tightly organized national system,(29) and 3) the weakness of towns and cities and the attendant lack of development of native middle classes and the bourgeosie.(30)

In short, it is safe to state that the classic model of feudalism, which certainly was valid in most of Western Europe, did not characterize the Eastern European developments. This lack of modernization of the state structure resulted in the creation of a growing gap between various segments of the national societies. The gap between the nobility and the aristocracy, on the one hand, and the peasantry, on the other, remained at the very core of the East European system. In retrospect, the separation of these two societies seems to have occurred as a natural process. It was guided by the perceived need of the aristocracy to maintain significant landholdings and it was aided by a process that can best be described as urban "illegitimacy" in the eyes of the countryside. The reasons for this perception are complex and space does not allow us to deal with this subject in extenso.(31) Nonetheless, the fact remains that urban populations in Eastern Europe tended to be associated with non-native existence. As the native dynasties in Poland, Hungary and Bohemia died out as a result of the rigorous application of the Slavic laws of inheritance, as a result of plagues, invasions, occupations and other historical events, foreign princes and dynasties were invited to ascend the thrones of these states. These princes brought with them their native advisors, native traditions and their native languages.

The differences between the language of the peasantry and the language of the urban hierarchy grew from century to century in parallel with their differences in life-style; Magyar, Polish or Czech became increasingly the language of the peasant, Latin the language of the clergy and of the administration, and the native language of the imported dynasties the language of the court. Even in southern Europe, this pattern seems to have dominated the development of dual cultures following the Turkish occupation of the region. The Turks lived in the cities and in the administrative centers, leaving those in the countryside free to speak their native language. As a result, the peasants of the entire region viewed the cities as urban centers occupied mostly by foreigners - Turks, Germans and Jews. It was not until the nineteenth century that a significant native burgher class, a native bourgeosie, began to develop.(32) For the peasants and the peasant economy, their relationship to the urban economic center, almost until the First World War, was clearly one of exploitation and the peasants existed at the mercy of landlords who were seldom identified with improvements in the lives of the rural poor.

The transformation of the economic basis of peasant society, as indeed that of the entire East European system, began with the demographic revolution of the late nineteenth century. As in Western Europe until the beginning of the nineteenth century, the average life expectancy of the people had been unchanged for the last few milennia; it was around twenty-five years of age. Starvation, plagues, extraordinary weather, and lack of hygiene had taken their toll throughout the ages. In a manner similar to the changes that had taken place in Western Europe in the 1800s, in Eastern Europe, in the second half of the nineteenth century, important demographic developments occurred. By the end of the century, the average life expectancy rose to between thirty-five and forty years of age and, as a result, the population of Eastern Europe increased by two and one half to three times.(33)   It was not until the last two decades of the nineteenth century, however,. that the rate of population growth exceeded that of Western Europe. Similarly, it must be noted that this excessive growth rate occurred at the same time that 20 to 30 percent of the natural growth in population was lost by emigration to the United States. It is safe to say that had the emigrants stayed, the average rate of natural increase would have been significantly higher. It should also be noted that nearly 70 percent of all emigrants from Eastern Europe came from rural peasant communities and that, therefore, the rate of natural growth in the urban areas was greater than in the rural environment.(34)

The demographic explosion in the Western European countries was coupled with an even greater degree of growth in life expectancy than occurred in Eastern Europe: the difference was at least ten years in the life of a generation. The reason for this variance was the difference in the level of civilization and the degree of urbanization existing in these regions. The difference in the degree of civilization can easily be observed by looking at the indexes of literacy in Eastern and Western Europe. In 1800 about sixty percent of the population of Western Europe was illiterate; by the turn of the century between one and twenty percent was illiterate. For example, in Switzerland, England, Germany and the Scandinavian states, only one to two percent of the adult population was illiterate. In Eastern Europe, the rate of illiteracy had remained much higher. In Hungary, for example, in 1800, about 80 percent of the population was illiterate, while by 1910 this percentage decreased to only 33 percent. The situation was still worse in other states in Eastern Europe. Thus, in 1908 in Bosnia-Herzegovina there was only enough space to educate 15 percent of all those students between six and ten years of age. In 1900 the percentage of illiterates in Serbia was 79 percent; in Romania, 78 percent; and in Bulgaria, 72 percent. Needless to say, most of those who remained illiterate were people who lived in nonurban localities, in other words, the peasantry as a whole.(35)

The demographic explosion in itself had enormous economic consequences, but to the demographic consequences of population increase, the results of agrarian development have to be added. The transformation of agriculture from economic domination to a supportive, productive role had occurred in Western Europe at the beginning of the nineteenth century. The modernization of agriculture according to the largely accepted Mantoux thesis is the very foundation of industrial development.(36) The modernization of agriculture, the so-called agrarian revolution, liberated the needed man-power that became the raw material out of which capital was formed and which became the prime motivator of the industrial revolution. The characteristic development of the moderniza-tion of agriculture took place in several steps, the first of which was the abolition of feudal relationships. The abolition of the three-field system, the creation of intensive livestock production, the increased use of soil improvement, the in-tensive use of irrigation and, of course, the enormous benefits of industrial techniques were also important developments in the agrarian revolution.

Agrarian development, however, could only be meaningful if it altered the traditional systems of land ownership. It is important to recall that in Eastern Europe two distinct types of land ownership patterns developed. In the Balkans, the native dynasties and native aristocracies had perished under Turkish rule. Hence, the peasants were able to own small amounts of land and were able to tend their herds, by and large for their own goals and purposes, as well as to maintain their life-style and economic activities for their own benefits. On the other hand, in the northern tier, in what was to become Poland, Czechoslovakia and Hungary, large land-holdings, owned and operated by frequently absentee land-lords, developed and only a few peasants were able to own minimal amounts of land.

Earlier West European developments did show some effect on the East European states as well, but until the third quarter of the nineteenth century the reformist aspirations in agriculture found only partial support in the ruling strata of the states of Eastern Europe. To be sure, serfdom was abolished and the demands for robot placed on the serfs and free peasants by the landed estate owners had been de-creased.(37) In spite of the abolition of serfdom and the subsequent division of some land, the peasantry failed to receive adequate landholdings for rent or use; and about 50 percent of the total arable land remained in the hands of the large estate holders. Table 5.1 indicates the East European structure of land ownership around the end of the nineteenth century. The same pattern of agrarian ownership prevailed in

THE PROCESS OF RURAL TRANSFORMATION

Table 5.1.   Structure of Land Ownership

Size of Estates in hectares	Percent of Estates	Percent of Total Land Area
Austria-Czech Lands (1899)		
0-5	71.8	66.9
5-100	25.5	
100-1000	0.6	15.6
1000 +	0.1	17.5
Hungary (1895)		
0-3	53.6	5.8
3-60	45.4	46.5
60-600	0.8	15.4
600 +	0.2	32.3
Romania (1899)		
0-5	77.2	25.9
5-10	18.2	14.7
10-100	4.0	11.1
100 +	0.6	48.3
Serbia (1897)		
0-5	52.8	62.1
5-20	43.1	35.6
20-50	3.8	2.2
50 +	0.3	0.1
Bulgaria (1899)		
0-10	67.3	49.0
10-100	32.6	44.5
100 +	0.1	6.5
Poland (1864 land reform)		
0-2	30	-
2-9	40	-
9 +	30	-

Source: Ivan T. Berend and Gyorgy Ranki, Kozep-Kelet-Europa gazdasagi fejlodese a 19.-20. szazadban [The economic development of central Eastern Europe in the eighteenth and nineteenth centuries] (Budapest: Kozgazdasagi es Jogi Konyv-kiado, 1976), pp. 60-69.

what was to become Poland, Czechoslovakia, Romania and Serbia. In Romania, at the end of the nineteenth century, estates that were larger than 1,500 acres comprised only 0.6 percent of the total number of estates but in acreage they accounted for 48.3 percent of the land; and 77.2 percent of the total number of farms were less than 15 acres. In Serbia this pattern remained the same; only in Bulgaria was the large estate type of farming not predominant.

Furthermore, unlike in Western Europe, more than 50 percent of the peasant farms were subsistence. In most countries the peasants remained, in some degree, economically dependent on their former feudal lords, including the maintenance of such obligations as certain numbers of work days they were required to work on the land of the former feudal owner.

The introduction of some land reforms and of the agrarian revolution in most states of Eastern Europe meant the transformation of the former feudal estates into semifeudal, semicapitalist farms and resulted in the continued impoverishment and landlessness of the peasantry. Only in a limited region, namely in Bohemia, did the West European pattern of agrarian development prevail. In Eastern Europe as a whole, until World War I, the agrarian system remained the peculiar mixture of feudalism and capitalism from which the landlords retained the benefits of both systems while the peasants retained the disadvantages of the same.

Two additional points characterized the Eastern European agrarian productive system. The first was the institution of leasing. At the end of the seventeenth century, between 20 and 60 percent of all large estates - depending on the individual state and its characteristics - were leased to individuals.(38) There were three types of lessees: small peasants; those who were not entitled to ownership of land, such as the Jews; and those to whom the land was only leased and not sold in order to preserve the fiction of ownership of members of the nobility for whom the theoretical ownership of land meant continued admission to the circle of aristocracy. Unlike in Western Europe, where often as much as 85 to 90 percent of the land was leased to individuals who undertook an extensive capitalist type of agricultural activity, in Eastern Europe, most of the lessees were small peasants who had paid for their land lease by working for the landlord on his land.(39)

Simultaneously with these developments one must also mention the rapid growth of mortgage loans that were inextricably coupled with the expansion and increased use of the monetary system, with the development of large-scale urban capitalism and with the growth of the financial institutions in the latter part of the nineteenth century. The industrialization of the agrarian sector, of course, had to be coupled with the infusion of capital, and capital could only be generated through these financial institutions. In 1907, for example, nearly 70 percent of all mortgages in the Hungarian part of the Austro-Hungarian monarchy were made available to agrarian producers. While this percentage was smaller in other states of the region, the advance of financial power over the agrarian productive units was observable everywhere.

Much of the reason for the backwardness of the agrarian modernization can be found in the fact that the East European financial institutions, contrary to their Western counterparts, still operated on traditional bases of usury rates, frequently reaching two hundred percent interest on loans to the small peasantry. In Bulgaria, for example, at the beginning of the twentieth century, of 1,200 villages included in a survey, 300 had to give their total annual production and 400 other villages gave 50 percent of their total annual production to banks from whom loans and credits were secured.(40) These loans, however, did not serve the purpose of agrarian investment; rather, they were given to assure the minimal level of survival of those to whom the loans were given. If we add the heavy, conservative taxation system that forced the peasants who either leased or owned the land to contribute between 15 and 30 percent of their income to the tax collectors and if we recall that even in the best small estates owned or leased by productive peasants, only 60 percent of the produce was ever shipped to the market, we can fully appreciate the extent of the backwardness of Eastern European agriculture.(41) In spite of enormous advances in the field of wheat and corn production and the rapid growth of slaughter animal production, the agrarian area at the turn of the century remained far more backward than in Western Europe. The peasantry, by and large, did not benefit significantly from the agrarian revolution. Unlike their Western European counterparts, the peasants remained backward, exploited and isolated. Because of the backwardness of the means of communications and the lack of adequate development in the road systems, only a weak network of communication existed, the main function of which was the establishment of the connection between the urban administrative centers.

Inevitably, these developments resulted in a rapid growth in the number of hired agrarian laborers who worked on the estates of others without the owning of any land themselves. Between 1850 and 1900 the number of hired laborers grew rapidly, and by the end of the nineteenth century, even in the most advanced Czech lands, 36 percent of the agrarian population lived and worked as hired hands or agrarian proletars.

The minimal modernization of agriculture and the very backwardness of the East European agrarian system can also be measured by the lack of modern machinery tilling the land.

While, for example, in the beginning of the twentieth century in Bulgaria, one steam tiller was available for every 15.6 hectares of land, in Germany that same machine would have had to till only 16.9 hectares and similar, though perhaps less extreme, ratios could be observed in all the Eastern European states.(42)

All these factors contributed significantly to the impoverishment of the peasant families that began to experience the effects of the demographic revolutions. By the end of the nineteenth century even the small peasant acreages began to be continually subdivided to feed more and more families, and when impoverishment reached intolerable levels, the surplus labor could only go to the urban, industrial centers or to the United States. Urban industrial activities began to employ increasing numbers of peasants. For example, in 1869 in Hungary, 75 percent of the people worked in agriculture; this percentage decreased to 64 in 1910. While this reduction may not seem very large, it must be read in conjunction with the fact that nearly 1.5 million people had left the country between 1869 and 1910 and that the population as a whole during this period increased by 35 percent. Similar data characterized most of the other East European states.

Unlike Western Europe, in Eastern Europe the radical change from a feudal agrarian to an industrial capitalist system did not take place. The agrarian revolution did begin to move Eastern Europe in the same direction as did the West, but these changes were not radical enough to alter the system of production as fundamentally as they did in Western Europe. By and large the East European states remained agrarian, with production providing subsistence and export to the West and agricultural production methods remaining quite primitive. And the peasantry, by and large, continued to pay the price of backwardness.

World War I caused a radical alteration of the entire political, economic and social structure of Eastern Europe. The Turkish, the Hapsburg and Romanov empires were broken up and replaced by independent states. But even these states were unable to represent the legitimate aspirations of the peasant class. In addition, the peasantry was dominated by the cities, by the rising urban bourgeoisie, and by urban cultures that regarded the peasantry as inferior, hostile, backward and indeed, stupid. The ruling classes were urban-oriented and hence, antipeasant.(43)

Thus, the problem of the peasantry in the interwar era was further complicated by the peculiar economic policies of the ruling classes. The purpose of these classes was to maintain their privileges, their wealth and hence, the ownership structure that was prevalent before the beginning of World War I. At the same time, there was a recognition that some land reform was essential, specifically in the states of the northern tier.

Consequently, following the disasters of the First World War, land reform programs were undertaken in most of the newly created states. To be sure, land reform was relatively easy in Romania, Czechoslovakia, Yugoslavia and Poland, where former "imperial" powers, such as Austria, Germany, Russia, and Hungary were expelled from the region. Since many of the landowners had belonged to the defeated imperial nations, after the creation of the new states most of the non-native former landowners were expelled and their estates were expropriated and divided among the land-hungry native peasantry. In Romania, Yugoslavia and Czechoslovakia, the Hungarian- or German-owned estates were broken up and the land divided among the peasants. In Poland a fairly liberal land reform program was planned, but the land reform itself was postponed for political reasons and was never completed during the interwar era. By far the least significant land reform was undertaken in Hungary where the old, land-owning aristocracy retained its political power and clung with every available means to their lands.(44)

As a result of these land reforms, some peasants were given land, but the land reforms in general failed to solve the problems of the peasantry because most of the new farms were too small to produce efficiently and extensively. For example, in Poland, 65 percent of all holdings were less than five hectares; in Romania, 75 percent; in Bulgaria, 62 percent; and in Czechoslovakia, 71 percent were less than five hectares. The most extreme case, again, was Hungary, where 85 percent of all farms were under five hectares.(45) The lack of capital further aggravated the problem of the peasantry. The "dwarf" farms were largely nonproductive or provided only subsistence level production for the peasants. The extremely high birth rate and the continued subdivision of landholdings among children resulted in fragmentation all over the region, perhaps with the exception of Bohemia, which continued to maintain the law of primogenitor in the ownership of land. Consequently, the rule of the large estates continued unabated and the Depression, coupled with the incredibly low food prices paid to the peasantry in the famous "scissors crisis" of the late 1920s, only worsened the lot of the peasantry.(46) During the interwar years the resulting impoverization of the peasants continued to take on even greater scope. Hired farm hands and small farmers alike worked on farms which belonged to large estate holders. The Catholic Church extracted labor for its giant holdings at almost less than subsistence wages and starvation began to force larger and larger numbers of peasants to seek nonagrarian employment. But unlike the pre-World War period there was no longer the opportunity to emigrate to America. Indeed, the surplus agrarian population in Eastern Europe began to increase steadily around 1920, interrupted only by World War II. This surplus population was somewhere between 25 and 35 percent of the population, or around nine to ten million people.(47)

World War II was one of the great disasters of the twentieth century. Urban and rural populations suffered equally from the stress and strain of raging warfare, occupying armies, and economic devastation. When World War II ended, new governments came to power all over Eastern Europe. Regardless of the type of government all members of the new ruling hierarchies agreed on one thing: the need for land reform. Table 5.2 illustrates the effects of land reform in Eastern Europe.

The most extreme cases of land reform occurred in those states where the greatest need for reform was evident, Poland and Hungary. In these states large numbers of peasants were given land practically overnight by the new land reforms.(48) Nowhere in Eastern Europe, however, can we see the importance of the agrarian reform more clearly than in the case of Hungary. The 1935 and 1948 land ownership patterns are illustrated in table 5.3. Thus, in 1935, of 4.6 million peasants, nearly three million, or 64 percent, had little or no land; in Czechoslovakia, only 28 percent; in Yugoslavia, only 9.3 percent; in Romania, only 8.9 percent; and in Bulgaria, only 5.1 percent of the peasants had any land. In Poland and Hungary, on the other hand, land had to be given to two-thirds of the peasantry. In addition, in Czechoslovakia, Romania and Yugoslavia, the land reform policies of the regime again benefited from the incorporation of formerly German and Hungarian occupied territories. In Czechoslovakia, for example, 122,000 families were given one million, forty thousand hectares of land, mostly from estates that were held in former enemy hands. The same was true in Romania where eight percent of all cultivatable land had been held by such owners; in Yugoslavia, where five percent of these lands were divided; and in Bulgaria, where 1.5 percent of all such cultivated lands were divided.(49) In Hungary, however, land was given to the peasants from estates that were forcibly expropriated from the native landed nobility. Thus, between 1945 and 1947 in Hungary, for example, new owners and heads of families were given land in one of the most massive agrarian land reforms.(50)

As indicated in table 5.2, similar land reforms took place in Poland as well. These land reforms, however, failed to adequately answer the problems of the peasantry. In Hungary the average size of a new estate was only three hectares while in Poland the average size of a new estate was slightly under that figure.(51)

As a result of these land reforms, some problems seemed to have been solved, but the problem of agrarian overpopulation could not be overcome. While some peasants were given land and others had sizable landholdings added to present

Table 5.2. Structure of Land Ownership (1) before World War II and (2) following the First Postwar Reforms (in Percent)

Size of Estates in Hectares	Czechoslovakia		Poland		Hungary		Romania		Bulgaria		Yugoslavia	
	1	2	1	2	1	2	1	2	1	2	1	2
0-2	7.8	7.9	25.1	6.0	10.9	23.1	12.8		5.3	6.7	6.5	7.6
2-5	14.3	17.9	32.5	21.5	9.2	27.3	15.2	57.5	24.7	30.9	21.5	28.3
5-50	61.9	74.2	15.7	72.5	33.5	49.6	39.8	39.3	68.4	62.4	62.4	64.1
50-100					5.5		4.5	3.0			3.2	
100 +	16.0		26.7		40.9		27.2		1.6		6.4	

Source: Berend and Ranki, Kozep-Kelet-Europa, p. 597.

Table 5.3.   The Distribution of Privately Owned Estates in Hungary in 1935 and 1948

1935

Size in Hectares[a]	Number of Estates	Percent of all Estates	Percent of Total Agricultural Land	Average Size of Estates in Hectares
0-3	1,184,783	75.2	10.1	0.8
3-6	204,471	12.5	9.2	4.0
6-12	144,186	8.8	12.6	8.0
12-30	73,663	4.5	13.5	17.0
30-60	15,240	0.9	6.5	39.0
60-120	5,792	0.3	5.0	79.0
120-600	5,202	0.3	13.2	235.0
600 +	1,070	0.2	29.9	2,476.0
Totals	1,634,407	100.0	100.0	

1948

0-3	1,406,325	68.1	17.9	1.2
3-6	388,179	18.8	21.1	5.0
6-12	175,428	8.5	17.3	9.1
12-30	71,164	3.4	14.7	19.1
30-60	14,864	0.7	8.1	50.1
60-120	5,525	0.3	4.4	74.4
120-600	4,034	0.2	8.4	192.8[b]
600 +	595	0.0	8.1	1,267.8
Totals	2,066,144	100.0	100.0	

---

[a] In Hungary the size of the estates were expressed in holds (0.575 hectares), hence, this category indicates approximate size.

[b] It must be emphasized that by 1948, all estates above 120 hectares were nationalized and were owned by the state.

Source: Sandor Orban, Ket agrarforradalom Magyarorszagon (Budapest: Akademiai Kiado, 1972), pp. 11, 61.

holdings, the problem of agrarian overpopulation remained. Furthermore, in Eastern Europe as a whole, the majority of the farms remained under five hectares, and in Hungary and Romania, the average size of peasant landholdings was under five acres, even after extensive land reform. The communist regimes that came to power in Eastern Europe in 1945-1948 claimed to provide the solution to the problem of the modernizing agriculture. They hoped to accomplish this type of rural transformation through forced collectivization.

The goals of the economic transformation of the rural sphere, of course, are well known. According to Kuznets, in strictly economic terms, the characteristics of economic development are rather universal. They are: 1) the rapid increase in per capita production; 2) a swift rise in labor efficiency; 3) an increased share of manufacturing and a decreased share of agricultural production in the output mix; 4) an increase in the size of the production units; 5) an increase in utilization of labor in urban versus rural environs; and 6) the extension of economic linkages.(52) The transformation of the agrarian aspects of economic life in Eastern Europe was thought to be best accomplished through the massive and forcible introduction of collective farming. However, precisely because collectivization began under communist auspices, certain important considerations defined this process. These considerations were significant; for example, when considering the role of ideology, it is essential for us to realize that communist collectivization measures were specifically different than the development measures of other economic systems. While Marxism-Leninism does follow the general aims of agricultural development - e.g., the mechanization of agriculture, a clearer delineation of the division of labor, a relatively planned and controlled method of execution - it also postulates certain measures:(53)

1. The prerequisites were the subordination of agrarian development to industrial development and hence, the exploitation of the countryside in favor of the city, the role of the state as a supreme proprietor and owner of the land, the role of central planning and allocation and finally, the deliberate social transformation of peasants into agrarian proletars.

2. Given the antipeasant basis of Marxist ideology, the collectivization measures were aimed not merely at economic results, but also at the breaking down of the peasant community, peasant values and peasant society in general. The communists have felt it necessary to create new value systems in the peasantry in order to satisfactorily control a portion of the population they regarded as backward.

3. Communist attitudes assigned an inordinately great role to central planning and attempted to establish such central organs of state control as machine tractor stations.

4. Finally, it is important to bear in mind that the collectivization of agriculture in Eastern Europe had to take place on the basis of the Soviet example. The reasons for following the Soviet model, of course, were complex. First of all, at the time of the collectivization measures, there was only one communist agrarian policy to follow, namely the Soviet model. The role of the Soviet Union and its apparent success – as evidenced by its victory in World War II – signified at least partial proof of the success of Soviet agrarian policies. Secondly, the governments of Eastern Europe, as led by the communist parties of the region, attempted to consciously emulate all Soviet policies. Thirdly, those people who dared suggest alternative ways of solving the land problem – Gomulka, Nagy and others – were generally out of power or in jail by the time the forced collectivization policy really got under way. And finally, Soviet agrarian policy had to be emulated because the Soviet leadership so decreed it and the Soviet Union had the power to enforce that decision.

The very fact that the governments emulated the Soviet model had immense consequences. After all, the Soviet model was not really applicable to Eastern Europe. Unlike the Soviet Union, the distances and scale were smaller. In contrast to the situation in historical Russia, communal ownership of land in Eastern Europe had been abandoned centuries before. Therefore, Lenin's threefold characterization of the peasantry as small, middle and rich peasants was not really applicable. Also, unlike Russia, some states of Eastern Europe, notably East Germany and Czechoslovakia, had relatively small peasant populations. There was certain resistance, even among the top leadership, to the deliberate policy practiced by the Soviet Union of leaving 50 percent of the population as backward muzhiks. The non-Soviet leaders had envisioned the collectivization of agriculture as one way of bringing the peasants into the mainstream of an integrated economy.

Aside from ideological considerations, the main reason for the creation of collective and state farms according to the Soviet model was the conviction, and the widely accepted economic verity, that the larger the production unit, the more efficient the production method. While today we are aware of certain doubts concerning this so-called economic truth, and there are a large number of reasons - high energy cost co-efficients, high costs of both infrastructural and operational factors, etc. - for questioning the projected "gigantism" of the Soviet model, few doubts were expressed in 1949-50 concerning this aspect of the goals of collectivization.

In spite of some recognition of the difficulties of following the Soviet model, the collectivization of land was begun in all of the East European states by 1949. According to Boguslaw Galeski, four types of collective farms can be created. The first type is based on an "ideological" or "religious" conviction that collectivization is the correct route to follow. The second type is created by landless families who could acquire land for communal purposes. The third type is forcibly organized by the government in order to reach certain national economic or political goals. And the fourth type is voluntarily organized by peasants who are able to join in order to take advantage of larger economic units of operation.(54)   In Eastern Europe, the collectivization efforts included a mixture of all four. It is important to note, however, that the most significant form of collectivization was the collective farm forcibly organized by the government, followed only by collective farms created by landless and land-poor peasants who believed that mutual forms of cooperation could be beneficial to them in the long run.

The necessity of forced collectivization in Eastern Europe stemmed from peasant reluctance to enter the cooperatives voluntarily. Indeed, the only peasants desiring to enter collectives (a) had little or no land of their own, (b) were unsuccessful as private farmers or, (c) were those who, by and large, could only benefit from collectivization.(55)   The process of collectivization usually took place through a combination of measures. Government recruiters and party "agit-prop" teams would harangue peasants at endless meetings to attain membership in the newly formed collective farms. Those individuals who opposed the collectives were arrested, beaten, occasionally killed and frequently shipped away to another part of the country or region and labeled kulaks. A machine tractor station would be established in or near each village. The station utilized machinery donated to it by the state or confiscated from the more successful peasants of the region; the residents of the station were charged with controlling the collectivization of the immediate area. Finally, peasants who refused to join would either be accused of "hoarding" and charged with a crime against the state or their taxes would be increased and their stock and household goods confiscated until they acceded to the demands of the organizers.(56)

Collectivization of agriculture implied having a dual structure of land ownership. There would be: 1) collective farms where land, while theoretically owned by the state as in the Soviet Union, would be leased to the collective farm in perpetuity and; 2) state farms were the land was owned and operated by a subdivision of the state. Theoretically, the difference was that a collective farm divided its earnings and profits among its members on the basis of the number of hours worked by them on the land, while members of the state farm were paid a simple wage. Because of the artificially low prices of agricultural goods set by the state, the minimal amount of work by peasants on collective lands, and considerations of political control of economic development, there was rarely, if ever, any profit made by the collective farm.(60) Hence, the differentiation was largely theoretical.

There is a great deal of debate concerning the exact type of the collective farms that were established. Depending on the state concerned there were three or four different types of collective farm associations. The difference in the type of the collective farm lies in the nature of the association of the members. At one end of the scale there was the most integrated collective farm, resembling to a great extent the Soviet kolkhozes. Everything was done in common, all work and all decision making was made by the "collective" - i.e., the local party secretary, the collective farm chairman, the agronomist, almost every implement was owned in common and members received more or less equitable remuneration for their work. At the other end of the scale there were the specialized cooperatives, where although everything was theoretically owned and accomplished in common, in reality the members farmed their "own" land, e.g., land that was originally allocated to them, and collective work and collective rewards were kept to a minimum.

Private land ownership, however, was not totally abolished. Indeed, the regime claimed that a minimal amount of land for household plots had to be given to each collective farm family. The location of these lands, however, was determined by political considerations. A peasant who was given distant, poor-quality land was not likely to produce excessively and, therefore, would represent no threat to the agrarian monopoly of the state. Through these measures of collectivization, the regime had primarily hoped to alter the peasants' attitudes toward the land. The "etatization" of the concept of land was intended to abolish once and for all the land hunger of the peasant through forcible means.

Collectivization was undertaken only on a very small scale in Bulgaria and Yugoslavia in 1945; in Poland, especially in the Western Territories that were expropriated from German farmers, a few state farms were established.(58) From 1948 to 1952, however, collectivization was undertaken on a full scale. Although forced collectivization was not as brutal in Eastern Europe during these years as it was in the Soviet Union during the 1930s, the experience was a traumatic one for the

peasant population. The regimes seemed to be determined to
attain complete collectivization eventually. By 1953, collective
farms of various kinds held 60 percent of the arable land in
Bulgaria,   33   percent   in   Czechoslovakia,   26   percent   in
Hungary,   21   percent   in   Yugoslavia,   12   percent   in   East
Germany,   11   percent   in   Albania,   and   7   percent   in
Romania.(59)   However, even if we add the state farms, the
results of forcible collectivization during these years could not
be   regarded   as   satisfactory   from   the   perspective   of   the
regimes in question.
     The   death   of   Stalin   and   Khrushchev's   rise   to   power
brought   distinct   changes   to   Eastern   Europe.   Forced   collectivization in Hungary was abolished and collective farms
were allowed to be dissolved on December 31, 1953, according
to the July 4, 1953, speech of Imre Nagy, the new Chairman
of   the   Council   of   Ministers   of   Hungary.   In   Czechoslovakia,
President Antonin Zapotocky, on August 1, 1953, advocated
the dissolution of some collective farms if their members so
desired.   On August 23, 1953, in Romania, Gheorghiu Dej
suggested a more lenient treatment of private farming and a
halfhearted   condemnation   of   forced   collectivization.(60)   In
Bulgaria, Albania, East Germany, and Poland, however, little
or no changes took place in agrarian policy.
     In Yugoslavia, the pattern was somewhat different.   In
1950 a major drought decimated the production capacity of the
land.   In 1951 there was nationwide peasant sabotage of agrarian production and, as a result of an additional drought the
following year, agricultural production in Yugoslavia dropped
to about 50 percent of the 1939 output.   Consequently, in
March 1953, a decree allowed peasants to dissolve the collectives if they so desired.   One-fifth of the approximately
7,000 collective farms organized by 1951 were dissolved by May
1953.   And by the end of 1956, the "socialist sector" accounted   only   for   22.9   percent   of   the   total   agricultural
area.(61)
     The most drastic changes took place in Polish agriculture.
There, Gomulka's rise to power brought with it a total decollectivization of agriculture.   Within one year, more than 93
percent of all agrarian holdings reverted to private hands;
only in the Western Territories were some large-scale agrarian
units maintained, mostly under state ownership.
     The   uncertain   agricultural   policies   of   1953-1956,   fol-
lowed by the revolutions in Hungary and Poland, were altered
very quickly all over the region starting in 1957.   As defined
by the Moscow Conference of 1957, the new agricultural policy
had to be based on massive, all-out collectivization.   Only
Gomulka and Tito remained behind the idea of truly voluntary
collectivization   measures.   All   other   East   European   leaders
began   a   determined   drive   to   collectivize   the   land.   Consequently, in Hungary dissolution of the collectives had taken

place for four years and where only 8.5 percent of the arable land in 1957 was held by the collective farms, in 1959 a two-year program was started to collectivize the land. Through a mixture of cajoling, incentives, persuasion and force, by 1962, 58.8 percent of the land belonged to the collective sector. While in 1957, 85 percent of the peasants were categorized as private farmers, by 1962, only 6.5 percent remained in that category.(62)

Similarly, by 1960 in East Germany, the share of the collective farms had been raised from 38 to 80 percent of the arable land. In Romania by 1960, 81.9 percent of all agricultural land was socialized and by 1962, only 5.9 percent of all agricultural land remained in the hands of private farmers.(63) By 1960 in Bulgaria, 84.6 percent of all arable land belonged to collective farms, 7.0 percent to state farms, and the amount of land owned by private farmers dipped to 0.8 percent(64) In Czechoslovakia by 1959-60, similar results were also announced. Only in Yugoslavia and Poland, as mentioned above, did the private farmers continue their domination of the agricultural sector.

Thus by 1963, the structure of the East European agricultural region had been relatively firmly developed. Some changes within the structure, however, have taken place, specifically in Bulgaria, where, by 1958 there were 3,290 collective farms, nearly one farm for every village. In 1959, an agglomeration of these farms reduced their number to 972, increasing their average size from 1,153 hectares to 4,186 hectares.(65) In Bulgaria, agro-industrial complexes which consisted of state or collective farms were introduced at the July 1968 plenum by Todor Zhivkov and implemented in April 1970. By 1971, there were 170 agro-industrial complexes in operation, including 73.5 percent of all arable land and utilizing 75 percent of all those permanently involved in agriculture. The average size of these agro-industrial complexes grew to 24,920 hectares by 1972.(66) Furthermore, some special industrial-agricultural complexes, such as the sugar-producing complexes, were also created in 1973, with even larger acreages frequently amounting to 50,000 hectares. These agro-industrial specialized complexes basically have operated as large farms which took advantage of large-scale industrial techniques and attempted to combine agrarian occupations with industrial planning operation.

The second structural change took place in Hungary in connection with the implementation of the 1968 New Economic Mechanism.(67) The purpose and goal of this change was the combination of personal incentives with socialist cooperation. Collective farms began to operate relatively freely, guided by market considerations, and approximately one-third of these collective farms found themselves in the enviable position, as a result of favorable government policy and good local leader-

ship, of producing exceedingly high earnings for the members
of these collectives. (68)

Collectivization had thus transformed the economic bases
of production in Eastern Europe and created the conditions for
the general rural transformation of the region. The evaluation
of this general process will be discussed in the following
section.

The successes of rural transformation of the economic
sphere, of course, can be measured through various indexes.
In our study, we will rely on the four agricultural indexes
that Kuznets identified as basic components of economic development. We shall examine: 1) the shift of population from
rural to urban locations; 2) the decline in the share of agriculture in total output; 3) the increased size of production
units; and 4) the increased mechanization of agriculture.

The first major consideration involves the shift in population from rural to urban centers. This shift was necessitated by the enormous rural agrarian surplus labor that
predominated in the economic production pattern all over the
region.(69) Tables 5.4 and 5.5 illustrate the changes in the
percent of the populations living in urban versus rural localities. These indexes illustrate widespread shifts in rural
population. Between the beginning of the collectivization
effort and the mid-1970s, nearly nine million people had
changed occupations or approximately 12 percent of the entire
population had moved from rural to urban locations. Rural
surplus population thus seems to have been effectively dealt
with and, judged from this perspective, the economic transformation of the countryside seems to have been successful.
The most dramatic shift, however, seems to have taken place
independent of the collectivization process. In Bulgaria,
where collectivization began very early, urban growth had
been nearly 20 percent between 1950 and 1975. Similarly, in
Poland, the size of the rural population declined from 61 to 46
percent. Here, however, we must note that the process of
collectivization had been minimal. Similar examples of massive
changes abound. Yugoslavia, with its minimal emphasis on
collectivization, and Romania, with its strong procollectivization
policies, had similar favorable urban growth rates. Thus, it
seems that the general trend of urbanization was not necessarily concomitant with or dependent upon collectivization
practices. The figures quoted above seem to indicate an
understandable and generally acceptable process of urban
growth that stemmed from both the desire of the governments
to utilize agrarian surplus labor and a strong dictatorial allocation of coercive measures against the rural population.

Reasonable questions can be raised concerning the type of
individuals who moved to the cities as a result of the
deliberate antirural policy. The individuals most likely to
move to the city were neither the best-trained peasants nor

Table 5.4. Distribution of Population in Eastern Europe (in Percent)
(1) Prewar, (2) 1970, and (3) 1976

	Bulgaria			Czechoslovakia			East Germany			Hungary			Poland			Romania			Yugoslavia		
	1	2	3	1	2	3	1	2	3	1	2	3	1	2	3	1	2	3	1	2	3
Urban	28	55	59	50	62	66	72	73	76	35	45	51	37	52	57	26	40	48	21	38	41
Rural	72	45	41	50	38	34	28	27	24	65	55	49	63	48	43	74	60	52	79	62	59

Source: National Statistical Yearbooks of individual countries, various years.

Table 5.5. Agricultural Employment as Percent of Actively Employed Population
(1) Prewar, and (2) 1976

	Bulgaria		Czechoslovakia		East Germany		Hungary		Poland		Romania		Yugoslavia	
	1	2	1	2	1	2	1	2	1	2	1	2	1	2
	79	24	28	16		12	51	22	65	35	74	57	80	45

Source: National Statistical Yearbooks of individual countries, various years.

those who had the greatest amount of ingenuity or desire to own and operate their own homesteads. Indeed, of the nearly one million peasants who had joined the industrial labor force in Hungary between 1949 and 1969, the vast majority seemed to have come from among those who formerly owned little or no land and therefore, were already semi-agrarian proletars.(70) These people, by and large, did not possess modern attitudes, their work habits lacked incentive and their work efficiency was comparatively low. Unlike the Yugoslav gastarbeitern who ventured forth to West European work situations for significant financial gain, the vast majority of the new East European urban population combined a large portion of the rural lumpen-proletariat with a sprinkling of former kulaks and middle peasants who had been forced to change occupations.

The second index used to measure economic successes in the sphere of rural transformation reflects the declining share of agriculture and the growing proportion of industry in the total output of the nation. Tables 5.6 and 5.7 depict the success of this effort for prewar years and for 1970. The changed character of production is clearly visible from these data. Thus, for example, the most dramatic increase of industrial production occurred in Romania, but the share of industrial production grew in all states including those that had employed little or no collectivization drive. Similarly, agrarian employment decreased dramatically in all the East European states. In Hungary, the decrease was one-quarter of the entire population and in Poland, nearly 30 percent. Naturally, the decrease was enormous, once again, regardless of the collectivization efforts and processes of the regime. Whatever methods of evaluation one uses to analyze the phenomenal shift from agriculture to industry, it becomes clear that the collectivization process was not an independent variable in the process of economic change, but that deliberate policies favoring industrialization seemed to have affected the rural sphere. Nonetheless, the decrease in the role of agriculture in general seems to be a significant part of the rural transformation process.

The third index of economic development is the increased size of production units. Economists concerned with the question of rural development have long argued that increased size of estates means greater productivity, since large-scale mechanical production techniques can be utilized to replace the expensive labor-intensive requirements of small-scale production units. If we examine the historical development of the East European estate structures, we find that in Poland and Hungary prior to World War II, larger estates predominated in national agrarian production. In these two countries, large estates had been responsible for at least two-thirds of the production output of the agrarian economy, while small estates, comprising only a small portion of the land area, were respon-

Table 5.6. Industrial Employment as Percent of Total Employment
(1) Prewar, (2) 1970, and (3) 1976

	Bulgaria			Czechoslovakia			East Germany			Hungary			Poland			Romania			Yugoslavia		
	1	2	3	1	2	3	1	2	3	1	2	3	1	2	3	1	2	3	1	2	3
	8	39	41	42	47	48	42	50	50	23	37	44	17	38	40	12	23	40	11	19	23

Source: National Statistical Yearbooks of individual countries, various years.

Table 5.7. Industry as Percent of Gross National Product,
1938, 1950, 1973, and 1976

	Bulgaria	Czechoslovakia	East Germany	Hungary	Poland	Romania	Yugoslavia
1938	28	53		36	32	28	21
1950	37	62	47	26	32	44	45*
1973	52	62	62	44	51	58	35
1976	51	68	61	47	52	57	38

*1950 including mining. Following the early and strikingly unpopular collectivization of Yugoslavia, the share of agriculture radically declined. It was this decline that caused the relative "advance" of the industrial sector; an advance that disappeared after decollectivization resulted in increased agricultural production.

Source: National Statistical Yearbooks of individual countries, various years.

sible for one-third or less of production needs. Elsewhere in Eastern Europe the production activities of the large estates were less significant, but even in Romania, Bohemia and in some areas of the Balkans, large estates were responsible for significant production patterns.

With collectivization, the size of the agricultural units increased significantly, reaching absolutely mammoth proportions in the agro-industrial combines of Bulgaria. These changes are depicted in tables 5.8. What is interesting to observe, however, is the persistence of small estates and their economic importance. Following the postwar land reforms and prior to the collectivization of the early 1950s, the small estates were the predominant production units. These small estates were usually less than two and one-half hectares and only the intensive work of the peasantry insured their economic viability. In spite of collectivization, however, it should be noted that even in the 1970s small estates, auxiliary farms and household plots retained their economic importance. Even in states where collectivization has been completed, the small auxiliary and household farms contribute an enormous share to the national economy, relative to their size. In Yugoslavia and in Poland this would be understandable, but in Hungary and Czechoslovakia this comes as somewhat of a surprise.(71)

Consequently, it is safe to assume that the communist regimes exhibited a great deal of success in their efforts to increase the size of the unit. The greatest successes were exhibited in Bulgaria, Czechoslovakia, East Germany, Romania and Hungary, but some advances can also be noted in the northern regions of Yugoslavia and in the Western Territories of Poland. It is important to bear in mind, however, that it remains evident that the economy of scale is not as important in agrarian productivity in Eastern Europe as the enormous success and continuous importance of small-scale farms.

Finally, we do have some data on the mechanization of agriculture as an indicator of rural transformation. It must be remembered that the region as a whole was undermechanized in the interwar period. Table 5.9 depicts very clearly the enormous increase in the number of tractors in use. The use of harvesters, depicted in table 5.10, shows a similar increase. Although we have no exact statistics regarding the number of harvester-thrashers available before World War II, the dramatic increase in equipment use of this type is clear from the preceding tables. If we compare our findings with other indicators, such as, for example, the fertilizer availability per hectare of arable land reported in table 5.11, we find that in regard to the modernization of agricultural production processes, the regimes attained remarkable successes. While it is true that other indexes, such as the growth of secondary road networks, refrigeration facilities, shipping capacities and technological advancements in production methods,

Table 5.8   Modal (A and B) and Average (C and D) Size of
Farms in Hectares Before the War, After the Land Reforms,
and in 1972

	A Prewar	B Post-1945 Land Reform	C 1972 State Farm	D 1972 Collective Farm
Bulgaria	5-50 (68.4%)	5-50 (62.4%)	3499	4426
Czechoslovakia	5-100 (61.9%)	5-50 (74.2%)	3321	614
East Germany			893	725
Hungary	5-100 (83.9%)	0-5 (50.4%)	3653	1653
Poland	0-50 (73.3%)	5-50 (72.5%)		
Romania	2-50 (55%)	0-50 (57.7%)	4572	1587
Yugoslavia	5-50 (68.4%)	5-50 (64.1%)		

Source: United   States,   Department   of   Agriculture,   Agricultural Statistics of Eastern Europe and the Soviet Union, 1950, 1970 (June 1973), pp. 19-20; Berend and Ranki, Kozep-Kelet-Europa, p. 697; and Everett M. Jacobs, "Organization and Management of Agriculture in Eastern Europe, 1967-1974," in Economic Development in the Soviet Union and Eastern Europe, vol. 2, ed. Zbigniew M. Fallenbuchi (New York: Praeger, 1974), p. 285.

117

Table 5.9.   Number of Tractors in Use

	1938	1952-56	1965	1969	1973	1976
Albania	200(?)	1,186	4,331	6,400	6,428[b]	9,000[d]
Bulgaria	1,000	11,193	40,040	53,000	57,400	65,600
Czechoslovakia	6,000	33,500	125,000	134,000	140,000	141,000
East Germany	38,400[a]	62,500	94,700	149,000	143,000	138,000
Hungary	7,000	22,266	63,506	66,606	64,800	61,500
Poland	3,000	44,612	124,106	186,000	315,000	444,000
Romania	5,700	23,811	81,356	102,000	116,000[c]	128,000
Yugoslavia	1,000	13,360	45,420	68,199	150,000	260,831

(a) 1949.
(b) 1971.
(c) 1973.
(d) 1975.

Source: Agricultural Statistics of Eastern Europe and the Soviet Union   (Washington: U.S.   Dept.   of Agriculture, 1973), p. 22; Ivan T. Berend and Gyorgy Ranki, Kozep-Kelet-Europa gazdasagi fejlodese a 19.-20. szazadban (Budapest: Kozgazdasagi es Jogi Konyvkiado, 1976), p. 81ff.; and Statistical Yearbooks of individual countries, various years.

Table 5.10. Number of Harvester-Threshers in Use

	1952-56	1965	1969	1973	1976
Albania	111	502	890[a]	936[b]	1,000
Bulgaria	2,462	6,892	9,393	10,100	10,500
Czechoslovakia	2,647	11,840	15,268	18,300	20,000
East Germany	1,200	12,500	17,900	12,000	12,300
Hungary	2,248	8,841	11,207	13,500	15,000
Poland	3,128	5,330	12,100	19,200	25,000
Romania	1,219	36,844	48,400	39,600[c]	39,000
Yugoslavia	-	11,293	11,793	11,092	11,079

[a]1970.
[b]1971.
[c]1972.

Source: Agricultural Statistics of Eastern Europe and the Soviet Union (Washington: U.S. Dept. of Agriculture, 1973), p. 23; Ivan T. Berend and Gyorgy Ranki, Kozep-Kelet-Europa gazdasagi fejlodese a 19.-20. szazadban (Budapest: Kozgazdasagi es Jogi Konyvkiado, 1976), p. 81ff.; and Statistical Yearbooks of individual countries, various years.

THE PROCESS OF RURAL TRANSFORMATION

Table 5.11. Fertilizer Availability per Hectare of Arable Land in Eastern Europe
(in Kilograms)

Year	Bulgaria	Czechoslovakia	East Germany	Hungary	Poland	Romania	Yugoslavia
1938	n.a.*	n.a.	n.a.	6	n.a.	n.a.	n.a.
1950	1.5	30	130	6	241	1	n.a.
1951	n.a.	39	120	8	n.a.	n.a.	n.a.
1952	4	38	134	8	n.a.	n.a.	n.a.
1953	n.a.	43	137	8	26	n.a.	n.a.
1954	n.a.	50	152	11	n.a.	n.a.	n.a.
1955	8	60	147	9	34	2	8
1956	11	64	157	10	36	n.a.	13
1957	16	73	168	13	39	n.a.	22
1958	18	77	184	18	36	n.a.	28
1959	45	94	189	30	40	n.a.	31
1960	34	92	188	29	46	7	34
1961	31	92	197	38	49	9	31
1962	33	102	194	49	56	10	39
1963	39	106	216	53	58	18	53
1964	62	125	240	61	62	18	55
1965	79	152	266	63	72	25	55
1966	105	167	274	69	85	32	61
1967	134	173	276	91	103	42	62
1968	185	176	n.a.	112	119	46	67
1969	152	209	n.a.	125	140	51	71
1970	159	223	319	146	158	56	77
1971	158	254	332	171	172	69	74
1972	161	263	334	183	196	72	63
1973	159	265	361	216	207	82	76
1974	140	275	376	245	228	88	53
1975	166	305	370	270	236	114	79
1976	161	319	361	254	244	109	74
1977	172	311	334	271	238	107	94

*n.a. = Not available.

Source: Agricultural Statistics of Eastern Europe and the Soviet Union (Washington: U.S. Dept. of Agriculture, 1973), pp. 25, 27; Ivan T. Berend and Gyorgy Ranki, Kozep-Kelet-Europa gazdasagi fejlodese a 19.-20. szazadban (Budapest: Kozgazdasagi es Jogi Konyvkiado, 1976), p. 81ff.; and Statistical Yearbooks of individual countries, various years.

have shown less dramatic improvements, even in these areas significant advances have been made.

The successes of the regimes in sheer economic terms are significant in light of the enormous transformation of the countryside. Today, in all East European states except Poland and Yugoslavia, the large collective farms dominate the production process, utilizing large-scale mechanization to attain maximum production efficiency. There has been a significant decline in the share and importance of agriculture compared to total output and there has been a tremendous out-migration from the village to the city.

In areas that are more difficult to quantify, however, we can also see evidence of significant changes in the rural economic environment. Although there is not space available to treat this subject extensively, we must briefly touch upon some of these transformations. The most obvious and conspicuous change has been the industrialization and administratization of the traditional peasant village. Urban factories moved to small villages in search of scarce labor and cooperative associations established headquarters in rural communities, "farming out" labor-intensive work from the cities and state organizations and establishing cottage industries in the agricultural sphere. The collective farms today employ an ever-growing number of people in nonagrarian occupations. In one farm in Hungary, for example, only about 25 percent of the active workers are employed in traditional peasant occupations; the rest are tractor and truck drivers or active industrial workers on the farm.(72) While the ratio is not as positive in all of Eastern Europe, this common element can be found in all of Eastern Europe.

The "administratization" of rural life is also noticeable. In the 1970s, the role of administrative authorities and administrative employment has increased enormously. For a more complex environment, more secretaries, more administrators and more officials are needed, and the white-collar employees are very much part of the new economic structure.

Traditional peasant farming is becoming rarer in the states of Eastern Europe where collectivization and mechanization were successful. But even in Poland and Yugoslavia, where collectivization did not take place, there have been enormous changes. Even private (uncollectivized) peasants are beginning to use sophisticated machinery, fertilizers and modern production techniques. While these family farms lack the basic characterisitics of truly large-scale capitalist enterprise and while they are still subsumed and subordinated to certain principles that determine the functioning of the economy as a whole, the peasants of Eastern Europe are no longer grouped primarily in traditional subsistence units and increasingly are no longer the sole source of family support.(73) More and more, in all of Eastern Europe, there are peasant

families with two incomes. The males usually work in the city
and commute daily, weekly, or monthly back to the village.
The phenomenon of peasant workers has been described in
great detail elsewhere. Suffice it to say that this change is
one of the most important steps in the modernization of the
rural landscape of Eastern Europe.(74) As large numbers of
workers become associated with both rural and urban occupations, the economic transformation process begins to merge
the rural and urban environments. And in this respect, the
policies of the East European communist states to achieve a
directed process of rural transformation seem to have
succeeded.

NOTES

(1) H. Mendras, Les Paysans et la Modernisation de l'agri-
     culture [Peasants and the modernization of agriculture]
     (Paris: C.N.R.S., 1958) p. 5.
(2) Boguslaw Galeski, "From Peasant Class to Stratum of
     Farmers," in Basic Concepts of Rural Sociology, ed.
     Boguslaw Galeski (London: Manchester University Press,
     1972), pp. 134-136.
(3) For a detailed bibliography on the enormously rich
     literature dealing with the peasantry, see the notes to
     Joel M. Halpern and John Brode, "Peasant Society:
     Economic Changes and Revolutionary Transformation," in
     Biennial Review of Anthropology, 1967, ed. Bernard J.
     Siegel and Alan R. Beals (Stanford, Calif.: Stanford
     University Press, 1967), pp. 116-139.
(4) Jerome Blum, Lord and Peasant in Russia from the Ninth
     to Nineteenth Century (New York: Atheneum, 1968) has
     the most extensive discussion of the concept in regard to
     Russian history.
(5) E. Norbeck, "Peasant Society," in A Dictionary of the
     Social Sciences, ed. J. Gould and W. Kolb (New York:
     Macmillan, 1964).
(6) M. Banton, "The Folk Society and Civilization," in Race
     6 (1964): 27-33.
(7) J. M. Halpern, "Yugoslav Peasant Society in Transition:
     Stability in Change," Anthropological Quarterly 36 (1963):
     156-182; and D. Warriner, ed., Contrasts in Emerging
     Societies (Bloomington: Indiana University Press, 1965).
(8) C. Wagley, "The Peasant," in Continuity and Change
     in Latin America, ed. J. J. Johnson (Stanford, Calif.:
     Stanford University Press, 1964).
(9) E. C. Banfield, The Moral Basis of a Backward Society
     (Glencoe, Ill.: Free Press, 1958).

(10) Karl Wittfogel, Oriental Despotism (New Haven: Yale University Press, 1957).

(11) J. M. Fitchen, "Peasantry as a Social Type" in Proceedings of the 1961 Meeting of the American Ethnographic Society, ed. V. E. Garfield (Seattle, Wash.: University of Washington Press, 1961).

(12) Stephen Fischer-Galati, "Peasant Movements in Central and Southeastern Europe," Balkan Studies 6 (1965): 358-61.

(13) E. R. Wolf, Peasants (Englewood Cliffs, N.J.: Prentice-Hall, 1966).

(14) See E. R. Wolf, "Types of Latin American Peasantry: A Preliminary Discussion," American Anthropology 57 (1955): 452-71; and J. Steward, Theory of Culture Change (Urbana: University of Illinois Press, 1955) for an extended discussion on the subject.

(15) K. C. Polanyi, C. A. Arensberg, and H. Pearson, eds., Trade and Market in the Early Empires (Glencoe, Ill.: Free Press, 1957).

(16) C. Dalton, "Primitive Money," American Anthropology 67 (1965): 44-65.

(17) M. D. Sahlins, "On the Sociology of Primitive Exchange," in The Relevance of Models for Social Anthropology (London: Tavistock, 1965).

(18) John F. Benton, Town Origins (Lexington, Mass.: D. C. Heath, 1956), p. x.

(19) Henri Pirenne, Economic and Social History of Medieval Europe (London: K. Paul, Trench, and Trubner, 1936).

(20) Lewis Mumford, The City in History (New York: Harcourt, Brace, and World, 1961).

(21) Harry A. Miskimin, The Economy of Early Renaissance Europe, 1300-1460 (Englewood Cliffs, N.J.: Prentice-Hall, 1969); and Cristobal Kay, "Comparative Development of the European Manorial System and the Latin American Hacienda System," Journal of Peasant Studies (Spring 1969): 69-95.

(22) Zsigmond Pal Pach, Nyugat-europai es magyarorszagi agrarfejlodes a XV. - XVII szaszadban [Western European and Hungarian agrarian development in the fifteenth and seventeenth centuries] (Budapest: Akademiai Kiado, 1964).

(23) See Marc Bloch, Feudal Society, 2 vols. (Chicago: Chicago University Press, 1961); and Jerome Blume, "The Rise of Serfdom in Eastern Europe," American Historical Review 4 (1957) for the best statements on this complex subject.

(24) A. de Maddalena, "Rural Europe, 1500-1750," in The Fontana Economic History of Europe, vol. 1, section 4 (London: Collins, 1970).

(25)　R. Hilton, A Medieval Society (London: Weidenfeld and Nicolson, 1936).

(26)　For the differences between the Gutsherren and the Grundsherren, see W. Abel, Geschichte der Deutschen Landwirtschaft (Stuttgart: Eugen Ulmer, 1967), pp. 206-08; and H. Maybaum's excellent study, "Die Enstehung der Gutsherrschaft im Nordwestlichen Mecklenburg," in Beihefte zur Vierteljahrschrift fur Sozial und Wirtschaftsgeschichte (Stuttgart: Kohlhammer, 1926).

(27)　Zsigmond Pal Pach, "The Development of Feudal Rent in Hungary in the XVth Century," Economic History Review 1 (1968).

(28)　J. Nichtweiss, "Zur Frage der zweiten Leibigens haft und des sogennanten preussichen Weges der Entwicklung des Kapitalismus in der Landwirtschaft Ostdeutschlands," Zeitschrift fur Geschichtswissenschaft 5 (1953): 694; W.E. Wright, Serf, Seigneur and Sovereign (Minneapolis: University of Minneapolis Press, 1966), pp. 8-9; and Jerome Blum, Noble Landowners and Agriculture in Austria, 1815-1848 (Baltimore: Johns Hopkins University Press, 1948), pp. 95-96.

(29)　F. L. Carsten, "The Origins of the Junkers," English Historical Review 243 (1947): 158.

(30)　I. Schoeffler, "The Second Serfdom in Eastern Europe as a Problem of Historical Explanation," Historical Studies (Melbourne) 3 (1969): 57.

(31)　Maddalena, "Rural Europe, 1500-1750."

(32)　Nichtweiss, "Zur Frage," pp. 691-96; and Blum, Lord and Peasant, p. 609.

(33)　Ivan T. Berend and Gyorgy Ranki, Kozep-Kelet-Europa gazdasagi fejlodese a 19. - 20. szazadban [The economic development of central Eastern Europe in the nineteenth and twentith centuries] (Budapest: Kozgazdasagi es Jogi Konyvkiado, 1976), p. 42; and the excellent study by W. Moore, Economic Demography of Eastern and Southern Europe (Geneva: League of Nations, 1945).

(34)　Berend and Ranki, Kozep - Kelet - Europa, pp. 45-46; and Julia Puskas, "Kivandorlas Magyarorszagrol az Egyesult Allamokba 1914 elott" [Emigration from Hungary to the United States prior to 1914], Tortenelmi Szemle, 1-2 (1974).

(35)　Berend and Ranki, Kozep- Kelet- Europa, pp. 51-53.

(36)　P. Mantoux, The Industrial Revolution in the 18th Century (London: J. Cape, 1961); and "Studies in the Industrial Revolution" in Essays Presented to T. S. Ashton, ed. L. S. Presnell, (London, 1961).

(37)　It is interesting to note, for example, that as late as 1831-32, the Reglement Organique for the territory of what was to become Romania defined 68 days as the maximum days of mandatory work the peasants were compelled to undertake on the land of the estate owner.

(38) R. Cameron, ed., Banking in the Early Stages of In-
      dustrialization (New York: Oxford University Press,
      1967).
(39) V. Liveanu, "Factorii determinanti ai variatlor arenzii
      taranesti la inceputal secolului al XX-lea in Romania,"
      Studii (Bucharest) 2 (1971).
(40) Berend and Ranki, Kozep-Kelet-Europa, p. 82.
(41) The extent of subsistence farming, of course, varied all
      over the region ranging from 15 to 25 percent of the
      product consumed by subsistence farming activities in
      Bohemia to 80 percent consumed by subsistence farming
      activities in Bulgaria around the turn of the century.
      (Ibid., p. 84)
(42) Ibid., p. 83.
(43) Joseph Rothschild, East Central Europe Between the Two
      World Wars (Seattle: University of Washington Press,
      1974), pp. 15-19.
(44) For detailed studies concerning the land reforms of the
      East European states see I. Evans, The Agrarian Revolu-
      tions in Roumania (Cambridge, England: The University
      Press, 1924).
(45) Berend and Ranki, Kozep-Kelet-Europa, pp. 285-6.
(46) In Hungary, for example, 0.5 percent of all estates with
      acreages above 100 hectares constituted 41.9 percent of
      arable land; in Romania 0.4 percent constituting 27.7
      percent fell in this category; while in Poland 0.3 percent
      of all estates with land above 50 hectares constituted 25.8
      percent of all arable land. (Ibid., p. 285).
(47) Paul N. Rosenstein-Rodan, "Problems of Industrialization
      of Eastern and South-Eastern Europe," Economic Journal
      53 (June-September 1943): 202-11.
(48) Berend and Ranki, Kozep-Kelet-Europa, p. 597.
(49) Berend and Ranki, Kozep-Kelet-Europa, pp. 593-595.
(50) Orban, Ket agrarforradalom, p. 42.
(51) Berend and Ranki, Kozep-Kelet-Europa, p. 593.
(52) S. Kuznets, Modern Economic Growth: Rate Structure
      and Spread (New Haven, Conn.: Yale University Press,
      1966).
(53) David Mitrany, Marx Against the Peasant (New York:
      Collier, 1961).
(54) Galeski, "Peasant Farming," in Basic Concepts of Rural
      Sociology, p. 15.
(55) Antal Vegh, "A bankett," in Okorsirato, ed., Antal Vegh
      (Budapest: Szepirodalmi Kiado, 1975), pp. 7-20; and
      Orban, Ket agrarforradalom, p. 42.
(56) Thus, for example, in Hungary compulsory deliveries
      from the estates of private peasants were raised by 300
      percent between 1949 and 1953 (Ibid., pp. 99-100).
(57) Ibid., p. 124.

(58) Andrzej Korbonski, "The Agricultural Problem in East
      Central Europe," Journal of International Affairs 20
      (1966): 72-88.
(59) H. Gordon Skilling, The Governments of Communist East
      Europe (New York: Thomas Y. Crowell, 1966), p. 189.
(60) For a more detailed account see Francois Fejto, A His-
      tory of the Peoples Democracies (New York: Praeger,
      1971), pp. 24-30.
(61) Stevan K. Pavolwitch, Yugoslavia (New York: Praeger,
      1971), p. 230.
(62) Orban, Ket agrarforradalom, p. 218.
(63) Ian M. Matley, Romania: A Profile (New York: Praeger,
      1970), p. 165.
(64) Statisticheski Godishnik, 1963 (Sofia, 1963), p. 186.
(65) Ibid., 1962, p. 213.
(66) Ibid., 1973, p. 265.
(67) For a good summary of the Hungarian New Economic
      Mechanism see Bela Csikos Nagy, Magyar gazdasagpolitika
      (Budapest: Kozgazdasagi Kiado, 1973), pp. 389 ff.; and
      William F. Robinson, The Pattern of Reform in Hungary
      (New York: Praeger, 1973), pp. 60-67.
(68) Gyorgy Enyedi, "A mezogazdasag szinvonal-zonai," in
      A magyar nepgazdasag fejlodesenek teruleti problemai, ed.
      Gyorgy Enyedi (Budapest: Akademiai Kiado, 1976), pp.
      175-186, categorized the types of agricultural activity on
      the bases of the latest techniques.
(69) According to Jozef Chalsinski, "The Young Generation of
      Rural Inhabitants in People's Poland as Seen from Their
      Life-Records," Polish Sociological Bulletin 2 (1964);
      Spoleczna geneologia inteligencji polskiej (Lodz: Czytelnik,
      1964): and Janusz Zarnowski, Spoleczenstwo Drugiej
      Rzeczypospolitej 1918-1939 (Warsaw: Panstwowe Wydaw-
      nictwo Naukow, 1973), especially pp. 115, 168. In
      Poland, forty percent of the peasants simply remained on
      the farm as surplus labor because there was no place to
      go. A similar situation prevailed in Hungary, Romania,
      Bulgaria and Yugoslavia and only in East Germany and
      the Czech part of Czechoslovakia was the rural over-
      population slightly less extreme.
(70) According to one source, in 1930 there were three million
      active peasants and 600,000 active workers in Hungary.
      Forty-five years later the ratio was reversed: there were
      three million active workers and 750,000 active peasants
      employed in the Hungarian economy. Most of those who
      became industrial laborers seem to have come from the
      ranks of landless peasants or those who possessed only
      minimal amounts of land. (Bela Iranyi Toth, "Uton,
      doccenokkel," Elet es Irodalom, May 17, 1977, p. 16.)
(71) Galeski lists a breakdown of the Polish ownership struc-
      ture basing his examples on two Polish provinces. Al-

though his sample is skewed by the fact that the provinces are located in the western and central regions, his research indicates that smallholding peasants in two modal communities, owning less than four hectares of land made up of 38.5 percent of total farm owners and hold only 8 percent of the land; 50.4 percent of all families had possessed lands between four and 25 hectares and held 87 percent of the land; while 1.1 percent of all peasants held 5.3 percent of the land. (Galeski, "The Social Structure" in Basic Concepts of Rural Sociology, pp. 123-124.)

(72) Ferenc Karinthy, "Talking to Erzsebet Galgoczi," New Hungarian Quarterly 65 (1977): 99.

(73) Galeski, "Peasant Farming," pp. 17-23.

(74) For a good basic sociological study, see Andrei Simic, Peasant Urbanites (New York: Seminar Press, 1973).

6 Current Development Patterns and Agrarian Policy in Latin America
William C. Thiesenhusen

The beginning of the last quarter of the twentieth century sees Latin America changed but hardly transformed from the century at midpoint. Those who predicted cataclysmic, widespread revolution have been disappointed or at least incorrect. But those who forecast that the Latin America of the late 1970s would be no different from that of the mid-1950s would be no different from that of the mid-1950s have likewise been proved wrong. Casual observers of the Latin American scene are astonished by what appears to be social and political fragility; those who study long-term trends by resilience and adaptability.

In the main, the elites of the subcontinent have been evolving slowly such that many of those with power or at least riches 25 years ago have, by and large, not been stripped of those trappings today. While there is less ostentation now, those in power have adapted to modernity in the beginning of the last half of the twentieth century in Latin America (with the exceptions of Cuba and, possibly, Bolivia) in the way in which the landed nobles seem to have thought they would during the era of the "Garibaldini" in Italy. The Latin American political prototype of mid-century and now may be somewhat whimsically personified by the Prince and his nephew Tancredi in di Lampedusa's fictionalized Il Gattopardo.(1) As readers are introduced to Tancredi, he is engaging in light-hearted conversation with his uncle about plans for joining the anti-Bourbon forces, but suddenly becomes serious when the Prince shows consternation tinged with disapproval. Among justifications for his proposed, almost treasonous, and certainly disloyal actions, Tancredi avers, "If we want things to stay as they are, things will have to change. D'you understand?" The older man does not at first, finding the words ambiguous nonsense. Only later he comprehends. And the landed aristocracy slowly receded in Sicilian life with more of a whimper than a bang.

What has changed Latin America lately has not been in-
vading forces or even civil uprisings that have the potential
for sparking more widespread strife, but industrialization and
the forces of modernization attendant upon it. Elites have
attempted to maintain their wealth and status not by battle,
but by subtle adaptation to the inevitable spread of industrialization and the locus therein of the subcontinent's economic
growth points. One obvious mechanism by which such accommodation has occurred, upon which many varying themes are
played, is that agricultural elites have bought into urban
poverty. In some cases this has brought the sons of former
agricultural gentry into the urban elite. As such they have
latched onto some of the dynamic elements found in manufacturing or its attendant technology or commerce, established
themselves or reaffirmed their positions in exporting, and/or
allied themselves with strong foreign elements.

What is important in the economic pattern that has
emerged is that in Latin America today there is still little
upward mobility in the system, if by that is meant opportunity
for those at the bottom of the socioeconomic structure to rise
to responsible positions in strata above them. And because of
the astounding rate of population growth since World War II
there are probably more poor and illiterate in Latin America
now than at mid-century. In an appendix on Latin America,
Gunnar Myrdal in his Challenge of World Poverty, concludes
that present trends are likely to continue however negative
they prove to be for human values. He predicts neither
evolution nor revolution.(2)

While his conclusion has proved true in the short run, it
bears fleshing out, for it there has been no evolution or
revolution, there certainly has been social alteration. Most of
this change relates in one way or another to the uneasy reality
that income distribution patterns - regional, country, family,
sectoral, etc. - apparently are becoming more unequal. While
income concentration and regional divergence have been
common historically in countries going through early industrialization, these trends seem to be so long standing in Latin
America that it is doubtful whether they are a necessary condition for industrialization.

1. There is an increased number of strong-man
    regimes, most of them rightist military, in Latin
    America and their durability seems to be in-
    creasing. "Democratic forms" of government
    are harder to find now than at mid-century.
    As civic violence increases, so does repression.
2. While the United States is still far and away the
    dominant foreign economic power in Latin Amer-
    ica, some stronger Latin American countries are
    increasingly assuming part of that role (which

has often been referred to as imperialism) by
encroaching on their poorer neighbors, for good
or ill. Brazil and Argentina in Paraguay and
Bolivia, Brazil in Uruguay, Venezuela in Colombia, and Mexico in Central America are some examples. Concomitantly, Japan and Western
Europe are also playing a more active economic
role in Latin America than in the past.

3. Population growth rates show some signs of
falling in some countries but not very rapidly;
the region continues to exhibit the highest
demographic increase of any in the world. But
Chile and Costa Rica are examples of countries
where dramatic drops in growth rates have been
recorded.

4. The press is becoming more government controlled and countries are becoming more isolated
from what is happening in their own countries
and in other parts of Latin America and the
world. The electronic media, including movie
news, whose influence has never been subject to
much scrutiny but is probably available to many
more people than television, are as subject to
this tendency as are the print media.

5. The number of countries undergoing balance-of-
payments problems is increasing. Among the
causal factors are that the market for traditional
exports (except for oil) has weakened, while
the market for new, often manufactured, export
goods has failed to show much strength.
Furthermore, the demand for imports has increased, the multinational corporations have not
picked up much of the slack, and long-standing
foreign debts have come due.

6. The domestic market also fails to show much
strength.

7. Inflation continues in some countries where it
was already endemic. Because of worldwide
tendencies, especially in the industrialized
countries, it is now a feature of nearly every
Latin American country. Meanwhile, unemployment, including underemployment, seems as
intransigent a problem as ever.

The most outstanding feature of Latin American economies
is not their lack of economic growth; it is the inequitable way
in which both income increments and resources are distributed.
The situation varies markedly from country to country, but
economic growth has, during the 1960s and first half of the
1970s, more than kept up with the demographic rate, which

averages about 2.5 percent. From 1968 to 1974 the average rate of growth of the gross domestic product (GDP) reached 6.9 percent per year.(3)   And one rate seems not to be related to the other. In Brazil the growth of gross domestic product per capita averaged 2.2 percent a year from 1963 to 1968 and a spectacular 7.2 percent a year from 1968 to 1973. Population growth averaged about 2.9 percent for the entire period. In Uruguay product growth rose from a negative 0.5 percent in 1963 to 1968 to 0.6 percent from 1968 to 1973, while population grew at only 1.2 percent in the decade beginning with 1963.(4)

In general, of course, the faster population grows the faster an economy's product must grow just so that everyone can stay at the same income level. But even if both rates stay about the same, all will not benefit equally. Economic growth rate is by itself an inadequate gauge of development because it says nothing about distribution: 1) growth is primarily an urban phenomenon and one that is concentrated in the small part of the agricultural sector that is commercially and/or export oriented; 2) its benefits may go to the segment of population that is numerically growing most slowly; 3) it may occur as a result of the "take-off" of but a few industries; 4) it may happen because of transient favorable conditions in one segment of the external market; and 5) it may be concentrated in the multinational segment of the economy.

A more adequate indication of welfare of the country's people, and, hence, "development," would have to be determined by formulating a composite of: 1) initial quantum of resources or product, including education; 2) how fast that product is growing, or resources are being depleted; and 3) how resources, product, and opportunities are distributed. We have no way of measuring initial endowment of resources or product except to observe that countries like Argentina, Venezuela, and Mexico have more to work with, and hence more product per person, than Bolivia, Honduras, and Paraguay. Distribution of resources and product is likewise difficult to discern. While data are generally poor, some observations can be made about the Latin American scene from tables 6.1 and 6.2.

1.   The bottom 60 percent of the population is relatively worse off than two decades ago and the bottom 10 or 20 percent may have a lower absolute income.

2.   In some countries the group just below the top 5 percent has benefited by an increase in its share of income; in some cases the top 5 percent have benefited in relative shares at the expense of all of the rest.

Table 6.1.   Distribution of Income for Selected Latin American Countries

	Year	Gini Index*	Income Share to Percentile of Recipients	
			Lower 60%	Upper 5%
Argentina	1953	0.41	31.9	27.3
	1959	0.45	28.6	31.8
	1961	0.42	30.5	29.3
Brazil	1960	0.49	25.4	27.9
	1970	0.56	20.8	34.9
Mexico	1950	0.53	24.6	40.0
	1957	0.55	21.2	37.0
	1963	0.55	20.8	38.3
Puerto Rico	1953	0.42	30.3	23.4
	1963	0.46	27.9	22.0

*The closer the index approaches one, the greater the inequality.

Source: Adapted from Richard Weisskoff and Adolfo Figueroa, "Traversing the Social Pyramid: A Comparative Review of Income Distribution in Latin America," Latin American Research Review 11 (1976), table M.

Table 6.2. Percentage Rural–Urban Population by Income Quartiles for Selected Countries

| | Year | Income Quartile | | | | | | | |
| | | I | | II | | III | | IV | |
		Rural	Urban	Rural	Urban	Rural	Urban	Rural	Urban
Colombia	1970	57	43	49	51	34	66	14	86
Costa Rica	1971	83	17	69	31	52	48	28	72
Mexico	1963	67	33	54	46	36	64	21	79
Peru	1961	89	11	69	31	43	57	28	72
Puerto Rico	1963	69	31	61	39	47	53	29	71
Average		73	27	60	40	42	58	24	76

Source: Adapted from Richard Weisskoff and Adolfo Figueroa, "Traversing the Social Pyramid: A Comparative Review of Income Distribution in Latin America," Latin American Research Review 11 (1976), table 4A.

133

   3.   Urban people dominate the upper half of the
        income distribution while rural people dominate
        the lower half. Family income is lower in the
        countryside but more equitably distributed.
   4.   The top income classes of the poorest countries
        command larger income shares than the corres-
        ponding groups of the richer nations.(5)

The case of Brazil is a good illustration of the inadequacy
of considering growth factors alone in determining whether a
country is "developing" or not. During the summer of 1976,
the newly founded International Food Policy Research Institute
predicted that food deficits in many poor tropical countries
could be double those in 1974-75 but that Brazil could turn
into an exporter.(6) If the 1961-65 agricultural output in
Brazil is represented by 100, in 1973 it was 131, 148 in 1974,
and 147 in 1975 - spectacular progress to be sure. Yields
have increased and more land has been brought under cultivation than anywhere else in the Americas. In the six years
ending in 1974, economic expansion ranged from 9 to 11 percent annually. The commerical agricultural sector received top
priority under government programs to increase exports,
reduce imports, and maintain food and industrial supplies.
Long-range programs to improve research and extension programs provided a basis for increasing productivity and the
government initiated a crop insurance program in 1975.
Agricultural credit has been increased markedly and a minimum
price program includes 32 commodities. According the to
United States Department of Agriculture, agriculture in Brazil
has also benefited from growing investments and progress in
improving transport, storage, and other infrastructure.(7)
     Yet a recent headline in the New York Times expressed a
problem that is often hidden in heady discussion on this kind
of progress, "Brazil's Agriculture Expands Fast, But Mostly
for Benefit of Well-to-Do." The article continues:

        Despite the country's rapid economic growth,
     the real wages of unskilled laborers have declined
     steeply because of inflation. And food prices have
     generally led the rise in the cost of living. As a
     result, nutritionists estimate that 40 percent of the
     110 million Brazilians are suffering from malnutrition.
     In the northeastern state of Bahia, the health secre-
     tariat listed malnutrition as the indirect cause of 80
     percent of the 17,000 child deaths in 1974.
        In Sao Paulo officials estimate that undernour-
     ishment accounts for more than 40 percent of the
     deaths registered among children 1 to 4 years of
     age.

The unbalanced development of agriculture is as apparent in the countryside as in the cities. About 50 million Brazilians still live in rural zones, and the vast majority of them eke out a living as ill-paid employees or as subsistence farmers.

Agrarian reform has never been carried out. A billion-dollar plan to redistribute land in the poverty-striken northeast was announced during the early 1970's, but it has not been carried out. An ambitious program to settle the vast Amazon area with landless peasants has also been largely abandoned because most of the jungle soil has proved too infertile for intensive agriculture.

Elsewhere in the country fertile land is considered too valuable to use on socially motivated reforms. (8)

During the 12 years of military rule, Brazil's gross national product increased more than 150 percent, but there has been a radical redistribution in favor of wealthier economic sectors:

1. Real wages for unskilled labor have declined almost 40 percent since 1964.
2. Skilled workers received a 2.6 percent increase per year.
3. Executives received an 8.1 percent increase. (9)

There is a temptation to translate these distributional phenomena into political terms, but if there is any lesson to the history of the past quarter century in Latin America, it is that there is peril in doing so. One cannot assume that the lower class, however repressed, will overturn the current order if for no other reasons than that the techniques of repression have been so refined and that potential power contenders can be bought off in a prolonged period of economic growth. Marshall Wolfe concludes:

The argument that critical poverty constitutes a threat to the existing order so serious that the dominant forces must eliminate it for their own self-preservation is...in most national settings unconvincing, although its disruptive potential does call for some combination of control and relief. The critically poor, whatever their number, become a serious threat only when a political system enters into crisis for reasons other than poverty. Even major famines do not necessarily goad the critically poor into anything more than easily repressed local disorders as long as the power structure remains

intact....In the world today, one finds countries
with a predatory elite ruling over a majority at the
lowest level of subsistence that are relatively stable
to outward appearance, while other societies in
which the dimensions of critical poverty are small,
are chronically disrupted by conflicts over the
distribution of income.(10)

Against this backdrop, one can view with more perspective
recent events in some countries. The governmental shake-up
in Peru, during the summer of 1976, merely continued a series
of rightward shifts; Chile's hosting of a major Organization of
American States (OAS) conference added a certain amount of
legitimacy to a repressive regime despite the denunciation of
the deprivation of civil rights the conferees delivered at an
inaugural session; and President Peron of Argentina was
replaced by a government that seems equally inept at maintaining civil order, let alone promoting basic change.
    Turning to the rural sector of Latin America, perhaps the
most telling indicator of tranformation would be the extent to
which countries have failed to institute agrarian reforms. With
the exception of Cuba, they have promulgated change but
hardly transformation. In Mexico and Bolivia, revolutions
occurred so long ago that they have been on a status quo or,
some say, a reverse track for years; Chile was on its way to
radical change and was stopped by the current military
government; Brazil and Paraguay had always been content to
deal with the rural problem through colonization. Peru's
accomplishments have not been very widespread in the
campesino sector, though, it's true, the oligarchs who ruled
by their control of land no longer have that option.
    The land tenure system of Latin America is still charac-
terized by the existence of latifundia and minifundia - that is,
the coexistence of very large landholdings, usually extensively
farmed, and a large number of very small-holdings, usually
located in marginal areas.
    In 1965 it was estimated that about 94 percent of the total
arable land in Latin America was owned by 7 percent of the
landholders. Since that time, populist governments have come
and gone; the Alliance for Progress spurned strongly reformist
pronouncements, some stemming from a fear of "another Cuba";
the plight of the poor in Latin America came to be recognized
as a serious and intransigent problem by international lending
and assistance agencies, especially in the early 1970s; campesino groups have spoken out for their rights, and traditionally conservative institutions in the region - parts of the military and the church - have seen the need for some change.
This interest seems to spring from the existential situation:

1. The population of the region is about 318 million
    now, it will probably reach 435 million in 1985,
    and 135 million will still depend on agriculture.
    Already 20 percent of the population suffers
    from serious malnutrition and rural under-
    employment is so large that nobody knows whose
    grim figures to believe. Industrial growth and
    growth of the services sector, while more rapid
    than agriculture, are not proceeding at a fast
    enough pace to absorb the excess farming
    population, let alone their own.
2. Services to farming areas - schools, health
    care, sanitation, etc. - are outstripped by new
    demands placed on them both by the increased
    population and by greater expectations.
3. Technological innovations - tractors, farm
    implements, etc. - are being adopted in agri-
    culture to raise production with little attention
    to what their use might mean in terms of in-
    creased unemployment, displacement of mini-
    fundios, and rural-to-urban migration.
4. The communications between the masses who
    aspire to a better life and the rising middle
    class in Latin America and the United States are
    increasing with the electronic and print media.
    Indeed, part of the repression that has oc-
    curred in Latin America recently is closing,
    through censorship, those "disruptive" informa-
    tional sources.

In the wake of the foregoing, it is rather surprising that with
few exceptions, the land tenure structure today remains pretty
much what it was in 1965. Expropriation has, according to the
United Nations Food and Agriculture Organization, (FAO)
reached barely 15 percent of the potential expropriable land
(under Agrarian Reform Laws passed in the 1960s by nearly
every Latin American country) and agrarian reform
beneficiaries are only about 22 percent of potential beneficiaries.(11) Even these figures appear somewhat high.
The reasons why so little has been accomplished is, as
alluded to earlier, that the real power structure in most countries of the region has changed little in the past several
decades. Therefore, the elite has been able to write laws -
even agrarian reform laws - which obfuscate the real issues,
and:

1. Diffuse calls for reform with such techniques as
    "planned colonization" of the frontiers or other
    marginal areas. These programs tend to be
    expensive on a per settler basis, to attract

wide publicity (such that some would-be reform-
ers are mollified into believing that the government is "doing something"), and largely to fail
in that participants default on loans, return to
old communities, and/or sell the plot they
cleared to a nearby rich neighbor.

2.   Discourage campesino organizations which would
     act as pressure groups.

3.   Monopolize services, marketing channels, educa-
     tional facilities, credit, etc. - even com-
     munication with the world outside the immediate
     locality.

4.   Channel new technology to its own use, at times
     threatening the rural poor with loss of jobs.

5.   Deflect demands for change with promises and
     small concessions.

6.   Engage in outright and brutal repression.

Examining these indicators and trends does not leave us filled
with optimism about the future of the poor - especially the
rural poor - in Latin America over the next decade or so.
And since so many are poor, how will the middle classes be
able to sustain impetus in economic growth with such a limited
market for goods they manufacture and such a limited export
market?

There are several possibilities, but the most probable is
that scattered uprisings will be quickly put down, alliances
between labor, including the agricultural poor, and intellectuals which might push for change will be discouraged by a
variety of techniques, the church will speak out more force-
fully against flagrant cases of the denial of civil rights by
those in power, and some industrialists will see some advantage
to a modicum of relief programs for the poor since that will
mean widening their markets. But this will happen slowly,
sometimes imperceptibly to outside observers. Di Lampedusa
offers a possible, plausible description as the Prince looks to
his future: "Much would happen, but all would be playacting:
a noisy, romantic play with a few spots of blood on the comic
costumes....For all will be the same. Just as it is now:
except for an imperceptible shifting of classes...."(12)

NOTES

(1) Giuseppe Tomasi di Lampedusa, Il Gattopardo (Milano,
     Italy: Feltrinelli Editore, 1959).
(2) Gunnar Myrdal, Challenge of World Poverty (New York:
     Pantheon Books, 1970).

(3) In 1975, however, most of the countries in Latin America experienced a sharp drop in their rates of economic growth and a substantial increase in their balance-of-payments deficit. Much of the problem can be traced to the adverse effects of the worst recession in industrial countries since World War II, the impact of higher costs for imported goods, and the energy crisis. (Inter-American Development Bank, Economic and Social Progress in Latin America, 1975 [Washington, D. C., 1976].)

(4) United Nations, Department of Economic and Social Affairs, 1974 Report on the World Social Situation, E/CN.5/512/Rev. 1; ST/ESA/24 (New York, 1975), table 9, p. 36, and table 10, p.38.

(5) For more on income distribution in Latin America, see Richard Weisskoff and Adolfo Figueroa, "Traversing the Social Pyramid: A Comparative Review of Income Distribution in Latin America," Latin American Research Review 11 (1976): 71-112

(6) Victor K. McElheny, "Doubling of Food Deficit of Tropical Nations Possible," New York Times, August 3, 1976.

(7) United States Department of Agriculture, Economic Research Service, The Agricultural Situation in the Western Hemisphere: Review of 1975 and Outlook for 1976, Foreign Agricultural Economic Report no. 122 (July 1976), table 2, pp. 15, 26.

(8) Jonathan Kandell, New York Times, August 16, 1976.

(9) Kandell, "Brazil Moves Toward State Capitalism," New York Times, September 12, 1976.

(10) Marshall Wolfe, "Poverty as a Social Phenomenon and as a Central Issue for Development Policy," ECLA/DRAFT/DS/133 (New York: United Nations Social Development Division, February 1976), p. 16.

(11) United Nations, FAO, ILO, Progress in Land Reform: Sixth Report, ST/ESA/32 (New York, 1976), p. 83.

(12) Di Lampedusa, Il Gattopardo.

7
The Family Farm in Australia: Land, Labor, Capital, and Management
Robert H.T. Smith

INTRODUCTION

It is said that the world recognizes Australia through rural
symbols, but these symbols are not part of the everyday experience of most Australians.(1) The fact is that most Australians live in urban areas; indeed, almost two thirds of the
total population is concentrated in the capital cities. In this
situation, it is a little too easy to overlook one of the classic
rural institutions, the family farm. Even the most aggres-
sively parochial Australian urbanite would agree that Australian agriculture is changing, although he or she may be a
little vague about the details. Urban Australians are being
reminded constantly about the trials and tribulations of rural
Australia: quotas on Japanese and United States imports of
beef, the threat to wool from synthetics, crisis in the dairy
industry, and the familiar droughts, floods, bush fires, and
cyclones. The ever-present Country Party is an enduring
symbol of Australia's rural backdrop.

There are several pervasive influences that have contributed in a continuing way to the shape of rural Australia.
Some of these, such as technological change - railroads,
roads, the conquest of the environment, etc. - are not dis-
tinctively Australian, but others, such as a federal con-
stitution and certain deeply held values and attitudes, are
peculiar to Australia. In particular, the widespread belief that
there is a wholesome quality about rural life, which stemmed
partly from appalling nineteenth century urban conditions in
Britain, coexists paradoxically with pronounced and continuous
urbanization. It is in this context of a decidedly uneasy
complacency that this study on rural transformation in
Australia is presented.

This study deliberately focuses on the family farm, in
particular on the economic aspects. The chapter proceeds
within the framework of the factors of production: land,
labor, capital, and management. Finally, the chapter concludes with a case study; this is based less on farm management and accounting details and more on a factual account of
what happened on one family farm during the quarter century
period from 1947.

For some time family farming has been under pressure to
become more capital intensive. Gruen has referred to the
"...relentless long-term economic pressure to substitute capital
equipment and industrial goods for labour,"(2) and this is
particularly true of family farming. This pressure is resisted
for a variety of reasons, perhaps the most important of which
is that family farming as a way of life has long had considerable appeal: the satisfaction from working one's own land
is not to be denied. This conflict between long-term economic
forces and prevailing attitudes can be phrased as a thesis
which is particularly appropriate to this study: developments
in the public and private sector that place emphasis upon land
and labor, rather than on capital and management, will inevitably lead to a proliferation of low standard-of-living,
high-cost, inefficient, low-income farms.(3)

LAND

Land as a factor of production in the rural industries can be
considered from several points of view: for example, land
quality, land use, land tenure, and the size of production
units. The ensuing discussion will be concerned largely with
land tenure and with farm size. These two characteristics of
land are particularly important to an entrepreneur in his
evaluation of a given parcel of land as a production unit.

The tenure disposition of land in Australia gives cause
for comment: as table 7.1 shows, only a little over one-eighth
of the total area has been alienated for private occupation, the
balance being designated Crown Land. The proportions vary
significantly from state to state: while almost two-thirds of
Victoria's land is under private ownership, both New South
Wales and Tasmania have experienced only moderate alienation.
Proportions in the remaining states are very small. Perhaps
more important than the proportion of land alienated is the
proportion leased or licensed to farmer-operators. More than
50 percent is in this category, with the state proportions
ranging from a low of 11 percent in Victoria to a high of 77
percent in Queensland. Clearly, much of Australia's farming
enterprise is conducted on publicly owned land, which suggests that land tenure is critical for an understanding of
changes in the Australian rural scene.

Table 7.1. Land Tenure in Australia, 1974
(in Percent)

State or Territory	Private Land		Crown Land			TOTAL	Percent Not in Rural Holdings[c]
	Alienated	In Process of Alienation	Leased	Other	Percent	Acres ('000)	
New South Wales[a]	32.0	1.9	55.8	10.3	100.0	198,037	13.9
Victoria[a]	59.7	0.6	10.8	28.9	100.0	56,246	42.7
Queensland[b]	7.3	9.5	77.4	5.8	100.0	426,880	10.7
South Australia[a]	6.4	0.1	61.3	32.2	100.0	243,245	33.8
Western Australia[b]	5.9	1.8	40.1	52.2	100.0	624,589	54.7
Tasmania[a]	40.0	2.0	29.6	28.4	100.0	16,885	61.8
Northern Territory[a]	0.1	0.0	58.2	41.7	100.0	332,979	42.2
Australian Capital Territory[a]	3.3	0.4	32.1	64.2	100.0	601	45.3
Australia	9.9	3.0	55.1	32.0	100.0	1,899,462	35.0

(a) as of June 30th, 1974.
(b) as of December 31st, 1974.

Source: Year Book Australia, 1975-1976 (Canberra: Australian Bureau of Statistics, 1977).

The history and sequence of Australian land settlement can be divided into five periods. In the first, experimental period, the population was relatively small: "...this was a phase of settlement which was limited in its extent and temporary in its occurrence."(4) After the physical barriers to the inland were breached, "...there emerged in Australia in the thirties a unique and unauthorized occupation of large provinces - 'Squatting',"(5) which constituted the second period (1831-1855). Pastoralists simply crossed the official boundary of settlement at will, established themselves and their flocks on the unused, unoccupied land. Squatting was an established fact by the end of the 1830s and, by the mid-1840s, the squatters themselves were agitating for protection of their de facto land titles.(6)

The third period of settlement (1855-1884) saw the emergence of agriculture, and pressures developed after 1850 to make more land available. The stereotype of the independent, self-supporting, sturdy, righteous, yeoman farmer appears at this time. Williams describes the theoretical and intellectual foundations for this movement, and suffice it to say that the purpose of legislative initiatives, for example, the Robertson land acts in New South Wales, during the ensuing decades "...was to intensify settlement by placing the small man on the land...there was the negative aim of stopping the squatter/speculator from subverting the main objective."(7) The degree to which these initiatives were successful varied enormously, and considerable ingenuity was exercised by squatters to subvert the efforts of government to preserve the claims of the "small" man. Nevertheless, as the end of the nineteenth century approached, an attitude of acceptance of "closer settlement" solidified; thus the fourth period (1884 to about 1955). Government initiatives during the late nineteenth and early twentieth centuries were directed toward adjustment in land tenure and occupation patterns to bring about a supposedly more equitable rural mosaic. This continued into the twentieth century with soldier settlement schemes after the two world wars. Peel has claimed that "provision of opportunities for 'small' men to go on the land became an end in itself, pursued too frequently with scant regard for economic efficiency, biological appropriateness or, ironically, human dignity."(8) Thus, when one contemplates the present-day stiuation, one can recognize that the array incorporates vestiges of the overriding preoccupation throughout Australian rural settlement history with the need to contain the squatter so as to be able to settle more people on smaller holdings. A fifth period, one of rural reconstruction, can be dated from about 1955 to the present.

This brief review of the historical foundations of closer settlement would be incomplete without some explicit attention to the procedures that developed to implement the policy.

Machinery had to be devised for survey and subdivision of unsettled lands. Given the implicit theme of "more and smaller is better,"(9) the agents of government became preoccupied with two considerations: the smallest unit of land that would serve the closer settlement purpose; and forms of land tenure that would discourage amalgamation and the gradual re-emergence of the abhorrent large estates. These two concerns were translated into concepts of a "living area," or in New South Wales, the "home maintenance area," and of various forms of leasehold tenure.

The Home Maintenance Area

The definition remained unchanged in New South Wales between 1908 and 1949. The home maintenance area was defined as "an area which when used for the purpose for which it was reasonably fitted would be sufficient for the maintenance in average seasons and circumstances of an average family."(10) Several significant features of the definition should be noted: the home maintenance area implies family farming; indeed, it makes an explicit reference to the "average family." There was an implicit long-term view, indicated by the reference to "average seasons and circumstances"; some seasons would be favorable, some unfavorable but, viewed as a series, the average output would maintain the average family. Observers have read further implications into the concept: the home maintenance area "... is not necessarily concerned with the most economic employment of land, labour and the other pro-ductive resources involved in farming. In fact, it can be shown that in many farming enterprises, the most economic unit is the relatively large farm making full use of mechaniza-tion and employing several hired hands who can more or less specialize in various farm tasks" [emphasis added].(11)

Land Tenure

The possibility of large-scale land aggregation can be reduced not only by firmly limiting holding size, but also by careful manipulation of the conditions of tenure. The squatting era implied an "effective occupation means ownership" type of land tenure that was anathema to the politicians and public officials of the late nineteenth and early twentieth centuries. As Lewis notes, "The locking up of land resources in large estates was seen as denying land to those not possessing large amounts of capital and as reducing incentives to rural development."(12)

Australia's land legislation is notoriously complex. While laws and regulations vary from state to state, and are different again for the Commonwealth, there are some common elements in the mainland eastern states which were originally the Colony of New South Wales. Here there are three agencies in addition to the Department of Lands that administer land tenure law (two state commissions, and the Commonwealth). At the most general level, land can be held in freehold (purchase) or leasehold, but beneath this, there are four distinct classes and several forms of land tenure: purchase (12 forms), perpetual leases (18 forms), lease for a limited period (16 forms), and permissive occupancy or tenancy at will. The most significant distinction is between alienated and leased land. Alienated land is purchased land held in freehold tenure (or in the process of alienation to freehold tenure). In general, land held in freehold tenure carries few if any restrictions on the rights to use, transfer, residence, improvement, and the use of timber or mineral resources on the land. In contrast, leases relating to public land vary in length and according to location; quality of land; purpose of occupation; rights to transfer; rights to use, e.g., minimum stocking rates; residence and improvement requirements; terms of purchase; and so on.

The implications of such a complicated pattern of land tenure for the rural sector generally, and for the family farm in particular, are enormous; only three will be discussed here.

First, while the productive capability of a parcel of land is unaffected by the terms used in the title description, the fact that one farm consists of several different parcels of land in terms of tenure can affect its value, especially to neighboring farmers who seek "to acquire additional land to build their properties up to a full living area."(13)

Second, fixed-period leases prevail in certain areas. It has been argued that fixed-period leases - common in Queensland and the Northern Territory - have effectively precluded improvement and maintenance of holdings,(14) thus hindering land development generally. While the objective of such a policy is to retain the flexibility to reserve large areas of land for closer settlement when the technological and economic conditions are appropriate, the effect is to dissuade the lessee from making investments to which he has no assured title beyond the end of the life of the lease.

Third, conditional purchase leases require the satisfaction of certain improvement and/or production targets. For example, in Western Australia, the requirements of a conditional purchase lease of grazing land were (a) a maximum of 2,500 acres to be allotted to any one person; and (b) certain improvements to be made in a specified period of time on pain of forfeiture of the lease.

Thus, land tenure restrictions can affect (a) the degree to which a given holding is viewed as a homogeneous or unified production unit, (b) the propensity of a lessee to ef-

fect improvements that could well affect the viability of the
unit as a family farm and (c) the efficiency with which the
farmer is able to conduct his enterprise. The point is not
that governments in Australia are or have been perverse in
the development and administration of land law. Rather, it is
that given the course of land settlement and the emergence of
a strong public commitment to closer settlement policies, land
tenure regulations have had some unexpectedly deleterious
effects on the viability of the family farm, especially as the
economic and technological environment has changed.

Farm Size

This characteristic of rural holdings can be examined from
several points of view: acreage, net income, or, for livestock
enterprises, herd or flock size. Clearly, two farms of the
same area may be very different in terms of productivity,
hence the income and herd/flock size dimensions of farm size.
It is useful to consider first the area characteristic of size.
    The preceding discussion emphasized the importance of
areal limits to farm size in early closer settlement initiatives.
"Small" and "large" have no real meaning in absolute terms,
but it is interesting to note that mean farm sizes from four
early twentieth-century closer settlement resumptions in what
is now called the wheat-sheep zone of New South Wales (see
grain/sheep zone, fig. 3.1) ranged from 415 acres near
Tamworth to 607 acres near Inverell and 454 and 588 near
Wagga Wagga.(15) Duggan suggested the following sizes of
home maintenance areas on the irrigation lands of southern
New South Wales: fresh vegetables, 10 acres; vegetables for
processing, 15-20 acres; fruits and vine, 25-40 acres; fat
lambs, 500-2,000 acres; and sheep for wool, 3,000-4,000
acres.(16) It is revealing that in the middle of the twentieth
century, serious arguments were advanced for holding less
than 50 acres.
    An alternative approach to the assessment of farm size is
to examine the evidence of economies of scale. This approach
seeks to identify the acreage - or herd or flock size, or the
level of total revenue - at which the long-run average cost
curve approaches a minimum. It has been observed "that long-
run average cost curves for rural industries commonly are
strongly downward sloping over the lower ranges of farm size
and that thereafter unit costs remain more or less constant."(17) A sheep enterprise needs to include 5,000 head,
with a total revenue of $20,000 before scale economies occur;
for wheat, 800-1,000 acres with an approximate yield of
25,000-30,000 bushels, with a total revenue of $30,000, is
necessary; economies of scale in beef cattle enterprises enter
at the 2,000-5,000 head size, involving a total revenue of

$40,000.(18)   Inevitably,   these   figures   mask   enormous
variations between different areas of Australia, but it gives a
useful national overview.

The well-intentioned policy makers of the early twentieth
century should not be castigated because of their failure to
anticipate the economic and technological forces that underlie
scale economies. Nevertheless, there is a "small-farm problem"
in Australia, and it can be best understood through an
examination of the characteristics of rural holdings. In many
countries, farm incomes are significantly lower than nonfarm
incomes,(19) but this is not the case in Australia.(20)
However, there are several potential problem characteristics of
farm income as revealed by a series through the 1950s and
1960s: they fluctuated about an upward trend, whereas
nonfarm income rose steadily upward in the same period;
annual fluctuations in average and aggregate farm incomes
were substantial; and farm incomes show a very wide dis-
persion about the mean.(21) The key element of all of these
characteristics is the emphasis on "fluctuations"; the Australian farmer may enjoy net incomes roughly comparable to
those of his nonfarming counterpart, but this masks the very
real - and, in Australia, ever-present - problem of susceptibility to variation because of climatic and market risk.(22)

McKay selected a net income of $2,000 as the criterion for
a low-income farm: "...the farmer has to meet, from the $2,000
or less, his family's living expenses, his interest payments,
and his fixed capital repayments, e.g. hire purchase. He
must also pay any income taxes...."(23) Survey data revealed
that the proportion of farms with net farm incomes less than
$2,000 varied from 7 percent in wheat to 92 percent in berry
fruit (see table 7.2). McKay estimates that of the roughly
50,000 farms not included in the survey table, 40 percent
(20,000) would be in the low-income category.(24) This gives
a combined total of 80,000 farms, almost one third of all
holdings. If the cut-off is lowered to $1,000 the number of
low-income - indeed, borderline poverty farms - is 45,000.
Perusal of table 7.2 shows that it is the dairy industry in
which there is the largest absolute number of low-income
farms; this is especially true in southern Queensland, northern
New South Wales and southwest Western Australia.

Table 7.2.   Low-Income Farms in Australia

Industry	Percentage less than $1000	$2000	Number
Wheat	4	7	32,294
Sheep	12	25	93,106
Potato	32	44	8,151
Dried vine fruit	17	47	3,084
Citrus fruit	28	50	3,375
Dairy	33	55	61,845
Banana	52	83	3,861
Berry fruit	75	92	658
All industries	19	34	206,374

Source: D.H. McKay, "The Small-Farm Problem in Australia," Australian Journal of Agricultural Economics 11 (December 1967): 118.

LABOR

The standard index of labor as a production factor in the Australian rural sector is the level of male farm employment (see table 7.3). Gruen's impressions of the composition of the farm labor force is best read with reference to the 1954 column of table 7.3: "The total Australian farm work force amounts to about 450,000. Over 60 percent (or 270,000) are employers or self-employed farmers. Less than 100,000 work as permanent farm and station employees; the balance of 80-90,000 are casual, temporary or seasonal workers. About 90 percent of the employees are men. The largest single group work for the pastoral industry amounting to perhaps 60,000....Twelve thousand were shearers and an equal number were other workers involved in shearing....The remainder were station hands."(25)

The level of male farm employment has declined steadily since 1954; indeed, the decline should be more correctly dated from 1933, when the level of male farm employment was half a million, slightly more than one fifth of the total male work force (see table 7.3). Part of the difference between the 1933 and 1947 figures may be attributed to the devastating effect on the rural labor force of World War II, but the burgeoning urbanization trends following the war must also be noted. The

Table 7.3.   Male Farm Employment in Australia
('000)

Item	Census Years						
	1921	1933	1947	1954	1961	1966	1971
1. Employers	57	103	57	62	56	73	50
2. Self-employed	162	155	200	200	191	149	135
3. Total farm operators	219	258	257	262	247	222	185
4. Employees	185	199	146	153	126	125	185
5. Helpers not receiving wages	28	35	21	15	11	8	113
6. Total employees	213	234	167	168	137	133	113
7. Total employees per farm operator	0.97	0.91	0.65	0.64	0.55	0.60	0.61
8. Unemployed and not stated	39	36	11	6	12	4	n.a.
9. Total	471	528	435	436	396	359	298*
10. Percentage of total male work force	25	22	18	15	13	11	8

*Unemployed and not stated excluded.
n.a. = Not available.

Sources: Rural Industry in Australia (Canberra: Bureau of Agricultural Economics, 1971), p. 20; and The Principles of Rural Policy in Australia (Canberra: Australian Government Publication Service, 1974), p. 14.

150   THE PROCESS OF RURAL TRANSFORMATION

vigorous immigration policy pursued in the postwar period did little to reverse this trend; migrants simply accentuated the familiar Australian pattern of movement from the country to the city to the suburbs. The vast majority of immigrants "...made directly for the employment hearths in the capitals and stayed there."(26) The male labor force in the early 1970s was in the vicinity of 300,000, less than 10 percent of the total male work force.   It is worth observing that this steady decline has occurred among both farm operators (see row 3 of table 7.3) and employees (rows 4, 5 and 6).   Further, the proportion of the population residing on farm holdings has also steadily declined in the last 20 years, from 11.5 percent in 1950 to 7 percent in 1971.(27)

The occupational status of farm operators has remained relatively stable (see row 1 of table 7.3), with approximately one-quarter of the farm operators being employer farmers.   A precipitate rise occurred in 1933 as unemployed urban labor sought rural employment.   Employees per farm operator (row 7 of table 7.3) declined steadily during the 40 years to 1961 and this index has remained relatively stable since that time.   A comparable trend can be observed for the average number of males engaged per rural holding: 2 in 1933, 1.6 in 1961.   With these trends as background, it should be no surprise to find that the rural male work force is also aging.   The 15-39 years age group, which accounted for almost 58 percent of the rural male employees in 1937, had declined to 47 percent 40 years later.   The 40-50 age group over the same 40 years increased from 31 to 39 percent.   This aging trend is, of course, inevitable when the work force is shrinking.

These bare statistics say little about concurrent change in productivity and in farm business organization.   The index of volume of rural production rose from 100 in 1921 to 291 in 1971,(28) thus indicating that a drastic decline in the rural labor force was not necessarily accompanied by a decline in the rural production.   In contrast, changes in farm business organization involving female participation in family partnerships have had little impact on the farm labor force.   It is useful at this juncture to consider briefly the antecedents to this situation.

Characteristics of the Rural Labor Force

There are several features of the Australian rural labor force that should be noted briefly.   It is overwhelmingly native-born and of British descent.   There is a prevalence of political conservatism among country people; it is quite pronounced in farm owners, and a little less so in farm laborers,(29) but the implications for the efficiency of labor are difficult to identify. At the farm owner/operator level, from which a large pro-

portion of rural labor is drawn, primary producer organizations
have tended to be narrowly sectional in outlook, although
Chislett suggests that these attitudes are changing.(30)
Unionism is not well entrenched among farm employees, partly
because of the difficulties of organizing members who work for
a large number of small, spatially separated employers, and
also perhaps because of the fact that job satisfaction for the
farm employee stems at least partly from the "way of life"
afforded by employment in rural areas.(31)   Farm employees
work under award wages set by arbitration tribunals, which
are related in one way or another to the Australian equivalent
of the minimum hourly wage, the Basic Wage.   Also, conditions
of accommodation, etc., have been specified, and this has
occasionally been given as the reason for the difficulty of small
family farms to continue to employ labor.(32)   The Australian
Workers Union, which grew out of the turbulent industrial
relations in the grazing industry in the 1890s, claimed a half
of the pastoral industry work force of 60,000, including a
large number of shearers, as members in 1960.(33)   Shearers
have traditionally been the most militant component of the rural
work force; given the backbreaking nature of the work, it is
not surprising that shearers are well paid by rural work force
standards ($5 per 100 in 1947, $56 per 100 in 1977) and that
conditions of work and employment have been carefully regulated by successive arbitration tribunals.(34)

Some observers have noted one aspect of the Australian
rural labor force of farm owners and employees that does have
implications for efficiency: there is a tendency for experience
to be more highly regarded than learning.(35)   This could well
be a reflection of several factors: the heroic pioneer notion of
the yeoman farmer and the itinerant bushman battling with
nature, untainted by urban civilization; the relative lack of
educational facilities in rural areas; and the relative newness
of a real concern for farm management training.(36)

Labor productivity in Australian rural industries has been
rising.   With a gradual increase in capital and equipment and a
matching gradual decline in the rural labor force, the index of
farm labor productivity has increased by a factor of three
since 1921.(37)   While this increase is substantial, Herr has
shown that the increase in labor productivity in the United
States over roughly the same period was considerably
greater.(38)   He argues that the difference stems largely from
structural differences in the two agricultural sectors; the
accumulated effect of the nineteenth- and early twentieth-
century closer-settlement policies has resulted in a lower rate
of out-migration from the Australian rural labor force.

As the absolute size of the rural labor force has declined
and, in particular, as the shortage of skilled workers has
become more pronounced, contract services have become
especially important.   Certain contract services, such as

shearing, fruit picking, cane cutting, bag sewing, wheat grading, wheat carting, potato digging, etc., have long been a feature of various rural industries. While some of these have been supplanted by technological developments, e.g., bag sewing and potato digging, several have increased enormously in recent decades: contract fencing, plowing, fertilizer spreading, pesticide spraying, and aerial top dressing.(39) The efficiencies that accrue through specialization and the economies in the use of capital equipment contribute in no small way to the improvment in farming efficiency and in labor productivity generally.

Many of the problems of life in rural areas stem from the fact that Australia is sparsely populated. Provision of the most basic services such as sealed roads, electricity, schools and basic urban amenities becomes a prohibitively costly proposition. Living costs are not necessarily less in rural areas and country towns than in urban Australia,(40) and the incidence of "poverty" is greater among rural nonfarm families than other families.(41)

In Australia, the rural labor force of farm owners and employees has steadily declined and, while labor productivity has increased, it has been constrained by the vestiges of past settlement policies. Contract services are becoming increasingly important in the rural sector. The rural-to-urban population drift continues apace and, while this is undoubtedly related to the changing production function of farming, it can also be seen in the context of the facilities and amenities available in rural areas.

CAPITAL

Discussion of capital as a factor of production is difficult because capital is of two types: financial capital and physical capital. Money capital is usually quite mobile and may be invested in almost any undertaking; the rural industries must compete with alternative uses. The more tangible and largely immobile form of capital, physical capital, takes the form of equipment and machinery, structures, and land. Access to a certain amount of financial capital is of course necessary to purchase or develop physical capital. It could be argued that the significant change that has occurred in the Australian family farm relates to the amount of financial capital necessary to obtain and sustain the physical capital necessary for the farming enterprise. The stereotype of the pioneer farmer literally creating a productive enterprise with little more than his bare hands has become less and less relevant with the passage of time; farming has indeed changed "...from a way of living to a way of making a living."(42)

The Family Farm and the Capital Market

The previous two sections have demonstrated that the family farm in Australia is relatively small and draws largely on the family unit as a source of labor. The central characteristic relating to capital as a factor of production stems from the fact that almost all productive units are unincorporated enterprises for which equity capital is not available.(43)   Unlike the company form of business organization, the family farm simply does not have access to the capital market, and sources of funds for family farming are thus rather narrowly circumscribed.   Further, the company form of enterprise organization, by separating ownership and control of productive assets, avoids the problems of intergeneration transfer of asset ownership.(44)

The family farm can seek financial capital from two general sources: those internal to the farm unit, including current income or past savings; and external sources, which include borrowing in one form or another from institutional and noninstitutional sources.   Institutional sources include such essentially private institutions as the trading banks, pastoral finance companies, and assurance societies, plus the various government and quasi-government sources such as federal and state banks, soldier settlement arrangements, etc.   Noninstitutional, external sources include hire purchase companies, trade creditors, and private lenders, e.g., solicitor's accounts.   Although a recent estimate suggested that one-third of commercial farms have no debts,(45) the level of gross rural indebtedness is substantial, and has been increasing steadily in the last 30 years.   (Pre-World War II comparisons are somewhat precarious if only because the figures for 1939 are given if ≸ A.)   Comparative yardsticks are difficult to identify and to use, but it is worth noting that while in 1955, net farm income exceeded rural indebtedness to major institutional lenders by almost $2 million, indebtedness was twice the value of net farm income in 1970.(46)

Without access to the capital market, internally generated income takes on enormous significance for the business activities of the family farm.   Apart from determining the standard of living of the farm family, the level of income has direct implications for both the amount available for reinvestment and for the farmer's ability to obtain and discharge loans.   While real incomes have shown little increase in recent decades, the financial requirements of the farm sector have been rising steadily.(47)

Farm Income in Australia

Farm incomes rose steadily through the decade of the 1940s so
that by the early 1950s, during the wool price boom, incomes
and average taxes of primary producers had caught up to
other nonemployees.(48)   However, during the next decade,
realized income of unincorporated farm enterprises declined,
from ₤585 million in 1952-53 to ₤453 million in 1961-62,(49) but
in terms of average actual income the comparable figures were
₤1,576 and ₤1,393, respectively.(50)   A recently published
series records real farm income as having declined from $1,637
million in 1952-53 to $1,455 million in 1972-73.(51)   Values in
all except four of the intervening years were less than $1,300
million.   During the same period, farm costs increased by
three times, dramatic evidence for the cost-price squeeze that
has plagued the Australian farmer since the 1950s.   An additional source of pressure on farm income from the economic
environment is the heavy reliance on export markets, where
prices tend to be substantially lower than on the domestic
market.(52)   When to this already difficult picture are added
the uncertainties that stem from climatic variabilities, the
instability of production and therefore of farm income can be
better appreciated.   Indeed, the farm income problem in Australia is less one of disparities between farm and nonfarm
sectors, and more one of gross fluctuations of income from
season to season.(53)

The Characteristics of Rural Credit

There are several quite distinct types of demands for rural
credit:(54)   "cushion"   finance to sustain production during
poor seasons, e.g., droughts, or in times of low prices, e.g.,
low wool prices due to synthetics competition; finance for a
capital-using innovation, e.g., improved pastures, specialized
shearing or milking machinery; finance for farm enlargement by
additional purchase or land clearing; and finance for inter-
generational transfers of ownership.   These demands vary in
the realistic term over which the debt will be repaid, and it is
this feature more than any other that differentiates the various
institutional lenders.   The family farm faces a particularly
difficult situation with respect to intergenerational transfers
because "...the farm has in practice, largely to be repur-
chased in each generation; farm liquidity is likely to come
under pressure again from time to time - leading to an increased demand for longer term loans."(55)   The loan term
criterion has been used to identify three different levels of
credit needs: short-term or production credit; intermediate-
term credit for farm development purposes; and long-term
credit for the purchase of rural properties.(56)

With this criterion in mind, the major sources of institutional credit can be divided into three categories. First, there are the trading banks and pastoral finance companies, the former providing capital via overdrafts, the latter by essentially short-term advances against anticipated income, such as an advance against a wool clip. Overdrafts normally have a maximum limit; they are effectively an open line of credit and in principle are repayable on demand. Interest is paid on the daily balance owing to the bank. While overdrafts may appear to be short term, they were in fact operated as long-term loans; periodic reductions in the level were required.(57) They are usually secured against the land, and the specter of foreclosure in bad seasons and difficult economic times was and is very real to many family farms. Over the last fifteen years, trading banks have come to regard their function as the provision of short-term working capital, so that the overdraft form of financing has become less accessible to the family farm. It was only the introduction of term loans and the farm development loan fund (FDLF) that led to the recent increase in the trading bank share of rural indebtedness. These are financed and executed by the trading banks; they are facilitated by the federal government's authorization of the release of Statutory Reserve Deposits of the trading bank for rural lending. They were designed to meet longer-term credit needs; the former have an eight-year maximum, while the latter has a 15-year or longer life. It is this source of credit that has been developed to fill the "major hiatus in credit facilities for rural development and property purchase" to which Lewis referred in 1961.(58)

The credit supplied by pastoral finance companies is largely for working capital, pending the sale of wool, livestock, or other produce. These loans are secured by a lien on the produce, rarely on land; interest rates are normally higher than on loans from trading banks. Most loans of this kind are made on the expectation that they will be repaid as soon as the produce is sold. Pastoral companies also finance short-term loans for property and livestock transfer but relatively few of the advances are tied up in long-term mortgages.(59) Thus, it is well to note that both the trading banks and the pastoral companies have become sources of predominantly short-term funds which, for the banks especially, is quite a change from their traditional role.

The second major source of institutional credit is the Commonwealth Development Bank (CDB). The essential difference between the CDB and the trading banks is that the former is less concerned with the value of the security available and more with the prospects of the enterprise becoming successful. Indeed, the CDB loans, which incorporated several features that set them apart from the traditional trading bank overdraft form of financing, were peculiarly appropriate to the longer-term financing needs of the family farm.(60)

The third major source of institutional credit includes the assurance societies, soldier settlement schemes, and other government agencies. In 1967 Jarrett suggested that "the Life Assurance Societies are relatively insignificant lenders to the farm sector," a conclusion that contrasts markedly with the United States experience.(61) Such mortgage loans as are made are usually of a long-term nature, frequently subject to renegotiation after an initial three- or five-year period, and carry higher interest rates than trading bank overdrafts. Public funds for soldiers' settlement reached a peak in 1960; with the gradual move away from closer settlement policies in general, and with the natural running down of the need for returned serviceman rehabilitation, borrowings in this category have steadily declined. Like most government-sponsored rural loan programs - through, for example, state banks and state savings banks - their terms were somewhat more favorable than in the private sector. However, restricted limits frequently applied, and loans tended to be for a fixed term over which the loan is to be amortized rather than an open line of credit as with trading bank overdrafts. Loans from these predominantly state institutions, which have increased markedly in the last decade, are made for such purposes as farm development, rural reconstruction, i.e., farm consolidation, sale or lease of Crown Land, and drought relief.(62)

The overall picture has changed little during the last 30 years; between two-thirds to three-quarters of rural indebtedness is to essentially private institutions, with the remainder to public agencies.

Physical Capital

This discussion would be incomplete without some reference to the physical capital stock of Australian farms. The capital value of beef cattle, sheep, and wheat farms is considerably greater than other enterprises.(63) That agriculture has become more capital intensive can be documented from many sources; this is in its simplest form a response to the "relentless long-term economic pressure to substitute capital equipment and industrial goods for labour."(64) The contribution of land to the capital structure is declining, while the importance of livestock, machinery and implements, and improvements are increasing. Several series are available to document the upward trend in sales of such farm equipment as tractors, shearing and milking machines, and combine grain drills; sales of superphosphate have likewise increased. Depreciation allowances have also recorded an upward trend, reflecting purchases of plant and equipment.

The family farm in Australia comes under particular pressure during droughts; livestock losses can be substantial

and replacement investment in livestock is not without implications for other forms of capital investment. Where the
objective of freedom from indebtedness has priority on the
family farm, the creation of physical capital inevitably is
slowed.

MANAGEMENT

Decision making is an essential ingredient in any productive
enterprise, and farmers in particular are constantly making
decisions about the way capital and labor are to be applied to
the land. These decisions are taken, at least partly, in the
light of the farmer's assessment of future economic and climatic
environments. In turn, these assessments will be conditioned
- again, at least partly - by the farmer's accumulated on-the-
job experience and by precise technical knowledge - from formal education, continuing education programs, or from agricultural extension sources. Thus, a discussion of "management"
as a factor of production in the farm sector necessarily involves attention to farmers per se, to farm business organization, and to public initiatives in the field of research and
development that are, in the final analysis, sources of knowledge for practicing farmers.

The Family Farm and the Family Farmer

There are three significant implications of the family farm type
of enterprise unit. First, it is difficult if not impossible to
separate the "farm" and the "family" for the purpose of
decision making: "...because the property is simultaneously a
unit of both production and domestic consumption of produce
or cash, goals related to consumption and capital accumulation
for the family will be intimately involved in production
decisions."(65) This is an inevitable characteristic of an enterprise in which the ownership and control of the production
unit is vested in the same person or group of persons.
Second, because of the time demands of the numerous manual
tasks required of the family farm owner/manager, the farmer
frequently has difficulty finding time for keeping records, let
alone for analysis and planning. The nature of farm labor
needs is such that there are few sequential and repetitive flow
patterns (an exception being milking on dairy farms), and "at
any one time there may be six jobs which urgently need doing,
or one job on which all hands are required."(66) Indeed, if
Gruen's observation that "hard work is identified with physical
effort and the importance of other types of work belittled"(67)

is accepted, the family farmer might well be relieved that there
is little time for the more clerical aspects of farm management.
In general, a disproportionate amount of emphasis has been
placed on technical skills rather than on managerial skills, in
formal training programs, e.g., agricultural diploma courses,
and in on-the-job training.

Third, the entry of new managers usually occurs with a
change in land ownership; "...traditionally this is by the
bequest of farm property from father to son."(68)   Thus, new
managers are, quite predictably, recruited largely from the
farm family, a form of recruitment that Schapper terms "highly
nepotic in character."(69)   While this is not necessarily bad,
there could well be an incentive for farmers' sons to enter the
family farm labor force on reaching the minimum school leaving
age.   The observation that "the vocational training of most
potential managers is conservative, coming from their fathers
and fathers' peers"(70) does not denigrate the management
abilities of the family farmer, but does emphasize that innovation in management practices is unlikely to occur when
experience gained on the job accounts for almost all of the new
manager's training.

It is difficult to document those less tangible management
characteristics of the Australian family farmer. In particular,
it is virtually impossible to answer the question: In relation to
the rate of return on invested capital, in relation to comparable farmers elsewhere, etc., do family farmers make good
managers?   They are said to be politically conservative and
therefore reluctant to change existing economic and political
institutions; self-reliant and adaptive, especially to natural
calamities; and prone to regard experience more highly than
learning.   The extent to which these attributes affect the
management efficiency of family farmers is unknown.

Farm Business Organization

The Australian family farm is conducted under several different forms of business organization (see table 7.4).   Of the
240-250 thousand rural holdings in Australia,(71) about one-
half are operated as partnerships.   In the 1940s, there were
relatively few companies in the rural sector, but by the early
1970s there were 7,400.   These are predominantly private,
family companies, with public companies being rather rare.
The number of trusts remained relatively stable during the
decade from 1965 and if anything has declined since the
mid-1960s.

The number of farms run by sole operators must be
inferred as the residual in table 7.4, and, not surprisingly, it
records a steady decline from approximately 178,000 in the
mid-1950s to a little over 100,000 in the early 1970s.   How-

Table 7.4. Farm Business Organization in Australia,
1944-45 to 1970-71

Year	Partnerships	Companies	Trusts	Subtotal	Operators
1944-45[a]	n.a.	695	n.a.	n.a.	n.a.
1949-50[a]	n.a.	1,104	n.a.	n.a.	n.a.
1954-55[b]	61,125	1,914	9,318	72,357	177,643
1959-60[b]	89,350	3,208	9,293	101,851	148,149
1964-65[b]	117,966	4,914	11,040	133,920	116,080
1970-71[c]	125,000	7,400	9,975[d]	143,375	106,625

n.a. = Not available.

Sources: [a] "Trends in Taxable Income: Companies Engaged in Primary Production," Quarterly Review of Agricultural Economics 7 (April 1954): 71-72.

[b] J.M. Wells an W.R. Bates, "Changes in Farm Business Organization in Australia," Quarterly Review of Agricultural Economics 22 (March 1969): 53-65.

[c] The Principles of Rural Policy in Australia (Canberra: Australian Government Publication Service, 1974), p. 17. Apparently this figure was 128,000 in 1968-69.

[d] 1965-66 figure.

ever, before it is concluded that these, the family farms proper, are being supplanted by different forms of farm business organization, it is necessary to identify the management implications of the several forms, and the reasons for the existence of alternatives to the sole-operator type of family farm. This is especially important as one authority has claimed that "the adjustments which have taken place in farm business organisation do not necessarily imply any change in the structure or management of the properties concerned. Mostly they represent a change in legal status rather than in basic organisation and the family farm remains by far the most important type of enterprise."(72)

Sole-Operator Family Farms

The implications of this form of farm business organization can be viewed in the short, medium and long term. In the first category, there are the day-to-day decisions concerning management and use of resources, such as livestock care decisions, crop preparation decisions, construction and maintenance of structures decisions. In the second category, there is the annual accounting of the farm enterprise and particularly the preparation and filing of income tax returns. The plans made by the farmer for retirement and disposal of the financial management of the farm business belong in the third category. The latter involves the transfer of ownership of future income streams, and of wealth; and the transfer of the decision-making function.(73) The sole-operator farmer pays individual income tax up to the moment of death. While the income tax law does include some concessions for primary producers, the Australian tax rates are quite progressive so that as incomes rise, especially as in recent years with rapid inflation, the amount of tax paid is substantial.

The estate of the sole operator is subject to death duties levied by both Commonwealth and state governments. Because a family farm business conducted by a sole operator is bound to have substantial assets, especially in land, death duties are quite high. Thus, while in 1970-71 primary producers constituted only about 5 percent of the income-tax-paying population and made a similar contribution to total income tax assessed, Commonwealth estate duty assessments of primary producers fluctuated between 32 percent and 39 percent of the total duties assessed to persons in all industries.(74)

Effective transfer of the decision-making function rarely occurs before death because "the pre-death transfer of the power to make the decisions is ... difficult for the ageing farmer to accept because he often, rightly or wrongly, sees his long experience on the family farm as the paramount qualification required for good managerial decision making."(75)

This situation is reinforced by the fact that life on the farm is such that a sole operator can continue active participation until well after the normally accepted retirement age. It is perhaps significant that the public discussions of a national super-annuation scheme conducted in the early 1970s made no mention of primary producers.

Partnerships

Most partnerships in the rural industries have only two partners, and the overwhelming majority are family, hus-band/wife partnerships. Thus, 71 percent of the two-member partnerships in the sheep industry in 1964 were husband/wife partnerships;(76) in the same year, the proportion of part-nerships tended to increase as net farm income increased, and the reverse was the case for sole operators.(77) The primary objective partnership formation seems to have been to minimize tax liability and, given the significance of farm income as a source of financial capital for on-farm investment, this must be seen as eminently rational economic behavior. The average rate of income tax is substantially lower when farm income is shared between two or more persons and when it can be shown that a partner does in fact have real and effective control and disposal over his or her share of the partnership.

Companies

Companies are far less numerous than partnerships in the rural sector, although the number has increased substantially since the mid-1960s (see table 7.4). Most of the companies are private, family ventures; public companies of the corporation farming type are not very numerous despite the fact that this form of organization is the only route to the wider equity capital market. Wells and Bates argued in 1969 that an "...important motive for the creation of private companies in the rural industries is the desire to reduce death duties."(78) One of the most common methods of reducing the cost of the intergenerational transfer of assets has been to sell the land and fixtures to a family company and to create a trading partnership which owns the livestock and machinery and rents the land from the family company. The major disadvantage of the company strategy is the relatively high level of income tax liability that the farm family might incur. The major ad-vantage of private companies over partnerships stems from the fact that farmers who form such companies are able to retain control over their property while divesting themselves of ownership.(79) Thus, as with partnerships, the form and style of farm management is substantially unchanged by the formation of a private company.

Trusts

All trusts involve the designation of one person, the trustee, as nominal owner of the property to be used for another's benefit. This form of farm business organization, especially where it concerns a husband and wife, can be established by a testamentary document. It avoids the payment of death duties on the same assets once when the husband dies and again when the wife dies, or vice versa. Other trusts can be established for the benefit of relatives while the contributor is still alive. The income tax regulations as they relate to trusts are rather precise, (80) and this form of farm business organization is less prevalent than partnerships and/or companies as a means of reducing income tax liability and the payment of death duties.

The inescapable conclusion from this discussion is that while at least half (and probably more) of Australian farms are conducted under a form of organization other than the sole operator, the managerial input is essentially the same as on sole-operator farms. In other words, the family farm type of business organization predominates in fact if not in name.

A FAMILY FARM, 1947-1973

This section describes in a qualitative and very personal way the experience of a farm family between 1947 and 1973. It is based upon discussions and correspondence with the farm family concerned.

Detailed financial management and accounting data are not available. The report outlines the actual case history on one Australian family farm under the headings used in the earlier part of this work. This is preceded by a brief discussion of several contextual matters: the nature of the farm and the district, the circumstances of the family, and so on.

Preamble

The property was located in the New South Wales grain/sheep zone, five miles east of a small service center, Warialda, of approximately 1,500 population, in what is often called the northwest slopes and plains of New South Wales. Sheep grazing for wool was the main activity of the district, although wheat growing, which was well established in the immediate post-World War II period, gained in importance during the period under review. Beef cattle raising was also quite widespread, especially on the western margin.

The topography is undulating, and basalt country -
black, stony basalt soil - prevails. This is interspersed with
tracts of fertile black and reddish loam, especially on lowlands,
and also sandy loam. Much of the land is heavily timbered
with various gums (eucalyptus) and pines. Certain areas are
covered wtih a dense wattle (acacia) scrub. Rainfall is in the
vicinity of 25 inches a year with a pronounced winter
maximum. It is good "dry sheep" country although sheep were
bred on many properties.

The route to the farm followed a quite narrow gravel-
surfaced road for five miles, which, in heavy rain, could be
impassable at at least one stream ford; final access to the farm
was via a private road through, first a neighboring property,
then a block of timbered Crown Land, and finally the farm
itself. The private road was maintained by the shire only as
far as the farm boundary. For much of its length this private
road traversed loose sandy loam, which could be a difficult
surface on which to drive even for experienced drivers when
dry. The house was more or less in the center of the
property. Adequate and reliable road access was a matter of
continuing concern. Mail was delivered three times a week to
a box placed at the private road junction. There was a
private telephone line to the Warialda manual telephone exchange.

The town of Warialda is located 80 miles west of the main
New England highway from Sydney to Brisbane (see figure
7.1A). A branch railway line from Moree passes through
Warialda and terminates at Inverell, 40 miles west of Glen
Innes and the main Sydney-Brisbane railway line. Moree is
connected to this main line at Werris Creek, almost 200 miles
southeast. Thus, Warialda's rail connections with the major
coastal cities are circuitous. Indeed, the town of Warialda is
three miles from the station which serves it, Warialda Railway,
a tiny village consisting of a general store, a hotel, a small
school, the wheat silo (elevator) and a few houses. The road
from Warialda to Inverell was not sealed until the 1950s, and
the road to Moree was sealed much later. This improvement in
access to larger towns, especially Inverell, more or less
stabilized Warialda's population and business turnover. It
remains a small rural service center: two hotels, one general
store, two banks, four service stations, and several agricultural machinery dealers.(81)

Both husband and wife came from farming families: One
family had grown wheat in South Australia and bought a sheep
property in northern New South Wales at about the time of
World War I: the other had won land in a ballot in 1906. They
were from the same general district to the northwest of
Warialda. After their marriage in 1930, they moved to the
north coast of New South Wales and leased a dairy farm.
Following the termination of their lease in 1932 at the height of

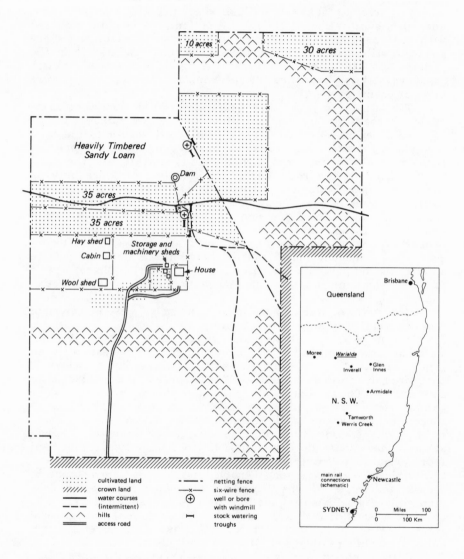

Fig. 7.1.   Plan and location of case-study family farm near
Warialda, New South Wales.

the Depression, they spent 15 years in casual rural labor. The farm under review was purchased in 1947.

Land

The land between Inverell and Moree was originally held by two or three large pastoral leases, and resumption into smaller family farms occurred largely in the late nineteenth and early twentieth centuries. The property was 1,628 acres in total area. It comprised seven portions held under three titles: freehold, 343 acres; conditional lease in perpetuity, 542 acres; and lease in perpetuity, 743 acres. The conditional perpetual lease was legally constituted "gazetted" prior to 1900, which meant among other things that conversion to conditional purchase would enable the owner to dispose of any salable timber for gain. The conversion procedure from conditional lease in perpetuity to conditional purchase required the owner to pay off the unimproved capital value set originally at 13 shillings (approximately A$1.30) per acre over a period of 23 years at a fixed rate nominated by the Crown Lands Department. At the end of the repayment period, a freehold title was granted. As the cash value of the timber, mostly cypress pine, was considerably greater than the conversion levy, the owners exercised this option and, by 1973, there was A$0.68 per acre outstanding. As the large 740-acre section of lease in perpetuity was gazetted after 1910, ownership rights of any salable timber were vested in the New South Wales Forestry Commission. Timber could only be used for improvements and structures on the actual section; hence, no attempt was made to convert this tract.

At the time of the case-study family's initial occupation, the farm consisted essentially of three large paddocks (fields) with some smaller fenced paddocks near the house (see fig. 7.1). The boundary fences were of wire netting sunk at least six inches into the ground. When kept in good repair, these fences were rabbit-proof, an important consideration at that time. Rabbits were a serious problem and remained so until the myxemytosis virus killed large numbers. Another serious problem was mintweed, a vigorous plant that not only spread rapidly in loose friable soils with little grass cover but was also fatal to livestock. Prickly pear and Darling pea, although not as serious as mintweed, were nevertheless a problem. Perhaps the most serious vegetation problem was presented by the presence of various varieties of scrub; hop bush and wattle were particularly well established. Mintweed, Darling pea, and Bathurst burr could be pulled by hand or hoed; scrub could only be cleared with an axe and mattock and this was a much more time-consuming proposition. Partly because of the prevalence of these various pests, the carrying capacity of the farm was limited to about 900 sheep at first.

Improvements to the land resources consisted almost entirely of clearing new land for cultivation and subdivision fencing. The front paddock remained virtually unchanged, but several additional cultivation tracts were prepared in the central part of the farm and in patches in the back paddock. The one major problem of these additional land resources was machinery access; roads within the farm were rudimentary, and it simply was not possible to get wheat-farming equipment out to the two back paddock sites; machinery had to follow a circuitous route through the adjoining properties.

The farm was not well supplied with water, there being only one well and one bore from which water was pumped by wind-driven pumps to livestock drinking troughs. There was a dam, but this, like the stream which ran through the center of the farms, did not provide a continuous supply of water. There was no permanent supply of water at the house; water from roof runoff was stored in galvanized iron tanks.

Labor

From 1947 until 1952, the farm labor force consisted of husband, wife and teenage son. A contract "rabbiter" was on the property for some time in the late 1940s but apart from this, almost all tasks were handled by the family unit. These tasks included care of sheep - attention to fly strike, crutching, shearing, lambing supervision, dosing, and marking; wheat and fodder crop cultivation - land preparation, planting, harvesting; and general maintenance - checking fences, rabbit and other pest control, and land clearing.

A second farm was purchased when the son married in the early 1950s. Construction of a small cottage in 1957 made the accommodation of hired help easier and, for the next ten years, there was usually a hired man present. During the early 1960s a retired farm neighbor occupied the cottage and assisted with some of the farm work. It was during this time that the labor problem became acute: The husband and wife had difficulty handling all the day-to-day operational work and they simply could not keep up with the continuing maintenance and land development chores such as scrub clearance. However, with rising costs and at best a stable income, regular help was simply out of the question. In terms of labor needs, the farm was just too large for one man to manage, but not large enough to support two families on a continuing basis (or one managerial family and a regular hired man on award wages). This situation was exacerbated by the enterprise choices dictated by the available land resources and by the economic climate: Much of the land was suitable only for sheep grazing, but additional enterprises such as wheat were necessary for survival. This mix of enterprise types made enormous demands on the limited available labor resources. Contract services did not provide a realistic alternative, largely because the tasks for which assistance was in greatest need were the day-to-day operational and maintenance jobs of a wheat sheep farm. The one need for which contract services might have been useful - land clearing - was not well served by existing technology; further, given the nature of the topography, use of machinery for this purpose would have been difficult if not impossible.

Capital

The purchase price of the farm was just under three pounds per acre, and involved a sum of ₤4,800. This sum included land and structures only, including the shearing plant; hence, separate provision had to be made for the purchase of livestock, in addition to the 400 sheep given to the partnership by the wife's father, and farming plant as well as "carry-on" expenses in the first few years. Equity in the farm of approximately ₤2,500 was provided by the proceeds of the sale of the couple's town house in 1947 plus a gift from the wife's father; overdraft finance from a local trading bank was guaranteed by the wife's father, a condition that continued until 1950. Capital improvements on the farm when purchased were: a four-room house; a wool shed with three shearing stands, engine, wool press, and associated yards; one well and one bore, each with a windmill, two storage tanks, and livestock watering troughs; netted boundary fencing; and six-wire subdivision fencing. (The back paddock was completely netting fenced.)

Capital as a production factor on the farm is best discussed under four headings: plant, structures, livestock, and land use. Initially, it was intended to farm with a horse team, but early in 1948 a kerosene-fueled lug-wheeled tractor was purchased which, along with a small eight-disc plough, combine seed drill, and five-foot harvester, comprised the farming plant for some years. Almost all of these items were purchased secondhand. The farming plant was never very extensive or sophisticated; the amount of cultivatable land available was not large enough to warrant the substantial investment that new farming machinery involved. Of course, as often as not, the wheat or oats crop served as green feed for lambing ewes and without a regular and anticipated income from grain, it was difficult to make anything but incremental adjustments to the farming plant; for example, the lug-wheeled tractor was eventually replaced with a rubber-tired tractor, and the harvester by an eight-foot header.

The shearing plant remained fundamentally unchanged during the 26 years of occupation. A concrete sheep-dip was built in the early 1950s to facilitate tick control; yards at the woodshed were extended, and new yards were built at several locations on the farm. As these projects used on-farm timber, they did not represent large additions to the capital stock of the farm. A small sawmill was installed in the late 1950s which facilitated the provision of a ready supply of rough lumber.

A considerable number of improvements and additions were made. The house underwent extensive – and necessary – remodeling which included such items as the installation of a home electric power plant, hot water system, and septic tank. However, a solution to the domestic water supply was never found. A large machinery shed was built about 1949, along with stables, storage sheds, and a new set of livestock yards. Two hay storage sheds were built, along with the small cottage to which reference has already been made. The developments associated with plant and machinery served largely to bring the farm up to a minimal level of operating efficiency, as it was woefully lacking in basic structures when first purchased.

Despite the changing fortunes of the various rural products over the quarter-century period, the farm remained predominantly a sheep farm. Initially, about 250 old ewes were bred, and they provided the nucleus of the stock. This pattern persisted, with the old ewes being sold after one and occasionally two lambings. It was more of a dry sheep than a breeding farm, hence the degree to which the flock size could be built up by breeding was limited. The number of sheep varied around 900 to 1,100, declining gradually as the cost structure of the sheep enterprise compared with wheat – and later cattle – became less favorable. The number of sheep also fluctuated seasonally, declining in dry times and droughts. During some dry periods, the family resorted to stock-route grazing.

Land development investments were limited to extension of the cultivated area. This usually involved stump removal and scrub clearing, but sometimes necessitated rock clearing as well. Some of these small areas were planted to lucerne (alfalfa), as a prime objective in such developments was to add to the supply of green feed for lambing ewes. Apart from the continuing efforts to keep the various plant pests under control, there was little land development activity, the main source of food for grazing livestock being the natural grasses.

Management

The farm was operated as a husband/wife partnership. The day-to-day operational decisions were made by the husband, but such matters as whether to buy or sell livestock or to alter the mix of enterprises – more wheat, fewer sheep, or to purchase a piece of machinery, or to consider changing the

account to a different bank, were subjects of discussion within
the partnership, however informal.   Both husband and wife
had considerable experience of mixed wheat and sheep farms
and there is no reason to believe that the efficiency of the
management procedures was any less than on many similar
farms in Australia.   There is no doubt that both were preoccupied with the debt level of the farm, but this was after all
entirely understandable: They had experienced the trauma of
financial loss in the Depression, and furthermore, they shared
with many other Australian family farmers a decided reluctance
to simply pay interest on the bank overdraft.

A second farm was purchased in 1954, when the son
married.   It was about 1,800 acres in area; it was quite hilly
and, as half of it was heavily timbered, it was very much a
dry sheep farm.   A family partnership involving father,
mother and a son was formed.   An attempt was made to integrate the operations of the two properites but the distance
separating the two farms (about 120 miles) reduced the effectiveness of this arrangement.   This partnership was dissolved in 1960 and the overdraft debt associated with the
second farm was consolidated with the overdraft on the original
farm.

Before much progress had been made to reduce the overdraft, the drought of 1965-66 occurred.   While its consequences were not exactly disastrous, it exacerbated an already
difficult situation: no crops, the necessity to hand-feed sheep,
and increasing insistence from the bank that the overdraft be
reduced.   Thus, the family farm closed out the 1960s on a
rather grim note.   Both husband and wife were now in their
early 60s and there were signs of some serious health difficulties; the debt situation had, if anything, worsened over
the previous 20 years; they were caught in the cost-price
squeeze, especially as they did not have the capital resources
to switch to beef; and it was becoming more and more difficult
to do the day-to-day work on the farm.   (Tasks for which
there was a continuing need, such as scrub clearing, were
simply neglected.)   They began giving serious consideration to
selling the farm in the early 1970s and after having had the
farm listed with several agents in the district and elsewhere, a
sale was made to a farmer from the Riverina in early 1973.
The proceeds were sufficient to release the overdraft and to
purchase a retirement house in Tamworth, 150 miles distant.
The farm changed hands a second time soon after and as of
early 1977 was not being worked.

This farm, and the experience of its owners is probably
typical of many such properties in the wheat/sheep belt:
Families come from a predominantly rural background, have a
shrewd appreciation of what the rural way of life involves, and
are attracted by the promise of independence.   Many are
undercapitalized, which, when combined with a farm size a

little too large for one person to work, but not large enough
to support two families, has long-term implications for their
ability to service the inevitable bank overdraft that is an
integral part of family farming. On the positive side, the farm
provided an adequate living for those involved. The sale of
the farm was not forced but was greeted with relief. The
negative side is more difficult to appraise because expectations
and aspirations vary. Perhaps the only useful speculation to
be offered is that given present aspiration levels, it seems
unlikely that many people would voluntarily duplicate the
experience outlined above. If this is the case, it is indeed
doubtful whether the family farm as it has been known in
Australia will survive.

NOTES

(1)   J. D. B. Miller, Australia (London: Thames and Hudson,
      1966), p. 10.
(2)   F. H. Gruen, "The Future of Family Farming," Journal
      of the Australian Institute of Agricultural Science   37
      (March 1971): 79.
(3)   Australian Institute of Agricultural Science, "Closer
      Settlement in the 1960's - Report of a Study Group,"
      Journal of the Australian Institute of Agricultural Science
      28 (September 1962): 10.
(4)   Michael Williams, "More and Smaller is Better: Australian
      Rural Settlement 1788-1914," in Australian Space: Aus-
      tralian Time; Geographical Perspectives,   ed.   J.   M.
      Powell and M. Williams (Melbourne: Oxford University
      Press, 1975), p. 65.
(5)   Stephen H. Roberts, History of Australian Land Settle-
      ment (Melbourne: MacMillan, 1968), p. 166.
(6)   Williams, "More and Smaller is Better," pp. 65-68.
(7)   Ibid., pp. 75-76.
(8)   Lynnette J. Peel, "History of the Australian Pastoral
      Industries to 1960," in The Pastoral Industries of Aus-
      tralia: Practice and Technology of Sheep and Cattle
      Production, ed. G. Alexander and O. B. Williams.
      (Sydney: Sydney University Press, 1973), p. 73.
(9)   Williams, "More and Smaller is Better."
(10) J. N. Lewis, "Land, Closer Settlement and Develop-
      ment," in D. Douglas, ed., National Rural Policy (Syd-
      ney: Department of Adult Education, University of Syd-
      ney, 1971), p. 67; and K. O. Campbell, "Land Policy,"
      in Agriculture in the Australian Economy, ed. D. B.
      Williams (Sydney: Sydney University Press, 1967), p.
      174.

(11) W. C. Duggan, "The Home Maintenance Area. Relation-
      ship to Irrigation Farming," Quarterly Review of Agri-
      cultural Economics 1 (October 1948): 15.
(12) Lewis, "Land, Closer Settlement and Development," p.
      67.
(13) A Review of Crown Lands Administration in New South
      Wales (Sydney: New South Wales Department of Lands,
      1970), p. 3.
(14) Campbell, "Land Policy," p. 175.
(15) C. J. King, "An Outline of Closer Settlement in New
      South Wales," Review of Marketing and Agricultural
      Economics 25 (September-December 1957): 188, 192, 195,
      207.
(16) Duggan, "The Home Maintenance Area."
(17) J. R. Anderson and R. A. Powell, "Economics of Size in
      Australian Farming," Australian Journal of Agricultural
      Economics 17 (April 1973): 6.
(18) Ibid.
(19) M. Slattery, "Relative Income of Farmers - Some Inter-
      national Comparisons," Quarterly Review of Agricultural
      Economics 19 (July 1966): 115-27.
(20) E. S. Hoffman and J. R. Hume, "Farm and Non-farm
      Income in Australia," Quarterly Review of Agricultural
      Economics 18 (July 1965): 121-35; and Bureau of Agri-
      cultural Economics, "Trends in Taxable Incomes of
      Primary Producers," Quarterly Review of Agricultural
      Economics 7 (January 1954): 11.
(21) D. H. McKay, "The Small-Farm Problem in Australia,"
      Australian Journal of Agricultural Economics 11 (December
      1967): 117.
(22) Keith O. Campbell, "The Challenge of Production In-
      stability in Australian Agriculture," Australian Journal of
      Agricultural Economics 2 (July 1958): 3-23.
(23) McKay, "The Small-Farm Problem in Australia," 11: 122.
(24) Ibid., p. 124.
(25) F. H. Gruen, "Rural Australia," in A. F. Davies and S.
      Encel, eds., Australian Society: A Sociological Introduc-
      tion, 2nd ed. (Melbourne: Cheshire, 1970), p. 356.
(26) J. M. Powell, "Introduction," in J. M. Powell, ed.,
      Urban and Industrial Australia (Melbourne: Sorrett,
      1974), p. 15.
(27) Agricultural Policy in Australia (Paris: OECD., 1973), p.
      28.
(28) Ibid., p. 40.
(29) Gruen, "Rural Australia," pp. 341-47.
(30) G. D. Chislett, "Primary Producer Organizations," in D.
      B. Williams, ed., Agriculture in the Australian Economy
      (Sydney: Sydney University Press, 1967), p. 127.
(31) Gruen, "Rural Australia," p. 357.

172   THE PROCESS OF RURAL TRANSFORMATION

(32) L. W. McLennan and E. A. Saxon, "Rural Labour Situation: Survey in MacIntyre Shire, New South Wales," Quarterly Review of Agricultural Economics 4 (April 1951): 77.
(33) Gruen, "Rural Australia," p. 356.
(34) Ibid., p. 357.
(35) Ibid., p. 350.
(36) J. N. Lewis, "Agricultural Adjustment in a Changing Institutional Setting," Journal of the Australian Institute of Agricultural Science 27 (December 1961): 217.
(37) Sheila B. Fraser, "Rural Labour in Australia: Progressive Increase in Productivity," Quarterly Review of Agricultural Economics 2 (October 1949): 127; Loreley Jackson, "Productivity of Rural Labour: Australia and United States Compared," Quarterly Review of Agricultural Economics 5 (April 1952): 70; and Agricultural Policy in Australia, p. 30.
(38) William M. Herr, "Technological Change in the Agriculture of the United States and Australia," Journal of Farm Economics 48 (May 1966): 264-71.
(39) The Principles of Rural Policy in Australia: A Discussion Paper (Canberra: Australian Government Publication Service, 1974); p. 90.
(40) B. R. Davidson and M. F. Tierman, "A Note on the Comparative Cost of Living in Sydney and Country Towns in New South Wales," Review of Marketing and Agricultural Economics 43 (1975): 126-39.
(41) The Principles of Rural Policy in Australia, p. 217.
(42) Lewis, "Agricultural Adjustment in a Changing Institutional Setting," 27: 216.
(43) J. N. Lewis, "Credit Facilities for Agriculture," Quarterly Review of Agricultural Economics 8 (October 1955): 158; and The Immediate and Longer Term Need for Debt Reconstruction and Farm Adjustment with Special Reference to the Sheep Industry (Canberra: Bureau of Agricultural Economics, 1971), p. 6.
(44) John W. Longworth, "Inter-Generational Transfer in the Rural Sector: A Review of Some Problems," Australian Journal of Agricultural Economics 16, (1972), 169-82.
(45) The Principles of Rural Policy in Australia, p. 17.
(46) Ibid., p. 292.
(47) Rural Industry in Australia (Canberra: Bureau of Agricultural Economics, 1971), p. 34.
(48) Australian Bureau of Agricultural Economics, "Trends in Taxable Incomes," p. 14.
(49) P. J. Dixon, "Australian Farm Income," Quarterly Review of Agricultural Economics 16 (July 1963): 133.
(50) Hoffman and Hume, "Farm and Non-farm Income in Australia," 18: 124.

THE FAMILY FARM IN AUSTRALIA   173

(51) The Principles of Rural Policy in Australia, p. 292.
(52) E. L. Jenkins, "The Economic Position of the Farming
      Community," in National Rural Policy, ed. Daryll Douglas
      (Sydney: Department of Adult Education; Sydney
      University, 1971), p. 39.
(53) James P. Houck, "Some Aspects of Income Stabilization
      for Primary Producers," Australian Journal of Agricultural
      Economics 17 (December 1973): 200-15.
(54) H. P. Schapper, "Rural Credit and Agricultural Policy,"
      in The Simple Fleece: Studies in the Australian Wool In-
      dustry, ed. Alan Barnard (Melbourne: Melbourne Univer-
      sity Press, 1962), p. 406.
(55) The Principles of Rural Policy in Australia, p. 106.
(56) Lewis, "Credit Facilities for Agriculture," 8: 158.
(57) F. G. Jarrett, "Credit and Agriculture," in Agriculture
      in the Australian Economy, ed. D. B. Williams (Sydney:
      Sydney University Press, 1967), pp. 217-18.
(58) Lewis, "Agricultural Adjustment in a Changing Institu-
      tional Setting," 27: 214.
(59) Jarrett, "Credit and Agriculture," p. 219.
(60) Lewis, "Agricultural Adjustment in a Changing Institu-
      tional Setting," 27: 216.
(61) Jarrett, "Credit and Agriculture," p. 219.
(62) Rural Industry in Australia, p. 36.
(63) Jenkins, "The Economic Position of the Farming Com-
      munity," p. 32.
(64) Gruen, "The Future of Family Farming," 37: 79.
(65) N. H. Sturgess, "Management Economics in the Pastoral
      Industries," in The Pastoral Industries of Australia:
      Practice and Technology of Sheep and Cattle Production,
      ed. G. Alexander and O. B. Williams (Sydney: Sydney
      University Press, 1973), p. 435.
(66) A. G. Lloyd, "The Economic Size of Farms," Journal of
      the Australian Institute of Agricultural Science 27 (Sep-
      tember 1961): 137.
(67) Gruen, "Rural Australia," p. 346.
(68) H. P. Schapper, "Rural Labour," in Agriculture in the
      Australian Economy, ed. D. B. Williams (Sydney: Sydney
      University Press, 1967), p. 192.
(69) Ibid.
(70) Sturgess, "Management Economics in the Pastoral In-
      dustries," p. 436.
(71) McKay, "The Small-Farm Problem in Australia," 11: 124;
      J. M. Wells and W. R. Bates, "Changes in Farm Business
      Organization in Australia," Quarterly Review of Agricul-
      tural Economics 22 (March 1969): 53; and The Principles
      of Rural Policy in Australia, p. 17.
(72) The Principles of Rural Policy in Australia, p. 17.
(73) Longworth, "Inter-Generational Transfer in the Rural
      Sector," p. 169.

(74) Ibid., p. 173; W. R. Bates, R. N. Sexton, and R. Jackson, "The Impact of Death Duties on the Rural Industries in Australia," Quarterly Review of Agricultural Economics 26, no. 1 (Jan. 1973): 31; The Principles of Rural Policy in Australia, p. 193.
(75) Longworth, "Inter-Generational Transfer in the Rural Sector," p. 179.
(76) Wells and Bates, "Changes in Farm Business Organization in Australia," p. 56.
(77) Rural Industry in Australia, p. 38.
(78) Wells and Bates, "Changes in Farm Business Organization in Australia," p. 62.
(79) Ibid.
(80) Longworth, "Inter-Generational Transfer in the Rural Sector," pp. 172-173.
(81) Robert H. T. Smith, "The Functions of Australian Towns," Tijdschrift voor Economische en Sociale Geografie 53, no. 3 (May-June 1965): 85, 91.

8 The Hungarian Tanyas: Persistence of an Anachronistic Settlement and Production Form

Nancy Volgyes

Since the communist takeover in 1949, Hungarian agriculture by and large has been characterized by state collective and cooperative farms. However, a peculiar exception to collectivized agriculture has been the persistence of small isolated private farms or tanyas whose stubborn survival has defied government efforts to abolish them. More recently, through revisions of government and administrative policy, tanyas have come to be regarded as desirable supplemental units of agrarian production in the ongoing transformation of Hungarian agriculture.

The origin of tanyas probably goes back to the tenth and eleventh centuries, but the system as we know it was fully developed only in the early eighteenth century. Since then the various governments have invariably viewed tanyas as undesirable due to 1) the difficulty in governing them, 2) cultural and educational backwardness of their occupants, 3) the relatively greater freedom of the tanya dwellers due to their isolation, and 4) the frequent harboring of outlaws and political criminals, which is made possible by the isolated and dispersed nature of tanyas. The various communist regimes have regarded the tanyas as ideologically unacceptable and until the early 1970s, undertook to eliminate them. However, despite determined efforts by various political regimes to abolish them, tanyas have survived to the present day.

The persistence of tanyas is due to a number of practical considerations and problems which the present regime has gradually recognized within the framework of reexamining its agricultural policies during the late 1960s. As a consequence of this reexamination, the unofficial policy toward their continuation has recently changed. Recognition of their importance in several forms of production has led to changes in government policy in assisting them. In addition, changes and adaptations in the traditional tanya forms have rendered them profitable to maintain as well as economically impossible to eliminate. Thus, the compromising of ideologies, due to practical considerations and economic limitations, has extended the life of tanyas in the official viewpoint. New assistance plans are now being offered to upgrade the still-backward tanya system following the rather unsuccessful earlier attempts to bring them into the "socialist sphere" of life. The various types of tanyas are adapting to new agricultural forms of production and they are likely to continue to function for years to come.

The purpose of this chapter is to: 1) offer a brief historical overview describing the evolution of the Hungarian tanyas; 2) outline government policies regarding them; 3) describe the presently existing forms of the tanyas; 4) analyze contemporary economic and social conditions on Hungarian tanyas; 5) examine the forces that encourage their persistence; 6) describe the attempts of the government to assist them as an alternative form within the Hungarian agricultural system; and 7) describe the dynamic relationship between ideology and practicality in reference to the persistence of the Hungarian tanya structure and the new policies of the current communist leadership.

HISTORICAL BACKGROUND

The Turkish occupation resulted in basic changes in the rural landscape of the Hungarian Great Plains. During the sixteenth and seventeenth centuries most of the small villages disappeared as their populations fled to rural market towns under loose Turkish occupation. The lands were either taken over by the Habsburgs or continued as property of the market towns, creating the large administrative areas associated with the Great Plains. The lands beyond town boundaries at this time were used for grazing.

The actual tanya system, as construed today, was a product of the introduction of capitalist agriculture at the beginning of the eighteenth century. The outlying lands were gradually acquired by peasants living in the rural market towns. The tanya structures emerged in the Great Plains as a reaction of the population to the great distances from the villages to their private landholdings, located sometimes up to 30 kilometers from their village houses. During the peak work periods, in order to eliminate valuable time spent commuting to the fields, temporary dwellings were constructed to house the owner and any workers, as well as draft animals needed for field work. For many years these structures remained temporary, and therefore quite crude, the owners maintaining

their permanent dwellings in the large villages. From the
eighteenth century onward, the tanya system spread throughout the entire country, but was most prominent on the Great
Plains, the Trans-Tisza region, the southern portion of the
Danube-Tisza Interfluve, the Nyirseg and in some of the
mountainous regions of northern and western Hungary (see
fig. 8.1).

Considerable changes were ushered in with the nineteenth
century. Several factors contributed to the altered tanya
structure. The demographic explosion promoted a need for
additional housing as well as food for the population. Agriculture, of necessity, became more intensive. In addition to
the usual task of tending animals on the outlying fields, wheat
cultivation, horticulture, and viticulture became important.
Consequently, there simply was so much work on the isolated
farms that the workers could not spare the time to commute
daily to and from the villages. The burgeoning population
strained the existing housing in the villages. These two
considerations combined to spark an exodus to the tanyas on a
more permanent basis after the 1850s. By the latter part of
the nineteenth century, most tanyas were occupied permanently
by one of three types of dwellers. The first type remained in
their houses in the village while the servants moved out to the
tanyas to tend the animals year-round and to engage in
gardening in the summer. The second type became the petite
bourgeoisie of agricultural towns or actually moved to other
areas, changing their life-styles. Their tanyas were then
leased to who ever wished to work the land. These rented
farms became the most rundown and backward settlements, the
owners declining to maintain the buildings and refusing to
improve infrastructural services such as roads. The third
type comprised those owners who were forced by economic
conditions to move out of their village houses to the tanyas,
either because they were unable to support their village house
or unable to support workers to tend the tanyas. Even after
such a permanent move, for many years these dwellers attempted to maintain social connections with their villages, an
effort doomed by distance and isolated conditions.

By the twentieth century the increasing agricultural
population and subsequent oversupply of agricultural labor
pushed more people out to the tanyas. Although the tanyas
were inferior to the villages - in terms of actual structure as
well as services, including medical service, schools, availability
of supplies and communications - they did offer a greater
freedom than enjoyed by villagers. Although most tanyas did
fall under the administration of nearby rural market towns,
many newer ones were beyond village jurisdiction. In both
cases, isolation made effective administration nearly impossible.

The problems created by rural overpopulation increased
from 1900-1945. While rural population increased during the

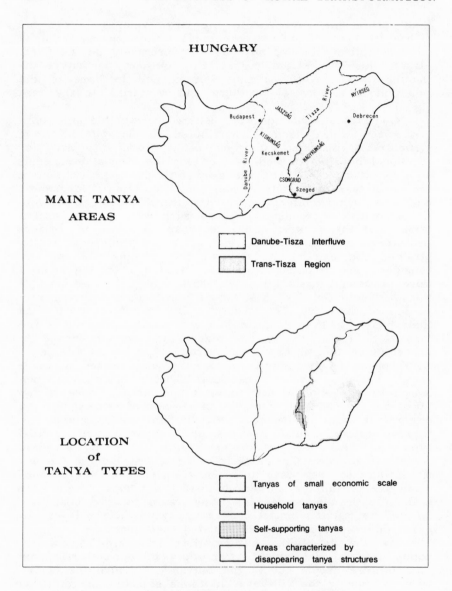

Fig. 8.1.

Source: derived   from   Pal   Romany,   A tanya rendszer ma,
Budapest: Kossuth, 1973.

period 1880-1945, from 3.6 million to 4.5 million, landholdings
per agrarian worker commensurately decreased from 6 to 4.7
acres per agrarian worker and an increasing percentage of the
rural populace was forced to move out of villages to tanyas.(1)
      Erdei identifies the three main types of "generic" tanyas
in existence by 1945. Most common were the "regular" or
"modal" tanyas in which production was carried on entirely on
the tanya proper. The harvest from the tanya land (frequently five to ten acres) was taken to the nearest large
market town for sale. These tanyas maintained close connections with the towns, and generally their development
paralleled the general agricultural development of the country
as a whole, incorporating improvements as their economic
prosperity permitted. Regular or modal tanyas were typical of
the southeastern corner of the Great Plains.
      The second type of tanya was characterized by those
very backward structures that developed from the leased
tanyas and by the poorer tanyas occupied by the owners.
They were primarily subsistence tanyas, specializing mainly in
animal production. These were found around Debrecen and
Nagykunsag.
      The third type, the "overdeveloped" tanya, specialized in
fruits and vegetables and their inhabitants, usually the
owners, labored tirelessly and prospered. The owners were
generally highly skilled in horticulture and readily adopted
modern agrarian techniques. These tanyas provided the most
advanced and profitable production of fruits and vegetables in
Hungary at that time.(2) These tanyas were specifically
characteristic of the regions around and to the north of
Kecskemet and sometimes around Szeged where highly
developed fishing tanyas dominated the riverbanks.

GOVERNMENT EFFORTS TO RESTRICT OR ABOLISH TANYAS

From the very inception of the tanyas, every regime in power
has opposed them and attempted various means to restrict and
eliminate them. These efforts have included national pro-
hibitions against construction of new tanyas and orders for the
destruction of existing ones. While the implementation of
various decrees failed, they had the unfortunate result of
aggravating the already backward economic and social conditions of the people involved. By the latter part of the
nineteenth century, the uncivilized, isolated nature of tanya
life and the lack of social services or schools became additional
reasons to attempt to eliminate the tanyas, although attempts
to resettle these people were consistently unsuccessful.
      The increasing economic and social backwardness of the
tanyas in the beginning of the twentieth century was evidenced
by poor communication and transportation systems, high il-

literacy rate, lack of schools, and high incidence of tuber-
culosis among tanya dwellers.(3) Especially when compared
with western Hungary's increasing prosperity, the backwardness and poverty of the Great Plains remained a thorn in the
side of rural development.

The 1945 Land Reform Act of the postwar regime created
75,000 new tanyas, many of which were occupied by former
tanya servants or by renters, indicating that the number of
tanya families did not increase to the same extent.(4)   Significantly, in 1949 there were more people employed in agriculture than in prewar Hungary, and fully 31 percent of these
lived on tanyas.(5)   But, by 1949, the new communist regime
committed itself to their abolition for four reasons.   First,
they were ideologically untenable as remnants of private
ownership violating socialist principles in an era characterized
by wholesale collectivization.   Second, they hampered efforts
to politically and economically control all areas of agrarian
production.   Third, it was financially impossible to serve the
tanyas in any large-scale network of social welfare programs to
which the state was committed in its efforts to improve rural
life.   Finally, as other regimes had discovered, it was impossible to control them through established administrative
channels.   Consequently, orders were issued against any
further construction or physical improvement of the tanya
structures.

The 1949 government decree on "tanya councils" created
special "microcenters" by the division of administrative areas
into smaller regions containing proposed small, new "model"
villages to which the tanya dwellers were supposed to move.(6)
The proposed creation of such model villages failed because
those who did leave the tanyas made a change in their life-
styles and jobs and simply moved to the larger industrial
centers.   At the same time, those who remained were no more
likely to be lured into a half-constructed new village a few
miles from their home than to the older existing villages.   To
be sure, during the early years of the regime, under forced
collectivization, many of the tanya lands were incorporated into
collective farms and lost the advantage of unity of place of
residence and place of work.   Table 8.1 indicates the decreasing population of the tanya resulting from communist
efforts to disperse the rural dwellers.   The partial success of
the initial thrust resulted in the fact that around 500,000
tanya dwellers were pushed into other occupations in the rapid
industrialization, some moving into industrial centers but many
remaining on the tanyas and commuting to work, returning
home daily, weekly or monthly.   But even in these cases,
gardening and the keeping of a few animals were very profitable.

Table 8.1.   Number of Tanya Residents in Hungary

Year	Tanya Dwellers
1949	1.7 - 1.8 million
1960	1.2 million
1970	800,000 - 900,000

Source: Pal Romany, A tanya rendszer ma [The tanya system today] (Budapest: Kossuth, 1973), pp. 38-39.

The official attitude toward the tanyas was a part of the general antipeasant, anti-agriculture Marxist policy characteristic of the 1950s; the tanyas were expected to die out of their own accord due to the confiscation of landholdings and the surfeit of agrarian labor.   The authorities, of course, overlooked the problem that even those tanya dwellers who wished to leave had nowhere to move.   Obtaining housing throughout the country was nearly impossible, and housing in the villages was no exception.   As a result of the official policy, the neglect of the tanya situation, within the context of the entire neglected agrarian development policy, continued until the late 1960s.   By the 1960s, the theoretical reasons for the existence of tanyas supposedly were eliminated; in theory, at least, the tanyas should have disappeared but they continued in fact to exist.

TANYAS TODAY: ADAPTATIONS FOR SURVIVAL
IN A CHANGING RURAL ENVIRONMENT

Despite past policies of all types of governments, including those of the postwar communist regime, to eliminate and discourage tanya settlements, over 800,000 people or eight percent of the population live on four main types of tanyas existing today (see fig. 8.1).   Many of these tanyas are considerably changed in form from prewar settlements.   Today the four main types are tanyas of small economic scale, household tanyas, self-supporting tanyas, and garden tanyas.(7) Efforts to abolish the tanyas have not been altogether unsuccessful.   With the modernization of agriculture, certain land previously characterized by tanyas has been very successfully collectivized.   For example, the area of the central Trans-Tisza region, characterized by fertile chernozem soil, is well

adapted for highly mechanized, collectivized wheat production.
This is an area where the tanyas are disappearing very
rapidly.

Tanyas of small economic scale are the private "farm
tanyas" in the old traditional sense. These provide much of
the fruit and vegetable produce sold privately in markets in
Hungary's towns and cities. Neither modern agricultural
techniques nor modern farm machinery are utilized to any
significant extent on them, although many persons use their
own cars to transport produce to market. As the owners
become more prosperous, they may build houses in nearby
towns, much like the original tanya dwellers, and a few individuals even hire day laborers to work just as some tanya
owners did in former times. These traditional tanyas of small
economic scale are found primarily near Szeged, in the
southern Danube-Tisza Interfluve, in areas of sandy soils, in
the Nyirseg, in the Jaszsag, and in hilly regions that may not
lend themselves to large-scale agriculture. Special cooperatives have encouraged labor-intensive fruit, vegetable,
and tobacco production in these areas.

Most widespread are the household tanyas which combine
certain modern aspects of production with traditional tanya
life-styles. Most of those dwelling on household tanyas work
on the collective farms and maintain their tanyas in a
traditional manner. They are often inhabited by younger
people who take advantage of the fact they they are able to
keep more animals there than if they lived in the villages.
This is due mainly to two facts. First of all, the preexisting
structures for keeping animals and poultry can be utilized;
and second, they receive animals from the cooperatives to
fatten, according to the capacity of the tanya - up to 50 or 60
swine yearly, in addition to large numbers of geese and
hens.(8) These people are not willing to move because of the
financial possibilities. A large percentage of these tanyas (40
percent in the Great Plains and 25 percent elsewhere) are
often improved and repaired, despite official prohibition.(9)
Household tanyas can be found in the southeastern Great
Plains where the loessial plains with rich chernozem soils are
well suited to corn production. Animal husbandry, particularly swine production, is encouraged on the tanyas in this
region to supplement the often insufficient swine production of
the collectives.

Self-supporting tanyas already mark a considerable
change from the former traditional tanya structures. People
who live on these tanyas are no longer employed in agriculture, but work in the primary industrial sector. They shop
in the towns for many goods but still rely heavily on their own
produce from the tanya. Often the grandparents continue the
farm work. Benefits are gleaned from being able to supply
their families with their own produce while earning a steady

and often greater income than obtainable from agrarian labor.
These tanyas frequently receive additional income by marketing
vegetables, domestic rabbits, and similar products in nearby
towns. Often these tanyas fall into the category of having
mixed incomes if one member, usually the wife, is employed by
the collective farm. The most prosperous self-supporting
tanyas are found in the regions of Csongrad, Kiskunsag, and
in the south-central Tisza River Valley.

Garden tanyas are a new type that have emerged since
about 1965. They are privately owned, isolated dwellings on
the unincorporated outskirts of towns, either newly built or
old renovated tanyas, constructed or rebuilt without legal
construction permits. In fact, quite often the monetary fines
levied by the state authorities for illegal construction are
calculated in the budget of the new building. Among such
tanyas are the typical garden settlements found outside many
larger towns and cities in the Great Plains. The garden
tanyas provide single-family gardens which are sometimes
tended on weekends or after work as a form of recreation and
for supplemental income, as well as providing the family with
some home-grown vegetable and fruit produce. The owners of
such garden tanyas either live in the village or occupy the
tanya on a permanent basis and are usually employed in
various spheres of the economy. Many of the inhabitants are
industrial workers who have returned to the countryside to
live, commuting daily to work. They have found that the
rural infrastructure is not as overworked as that in the
workers' districts of bulging cities. On these tanyas they are
able to raise a few animals and carry on some gardening, in
many cases returning to their original peasant life-style.(10)

ECONOMIC AND SOCIAL CONDITIONS ON THE TANYAS

The tanyas have for centuries been a thorn in the side of
modernization, giving successive regimes one more reason for
their elimination. A closer examination of presently existing
economic and social conditions must be made before further
elaborating the reasons for the persistence of such structures.
Only through a clear appreciation of these conditions can
government actions be understood.

The 800,000 people living on the tanyas present a mosaic
of demographic, occupational, and educational characteristics
that are divergent from the national pattern. Tanya families
tend to have more children than the national average. Unlike
the "modal" Hungarian family that is content with 1.5 children
per family,(11) fully 41.9 percent of all rural tanya families
have 2 to 3 children and only 23.1 percent of such families are
content with having only one child. Moreover, contrary to

popular misconception, the tanya population is a relatively
young one; fully 37.6 percent of the population is below 20
years of age, in contrast to the 32.2 percent of the population
in the same age group in the national sample. In addition to
having enough young people on the tanyas, people above 61
years of age comprise only 10.2 percent of the total, in
contrast to 15.0 percent nationally.(12)

The occupational breakdown of tanya families indicates
fundamental changes that have taken place in the rural sector
since around 1950. Of those tanya dwellers living on settlements that are by definition "isolated and rural," only 71.3
percent work in agriculture. In one out of every five Tanya
families, one member, usually the husband, works in a nonagrarian occupation. The facts that 7.4 percent of all families
are employed totally in the nonagrarian sector, and that fully
60 percent of all tanya families in the 1970s derive some income
from nonagrarian sources, such as from cottage industry,
service sector, construction or industry, further amplify the
process of rural transformation.(13)

Tanya dwellers' incomes come from the following sources:
36.8 percent from the household plots, 37.3 percent from
collective farms, and 25.9 percent from other sources including
industry. The fact that nearly two-thirds of all income is
derived from noncollective farm sources illustrates the relative
independence of the tanya inhabitants.(14)

While the above indexes show the positive side of the
existing economic development of the tanyas, social conditions
on these homesteads are still far below the national average.
The years of purposeful administrative neglect - both non-
communist and communist - have had their impact. Rural
electrification in the tanya regions is only about 14 percent,
preventing modernization and improvements of life-styles.(15)
The undeveloped transportation network continues the isolation
of the tanyas, much as it has for centuries. Around 80 percent of all tanyas are located at least three kilometers away
from the nearest incorporated settlement.(16) Bicycles, motor-
cycles, and horse-drawn conveyances are the main modes of
transportation. The muddy, unimproved roads near tanyas
remain the most effective deterrent to the use of automobiles
and the full integration of the scattered settlements into the
rural social and economic system.

Perhaps the greatest social problem on the tanyas remains
that of education. The present regime is committed to education and has tried to solve the problem with a limited degree
of success. The isolation, backwardness and poor pay of the
tanya schools do not attract the most talented teachers, and
the schools are rarely able to retain teachers for more than a
couple of years. The teachers are not trained to use the
modern learning equipment sometimes supplied by educational
authorities(17) and the recent introduction of televised lessons

has not been as successful as hoped since the one-room
schools house eight grades, causing obvious problems for such
a mixed audience.(18)   Moreover, very frequently the lack of
electricity renders even the available instruments useless.
The school buildings themselves are often old barns, col-
lapsing, abandoned houses, generally without electricity, often
poorly heated, with dirt floors.   The children are reluctantly
allowed to attend school only when they are not needed to
work at home.   Table 8.2 suggests the severity of educational
failings on the tanyas at the beginning of the 1970s.

Table 8.2.   Educational Level of Tanya Dwellers

Level Achieved	Percent
Illiterate	6.7
Finished grades 1-5	40.0
Finished grades 6-7	36.8
Eighth grade education	13.1
Finished 1-4 years of high school	1.2
High school diploma	1.7
Attended university or technical high school	0.5

Source: Jozsef Fekete and Gyula Pocs, "Tanyavilag es ifjusag"
[The tanya world and youth], Valosag (1970): 103.

        Some degree of success has been achieved by educating
the tanya children in boarding schools located in nearby villages and towns.   Today there are ninety boarding schools,
educating 6,000 children coming from isolated tanyas.(19)   The
most important aspect of these schools has been their success
in "civilizing" the children, teaching them such social amenities
as eating with a knife and fork, using indoor plumbing,
washing themselves and their clothes, using minimal dental
hygiene, and of course giving them proper medical attention
and the benefits of a nutritional diet.   The children educated
in boarding schools, however, do pose a problem for their
parents, who most often do not believe in education anyway.
The children from these boarding schools often return to the
tanya but serve as the key for modernizing the life-style
there.(20)
        The tanya structure, even today, is marked by its social
and educational backwardness, which in part explains why
every political regime has attempted to eliminate it; but the

persistence of the tanyas, in the face of all such attempts, has
been remarkable.

PERSISTENCE OF THE TANYAS: REASONS AND RATIONALE

There are two main reasons why the tanya system has persisted.   First   of   all,   the   government   has   simply   found   it
economically   impossible   to   relocate   nearly   1,000,000   tanya
dwellers into villages and towns.   Second, the tanyas, through
adaptations   described   earlier,   now   engage   in   types   of   production   activities   not   satisfied   by   other   forms   of   agriculture
and that are beneficial to the state.
      Following   the   destruction   of   much   of   Hungary   in   World
War   II,   and   much   of   Budapest   in   1956,   reconstruction   of
housing   throughout   the   1950s   and   1960s   proceeded   at   a   very
slow   pace   as   government   placed   high   priority   on   building   an
industrial   infrastructure.   Not   only   the   cities   but   the   villages
suffered   as   well.   While   prohibiting   any   improvements   or
repairs   on   the   tanyas,   officials   have   placed   tanya   dwellers   in   a
double   squeeze   by   not   constructing   enough   housing   in   the
villages   to   accommodate   those   who   might   wish   to   move   into
towns.   With   the   recognition   of   the   necessity   for   increased
agricultural   production   in   the   late   1960s,   concerted   efforts
were   made   to   construct   multistoried   and   other   types   of   modern
apartments   in   the   villages   and   towns.   While   this   type   of
housing   is   obviously   more   socially   acceptable   to   the   communist
regime,   the   overriding   advantage   is   its   lower   cost.   There   are
long   waiting   lists   to   get   into   such   new   housing.   Even   so,   this
newer   housing   is   no   solution   for   the   tanya   dwellers,   who   are
used   to   their   own   private   houses   and   are   not   likely   to   be
satisfied   in   such   a   confined   space.   The   larger   average   size   of
tanya   families   creates   further   problems   as   apartments   are   built
for   families   of   three   to   four   members.   In   addition,   the   cost   of
village   housing   is   generally   prohibitively   high   for   a   tanya
dweller.   Thus,   it   is   clear   that   one   primary   factor   that   keeps
inhabitants   on   the   tanyas   remains   the   housing   shortage.
      The   increased   prosperity   of   the   tanyas   over   the   past   five
to   ten   years   has   become   the   second   major   factor   in   their
persistence.   The   original   advantage   of   proximity   of   work   and
residence   has   remained   an   attraction   for   the   tanyas   of   small-
scale   economy   and   even   for   those   tanya   dwellers   who   have   to
work   for   the   special   cooperatives   on   adjacent   land.(21)   In
addition,   the   household   tanyas   have   reached   an   unprecedented
level   of   prosperity   in   relation   to   the   limited   amount   of   produce
they   might   be   able   to   raise   and   cultivate   in   the   villages.
While   the   village   and   cooperative   household   plots   are   legally   no
larger   than   those   of   the   tanyas,   the   buildings   already   existing
on   the   tanyas   provide   advantages   for   animal   production,   en-

abling the occupants to raise more animals than agrarian
workers on the cooperatives or in the villages. The tanyas
are also aided by using the cooperative lands after harvesting
for fodder, and up until the most recent agreements reached
with cooperative farms for purchasing feed at reduced costs,
wholesale thievery of feed from the cooperatives helped to
fatten livestock and feed poultry.(22) In the 1970s many
collectives sell young animals to the peasants - both on the
tanyas and in the villages - to fatten, then buy them back at
a fair market price when they have matured, thus allowing the
peasant to pocket a decent profit from the arrangement.
     Dairy cattle are kept mainly for private needs of the
tanya, while swine remain one of the most important market
products. Poultry serves the tanyas as well as providing cash
income. When it is remembered that in Hungary 15 percent of
the land is farmed in small-scale private plots, household
plots, or auxiliary plots producing 36 percent of the agricultural produce, the tanyas' importance to the national
economy cannot be emphasized enough.(23)   Indeed, the
current Minister of Agriculture, Pal Romany - who is
Hungary's best specialist on the problem of the tanyas - claims
that in 1971 alone, the number of swine fattened for market on
the tanyas would have required a state investment in the
large-scale farming sector - e.g., collectives and cooperatives
- of five billion forints.(24)   Thus, in terms of the possible
loss of agricultural production alone, the government can no
longer afford to indiscriminately abolish the tanyas.
     Finally, it would be an oversight not to mention that fully
60 percent of the tanya inhabitants simply do not wish to leave
the tanyas.(25) The advantages of production, the private
single-family dwellings, and the age-old traditions continue to
hold many, especially among the mature inhabitants, to the old
life-style.

GOVERNMENT POLICY CHANGES TOWARD THE TANYAS

For the reasons given above, the government has digressed
markedly from its strict ideology to a reassessment of tanya
policies in the early 1970s. Through 1959-1968 the at-
trition rate of tanyas was 0.7 to 0.8 percent per annum, or
2,100 to 2,400 scattered settlements annually.(26) As mentioned earlier, despite ordinances against renovation during
these years, fully 25 percent of the tanyas between the
Danube and the Tisza rivers, in the Nyirseg, and 40 percent
of those in the Great Plains have been repaired or renovated.
At the same time, 25 percent of all tanyas have deteriorated to
the extent that today they are considered uninhabitable.(27)
Consequently, at the direction of the present Minister of

Agriculture, Pal Romany, a thorough reexamination of the tanya policy took place. In so doing, the government found many inconsistencies in policy and considerable confusion in the laws regarding the tanyas.

A number of problems needed planning attention. For years local councils have neglected paving the roads near tanyas. Consequently, persons far from highways still have to go by foot or by horse cart since mud prohibits use of motorized vehicles much of the time. One absurdity here is that the tax on a horse is higher than the tax on a 1972 private car.(28) While tanya dwellers do pay local "improvement taxes," they have reaped little or no infrastructural benefits. Even though official policies place an emphasis on the development of adequate retail distribution networks, the tanya stores have been a highly visible failure. Some tanya dwellers are not served by any store at all; for others there are continual shortages of essentials such as petroleum lamps and petrol for them, spare parts for horse carts, or small machinery for small-scale agriculture, and the prices of these and other goods are consistently higher in stores supplying tanyas.(29) The requirement for rural electrification - for one kilometer of lines there must be thirty users - has proved impossible to follow throughout most of rural Hungary. In order to implement rural electrification, the regulation is ignored in most areas, with the exception of tanya regions where it is used as a bureaucratic rationale against electrification.(30) Other policy "inconsistencies" include the unavailability of credit for tanya agriculture or building renovation and the "neglect" of social services - or more accurately, inability and unwillingness to finance them.

The result of the agrarian reevaluation has been the quiet adoption of a new overall plan wherein the "main task of regional development policy in Hungary is to reduce the appreciable regional differences in living conditions."(31) Romany followed this policy declaration by stating even more clearly that, "we are not so rich that we can decline the produce from the tanyas, nor so poor that we cannot afford to help support and develop the tanya [as an agrarian unit]."(32) Included in the political decision to improve the tanyas was the proposed upgrading of social and living conditions through increased attempts at electrification, and the better supplying of tanyas with grocery and general stores, running water, and improved roads.(33) The success of these policies remains to be seen. So far, the implementation has been sporadic and uncoordinated, and faced with considerable opposition by local village councils.

It is clear that the tanyas are likely to continue to exist for some time. The matter of ideological acceptance of them is precarious. While the regime may have stopped overt campaigning against them, it has a long way to go before this form of economic activity is regarded as ideologically legitimate. It is currently accepted as a compromise. Faced with the financial impossibility of eliminating the tanyas, the leadership has accepted their existence out of practical necessity. It remains to be seen whether proposed social improvements will actually be implemented. Whatever ideological stance is taken, however, the tanyas are likely to continue to exist much as they have for two hundred years.

NOTES

(1) Pal Romany, A tanya rendszer ma [The tanya system today] (Budapest: Kossuth, 1973), p. 16.

(2) Ferenc Erdei, Magyar Tanyak [Hungarian tanyas] (Budapest: Akademiai Kiado, 1976), p. 212.

(3) See Ferenc Erdei, Futohomok [Drifting sand] (Budapest: Athenaeum, 1943), p. 77; Geza Feja, Viharsarok [Stormy corner] (Budapest: Athenaeum, 1941), p. 114; and Geza Mille, Gyakorlati Gazdalexikon [Practical dictionary for farmers] (Budapest: Sylvester Kiado, 1927), p. 883.

(4) Jozsef Becsei, A tanyai telepules nehany kerdeserol [Some questions concerning tanya settlements] (Budapest: Akademiai Kiado, 1966), p. 389.

(5) Ibid., pp. 388-89.

(6) Romany, A tanya rendszer ma, p. 31.

(7) Pal Romany, "Mai tanyak" [Today's tanyas], Valosag 12 (1972): 62-65.

(8) Romany, A tanya rendszer ma, p. 42.

(9) Ibid., p. 53.

(10) Interview with Gyorgy Enyedi, January 10, 1977, Budapest.

(11) Magyar Statisztikai Zsebkonyv, 1976 [Hungarian statistical pocketbook] (Budapest: Statisztikai Kiado, 1976), p. 38.

(12) Mihaly Kerek, "A tanyai lakossag telepulesi es elet korulmenyeinek vizsgalata" [An examination of settlement and living conditions of tanya inhabitants] mimeographed (Budapest: Varosepito Tudomanyos es Tervezo Intezet, 1970), pp. 108-10.

(13) Ibid., pp. 119, 137, 211.

(14) Ibid., p. 137.

(15) Romany, A tanya rendszer ma, p. 54. See, Jozsef Fekete and Gyula Pocs, "Tanyavilag es ifjusag" [The tanya world and youth], Valosag 7 (1970): 102.

(16) Kerek, "A tanyai lakossag," pp. 51, 167.

(17) Fekete and Pocs, "Tanyavilag es ifjusag," 7: 102.

(18) "Televizio a tanteremben" [Television in the classroom], Nok Lapja, September 11, 1976.

190   THE PROCESS OF RURAL TRANSFORMATION

(19) Laszlo Siklos, "Children from the Tanya," New Hungarian
      Quarterly 11 (1970): 20.
(20) Ibid., pp. 16-25. See also Laszlo Garami, "Tanyai
      kollegiumban" [In a tanya boarding school], Tukor,
      February 26, 1977, p. 7.
(21) Romany, A tanya rendszer ma, p. 70.
(22) Antal Vegh, Okorsirato [Mourning for the ox] (Buda-
      pest: Szepirodalmi Konyvkiado, 1975), pp. 54-58.
(23) Istvan Lazar, "The Collective Farm and the Private
      Plot," New Hungarian Quarterly 17 (1976): 73.
(24) Romany, A tanya rendszer ma, p. 71.
(25) Kerek, "A tanyai lakossag." p. 182.
(26) Ibid., p. 195.
(27) Romany, A tanya rendszer ma, p. 53.
(28) Ibid., p. 69.
(29) Fekete and Pocs, "Tanyavilag es ifjusag," 7: 102.
(30) Romany, A tanya rendszer ma, p. 88.
(31) L. Lacko, "The Hamlet and Farmstead Regions of Hun-
      gary: Planning Problems," in Gyorgy Enyedi, Rural
      Transformation in Hungary (Budapest: Akademiai Kiado,
      1976), p. 68.
(32) Romany, A tanya rendszer ma, p. 91.
(33) Interview with Gyorgy Enyedi, January 10, 1976, Buda-
      pest. See also Magyar Nemzet, October 28, 1977.

IV

Political and Social
Change Among
the Peasantry

9 Electoral Behavior Among Peasants
John Duncan Powell

The systematic comparative study of peasant or, more generally, rural electoral behavior is in its infancy. There are a
number of apparent reasons for this state of affairs. The
comparative empirical study of voting behavior in general is of
relatively recent origin within the political science discipline,
and its practitioners tend toward emphasis on aggregate
cross-national data analyses, obscuring or glossing over significant conceptual variables such as time sequences, rates of
process change, and social structures.(1) Several years ago
Stein Rokkan argued that the incorporation of these variables
into a systematic comparative analysis of urban-rural lags and
cleavages appeared to be one of the most promising research
strategies available to social scientists interested in development, and he and Lipset asserted that the dearth of such
studies was "one of the great lacunae in empirical political
sociology." A lack of enthusiasm for the study of the historic
dimensions of development on the part of many data analysts,
combined with the absence of a widely agreed upon and
utilized typology of comparative agrarian structural variables -
despite the fact that such variables are commonly recognized
as decisive in rural political analyses - have perpetuated this
particular lacuna. This chapter attempts to take a modest step
toward at least reducing its dimensions. A useful starting
point for this attempt will be laying out and discussing some
of the general themes and problems encountered in the study
of electoral behavior in rural areas.

THE URBAN RURAL LAG

The first theme I wish to explore concerns the common notion -
often implicit and untested - that rural areas and peasants lag
behind urban areas and workers in terms of participation in
electoral processes. There are a number of dimensions which
enter into this notion of an urban-rural lag: political party
activities and suffrage were historically born in the city and
extended to the countryside later in time; rates of rural participation in the electoral process, measured by percentage
turnout of eligible voters, were initiated at lower rates than
previously existing urban participation rates, and only slowly
and gradually approached the same levels; and, finally, there
is implicit in much of the literature on electoral behavior the
idea that the quality of electoral participation shifted more
slowly in rural areas than in urban areas, that is, that class-
based voting grew more slowly in rural than in urban areas.
Taken together, these three dimensions comprise the content of
the widely held notion that rural electoral behavior and processes lag behind their urban counterparts.(3)   Each of them
needs to be probed in order to more exactly specify their
meaning and explore their empirical underpinnings.
     The idea that parties and elections were initiated in urban
areas and penetrated into rural areas later is built into much
of our understanding of Western European developments. As
Huntington summarizes this notion: "The expansion of participation in Europe meant the gradual extension of the
suffrage for the assembly from the aristocracy to upper
bourgeoisie, lower bourgeoisie, peasants and urban
workers."(4)   The development of parties similarly can be
traced from caucuses of notables toward the mass party model
which gradually incorporates lower and lower social strata into
the electoral process.(5)   Several qualifications need to be
taken into account, however, before one accepts these sequential events as the basis for an urban-rural lag. First, to
the extent that the aristocracy which initially achieved a
rudimentary electoral participation in these systems was a
land-based aristocracy, rural participation - of its upper
stratum - was either coincidental with or even preceded participation by an urban-based aristocracy or upper bourgeoisie.
Second, in the earliest extensions of suffrage (such as the
Norwegian process studied by Rokkan) to the peasantry, it
was the substantial, property-owning stratum of peasantry
which achieved access prior to the urban working class. The
"dwarfholding" or landless types of peasants lagged behind
both of these groups in gaining suffrage, being indeed one of
the last social groups to achieve it.(6)   Here we have the
basis for a qualified acceptance of the idea that participation
by lower social strata in rural areas lagged behind participa-

tion by lower strata in urban areas. Suffrage limitations
based on literacy requirements, whether intentionally or not,
reinforced the earlier and more extensive participation of the
urban dweller relative to his rural cousins. On the other
hand, if literacy requirements are subsequently removed as a
basis for suffrage, the leap forward in access to the electoral
process is far greater in rural areas than in urban areas.

This brings up a point made persuasively by Nordlinger
in his article on time sequences and rates of change as explanatory concepts in political development. He argues that in
many non-Western European systems, sequences such as those
described above might occur in a different order, and the
rates of change within a given dimension might be different
(e.g., suffrage extensions could be much more wholesale and
rapid, literally occurring overnight), and that these differences are useful in explaining outcome variations in terms of
system stability and the democratic nature of governing
regimes. This suggests that even if one accepts the qualified
notion of an urban-rural lag in the developmental processes of
carefully studied Western European countries, it is an open
empirical question of whether, and to what extent, similar lags
occurred in other areas of the world, especially in excolonial
areas.(7) The notion of an urban-rural time lag between the
initiation of mass urban and rural participation may indeed be
a useful indication of general realities, but it is a notion which
needs to be empirically specified, not assumed.

The second dimension incorporated in the general notion
of an urban-rural lag in electoral politics concerns the rate of
turnout for elections. Rokkan linked this dimension to the
first dimension explored above, and presented data which
showed that Norwegian rural turnout rates - as suffrage was
completely extended to all social groups in the rural areas -
lagged behind urban turnout rates over time, although the gap
was steadily closed between the two.(8) The same general
pattern has been found in the United States, Germany, and
Finland, and is also reported by Weiner and Field for India
since independence.(9) This dimension of an urban-rural lag
is open to serious question. There are significant counter-
examples in which aggregate turnout rates for elections are
consistently higher (for post-World War II elections) in rural
areas than in urban areas: France, Japan, and Turkey are
three cases which have been documented, and there may be
others.(10) Other bits of data indicate that rural and urban
turnout ratios may shift over time. In Chile, for example,
rural turnout rates exceeded urban turnout rates during the
1920s and early 1930s, but this situation has been reversed
since then. Variation between countries, and over time in
individual countries, then, should be anticipated in measuring
turnout rate differences between urban and rural constituencies. Systematic empirical study may eventually pin

down consistent urban-rural differences, and in the aggregate sense, a general urban-rural lag may be demonstrated, but this remains to be done.(11)

Weiner and Field found that in India great variations existed in turnout levels of urban and rural constituencies for the same election, and within individual constituencies over time. For a given election, although the national urban mean turnout was higher than its rural counterpart, a large number of important rural areas had higher turnout rates than a number of important urban areas; and over time, there was a wide range of turnout variance within individual constituencies, both urban and rural. They also found that urban and rural turnout rates tended to covary state by state, so that for a given election, high-turnout urban areas were associated with high-turnout rural areas in the same state, and that the state variable explained a larger proportion of national turnout variance than the urbanity measure. While Weiner and Field concluded that the data available to them did not permit a causal explanation of the covariance of urban and rural turnouts by state, they did find that in three of the four states where rural turnout has exceeded urban turnout since 1967, running counter to the aggregate mean findings, there was a well-developed, active Communist Party.(12) Surely this is a more significant and interesting finding than the fact that national turnout rates for urban areas were on the average higher than for rural areas. And surely, what is interesting to explain is not the question of why this should be so, but why there were wide turnout fluctuations in both urban and rural constituencies.

An additional reason for doubting the importance of mean turnout differentials between urban and rural constituencies was suggested by studies of elections in Japan, where rural turnouts have been consistently higher than urban turnouts in a series of postwar elections. Kyogoku and Ike, in their analysis of six elections for the Japanese House of Representatives, based on electoral district data, compared urban and rural differences along a metropolitan/urban/semirural/rural continuum, finding that turnout varied inversely with degree of urbanization. But more interestingly, they reported different levels of turnout for different types of elections within both urban and rural districts. Turnout levels were highest in rural areas for local elections. Turnout rates in rural areas dropped off for regional assembly elections and even further for national level elections. Turnout rates in urban districts similarly dropped off in a local-regional-national election pattern, but not as sharply as in rural areas. The search for causal explanations of the differences in electoral districts at local, regional, and national levels of electoral competition would seem to be a more interesting pursuit than a search for the cause of higher rural than urban mean turnouts, even though this runs counter to the conventional urban-rural-lag wisdom. Adding spice to the interesting finding that turnouts dropped off sharply from local to regional to national elections in rural areas was the fact that Japanese rural voters showed a distinct pattern of shifting party preferences as they voted in elections at different levels.(13) In general, rural voters preferred conservative candidates in local elections and moved steadily to the Left in supporting candidates for regional and national offices, a finding paralleled in French rural constituencies and interpreted by Linz as "an expression of hostility to the ruling classes and the state."(14)

This brings us to the third dimension bound up in the idea of an urban-rural lag, namely the degree of voluntarism involved in electoral participation in rural areas, the general impression being that voting behavior is more a matter of individual choice in urban areas than in rural areas, and that in some sense this represents a lag in developmental terms. Actually, this question opens up a wide range of themes and problems encountered in the study of electoral behavior in rural areas: patterns of consensus and cleavage, problems of coercion and corruption in electoral processes, economic dependency and "clientelism" as critical variables in rural elections, the idea that peasant politics often approximate a rural "mafia" style of control and organization, and the entire question of class-consciousness among peasants. These topics are of great importance in understanding electoral behavior among peasants. One need not, however, approach these problems with any assumptions of urban "lead" or rural "lag."

COERCION, CHOICE AND CORRUPTION IN RURAL ELECTIONS

There are two contrasting patterns of voting behavior - taking the village as the unit of analysis for the moment - which are frequently encountered in studies of rural electoral behavior: one reflecting villagewide solidarity and homogeneity in turnout and party preferences, and one reflecting great variation and factionalism in terms of participation and party preferences. Turning first to the village or community solidarity pattern, one finds it exhibited under two different sets of conditions: when there is a high degree of inequality in landholding patterns and dominance by one or very few large landlords, and - at the other extreme - when there is a very low degree of landholding inequality, and the corporate village pattern is approximated. In both of these cases, there is an inevitable degree of coercion or compulsion involved, but in neither case can a satisfactory explanation of communal solidarity be made exclusively in terms of coercion.

Studies in Turkey, India, and Pakistan indicate that in isolated villages where powerful landlords reside, remarkably high turnout rates can be achieved, and near-unanimous patterns of electoral preferences exhibited. Despite the widely accepted assumption that large landlords intimidate their peasants into voting the way they are told, it is by no means clear that coercion by landlords is primarily responsible for the degree of cohesion exhibited.(15) In most of these reported cases, the participation by peasants is an integral part of the patron-client exchange process, and the indication is that it is chiefly when the landlord himself is directly interested or involved in the election - standing as a candidate or serving as a party organizer - that the near-perfect mobilization of his economic dependents occurs.(16) A further indication of the bargaining or brokerage nature of the landlord's role is reflected in the fact that many of these local candidacies are run on a nonpartisan, or independent basis, with the local landlord being sent to the municipal council or regional legislative assembly with the room for maneuver required to achieve the most profitable alliances or "log-rolling" arrangements he can with any of the parties in the system.(17) Patron-client politics, with its mutual benefits to each party, and neither sheer coercion on the part of the landlord nor traditional deference on the part of the peasant, are what are normally discovered at the root of the widely noted ability of landlords to influence peasants in a conservative direction in their electoral preferences.(18) Furthermore, there is some evidence that latifundia peasants may at times vote "with" their landlord not because of coercion, patronage or deference, but because they believe it is their own interest to do so. This occurs, ironically when agrarian reform becomes a salient issue in national politics. The landlords may have little difficulty in persuading their resident peasants that rather than gain by agrarian reform, they stand to lose by it. This argument carries weight in communities in which there is great inequality of landholdings combined with considerable demographic pressure, with large numbers of landless and dwarfholding subsubsistence peasants in the immediate vicinity of the latifundia. The latifundia peasantry is easily convinced that agrarian reform would mean the distribution of the large holdings among all the peasants in the area, and not simply among the residents. This has been suggested for parts of Peru, and has become an important issue, for example, in the Chilean agrarian reform process as peasants settled on fundos sought to exclude the afuerinos (seasonal and migrant day laborers) from the right of settlement.(19)

To the extent that prereform political campaigns are waged among the sub-subsistence peasantry in such circumstances, promising them the distribution of the large estates in their vicinity, the issue does not even need to be initiated by the large landlords - the political parties both initiate and emphasize it. The result, as in Peru and Chile, may be to turn the latifundia peasantry against the sub-subsistence peasantry, and consequently to affect patterns of electoral preference. Thus, for example, in the 1953 presidential election in the Philippines, the outspoken proponent of agrarian reform, Ramon Magsaysay, ran far below his national average rate in those districts in central Luzon dominated by the great landed estates.(20) And unless we argue for fraud or coercion on a massive scale - both doubtful, since Magsaysay's support among the military in this area was very strong - we must remain open to the possibility that latifundia peasants voted against the agrarian reform candidate because they felt it was in their interest to do so; and hence conclude this discussion of peasant solidarity patterns in landlord-dominated local communities with the observation that for the most part they stem from a blend of compulsion and calculated self-interest.

The same pattern - high turnouts and almost perfect concensus in electoral preferences - is frequently encountered in villages or communities without large landlords, where the distribution of wealth is fairly equal, and where what we have identified as subsistence peasants dominate the community. Rural studies in Germany, Japan, and central Italy demon-strate this peer-solidarity electoral pattern.(21) While group solidarity in landlord-dominated villages cannot be exclusively traced to coercion, but is usually laced with a dose of self-interest, neither can solidarity in these communities of peasant equals be primarily explained in terms of self- (or even col-lective) interest. In fact, it is often based on clearly coercive practices, ranging from overt violence, as in the German villages studied by Heberle, to more subtle, implicit threats of ostracism by the members of the community, as reported in Japanese villages by Kyogoku and Ike.(22) The point needs to be made here, I think, that the corporate village community in general - with widespread participation in decision making, a high degree of equality in the distribution of wealth, and a highly developed sense of "we/they" communal solidarity - is thoroughly permeated with authoritarian and coercive practices as far as the resident individual is concerned. Unlike the landlord-dominated village, there is little direct coercion by powerful nonpeasants, but there is a great deal of pressure from one's fellow peasants to conform to a wide range of behavioral limitations and prescriptions. It is because of, and not in spite of, this internal authoritarianism that the cor-porate community is able to persist as an autonomous unit and exhibit such solidarity to the world outside.(23)

Having made the general point that coercion should not be thought of as an exclusive property of landlord-dominated politics, and that a blend of coercion and self-interest is often involved in producing rural patterns of high participation rates and communitywide consensus in terms of electoral preferences, one other explanatory factor should be mentioned in regard to patterns of solidarity before turning to a discussion of the patterns of factionalism in village voting. This factor, which Tarrow refers to as an "ecological" set of variables, turns on the size of the social community in rural areas; local politics are personal and individuals in these communities highly visible to one another, and due to the small size of the village, there will tend to be a higher proportion of formal political role holders in its population than in urban areas. He reports, for example, that in a nationwide French survey, 21 percent of the husbands among peasant families were or had been members of a municipal council, compared to the nationwide figure of 1.8 percent.(24) In my study of local peasant union leaders in Venezuela, I found that 15.2 percent of them had been elected to local public offices, and 39.1 percent had held or were holding appointive offices as well.(25) How does this fact relate to high turnouts and patterns of community solidarity in voting? It is often through clientelistic cal-culations that entire villages vote for a candidate known to them, especially if he is a member of their village. Sometimes this is reported in terms of upholding village prestige by voting for a native son, but more often it is tied explicitly to patron-client considerations. Whether as a peer, in corporate villages, or as an economic dependent, in landlord-dominated villages, if a peasant knows a candidate personally who is standing for an elective office, he might be able to put that acquaintance to good use in case of trouble or need. In landlord-dominated village politics, even when the villager may not particularly like or respect his landlord, he may prefer him to some other village's landlord. Sertel brought out some of these elements in the pithy responses of villagers who were asked why they actively campaigned and voted for the landlord who dominated their Turkish village:

> There were those who summarily explained their support by remarking "someone else's dog is going to be no better than your own," or "why feed an-other's dog when you have your own," while some equated their support of the bey to defending the "honor" of the village.(26)

The pattern of village cohesion, as I have suggested, depends on one of two structural conditions: a very high degree of inequality, with a single large landholder dominating politics, or a very low degree of inequality, with a peer-enforced corporate domination of political processes. These structural conditions are less likely to be encountered than a more diverse structural situation in which there is more than one substantial landholding family in a local community, and there are several strata among the rest of the populace. Accordingly, village factionalism, the pattern of electoral behavior encountered under these conditions, is a more common one than village cohesion. Village factions and their function in the electoral process have been given a central place in studies of rural India, Pakistan, Turkey, Egypt, Peru, Taiwan, and the Philippines.(27) Factionalism is based on three key factors: economic competition among local elites, economic dependency of local peasants, and kinship structures. Taken together, they make up the familiar pattern of clientelistic politics.

The economic factors involved in village factionalism go together. Two or more families in a local community will typically have control over a considerable proportion of the primary economic resource, access to land and water. This control over resources generates in turn economic dependency on these families among the local peasantry, who require access to land and water for survival, whether through direct cultivation or employment as agricultural laborers. Economic competition among the landholding elites in rural communities is what provides the motive for political competition, or factionalism. It is repeatedly stressed in studies of village factionalism that there is little or no doctrinal or partisan-preference basis for the fragmentation of the vote in such villages. In fact, candidates often stand as independents, or as representatives of minor, little-known, or ephemeral parties. What counts are not national issues and party policies, but historic patterns of elite family conflicts and loyalties and the nature and size of their peasant followings. The pattern of factionalism does not seem to be confined to the most backward and traditional communities, but may persist for some time under the impact of economic modernization if intra-elite local competition revolves around a limited number of activities. There is evidence, however, that as economic modernization further proceeds, drawing local elites into what may be specialized roles that complement, rather than compete or conflict with one another, then local electoral patterns may shift away from elite mobilization of peasant dependents toward a class-conflict pattern.(28) There is some indication that patterns of local, faction-based support for village elites may coexist with an underlying feeling of class conflict. This is demonstrated by village elections in which local elites are supported for local elections (peasants voting conservative), yet class hostility may be expressed in national electoral preferences (peasants voting radical Left). Village factionalism can not only be undermined by changing economic circumstances, but can be shifted rapidly by changes in electoral regulations and procedures. Thus, in Taiwan, clear-cut patterns of elite-generated factionalism faded quickly when the locus of local political competition was shifted from a village base to a regional unit combining several villages; and in India, the casting of votes by a show of hands (in the presence of all village members, including the large landlords) produced support for landlord-backed candidates, but the use of secret ballots produced support for the Communist Party by the same agricultural laborers who had dared not defy their economic patrons in public.(29)

Kinship patterns among the peasant electorate also seem to play a crucial role in factional politics according to studies conducted in Turkey, Egypt, and West Pakistan.(30) Research in these countries indicates that clans, or lineages, among the peasant populace are sought after as building blocks by factional leaders. Landholding lineages of subsistence or family-farm peasants, only marginally dependent on large landlords, may find their political bargaining power increased as a result of their ability to cohere as a unit for either protective purposes or for patronage purposes. Dependent lineages of resident latifundia peasants, on the other hand, may find their political bargaining power at a minimum, since their collective vulnerability is very great. The sub-subsistence or poor peasants often find themselves in a situation of cross-pressures, wherein some lineage members are economic dependents of the leaders of one faction, and other lineage members the dependents of competing factional leaders for employment, loans, or leases of parcels of land. In this situation, intense pressures mount inside the lineage and within single families and individuals, as the principles of economic dependency and kin dependency collide, often viciously.

There hangs over this entire discussion the distinct hint of violence, bloodshed, and even death. This will become more evident in subsequent discussions of organizational behavior and forms of direct political action among peasants. Although this factor is seldom the subject of systematic investigation, it turns up often enough to be considered an important background variable in exploring peasant electoral behavior. Vigilantism among peasants may be directed toward other peasants in order to enforce corporate or communal norms, or toward local elites or their representatives engaged in serious conflict with a peasant community. The employment of henchmen by local agrarian elites is a well-established and well-known factor throughout much of rural Latin America and is common in some parts of South and Southeast Asia as well. After all, terms like "thugs" and "goons" (from goondas) originated in the Indian subcontinent. And according to Alavi the activities of goondas in West Pakistan remain key explanatory variables in the organization of political life, including elections.(31) There are hints, in fact, almost everywhere when one penetrates beneath the surface of political behavior in rural areas of the developing countries, of a style of politics which can be labeled a "rural mafia" system.

This kind of shadowy variable is not only difficult to study systematically (for perfectly obvious reasons), but it is difficult to conceptualize systematically even if one wanted to attempt a study. Nonetheless, it does seem to have an effect on peasant electoral behavior, whether one conceptualizes the study of it in terms of social coercion or corruption of the electoral process.(32)   For example, in Japan it is reported that local political leaders instruct peasant voters how to cast their ballots.   Subsequently,

> ...it is not difficult for henchmen of local leaders to station themselves near polling booths and watch the facial expressions of the voters as they come and go.   Those who have not obeyed instructions are likely to give themselves away when they are so confronted.   The result is that in rural districts the final tally can often be predicted with some accuracy.(33)

Of course, it may be peculiar to Japanese culture, in which norms of integrity and ethical compulsion are so strong that violation of an agreement with a local leader can produce such an internal struggle as to be detected by observers of facial expressions.   In any case, violation is a less likely outcome than compliance, when voters are faced with the visible presence of local elite representatives outside the polling stations, as in this case, or inside as poll watchers, as was reported in Puerto Rico.   In Puerto Rico, the resident workers of the sugar corporation, when they reached the polling place, found the corporation foreman sitting at the table set aside for electoral officials and party representatives.(34)   It is difficult to say how individuals react to such pressures, especially if the local leaders have spread the word that they have ways of finding out how individuals voted, even if a secret ballot method is used.   And of course, if such subtle tactics do not succeed in corrupting the process of electoral choice among vulnerable peasants, the tried and true method of outright fraud may be available.   Tawfiq al-Hakim, recording the statement of an Egyptian ma'mur (district representative of the Ministry of Interior) brings out this factor in the undisguised cupidity of the official's own anecdote:

> Please believe me.   I am a ma'mur with a sense of honor.   I am not the usual sort of ma'mur.   I never interfere in elections and never say "Vote for this man!"   Nothing of the kind.   My principle is - leave folk along to vote for whomever they want....Well, that's my method with elections. Complete freedom.   I let people vote as they like - right up to the end of the election.   Then I simply

take the ballot box and throw it in the river and
calmly replace it with the box which we prepare
ourselves.(35)

On this uncertain note, I conclude my exploration of some of
the common themes and problems encountered in the study of
rural electoral behavior. On the basis of admittedly scattered
and unsystematically comparative bits and pieces of data, I
have attempted to establish a background level of caution and
skepticism regarding the significance of electoral behavior
among peasants. Emphasis thus far has been placed on
caveats and not on positive findings. Had I proceeded further
along this path, we might be placed in a position of questioning the validity of all electoral data emanating from rural
areas, and especially peasant communities. But building a
case for the rejection of rural electoral data has not been my
objective; building a conceptual sensitivity to the subtleties
and complexities of the electoral process in rural areas, and
particularly among peasant communities, has. In the belief
that this sensitivity has been sufficiently aroused, we are now
in a position to turn to the evidence of electoral behavior
among peasants in a more positive context, seeking to cull
from the available evidence the genesis and explanation of
issue saliency and party preference patterns among various
types of peasants. Thus we can begin to explore voting, the
"democratic translation of the class struggle."(36) How do
different peasant groups, with identifiably different economic
interests, go about the pursuit of those interests through the
electoral process?
    The party preferences of peasants, as expressed in their
patterns of electoral support, have covered the entire
spectrum of choice, from the most conservative to the most
radical, change-oriented parties of the Left. This spectrum
can be analytically collapsed, however, into three distinct
orientations which manage to encompass the primary thrusts of
peasant electoral behavior: an agrarian-populist pattern, a
radical-leftist pattern, and an electoral-machine pattern.
Taking each in turn, we shall explore the structural characteristics of the rural areas in which support for each pattern
occurs, the types of peasants who give such support and/or
provide local leadership for it, and finally, the historic
circumstances under which such patterns tend to emerge and
decline, relating these circumstances to the apparent electoral
objectives of peasant voters.

THE AGRARIAN-POPULIST PATTERN

The agrarian-populist pattern of electoral behavior among peasants is a phenomenon which blossomed in Central and Eastern Europe during the interwar period. This pattern is frequently, but not necessarily, tied to agrarian or peasant parties, examples of which would include the Norwegian Agrarian Party, the Finnish Agrarian Union, the German Landespartei, the Czechoslovak Republican Party of Small Farmers and Peasants, the Bulgarian Agrarian Union, the Polish Piast Peasant Party, the Croatian Peasant Party and the Rumanian National Peasant Party.(37) Though the life cycles of these parties vary, they have strikingly common origins. They all drew their support from certain types of rural communities experiencing the impact of international and domestic market forces at a relatively early stage of economic modernization. The emergency of these electoral movements can, I think, best be understood as a defensive, corporative response to the destabilizing pressures exerted in traditional rural societies by the development of an urban-based, modern economic system.

The agrarian-populist pattern of electoral behavior seems to develop in areas and communities which are relatively isolated in geographic terms and which exhibit strong attachments to traditional values, in particular to Catholicism. The social structure within such communities is marked by a dominant stratum of family farm peasants, primarily oriented toward self-sufficiency, but gradually being drawn into the marketplace by an active stratum of rich peasants. Latifundia often coexist in such communities. But for agrarian-populist politics to emerge, the estate owners are very likely to be resident farmers, sharing most of the community's traditional values, and not a culturally distinct elite, or an absentee or rentier class.(38) Although family farm peasants dominate the local community, there are usually a number of poor peasants present, also engaged in the kind of diverse multiculture which marks the family farm peasant enterprise. Finally, in combination with relative community isolation, and diversity of social structure and agricultural activities, the emergence of the agrarian-populist pattern is often associated with an increasing peasant population pressure on its relatively fixed land resource base. This final factor tends to produce a process of land fragmentation through peasant inheritance practices, resulting in downward mobility into the poor peasant stratum for a growing number of family farm peasants.

In areas where these conditions hold, agrarian-populist peasant movements have emerged which bring together - or attempt to do so under such mottoes as "Unite all those who live from the land," and "The village is a single family" - all rural social strata into a kind of holding action by the rural society against the onslaught of economic modernization emanating from either national urban centers of commerce and industry, or from foreign trading partners whose policy and market impact are transmitted to the countryside through the urban enclaves of modern economic activities.(39) Cross-class alliances are possible under these conditions, with paternalistic latifundia owners incorporated into, or even taking the lead in, the same movements alongside vigorous rich peasant leaders, and family farm peasants who typically provide the organizational muscle for such movements, bringing along with them the poor peasants, for whom they are the models of virtue and success. Agrarian-populist electoral movements initially seek through democratic means a way to limit and control the advance of modern industrialism and to cushion the impact, in traditional rural communities, of the entire commercial-corporate-capitalist-market nexus. Frequently rooted in moral or religious values which legitimate and laud agriculture as a way of life and family-oriented private property as an institution, agrarian-populist electoral movements develop programs emphasizing the formation of co-operatives, low tariff policies, the protection of domestic agriculture from foreign competition, programs of social insurance, a technically rational vocational education for the farm populace, and agrarian reforms. Once established, agrarian-populist electoral movements tend to move in one of two directions: one, an increasingly authoritarian, radical right-wing trend toward drastic, dictatorial solutions to rural economic problems; the other, a drift toward increasing conservatism and compromise within the existing electoral framework. Different types of peasants play importantly different roles in determining which of these directions will be followed.

Heberle's ecological study of electoral trends in interwar Schleswig-Holstein provides a very interesting example of the development toward right-wing authoritarianism from an agrarian-populist base.(40) In interwar Schleswig-Holstein, Heberle's data indicate, there were three distinct zones: one dominated by small-scale capitalist agriculture (a rich peasantry as I have defined it), a second dominated very markedly by family farm peasant agriculture (oriented toward the marketplace), and a third zone with a more mixed tenurial pattern marked by the presence of latifundia. Postwar economic problems deeply concerned the rich peasantry and particularly the family farm peasantry. Shrinking supplies of credit combined with foreign agricultural competition to squeeze inputs and drop the prices of farm produce. Under governments and banks with rather inflexible attitudes toward foreclosures and debt moratoria, family farmers in particular faced economic ruin as postwar recovery problems were aggravated by the impending Depression. Artisan and cottage industries which had provided a cushion for the family farm peasant household were steadily driven out of existence by manufactured - and often foreign - imports. Such conditions were ideal for the emergence of an agrarian-populist movement which was at once anti-imperialist and anti-big business, antisocialist, and infused with a strong ethnic or "folk" identity with the peasant corporate village as the model of the just society. The German Democratic Party and the short-lived Agrarian Party (Landespartei) based their campaigns in 1919 and 1921 on programs responsive to agrarian-populist concerns. Both parties failed to institutionalize and consolidate this appeal into a single, effective, electoral movement, however, and under the relentless continuation of mounting economic pressures, a massive electoral movement toward the Right - toward the Nazis - occurred in the 1930 and 1932 elections. The most dramatic movement to the Right occurred in the zone dominated by the most vulnerable peasant stratum, the family farm peasantry. Movement in this direction also occurred among the rich peasantry, but to a much lesser extent, which is perhaps a reflection of this stratum's ability to more successfully cope with economic pressures for a longer period of time without striking out for drastic solutions. Table 9.1, based on Heberle's data, clearly indicates the anti-conservative, antisocialist, agrarian-populist tendency to move toward the Right under continued economic pressures, particularly among family farm peasants.

Aleksandur Stamboliiski's Bulgarian Agrarian Union (BAU) illustrates the tendency toward authoritarianism in agrarian-populist electoral movements in a somewhat different manner, since his party did become institutionalized and succeeded in gaining power through the electoral process.(41) In a series of elections, the BAU won 85 of the 245 seats in the Subranie in the first postwar contest; 110 in the 1920 election; and 212 in the 1923 election, bringing the "agrarian messiah" into government power in an atmosphere of impending political crisis. Stamboliiski was so anti-urban oriented that he considered all urban groups social parasites in comparison with the peasantry, and even the urban working class merited little more than his pity. His constituency was very largely a class of family farm peasants being squeezed down into a poor peasant status by growing population pressures and the onset of economic modernization radiating outward from the urban centers of the country. (Bulgaria was not a land of large estates.) Stamboliiski's rise to power is one of the clearest cases of an agrarian-populist electoral movement based on a traditional family farm peasantry directly confronting and challenging the modernizing urban elites of a country in the early stages of development. Of course, Stamboliiski's flamboyant personality complicates this case. Nonetheless, once in power, his agrarian-populist government took a marked turn

Table 9.1.   Spearman Rank-Order Correlations Between
Party Vote and Type of Peasant, Schleswig-Holstein,
1919-1932

Party and Year of Election		Type of Peasant Voter[a]	
		Family Farm (Kleinbaurn)	Rich (Grossbaurn)
Conservatives	1919	- 0.70	- 0.34
	1921	- 0.19	- 0.04
	1930	- 0.60	- 0.49
	1932	- 0.80	- 0.40
Socialists	1919	- 0.97	- 0.43
	1921	- 0.98	- 0.45
	1930	- 0.92	- 0.43
	1932	- 0.80	- 0.40
Democrats & Agrarian Party	1919	+ 0.89	+ 0.52
	1921	+ 0.80	+ 0.34
	1930	(b)	(b)
	1932	(b)	(b)
Nazis	1919	(b)	(b)
	1921	(b)	(b)
	1930	+ 0.43	+ 0.26
	1932	+ 0.85	+ 0.49

[a] The actual measure used was local electoral-unit proportion of agriculturalists on farms of a specified size, being 2-20 hectares for what Heberle called kleinbaurn, and 20-100 hectares for what he called grossbaurn. His description of their activities fits them nicely into my categories.

[b] Party did not exist.

Source: Adapted from Rudolf Heberle, From Democracy to Nazism (Baton Rouge: Louisiana State University Press, 1945), table 8, p. 114.

toward authoritarian practices in dealing with its urban ad-
versaries, claiming that the BAU would rule the country for at
least 40 years, threatening a peasant dictatorship, and organizing an "Orange Guard" to beat and terrorize opposition
leaders of both the Left and Right. His regime was over-
thrown within the year by an alliance among the police, the
army, and a regional revolutionary movement in Macedonia
which Stamboliiski had persecuted.

The second and more common historic trend in agrarian-
populist parties, once they have emerged, is toward an increasing moderation and eventual conservatism in electoral and
parliamentary behavior. This pattern is illustrated by the
Finnish Agrarian Union, and is particularly clear in the case
of the Czechoslovak Republican Party of Small Farmers and
Peasants. It is also reflected, but to a lesser extent – due to
the shorter life cycle of the parties – by the Rumanian
National Peasant Party, which held power from 1928 to 1930;
the Polish Piast Peasant Party, in power from 1920 to 1923;
and the Croatian Peasant Party, which formed a government
from 1925 to 1927.(42)

The Finnish and Czech agrarian parties, unlike these
others, managed to survive and participate in governments
over quite lengthy periods of time: from 1919 to 1962 in Finland, and from 1919 to 1938 in Czechoslovakia. In fact, not
only did these two parties participate, they became the
strategic linchpins for most of the various coalition governments formed during these periods, developing remarkable
parliamentary and leadership skills along the way. But in
effect, their function was transformed from representation of
agrarian-populist peasant electorates to one of making
democracy work in their respective parliamentary systems.
The beginnings of this process were engineered by a vigorous
leadership stratum of rich peasants, who achieved dominance
over the family farm and poor peasant strata in the movement
and gradually began to back away from positions initially
fostered by the agrarian-populists, such as radical agrarian
reform. As time passed and the leadership of such parties
became increasingly oriented toward the politics of the center,
they came to win the increasing approval and support of
latifundia owners and other upper-class representatives who
themselves began to participate in the leadership of the
parties. In Finland, for example, where the Agrarian Union
consistently won some 20 to 30 percent of the national votes
from 1919 to 1962, the studies of Allardt and Pesonen revealed
that upper-class leadership within the parliamentary delegation
of the Agrarian Party (42 percent), was second only to the
Conservative Party (93 percent).(43) In Czechoslovakia, a
different type of data reveals the same phenomena, along with
another very important aspect of the process of gradual movement toward conservatism: the eventual withering away of

210   THE PROCESS OF RURAL TRANSFORMATION

peasant support for the party, which increasingly failed to represent their interests. A regional comparison of the elections of 1920, 1925, 1929, and 1935 (see table 9.2) indicates

Table 9.2. Support for Agrarian Party According to Dominant Agrarian Stratum in Four Regions of Czechoslovakia, 1920-1935
(Percent Total Vote)

Year of Election	Dominant Stratum by Region			
	Family Farm and Rich Peasants		Latifundia	Peasants
	Bohemia	Silesia	Slovakia	Ruthenia
1920	19	18	24	–
1925	23	19	26	44
1929	23	19	28	44
1935	13	14	18	20

Source: Adapted from Carol Skalnik, "Patterns of Peasant Political Behavior in the Czechoslovak Republic," Government Department, Harvard University, January 1970, p. 37.

that support for the agrarian-populist party reached its peak not in areas dominated by family farm and rich peasant farming, but in the areas of the great landed estates, where Magyar latifundia owners initially perceived - and had the perception validated in the first five years' experience with the leadership of the Czech Agrarian Party - that not only did they not have to fear a drastic agrarian reform, but that they had their interests rather well represented by the agrarian party, and therefore influenced the voting of their resident peasants in that direction. At the same time, the primary electoral competition in these areas came from the Communist Party, which appealed heavily to the landless and dwarfholding populations surrounding the Magyar estates, particularly in Ruthenia. In these circumstances, the Magyar landlords may have been able to convince their resident peasants that they stood to lose more if the communists came into power than if the more conservative agrarian party continued to rule - and continued to ignore its early position on agrarian reform. In any case, in the contrasting parts of Czechoslovakia where the family farm and rich peasantry dominated, support for the agrarian party leveled off and then declined as it became increasingly a conservative choice in the electoral system.

The analysis of electoral support for agrarian parties cannot, of course, be taken in abstracto, since, as already indicated, the note in Ruthenia was conditioned by the electoral threat posed by a militant Communist Party movement among poor peasants. Both the Communist Party, and during the same period in Czech politics the Social Democrats, provided a more militant, left-wing alternative to peasant voters than the Agrarian Party. I shall turn to a consideration of this alternative, after concluding the analysis of the agrarian-populist pattern of electoral behavior among peasants, by pointing out that such movements declined not only because they departed from their initial objectives or because their pursuit of those objectives was insufficiently drastic, but because in the long run those objectives - the limitation and control of the impact of economic modernization on the local farm community - were unobtainable. The forces behind economic modernization in the twentieth century were simply too powerful to be resisted by traditional rural societies.

THE RADICAL-LEFTIST PATTERN

By radical-leftist, I refer mainly to communist parties under a variety of labels, but also to other militant, aggressive parties of the socialist Left, which in fact are at times more radical in their electoral and parliamentary behavior than the communists. This type of electoral pattern emerges in quite a different type of community than that in which agrarian populism emerges, although in some cases it emerges within the same set of destabilizing conditions at the onset of the processes of economic modernization. Unlike agrarian populism, the radical-leftist pattern may persist - or emerge for the first time - at a much later stage of capitalistic penetration of the agrarian economy. Thus our examples of this pattern are drawn from certain parts of Germany, Poland, and Czechoslovakia during the 1920s and early 1930s, and from post-World War II France, Italy, India, and Chile.(44)

The rural areas in which this pattern occurs are highly polarized communities, with a small elite controlling large portions of strategic resources, combined with a large poor peasantry, including a very substantial number of landless peasants who are faced with periodic unemployment. The stratum of family farm peasants is relatively small, and in no case dominant or even very influential in local community affairs. The latifundia or large-scale capitalist elite stratum is nonpaternalistic, either through default or by choice, and in either case is perceived by the peasantry to be essentially parasitic or exploitative. Because of the great inequalities in the ownership and control of land and water resources, there is a high degree of demographic pressure on the resource base, both in a relative sense (large numbers of peasants on a small peasant-controlled land base) and often in an absolute sense (large numbers of peasants on the total land resource base). Where such conditions exist, and where radical-leftist political party presence is possible, then this radical-leftist pattern of electoral behavior among poor peasantry may emerge.

Indeed, such highly polarized communities would seem to be ideal settings for radical-leftist electoral movements to flourish among peasants. On the one hand, the explicit socioeconomic stratification patterns are clear-cut and comprehensible by the lower orders of the peasantry; it is easy to distinguish the interests of one's own group from those of the elite, and to frame those perceptions in terms of "class" and "conflict." On the other hand, the ideological predispositions of radical-leftist party organizers lead them to seek out such communities as their natural habitat; they will tend to focus on those rural areas in which a large mass of peasants (rural proletariat) confronts a highly privileged elite (primitive or modern capitalists). The perceptions of reality among the peasantry coincide nicely wiith the ideologically derived perceptions of the radical-leftist organizer. Each makes "sense" to the other, and communication is relatively easy, clear, and accurate, in terms of the problematic situation of the peasantry.(45)   But it is a long step from a common recognition of problem conditions to a common commitment to political goals. What is fascinating about the pattern of radical-leftist electoral behavior among peasants is the degree to which it seems to be divorced from the programmatic objectives of the ideologues who organize and direct it. In some cases, there is an observable difference between the ideological content of the programs espoused by radical-leftist party organizers and their own political behavior in the local community and in the legislative arena.

The following section explains: 1) the extent to which peasant electoral support for the various communist parties of Eastern Europe during the interwar period was based on ethnic, rather than class cleavages; 2) the extent to which voting for radical-leftist parties in post-World War II Italy and France can be traced to local historic circumstances and traditions rather than to class struggle; 3) the extent to which radical-leftist political parties in southern Italy and in Chile, for example, really differ, in terms of the actual behavior of their local organizers and parliamentary representatives, from their counterparts in more moderate reform parties; and 4) whether radical-leftist voting among tenant farmers in India and central Italy has as much to do with pragmatic, concrete material interests as it does with the overthrow of capitalism.

No attempt will be made to prove or disprove common assumptions or theories about class-consciousness among peasants, because that is a matter of degree to be established through empirical research. The objective will be simply to explore the mixture of motives and objectives which are characteristic of radical-leftist electoral behavior among peasants.

What is striking about the appearance of this pattern in interwar Eastern Europe, for example, is how frequently ethnic or nationalities cleavages crop up as a significant explanatory variable. In Czechoslovakia, comparing the 1925, 1929, and 1935 elections, the region in which the Communist Party (KSC) drew its greatest support - Subcarpathian Ruthenia - is one in which a Slovakian peasantry was dominated by an exclusively Magyar landed elite. In Bohemia and Moravia-Silesia, poor peasants tended to follow the lead of the family farm peasantry in support of the Agrarian Party, or the Social Democrats. In these two areas, the landed elites were largely, but not exclusively, German, yet issues like the language of instruction in schools or on legal documents did not arise as they did in the Magyar-dominated areas.(46) The appeal of the Communist Party was identical in both areas, and if peasants acted on the basis of the Comintern-derived agrarian program of the communists - that is, in a class conflict-oriented manner - they might have been expected to respond uniformly. But the fact is that poor peasant responsiveness in Ruthenia was based primarily on the party's position on the nationalities question, not the agrarian question. Czech leaders in fact struggled bitterly over the agrarian theses in the Comintern, because landless peasants wanted land, and not "factories in the field," which was the line eventually triumphant in the agrarian theses. But dissenting Ruthenian communist leaders felt they had to respond to the demands among their landless and dwarfholding constituencies for land, and the resulting potent combination - a program to divide the Magyar estates among the total Slovakian peasant populace - was so successful that, as we have seen, it frightened the latifundia resident peasantry into support for the conservative Agrarian Party. It also resulted in heated friction with the Comintern.(47)

Ethnic cleavages in Poland also tended to override class cleavages in influencing the electoral behavior of peasants during this period. Thus, in eastern Poland, the communists - or regional-ethnic parties aligned with the Comintern - derived their main support from the peasantry on the basis of their championship of the minority nationalities - Belorussians, Ukranians, and others - within the Polish state; while in western Poland, where the peasantry was Polish, the Communist Party found little support in the countryside. This showed up most clearly in the 1928 elections, when the communist vote in the western part was concentrated in the cities, while in the eastern part it came overwhelmingly from the countryside. Ethnic or nationalities cleavages appeared to be stronger than class cleavages as a basis for electoral mobilization. This particular finding, however, is complicated by the presence of two other factors which may also have had considerable influence in establishing the electoral preference patterns among the Polish peasantry, and both of them are compatible with a class-conflict interpretation of the vote of 1928. In the western areas of rural Poland, electoral support went to the Piast Peasant Party, the agrarian-populist party led by Wladislaw Witos. Community organization differed in east and west, where the kind of communities described in the last section - dominated by family farm peasants with a resident stratum of traditional landlords - existed. In the east, the great estates predominated, often owned by absentee or rentier landlords. Therefore, there may have been in fact a greater basis for class struggle and conflict in the east than in the west. This factor in turn was reinforced by a second factor, that of differing historic experiences between east and west Poland, the former occupied by Czarist Russia and the latter by the Prussians and Austrians. The kind of difference these contrasting administrations made to peasants and peasant leadership was emphasized by Thugutt, a principal leader of Wyzwolenie, an eastern Polish militant counterpart to the moderate, western-based Piast:

> Nowhere as much as in politics is the question so vital as to whether someone began his political activities under the Russians or under the Austrians, that is to say, whether in the tradition of the insurrectionary struggle and underground conspiratorial work or in an atmosphere of petty skirmishes for the attainment of very secondary ends.(48)

In seeking to establish conclusively the weight attached to the various factors which led various Eastern European peasantries to support communist parties during the interwar period, Jackson, in his careful study, comes out clearly for the salience of the ethnic-nationalities factor. He delineates the cross-cutting pressures which resulted from the parties; positions on the agrarian question (eliminating the private great estates) and the nationalities question (advocating self-determination), and concluded that the result meant communist success where the peasants were an ethnic or cultural minority group, but failure where they were part of the culturally dominant national majority.(49)

Taking a somewhat different tack, Burks sought to explain the high proportions (69 percent to 72 percent) of the total Communist Party vote which were produced in the rural areas of Bulgaria, Czechoslovakia, and Poland in the 1923, 1925, and 1928 elections, respectively. Noting that the common assumption was that this rural vote came from the landless and dwarfholding strata of the peasantry, Burks argued that in fact the presence of these poor peasants correlated with a socialist, not a communist, vote, and that the communist vote in fact came from single cash-crop family farm peasants and agricultural specialists such as tobacco workers.(50)   This finding parallels exactly the contention of Lipset that single cash-crop farmers (peasant or nonpeasant) and members of what he called "an occupational community" - fishermen, miners, sheepshearers, lumbermen (and I would add the tobacco sorters described by Burks) - consistently exhibited a tendency to vote more leftist than most other social groups, a fact which Lipset assigned to their insecurity of income.(51)   In a similar vein, Burks concluded that

> ...a proper explanation of Communism in eastern Europe would begin, not with the industrial proletariat and the class struggle but with the reaction of the economically poorer and less sophisticated cultures to the West, as that contract affects persons and groups subjected through social disorganization to great personal insecurity.(52)

In short, ethnic-nationalities cleavages and personal economic insecurities experienced by special socioeconomic groups may have been more important determinants in producing a radical-leftist pattern of electoral behavior among certain peasants than class cleavages.   But perhaps these factors are peculiar to the conditions existing in Eastern Europe during the early advance of capitalist economic penetration.   What of the appearance of radical-leftist electoral patterns in more recent times in countries under conditions of a more advanced and thorough penetration of capitalism?

Dogan's study of electoral support for the Communist and Socialist parties in postwar France and Italy focused on patterns of rural stratification associated with these votes. Distinguishing, by means of a variety of data, among small farmers, great and middle-class landowners, tenant farmers, and hired hands, Dogan pointed out that in Italy, small farmers tended to support the Christian Democratic government, along with middle and great landowners, while the tenants and hired hands supported the communists and socialists.   In France, however, tenants did not tend to support these parties, which drew their primary support from agricultural laborers on the highly capitalized, large-scale farms of northeastern France, and also from among scattered groups of small farmers throughout rural France.   In seeking explanations for these patterns of voting, Dogan offered a

wide range of explanatory variables: ties with prior organizational mobilizations which had been dominated by the
Communist or Socialist parties, distinctive community histories
of clericalism and anticlericalism, and such widely varied
electoral appeals employed by the two parties that Dogan
concluded that

> ...the vote for the same party does not have
> the same meaning everywhere. It is differently
> colored from one region to another, according to the
> dominant social category or the balance of power of
> the opposing political forces. Moreover, the party
> leaders cultivate this polymorphism by adapting their
> programs to regional contexts.(53)

The impact of localistic traditions on electoral patterns of
behavior is peculiarly marked in rural France. Berger, echo-
ing Dogan's contention, points out:

> Voting for the Communist Party has a range of
> different meanings for French electors. For some
> groups a Communist vote expresses a preference for
> collectivist economic and social alternatives; else-
> where a Communist vote is intended purely as a
> protest against "the system." For still another
> substantial part of the French Communist electorate,
> to vote Communist is to identify with a Left tradition
> whose core values are drawn from the Jacobin
> revolutionary heritage. In many parts of the coun-
> tryside, as Edgar Morin points out for the Plodemet
> Communists, the Communist Party is regarded as the
> authentic heir of the Left that defended republican-
> ism and the public school in the Third Republic, and
> voting for it is a way of expressing a commitment to
> the same institutions and values.(54)

Does this mean that we cannot interpret the meaning of the
radical-leftist electoral pattern among various types of
peasants? To the contrary, the meaning of such votes may be
simple and clear. But the meaning may also be highly par-
ticularized in time and space, and frustratingly resistant to
generalizations of the class-conflict variety. The truth of this
statement is borne out strikingly in cases where the Communist
Party and other radical-leftist parties accommodate themselves
to the varieties of particular situations in the countryside,
tailoring their appeals and activities accordingly, and behave
very much like any other political party interested in winning
rural elections rather than like revolutionary vanguards. Such
seems to have been the case in southern Italy and in Chile.

Tarrow's study of peasant communism in southern Italy makes it abundantly clear that the organizational and electoral successes scored by the Italian Communist Party (PCI) beginning in the early 1950s was based on a pragmatic brand of patronage, or the typical clientelist politics of the south, even though it occurred in highly polarized local communities which might be thought to lend themselves to an organized class struggle. Responding to the desperate plight of the southern peasantry in the postwar period, the PCI took the lead in sponsoring and organizing land invasions in the south, incorporating peasant groups into unions and directing their electoral support toward the PCI. The objective of participating peasants was ownership of land, however, and not the overthrow of capitalism. The PCI's initial success was not followed up by an effective program of raising the class-consciousness of the southern peasantry, as pointed out in the bitter criticisms leveled at the southern communist leaders by their northern counterparts. Southern Italian communist leaders never managed to transcend the clientelist political culture in which they found themselves, nor to alter the patron-seeking behavior patterns of their peasant membership. Thus, when the Christian Democratic-dominated governments passed a de jure agrarian reform and established programs for the economic development of the south, the same peasant leaders and members who had supported the PCI flocked into the Christian Democratic-affiliated peasant unions and diverted electoral support away from the PCI in order to ratify their ownership of land through the agrarian reform, and to gain access to the jobs, favors, and material benefits flowing from the national Christian Democratic government into the region. As Tarrow summarized this ironic situation, explaining the shift of peasants from a communist affiliation toward a Christian Democratic one:

> ..the Catholic Confederation of Direct Cultivators is really a corporate arm of the government which dispenses patronage to peasants through a complicated system of interlocking directorates with the provincial agricultural syndicates....The chain of causation is revealing. In leading the struggle for land, the Communists forced the Agrarian Reform; but in the achievements of the Reform, many peasants became dependents of the Christian Democrats and of the state.(55)

While the southern Italian case does not warrant the proposition that there is no class-consciousness among peasants, for this would have to be established empirically, and remains an open question, neither does it warrant the proposition that membership in a communist peasant union and voting for the

PCI in the 1950s was an indicator of class consciousness and struggle. The behavioral evidence shows that the southern Italian peasants acted in a typically clientelist fashion, and the southern branches of the PCI acted in a typically patronage-oriented fashion. The PCI's troubles began when their competitors - practically indistinguishable from the PCI in their actual behavior - gained superior access to the resources of the state.(56)

The Chilean case also illustrates some ambiguities concerning the ideological significance of peasant voting for radical-leftist political parties. The case for an increasing Marxist class-consciousness among Chile's poor peasants - particularly the landless wage laborers - has been made by Petras and Zeitlin in their study of agrarian radicalism in Chile. By means of an ecological analysis, and using municipal voting data, they demonstrated that electoral support for the Popular Action Front (FRAP) - which coalesced Socialist and Communist parties behind the candidacy of Socialist Senator Salvador Allende in the 1958, 1964 and 1970 elections - was rather strongly and positively related to the proportion of the agricultural labor force in the municipality classified as agricultural laborers, and weakly related to the proportion of the agricultural labor force classified as agricultural proprietors (family farm and rich peasants). In summarizing these findings they state that

> ... while FRAP has increasingly gained support among the peasantry as a whole, its program has had its greatest and increasing electoral success precisely in the agrarian stratum conforming most closely to the classical Marxist model - the property-less proletariat of the countryside.(57)

Petras and Zeitlin do not automatically impute a causal linkage between this pattern of electoral support and a heightened peasant class-consciousness. But they do point out that the ideological predispositions of the radical-leftist parties induce them to seek out the landless laboring class as an organizational target, and that a growth in class-consciousness is a process in which the individual's life experience interacts with exposure to the kind of consciousness-raising socialization which goes along with membership in a socialist or communist agrarian union movement. Logically, this portends an increasing tendency among the poor peasantry - and with some organizational effort among the family farm peasantry as well - to analyze and behave in conformance with a class-conflict orientation toward politics.

The Chilean case presents us with no intervening variables such as an ethnic-nationalities cleavage, which casts doubt on the Marxist interpretation of the Eastern European

peasant communist vote, nor the complicating Italian factor of
party competitors in command of sufficient governmental resources and patronage to lure peasant supporters away from
communist and radical-left peasant unions and voting preferences.   The agrarian reform under the Chilean Christian
Democrats never reached a sufficiently high volume of benefit
flows prior to the election of Allende in 1970 to permit this.
Thus a peasant electorate which prior to 1958 was apparently a
tool of the conservative stratum of latifundia elites, voting in
a direction consistent with that elite's interests, has shifted
steadily away from the old pattern and toward one of radical-
leftist support.   Is this then finally a clear case of true
peasant radicalization?   In the absence of systematic empirical
data on peasant attitudes, we are forced to rely on the observable behavior of the radical-leftist parties in Chile to help
answer this question.
     There is much evidence (prior to 1970) that in both local
organizational activities and in legislative activities, the
Chilean radical-leftist parties have not differed markedly from
their non-Marxist clientelistic counterparts in the system.
Chilean leftists have consistently criticized the radical-left
parties for becoming part of the "establishment" since the
Popular Action Front victory in 1939.   In their willingness to
participate responsibly in coalition governments and legislative
accomplishments, in their patterns of particularistic clienteles
built around the figures of elected officials, in their eschewing
of radical and direct political confrontation in the streets, in
their capacity to coopt militant, ideologically extreme young
leaders into conformity with the clientelist pathway to ad-
vancement, the Socialist and Communist parties in Chile were
not that different from the radicals and more recently the
Christian Democrats.   Kaufman, in pointing out these historic
patterns within the radical-leftist parties, notes that the
ideological climate within the Chilean political system began to
grow distinctly more extreme beginning in the late 1950s, and
that the socialists, in particular, were on the growing edge of
that increasing radicalization.
     Nevertheless, as attested by their observable behavior
under the Frei regime, neither party departed far from its old
ways.   The FRAP congressional coalition was conciliatory and
supportive of Frei's agrarian reform legislation, going so far
at one point as to express the sentiment that there should be
"concessions to the owners of latifundia of [an area] sufficient
to work and live with their families.   The poor and medium
peasants and even the rich farmers who work their land
rationally have nothing to fear.   On the contrary, they will
count on the aid of the state to achieve an increase in the
productivity of their land."(58)   And on the local level,
clientelistic patterns of behavior persisted:

Other, less formal means of bringing peasants into the political process reflected the same tendencies. In local areas, the Marxist politicians elected to municipal councils frequently built amorphous lower-class clienteles by taking up the cause of individual peasants before the local police, landowners, or government agencies. On the national level, several Socialist Deputies were also noted for their capacity to establish close, personal ties with a heterogeneous peasant following.... Most of the Marxist elite performed similar brokerage functions; large numbers of peasants could usually be seen in the waiting room of most Socialist and Communist congressmen, awaiting their help in obtaining the payment of social security benefits, protesting a dismissal, or securing a property title, through a phone call to officials in the CORE [Agrarian Reform Agency] or the Ministry of Labor.(59)

In drawing the parallels between the Chilean radical-left and the Communist Party of southern Italy, and seeking to balance a judgment on the class struggle versus clientelist interpretation, Kaufman concludes:

In distinguishing between FRAP's apparently broad class-based electoral support and these more "vertical," particularistic forms of representation, one cannot ignore the possibility that the latter will disappear as the workers and peasants become more class conscious and more disaffected. At the same time, however, the obvious similarities between these forms of representation and the FRAP's own earlier behavior in the cities suggests that they may be an enduring aspect of the Chilean political system.(60)

Although we have at hand no systematic studies of peasant political behavior under the Allende regime, what data we do have do not indicate a drastic movement of the Chilean radical-leftist parties away from clientelistic practices toward a different pattern, in spite of the increase in militant activities at the national and local levels. Local agrarian union activities of the radical-leftist affiliates did not seem to differ markedly from those associated with the Christian Democrats or independently organized unions. Even prior to the Allende regime, the growth and increasing activity of the peasant union movement had been considerable; from a total of 24 agrarian unions in 1964, the movement had grown to a total of 488 unions with 127,688 members by the time Allende took office. Gazmuri, comparing the 1960-66 period to the 1967-68 period (immediately following the liberalization of the agricultural labor code in April 1967), points out that local activities had increased dramatically: farm invasions increased from four during the 1960-66 period to 18 in 1967-68, strikes from 100 in the earlier period to 586 in 1967-68, and petitions for benefits or to express grievances increased from 140 in 1960-66 to 1,513 in 1967-68.(61)

Two facts concern us here. One, there is no evidence that the radical-leftist unions engaged more in farm takeovers than in strikes or the submission of petitions. All local unions seem to have acted in a similar manner. Two, the greatest increase in activities, it will be noted, is in the submission of petitions, a strong indicator of clientelistic politics in action, as the Venezuelan case convincingly demonstrated.(62) What data we have for such activities under the Allende regime are incomplete, but there has been a great increase in the number of farm invasions, reportedly 339 in Allende's first year in office. Farm invasions, however, are not unambiguous indicators of class struggle under the hegemony of radical-leftist parties. Not all of them were led by such leaders. Rather, just as land invasions were sponsored by all parties in rural Venezuela during the turbulent 1959-60 period, Chilean farm invasions seem to have been organized by a wide spectrum of party leaders. Furthermore, it seems that in Chile many medium-sized farms have been invaded rather than the great fundos which one would expect to be the object of class struggle-inspired takeovers. In addition, again reminiscent of what occurred in Venezuela under Romulo Betancourt - who as a result of his action is excoriated by Chilean and other radicals - Allende had to call for a cessation of farm invasions because of the political reaction they were stirring up among the middle class, the conservatives, and the military.(63)

In short, in the absence of direct evidence of increasing class-consciousness-based behavior on the part of peasants, one cannot easily make a case for such behavior from the observable activities of certain radical-leftist parties which lead those peasants, since - at least in southern Italy, and so far as we know until the early 1970s in Chile - they were not distinguishable in any significant behavioral sense from more moderate, democratic-reform parties operating in the identical context.

Having explored the relationships between radical-leftist electoral behavior and ethnic-nationalities cleavages, localistic traditions, and the behavior of radical-leftist parties and party leaders in local and national politics, we now turn to the question of the relationship between tenancy and radical-leftist electoral behavior in central Italy and parts of India where the two are closely related. The conditions under which tenancy is associated with radical-leftist electoral preferences can be stated with some precision, since they are virtually identical, according to findings of studies of mezzadria (share tenancy) in Toscana, parts of Umbria and the Emilia-Romagna red belt of Italy, and in communist-voting parts of the Indian states of Kerala, West Bengal, and Andhra.(64) The two necessary conditions for the emergence of radical-leftist voting in these areas are a relatively high population density combined with a high proportion of farm units operated under share-tendency arrangements. More precisely, it is not tenancy (or even the sharecropping form of tenancy) per se which is associated with landlord-tenant tensions or violent conflict, as Russett's study indicated. Rather it is family-size farm tenancy under share-cropping arrangements which is the critical type of relation-ship: smaller sized and larger sized units farmed under share-cropping arrangements do not characteristically produce the landlord-tenant conflicts associated with radical-leftist electoral behavior among peasants, nor does family-sized tenancy under a fixed payment (in cash or kind) or lease basis.

Studies of the mezzadro system establish clearly that it is family-sized units - what have been referred to in this study as family farm peasant holdings - which are the norm in the parts of Italy producing strong radical-leftist voting pat-terns.(65) Zagoria's study indicates that in India, on the other hand, the share-tenants who support the Communist Party are what I have called poor peasants; that is, they also need to work as wage laborers in addition to farming their shared plot in order to gain a survival income for their families. In discussing them, Zagoria favors the phrase, "propertied proletariat" coined by Tawney for the type of peasant he studied in China - the kind of combination dwarf-holder, tenant, and wage laborer that clearly fits into the poor peasant category.(66) Zagoria's data are ecological and not the result of field research on the individual tenant's opera-tions, and therefore we cannot say how close these peasants are to being family farm peasants. However, I would hypoth-esize that the tenants he refers to are poor peasant tenants who manage to combine, through ownership of their own shared along with sharecropping of a landlord's parcel, almost the amount of land needed to put them firmly in the family farm category; but falling just short of that amount, they are compelled to supplement the family income through wage labor. This "threshold" or near-family farm status is one associated with exceedingly high internal tensions in the peasant family as the head of the household strives to maximize his control over both land resources and his available family labor units to move up across the boundary into the family farm status. Accordingly, one would expect that any landlord-tenant relationships incorporated into such a situation would be potentially explosive, as indeed it seems to be in the Indian case.

One more necessary condition is needed in addition to the ones already specified as conditions for radical-leftist electoral behavior among peasants: a certain type of landlord. If the owner of the land which is sharecropped is a local resident farmer, firmly embedded in the community and actively engaged in and knowledgeable about the farm enterprise, the landlord-tenant relationship may well be a mutually supportive and harmonious one, legitimated through custom and usage and respected and cared for by both parties. Under these conditions we might expect an agrarian-populist kind of politics, or clientelistic patterns of democratic-reform politics, but not radical-leftist politics among the peasant sharecroppers. On the other hand, if the landowner is a nonfarmer and a nonresident of the local community - typically this in effect means a petit bourgeois town dweller or professional holding land for profit or speculative investment - then all of the necessary conditions will have been met for the emergence of a radical-leftist electoral response among the peasantry. The entry into such a community of a competent radical-leftist party organizer will then be sufficient to produce the expected result.

Silverman's careful analysis of the mezzadria relationship in an Umbrian community stressed the critical nature of the landlord's performance in producing satisfaction or dissatisfaction on the part of the tenant. According to the traditional, legitimate role model, the landlord had important social obligations to perform for the rural community:(67)

1. Economic: The landlord group provided funds for various public services, e.g., administrative offices and officials, roads, public gardens, schools, medical services and various charities.
2. Political: They were the major political functionaries, both as bureaucrats for the state and as advocates and mediators for the community to the powers outside.
3. Community-level organization: They provided the economic support and the leadership for local associations and community secular activities.
4. Ceremonial: They provided the economic and leadership foundation of the local church and the funds and leadership for the ceremonial cycle.
5. Identity: The landlord group was strategic to and symbolic of the identity of their community.

In short, the traditional landlord was a true signor, capable of and interested in playing an active role as a patron for his peasant clients - providing protection, loans in time of crisis, and brokerage services - as well as playing a constructive part in the farm enterprise in which he and his tenants collaborated.

The "new" landlords who replaced the "traditionals" did so under conditions of the competitive commercialization of agriculture, requiring higher capital investments and more advanced technologies than the traditional landlords were capable of supplying. Significantly, however, the new landlords - mostly small businessmen and artisans who bought land as an investment commodity - also failed to supply adequate capital and technical knowledge, and as a result the agriculture in this region of Italy stagnated. Unlike the traditional landlords, who brought to the tenancy relationship the performance of social functions, which the peasant portion of the community was incapable of performing, yet valued, the new landlords tended to reduce the <u>mazzadria</u> relationship to a formal, contractual tie of an exclusively economic nature. Over time, due to organized pressures from the peasantry and the intervention of the state, the material terms of this contractual relationship actually shifted in favor of the tenant, reducing the proportion of the crop allowable for rent, requiring a minimal level of the landlord's profit to be plowed back into the farm enterprise, formalizing the requirements for notification of termination of the contract or eviction, and so forth. And yet, in spite of this, tenants became increasingly dissatisfied with the relationship, coming eventually to characterize it as "exploitation." This led in turn to the organizational and electoral responsivemess to radical-leftist political organizers. When one considers not just the narrow, economic-contractual relationship which ties landlord and tenant together, but the total social fabric of the local community and its need for security, ritual, and identity, the new landlords were in fact exploiting their tenants in comparison with the traditional landlords. As Silverman concluded:

> In each aspect of the landlord-peasant relationship, the contributions from and returns to each party have changed, to the overall detriment of the peasant. In effect, there has been an objective increase in the exploitation of the peasant. Thus, the popular ideology is essentially correct, however inexplicit. The landlords no longer provide many of their previous contributions, both those that were strictly economic and those that were subsidiary but nevertheless essential social functions. At the same time, while the landlords do not extract more surplus, the peasants' net return, in relation to needs created by the intrusion of the market, is diminished.(68)

As to the question of whether voting for radical-leftist political parties under these conditions reflects a situation of conscious class conflict on the part of the peasant tenants, once again we have no direct empirical evidence one way or the other. But in their apparent pursuit of personal, family, and community security through organizational and electoral activity, the radical-leftist voting peasants of Italy and India differ very little from peasants in other parts of the world pursuing identical objectives under democratic-reform leadership.

THE ELECTORAL MACHINE PATTERN

By far the most common pattern of peasant electoral behavior encountered in the post-World War II era is the electoral machine pattern. Indeed, certain aspects of agrarian-populist and radical-leftist electoral behavior were seen to be colored by machinelike characteristics. In what I am labeling the electoral machine pattern, however, the party organizations connected with such behavior are more moderate, middle-of-the-road, pragmatic in program and leadership, and less explicit in ideology than either agrarian-populist or radical-leftist parties. They are frequently referred to in the literature as democratic-reform parties. Nevertheless, as will be shown, there are variations within the electoral machine pattern that begin to resemble the agrarian-populist pattern on the conservative end of the political spectrum and the radical-leftist pattern on the liberal end.
     Many of the community characteristics which produced the radical-leftist patterns are also conducive to the electoral machine pattern. As a matter of fact, in many countries - Italy, France, Chile, and India - the same patterns appear at the same time, and even competitively coexist within the same local communities or agricultural regions. While the agrarian-populist pattern is associated with either the earliest stages of capitalist-commercial advances into the countryside, or with given geographic locales where such advances are feeble, the radical-leftist and the electoral machine patterns tend to be associated with a more advanced, complete, and mature stage of penetration of the modern market. As one result of such a stage, family farm peasants and latifundia steadily disappear, leaving behind an overwhelming proportion of poor peasants that gradually become the dominant social stratum in the local community.(69)
     But "capitalist penetration," or commercialization of agricultural life is nowhere and never entirely homogeneous and uniform across national territories. Several slightly different variations may exist in postpenetration communities dominated demographically by a sub-subsistence peasantry. If the com-

mercialization of agriculture is successful and vigorous, a
dynamic stratum of rich peasants may crystallize, and together
with large-scale capitalist agricultural operations and other
commercial and governmental enterprises, provide the employment opportunities needed by the poor peasant labor pool.
On the other hand, the area may become or remain economically stagnant for a variety of reasons, creating either a
mixture of poor peasants and a decaying rural aristocracy, or
an almost uniform population of poor peasants. In given
countries, such as India, Turkey, Italy, all of these variations
may exist simultaneously, with their exact location and distribution depending on a complex set of ecological and market
variables.

In order to have electoral machine patterns of political
behavior among significant numbers of peasants, certain very
broad, general conditions have to be manifest on the national
level. Economically, as we have already suggested, there must
have been significant movement toward modern economic
development within which private initiative is predominant.
Politically, of course, competitive elections must hold a central
place in the political processes of the country in question. In
addition, there must exist a certain degree of power decentralization, with regional, city, town, and local community
authorities exercising control over significant resources in
addition to those controlled by the central authorities and their
bureaucratic representatives throughout the nation. Socially,
the penetration of modern economic forces into traditional
agriculture, combined with the decentralization of resource
control - that is, the relative ineffectiveness of the central
authorities in dealing with the social impact of economic
modernization - tends to produce among the poor peasantry a
marked degree of social disorganization, personal insecurity,
and a perceived lack of dynamic upward-mobility prospects.(70) In confronting these problematic conditions, the
poor peasantry finds that governmental, rationally administered
(in the Weberian sense), public law-backed mechanisms or
programs are inadequate to deal with these problems on their
behalf. Furthermore, traditional elites and self-help kinship
mechanisms which ameliorated habitual problems are no longer
able to cope with the scope and intensity of the different set
of problems associated with the movement toward economic
modernization.(71) Under the combination of all these conditions - economic, political, and social - the electoral machine
pattern may emerge, as it has on a large scale in countries
such as Italy, Venezuela, India, Turkey, Colombia, the
Philippines, and others.

Within peasant-based electoral machines, three distinct
types of ties are encountered which may bond the participants
together: primordial ties, secular ties, and ideological ties.
Primordial ties refer to bonds based on kinship, religion, or

traditional status hierarchies. Secular ties refer to jobs, money, favors, public-works goods and services, and access to resources such as land, water, credit, marketing assistance, information, and technologies. Ideological ties refer to common adherence to ideas, programs, and analyses, along with loyalties to the political parties which are their symbolic carriers and promulgators. As data gathered by Nicholas demonstrates, the Indian Congress Party built its following out of all three types of loyalties (as well as others) but secular ties between leaders and followers at the local level tended to be dominant. He found, for example, in a survey of village voters in Govindapur, West Bengal, that Congress Party faction leaders claimed loyalty and votes from peasant followers by virtue of the following bonds: kinship with 13 percent of their followers; caste ties with 7 percent; economic dependency ties with 44 percent; traditional deference (for neighborhood headmen) in 17 percent; and finally, the fact that they shared mutual enemies bonded 19 percent of the Congress Party peasant followers to their local leaders.(72) Clearly such machines as the Congress Party incorporate within them complex patterns of binding loyalties between local peasant voters and local leaders, between local leaders , and between local leaders and national-level leadership. A brief description of some almost "pure" cases in which one or another type of bond exists will help to illuminate some of the political implications which flow from their possible variations.

The pure primordial electoral machine is one which is formed by traditional local leaders on the basis of inherited status and respect in the local community, religious leadership, leadership of community kinship structures such as lineages, clans, or tribes, or some combination of these. Ozbudun and Sertal, among others, have demonstrated that this type of electoral machine flourished in eastern Turkey during the 1960s, the high-tide period of competitive elections dominated by the Justice Party and the Republican People's Party.(73) In this area, both inherited local elites (agas) and religious leaders organized electoral competition for both parties. Each type of leader, moreover, utilized lineage cohesion among peasant tenants and smallholders to mobilize entire blocs of voters under the leadership of the lineage elders. At times, however, lineages, especially among tenant peasants, were split because of dependency ties to competing agas or large landlords, a situation described in detail by Alavi for Punjabi villagers, also.(74)

There are clear-cut African examples of such primitive electoral machines dominated by local traditional elites. Whitaker's study of northern Nigeria carefully documents one such case, and Lemarchand mentions the Union Progressiste Senegalaise as another, as well as religious-based (maraboutic) types elsewhere in Africa.(75) I mentioned earlier the existence of such electoral machines in parts of princely India, where the descendants of hereditary elites can still capitalize on their standing and influence among local peasants to mobilize and control large and effective blocs of peasant voters. Scott describes a number of such machines in Southeast Asia, such as those in the Outer Islands of Indonesia during the 1950s. Similarly, in Burma during the 1960s, U Nu's faction of the Anti-Fascist People's Freedom League built its strength in upper Burma on the basis of recruiting traditional leadership which brought along with it its traditional peasant following. The National Party in the Philippines followed a similar strategy in Mindanao.(76)

In most of these cases, the communities involved were either relatively isolated from, or only in the earliest stages of, exposure to the forces of economic modernization that underlie the electoral machine pattern. This helps explain the continued existence and influence of the traditional authorities which lead primitive machines at the local level. In a significant sense, such local leaders are still performing one of their traditional functions - mediating between the local populations and outside actors and institutions - when they take over the role of local electoral mobilizers. They have traditionally been looked up to and expected to protect and benefit the local peasantry, and their linkages with national political parties significantly extend their range of instrumental resources. Little wonder, then, that in areas where such local notables exist, their services are assiduously sought by competing parties.

To maintain a proper perspective on the existence of primitive electoral machines, one should note that in most of the cases we have been discussing - Turkey during the 1960s, India since independence, Burma in the 1960s, Indonesia during the 1950s, and the Philippines traditionally - the primitive electoral machines merely formed cells or segments of far larger machine organizations which operated at the national level. These national machines were based predominantly not upon traditional - hereditary, religious, or kinship - considerations, but upon much more mundane specie.

The pure secular machine is a reasonably well-known phenomenon to political scientists. Its functional cement is the trading of votes for material incentives: jobs, favors, loans, credits or gifts, public-works projects or services, land grants under agrarian reform programs and the regular access to and influence in decision-making centers necessary to secure and, if possible, to institutionalize and perpetuate the flow of such incentives to local followers through the hands of local machine leaders. In an ideal-typical sense - and the Philippines approaches this status -such a machine is almost entirely devoid of programmatic content or loyalty to any particular party. It is marked by a naked market mentality. Local leaders sell the

votes they control to the party which makes the most attractive offer.(77)   This is a relatively rare case, however,
for to the extent that secular machines share characteristics of
either primordial or ideological machines, this naked selling of
votes is constrained.   Toward the primordial end of the
spectrum, local leaders are not entirely dependent upon
material inducements or incentives to their followers.   Therefore party switching or running local notables as independents
is possible, but not regularly forced by the demands from
below for the maximum possible flow of benefits from whichever
party seems most likely to provide it.   Toward the ideological
end of the machine spectrum, the extent of peasant adherence
to ideas, programs, and particular parties which symbolize
them restricts leaders in their ability to swing their peasant
voters from one party to another for tactical advantage in the
bargaining process.

As I have stressed elsewhere, however, pure ideological
machines based on peasants seem to be short-lived phenomena,
for a quite basic reason.   The material needs of poor peasants
are so acute and so manifest that the would-be ideologically
pure party (the Italian Communist Party is an excellent
example) which operates in an impoverished peasant milieu
(such as southern Italy) comes under very great pressure to
secure material benefits, just as their secular competitors do.
While local leaders may not switch parties, local followers may.
Yet to the extent that local ideological machine leaders attempt
to respond to the material needs of their local clienteles by
playing the same type of patronage game as their secular
counterparts, they are likely to come under fire from ideological purists in the party's national hierarchy, as occurred
in Italy during the 1960s.   No matter which way local leaders
try to move - sell their followers an ideology or respond to
their material needs - they are likely to weaken the party's
national effectiveness as an electoral mobilizer, and they may
become either an ideologically pure party without a mass following, and therefore no longer a machine of any kind, or a
machine of the more predominantly secular type, de-
emphasizing or bastardizing their ideology in the process.(78)

It seems clear that the most successful of the peasant-
based electoral machine parties in recent times (I am thinking
of the Congress Party in India, and the Democratic Action
Party of Venezuela, and to some extent the PRI in Mexico)
have achieved viable blends of secular and ideological appeals
which bond together in various ways local leaders and followers as well as the party leadership.(79)   Similar tendencies
may be found in Colombia, Italy, Chile, Japan and Bolivia,
although the success of the parties in these countries in
winning elections and forming stable governments has been less
striking.(80)

The existence of such large-scale machines has important implications for a number of issues besides electoral success and governmental stability, including matters of public policy, distributive justice, and the meaning of democracy itself. Before turning to a consideration of these issues, I will take a somewhat closer look at the kind of local leadership involved in the electoral machine pattern of peasant political behavior.

Since empirical studies of local machine leaders are rather rare, I shall have to rely heavily on my own data, gathered in rural Venezuela and Colombia.(81) No "primordial" leaders were encountered in my samples. On the contrary, the local leaders found by random sampling techniques turned out to be poor peasants themselves. Over 80 percent gave "small farmer" as their own occupation, and that of their father as well. Local machine leaders were well-established members of their communities; more than 60 percent had resided in the community in which they were interviewed for more than 10 years, with almost 30 percent having been born there. As demonstrated by my Colombian data, however, local leaders differed from local followers in their material standards of living (type of housing, roofing, household amenities), scoring significantly higher on an index measurement. Local machine leaders, in short, were drawn from among the most well-to-do peasants in the sub-subsistence stratum.

But while local machine leaders were drawn from and anchored in the peasant stratum they represented, they exhibited significantly different characteristics from their followers along a number of dimensions. They were twice as likely to have attended school, and among all those who had some schooling, the leaders were six times more likely to have finished the primary grades. Their exposure to radio programs was higher than normal, and they were twice as likely to have read newspapers regularly. Along another dimension - exposure to urban life - local machine leaders had traveled more widely and extensively than local followers, and, at least in Venezuela, many had even migrated to a city or cities for a period earlier in their lives - more than one-third had lived in urban areas for up to ten years, and 12.7 percent for more than ten years. Most importantly in terms of how machine organizations work, local peasant machine leaders exhibited a strikingly higher rate of regular contact with nonpeasants - teachers, local governmental officials, bureaucrats in national institutions, commercial middlemen, and political party officials - than local followers. In short, there is solid contextual evidence of their performance of the brokerage role for their peasant followers which is so characteristic of machine, or clientelist politics. Local leaders act as the transmission belts for peasant requests for jobs, favors, information, material help for individuals and groups, and as the mediators or go-betweens for the downward flow of

such incentives and payoffs from political parties, governmental agencies, and local economic influentials. Such local
leaders (and I have reason to believe that they are rather
typical), functioning in a coordinated fashion, provide the
means whereby sufficient sub-subsistence peasant votes are
collected to elect governments which are to some degree
responsive to the material needs and problems of their peasant
electors. This responsiveness, in the form of agrarian reform,
agricultural credit, rural public works, community development, public health and other programs, leads most observers
to characterize such parties and electoral systems as
democratic-reform in nature.

There is a wide range of opinion reflected in recent
literature on patron-client politics, or political clientelism,
regarding the functionality of electoral machine behavior in the
developmental or modernization process.(82) Beginning at the
level of the individual voter in peasant-based systems, there is
agreement that machine participants in fact receive tangible
benefits in return for their votes, and that the material and
other needs of such voters are excruciating. On the other
hand, public benefits under such machines tend to be particularistic, going either to favored individuals or selected
families and local communities. While some benefit, others do
not. Indeed, to the extent that electoral payoffs consume
public resources which might be distributed more universal-
istically, nonmembers of electoral machines may suffer to pay
the price of the benefiting members. Political parties of the
electoral machine type are on the one hand viewed as successful, aggregating, broadly integrating organizations which
have a proven record of ability to win elections and govern
over extended periods of time without excessive fraud,
coercion, or corruption. Furthermore, they organize flows of
tangible benefits to the most needy social strata in their
societies, and in this sense are functional in redistributive
justice terms. On the other hand, it is noted that such
parties exact a price. The political leadership benefits dis-
proportionately, and broad, collectively oriented public policies
are seldom formulated by the governments brought to power by
such machines due to the pressures for particularistic payoffs
to party supporters, communities, and regions. The dilemma
inherent in this situation is quite clear: electoral machines do
respond to real human needs, but they do so in a selective
and possibly wasteful fashion. Compared to traditional,
authoritarian systems, their distributive efforts are laudable.
Compared to modern, rationally administered democracies, their
distributive efforts are corruptly partisan.

At the most abstract level of analysis, electoral machines
appear on the one hand to be a viable alternative to violent
revolutionary change. They integrate the most disadvantaged
stratum of the population, the peasantry, and socialize it into

democratic, electoral forms of behavior. In return for the electoral support of the peasantry, such systems are responsive, to a reasonable degree, to peasant material and organizational needs. Furthermore, electoral machine-based political systems by their nature incorporate, build upon, and reflect cross-class alliances of individual patrons and clients and similarly related groups in society, thereby promoting political stability. On the other hand, built as they are upon preexisting social inequalities, patron-client systems and machine-based governments tend to perpetuate and in some cases exaggerate social stratification processes and structures of unequal distribution. Furthermore, in siphoning off large amounts of public resources for the private benefit of machine leaders and particularistic benefits for machine followers, governmental machines reduce the resources available for long-range, economically productive public investments. As a result, a situation of economic stagnation is foreordained, and the multiclass "terms of trade" of distributive justice are steadily worsened by the system, with leadership consuming ever greater amounts of existing productive benefits.

Ultimately, such systems must collapse, either under the weight of their own internal corruption and ineptitude in leading their country to economic development, or as a result of massive lower strata reaction to increasing stratification and their own immiserization, or both. While my own personal evaluations lean in the direction of the more positive view of peasant-based electoral politics, the counterarguments give serious pause. Within the basic context of dilemma inherent in machine politics, one matter is entirely clear: none of these contending points of view is entirely persuasive, and none will be persuasive until a great deal of carefully gathered and systematically analyzed data are in hand.

NOTES

(1)   Sorokin et al. made an attempt, more than 40 years ago, to summarze the electoral behavior of farmers and peasants in volume two of their Source Book. The effort fell far short of being an adequate comparative statement, however, even for the period; there was an undue reliance on studies of United States rural areas for quantitative data, which were rare for other parts of the world. See P. A. Sorokin, C. C. Zimmerman, and C. J. Galpin, eds., A Systematic Source Book in Rural Sociology (Minneapolis: University of Minnesota Press, 1931), vol. II, pp. 538-677.

Some 20 years ago, another effort was made to summarize the European data on peasant electoral behavior by Juan Linz, in "Patterns of Land Tenure and Division of Labor and Politics," (unpublished manuscript, Yale University, made available to me by courtesy of Professor Linz), in which he employed the rather cumbersome typology of rural strata developed by Sorokin et et. in A Systematic Source Book, vol. I, pp. 363-65.

Seymour M. Lipset discussed farmer and peasant voting in general terms under the topic of leftist voting versus traditionalism in "Elections: The Expression of the Democratic Class Struggle," in Political Man (New York: Doubleday, 1959), pp. 230-78.

Finally, Arthur L. Stinchcombe offered some generalizations on peasant political and electoral behavior in his article, "Agricultural Enterprise and Rural Class Relations," American Journal of Sociology 67 (September 1961): 165-176. In each of these earlier studies, the authors emphasized the lack of both data and a comparative framework for the study of peasant electoral behavior, although Sorokin et al. and Stinchcombe attempted to formulate such frameworks.

On the utility and limitations of aggregate data analyses versus process modeling analyses, see Ronald Brunner and Garry Brewer, Organized Complexity: Empirical Theories of Political Development (New York: Free Press, 1971); and for a very shrewd essay on sequence and rate considerations, see Eric A. Nordlinger, "Political Development: Time Sequences and Rates of Change," in Politics and Society: Studies in Political Sociology, ed. Eric A. Nordlinger (Englewood Cliffs, N. J.: Prentice-Hall, 1970), pp. 329-47.

(2) See Stein Rokkan, "Electoral Mobilization, Party Competition, and National Integration," in Political Parties and Political Development, ed. Joseph LaPalombara and Myron Weiner (Princeton, N. J.: Princeton University Press, 1966), pp. 241-65, especially pp. 260-65. The quote is taken from the Introduction by S. M. Lipset and Stein Rokkan, ed., Party Systems and Voter Alignment: Cross-National Perspectives (New York: Free Press, 1967), p. 53.

(3) One of the first writers to attempt to develop systematically and demonstrate empirically the urban-rural lag concept was Stein Rokkan in "Geography, Religion, and Social Class: Crosscutting Cleavages in Norwegian Politics," in Lipset and Rokkan, eds., Party Systems, pp. 367-444.

(4) Samuel P. Huntington, Political Order in Changing Societies (New Haven, Conn.: Yale University Press, 1968), p. 127.

(5)   Maurice Duverger, Political Parties (New York: John Wiley, 1954).
(6)   Rokkan, "Geography, Religion, and Social Class," p. 383.
(7)   Nordlinger, "Political Development."
(8)   Rokkan, "Geography, Religion, and Social Class."
(9)   See Sidney Tarrow, "The Urban-Rural Cleavage in Political Involvement: The Case of France," American Political Science Review 65, (June 1971): 341-357, especially p. 345; and Myron Weiner and John Osgood Field, "India's Urban Constituencies" (Paper presented to the Seminar on Electoral Patterns in the Indian States, Boston, June 1972).
(10) On France, see Tarrow, "The Urban-Rural Cleavage"; for Japan, see Jun'ichi Kyogoku and Nobutaka Ike, "Urban-Rural Differences in Voting Behavior in Postwar Japan," and Robert E. Ward, "Urban-Rural Differences and the Process of Political Modernization in Japan: A Case Study," both found in Economic Development and Cultural Change 9, part 2 (October 1960), pp. 167-85 and 135-65, respectively; for Turkey, see Ergun Ozbudun, "Participation Patterns in Rural Turkey: Some Preliminary Observations" (Paper presented to Colloquium on Turkey, Princeton, N. J., May 1972).
(11) Sorokin et al. made essentially the same points in 1931; confronted with the great variation in urban-rural turnout data available to them, they felt compelled to "conclude, therefore, that whatever relationship exists between urbanization and the size of the vote is purely temporary and characteristic only of the individual country." (Sorokin, A Systematic Source Book, vol. 2, p. 549.)
(12) Weiner and Field, "India's Urban Constituencies."
(13) Kyogoku and Ike, "Urban-Rural Differences," and Ward, "Urban-Rural Differences and the Process of Political Modernization," especially pp. 162-65, where such findings are summarized.
(14) Linz, "Patterns of Land Tenure," p. 74. The rationale for such voting patterns is explored further in this chapter.
(15) For Turkey, see Ozbudun, "Participation Patterns," and Ayse Kudat Sertel, "Peasant Conceptions of Community Power Structure: A Comparative Study of Two Turkish Villages" (Ph.D. diss., Harvard University, 1971); for India, see David J. Elkins, "Social Mobilization, Social Structure, and Politics: Evidence and Qualifications" (Paper presented to the American Political Science Association Meeting, Chicago, September 1971), and William L. Richter, "Electoral Patterns in Princely India" (Paper presented to the Seminar on Electoral Patterns in the Indian States, Boston, June 1972); for Pakistan, see

Hamza Alavi, "Political Structures and Economic Development in Rural West Pakistan," Institute of Development Studies, University of Sussex (Brighton: n.d.).
(16)   This is one of the chief findings in Richter, "Electoral Patterns in Princely India." Additional evidence of very high mobilization rates in India is included in Albert Hadley Cantril, Jr., "Political Involvement in Four Indian Villages" (Ph.D. diss., Massachusetts Institute of Technology, 1966). Cantril found, for example, in his random sample of Rajasthan peasants, that 63 percent had attended political rallies, 42 percent had worked for a candidate in a campaign, and 23 percent had even contributed financially to political campaigns. These percentages are far higher than those for a national sample of United States, United Kingdom, German, Italian, and Mexican (urban only) citizens. See Gabriel Almond and Sidney Verba, The Civic Culture (Princeton, N. J.: Princeton University, 1963), pp. 302, 308.
(17)   For Turkey, see Ozbudun, "Participation Patterns," and also Ayse Kudat Sertel, "Patron-Client Relations: The State of the Art and Research in Eastern Turkey" (Massachusetts Institute of Technology, 1972); for Japan, see Ward, "Urban-Rural Differences and the Process of Political Modernization," 9: 163.
(18)   Huntington, Political Order, pp. 443-44, cites evidence from Germany, England, Brazil, Ceylon, and Turkey emphasizing the ability of traditional elites such as landlords to influence the electoral choices of their underlings. The clientelist pattern of voting behavior will be considered at length at the end of this chapter.
(19)   See Edward Dew, Politics in the Altiplano: The Dynamics of Change in Rural Peru (Austin: University of Texas Press, 1969), p. 78; and Robert R. Kaufman, The Politics of Land Reform in Chile 1950-1970 (Cambridge, Mass.: Harvard University Press, 1972), pp. 119-23. In a few reported instances, right-wing politicians took advantage of the fears of the latifundia peasants by inducing them to "invade" fundos in order to prevent the Agrarian Reform Agency from expropriating the land and "allowing the selection of outside peasants as settlers" (p. 120).
(20)   Frances Lucille Starner, Magsaysay and the Philippine Peasantry: The Agrarian Impact on Philippine Politics, 1953-1956 (Berkeley: University of California Press, 1961), pp. 65-66, 78-79.
(21)   Rudolf Heberle, From Democracy to Nazism (Baton Rouge: Louisiana State University Press, 1945); Kyogoku and Ike, "Urban-Rural Differences"; Ward, "Urban-Rural Differences and the Process of Political Modernization"; Sydel F. Silverman, "Agricultural Organization, Social Structure, and Values in Italy: Amoral Familism Re-

considered," American Anthropologist 70 (February 1968):
1-20; and J. S. Macdonald, "Agricultural Organization,
Migration and Labour Militance in Rural Italy," Economic
History Review 16 (August 1963): 61-75. The case of
Colombia is an unusual one in that local solidarity patterns exist, it seems, in both landlord-dominated and in
peer-dominated communities (in which landlords may have
historically established the pattern of support for one of
the traditional parties), and such patterns became so
deeply rooted that landlord influence was no longer
necessary to maintain them, as some of the intervillage
warfare during the period of la violencia suggests. See
John R. Mathiason and John D. Powell, "Participation and
Efficacy: Aspects of Peasant Involvement in Political
Mobilization," Comparative Politics 4 (April 1972): 303-29,
especially pp. 308-13 for comment and further references.
(22)   Heberle, From Democracy to Nazism, pp. 89, 108, 111;
and Kyogoku & Ike, "Urban-rural Differences," p. 173.
(23)   For an extensive treatment and analysis of the subject of
corporate village solidarity patterns, their origins and
conditions of decline, see Joel Samuel Migdal, "Peasants in
a Shrinking World: The Socio-Economic Basis of Political
Change" (Ph.D. diss., Harvard University, 1972).
(24)   Tarrow, "The Urban-Rural Cleavage," pp. 355-56.
(25)   John Duncan Powell, Political Mobilization of the Venezuelan Peasant (Cambridge: Harvard University Press,
1971), chap. 6.
(26)   Sertel, "Peasant Conceptions," pp. 34-35; and Sertel,
"Patron-Client Relations," p. 45.
(27)   See inter alia for India, Myron Weiner, "Village and
Party Factionalsim in Andhra: Ponnur Constituency," in
Indian Voting Behaviour, ed. Myron Weiner and Rajni
Kothari (Calcutta: F. K. L. Mukhopadhayay, 1965), pp.
177-202; Mary C. Carras, "Congress Factionalism in
Maharashtra: A Case Study of the Akola Zilla Parishad,"
Asian Survey 10 (May 1970): 410-426; and David J.
Elkins, "Social Mobilization and the Nature of Society: A
Reassessment Using Indian Data" (University of British
Columbia, Vancouver, Canada). On Pakistani patterns of
local factionalism, see Alavi, "Political Structures." For
Turkey, see Joseph Szyliowicz, Political Change in Rural
Turkey: Erdemli (The Hague: Mouton, 1966); Jan
Hinderink and Mubeccel Kiray, Social Stratification as an
Obstacle to Development: A Study of Four Turkish Vil-
lages (New York: Praeger, 1970); and Frederick W. Frey
and Leslie L. Roos, "Social Structure and Community
Development in Rural Turkey: Village and Elite Leader-
ship Relations," Report no. 10, Rural Development
Research Project, Massachusetts Institute of Technology,
Cambridge, Mass., 1967. See also James B. Mayfield,

Rural Politics in Nasser's Egypt (Austin: University of
Texas Press, 1971); Dew, Politics in the Altiplano, and
F. LaMond Tullis, Lord and Peasant in Peru (Cambridge,
Mass.: Harvard University Press, 1970); Bernard Gallin,
"Political Factionalism and Its Impact on Chinese Village
School Organization in Taiwan," in Local Level Politics,
ed. Marc J. Swartz (Chicago: Aldine, 1968), pp. 377-400.
On the Philippines, see Carl Lande, Leaders, Factions and
Parties: The Structure of Philippine Politics, Monograph
no. 6 (New Haven, Conn.: Yale Southeast Asia Studies,
1965);and "Networks and Groups in Southeast Asia: Some
Observations on the Group Theory of Politics" (Paper
presented to the SEADAG Political Development Seminar,
Asia Society, New York, March 1970). Good comparative
analyses of factionalism include Ralph Nicholas, "Factions:
A Comparative Analysis," in Political Systems and the
Distribution of Power, ed. Max Gluckman and Fred Eggan
(London: Tavistock, 1965), pp. 21-62; and F. G. Bailey,
Stratagems and Spoils: A Social Anthropology of Politics
(Oxford: Basil Blackwell, 1969).
(28) Hinderink and Kiray, Social Stratification, pp. 225-40.
(29) Gallin, "Political Factionalism"; and Weiner, "Village and
Party Factionalism," p. 195.
(30) Szyliwocz, Political Change, pp. 151-53; Mayfield, Rural
Politics, pp. 76-99; and Alavi, "Political Structures."
Sorokin et al., A Systematic Source Book, also puts great
emphasis on family ties in rural political behavior (vol. 2,
pp. 540-45) as well as in all other aspects of rural life.
(31) Alavi, "Political Sturctures."
(32) Ernest Feder, The Rape of the Peasantry: Latin America's Landholding System (Garden City: Doubleday, 1971),
emphasizes and presents evidence for the employment of
violence by landlords in order to coerce their peasants.
The kind of violence and coercion I am referring to here
is an even more diffuse characteristic of the entire social
and political system, as studies of the mafia in rural
Sicily have described.
(33) Kyogoku and Ike, "Urban-Rural Differences," 9: 173.
(34) Sidney W. Mintz, Worker in the Cane (New Haven,
Conn.: Yale University Press, 1960), pp. 149-151.
(35) Mayfield, Rural Politics, pp. 48-49.
(36) Lipset, Political Man, p. 230.
(37) See Rokkan, "Geography, Religion and Social Class"
(Norway); Erik Allardt and Pertti Pesonen, "Cleavages in
Finnish Politics," in Lipset and Rokkan, Party Systems
and Voter Alignments, pp. 325-66; for Germany, see
Heberle, From Democracy to Nazism. The most useful
single volume for the Eastern European parties is George
D. Jackson, Jr., Comintern and Peasant in Eastern
Europe 1919-1930 (New York: Columbia University Press,
1966). See also David Mitrany, Marx Against the Peasant

238 THE PROCESS OF RURAL TRANSFORMATION

(Chapel Hill: University of North Carolina Press, 1951) for additional insight into the East European situation; and Sorokin et al., A Systematic Source Book, vol. 2, pp. 618-77 for brief descriptions of a number of European agrarian parties and movements. For further information and insight into the Croatian Peasant Party, see Vladko Macek, In the Struggle for Freedom (University Park, Pa.: Pennsylvania State University Press, 1957). Macek took over the party following the assassination of its founding leader, Stjepan Radic.

(38) Suzanne Berger's study of rural organizations in Brittany illustrates (in the case of Finistere) a corporate agrarian response led by local elites without linkages to a national agrarian or peasant party. See Suzanne Berger, Peasants Against Politics (Cambridge, Mass.: Harvard University Press, 1972).

(39) See Berger, Peasants Against Politics, pp. 65-75, especially p. 72; and Jackson, Comintern and Peasant, pp. 278-79, for the contrast between the appeal of the Czech agrarians for social harmony and the communists' highlighting of rural stratification phenomena.

(40) Heberle, From Democracy to Nazism.

(41) See Jackson, Comintern and Peasant, pp. 159-80.

(42) Allardt and Pesonen, "Cleavages in Finnish Politics"; and Jackson, Comintern and Peasant, pp. 266-97 (Czechoslovakia), pp. 237-65 (Rumania), pp. 181-214 (Poland); and pp. 215-36 (Yugoslavia).

(43) Allardt and Pesonen, "Cleavages in Finnish Politics," p. 338.

(44) Heberle, From Nazism to Democracy; Jackson, Comintern and Peasant; Carol Skalnik, "Patterns of Peasant Political Behavior in the Czechoslovak Republic" (Government Department, Harvard University, January 1970); R. V. Burks, The Dynamics of Communism in Eastern Europe (Princeton, N. J.: Princeton University Press, 1961); Mattei Doggan, "Political Cleavage and Social Stratification in France and Italy," in Lipset & Rokkan, Party Systems and Voter Alignments, pp. 129-95; Sidney Tarrow, Peasant Communism in Southern Italy (New Haven, Conn.: Yale University Press, 1967); Linz, "Patterns of Land Tenure"; Donald S. Zagoria, "The Ecology of Peasant Communism in India," American Political Science Review 65 (March 1971): 144-60; James Petras and Maurice Zeitlin, "Agrarian Radicalism in Chile," in Agrarian Problems & Peasant Movements in Latin America, ed. Rodolfo Stavenhagen (Garden City: Doubleday, 1970); and Kaufman, The Politics of Land Reform in Chile.

(45) Petras and Zeitlin, "Agrarian Radicalism in Chile," pp. 527-31.

(46) Skalnik, "Patterns of Peasant Political Behavior."

Political Factor in Mexico, Bolivia, and Venezuela,"
Research paper no. 35. (Madison: Land Tenure Center,
University of Wisconsin, 1965).

(80)   Robert Dix, Colombia: The Political Dimensions of Change
(New Haven, Conn.: Yale University Press, 1967); Sidney
Tarrow, Peasant Communism in Southern Italy (New
Haven, Conn.: Yale University Press, 1967); Kaufman,
The Politics of Land Reform in Chile; Nobutaka Ike,
Japanese Politics: Patron-Client Democracy (New York:
Alfred Knopf, 1972), and James M. Malloy, Boliva: The
Uncompleted Revolution (Pittsburgh: Pittsburgh Univer-
sity Press, 1970).

(81)   Powell, Political Mobilization, John Duncan Powell, "Organizing Colombian Peasants," Cambridge, Mass.: Center
for Rural Development, 1968; and Mathiason and Powell,
Participation and Efficacy," pp. 303-39.

(82)   For essentially "pro" interpretations, see Powell,
"Peasant Society," and Political Mobilization; Rudolph and
Rudolph, The Modernity of Tradition; Myron Weiner,
Party Building in a New Nation: The Indian National
Congress (Chicago: University of Chicago Press, 1967);
and Ike, Japanese Politics. For essentially "con" in-
terpretations, see Francine R. Frankel, "Democracy and
Development" Perspectives from the Indian Experience,"
World Politics 21 (April 1969): 448-68; and Luigi Graziano,
"Patron-Client Relationships in Southern Italy" (Paper
Prepared for the 1972 annual meeting of the American
Political Science Association, Washington, D.C., Septem-
ber 5-9, 1972). For interpretations which seem to in-
dicate that clientelism may be functional under some
circumstances (or at certain stages of development) but
not others, see James C. Scott, "Corruption"; Rene
Lemarchand and Keith Legg, "Political Clientelism and
Development: A Preliminary Analysis," Comparative
Politics 4 (January 1972): 149-78.

10 Memories of Recent Change: Some East European Perspectives*

Joel Martin Halpern

Perhaps the most outstanding fact about East European rural communities and to a great extent East European societies in general has been their transformation from countries which were dominated by what has generally been called a traditional peasant economy to an industrially based region. This is not to say that peasants or peasant-linked value systems have disappeared in this area but rather that family-based agricultural production relying principally on human and animal power is no longer a major focus of the economic systems of these countries. This process of modernization may turn out to be more significant, when viewed from a future long-range perspective, than the specifics of the various socialist-communist ideologies which now predominate in Eastern Europe. This does not minimize the very great impact of these ideologies and the fact of the implementation of the governmental systems which have brought them into practice but rather to stress

---

*This paper is based on data derived from a long-term research project on rural change in Yugoslavia. The research has been financed, in part, by grants from the National Science Foundation and the National Institutes of Health.
As a survey article based on a primary source, supplementary references have not been included. However, a recent excellent survey of the literature, incorporating materials in English as well as in the local languages, is available in Irwin T. Sanders, Roger Whitaker, and Walter C. Bisselle, comps., East European Peasantries: Social Relations: An Annotated Bibliography of Periodical Articles (Boston: G. K. Hall, 1976).

that the processes of modernization, industrialization and urbanization which have occurred are part of a world-wide transformation. Although these processes appear irreversible we
are now more skeptical about the possibilities of maximizing
such change than we were a decade or so ago. "Traditional"
used to be a synonym for backward, "modernization" for progress, and urbanization and industrialization were viewed as
signs of positive achievement. Today the smoking factory
chimney can more often mean pollution than the attainment of a
higher standard of living. At the same time certain aspects of
old peasant ways are now romanticized as in food, dance, and
music. Given these attitudes we need more than ever to try
to attain some concrete perspective on where we have come
from in order to assess where we may be going.

I say "we" because in talking about recent rural pasts
the discussion must necessarily have a universal character
especially as far as Europeans and Americans are concerned.
Not only did many East Europeans come from farms in the Old
World to find a new life in the cities of North America but,
even though North American farmers have experienced different life-styles than East European farmers, there is no small
overlap.

A vivid example of this is provided in President Carter's
campaign autobiography as described by Norman Mailer:

> "My life," wrote Carter, "during the Great
> Depression more nearly resembled farm life of fully
> 2,000 years ago than farm life today."
> There was no electricity. He lived in a house
> heated by fireplaces and a wood stove in the kitch-
> en. He used an outdoor privy and a hand pump.
> Chickens, ducks, dogs and geese wandered through
> the yards. With his playmates, who were black, he
> brought water to the farmworkers in the field,
> "mopped the cotton, turned sweet potato and water-
> melon vines, pruned the deformed young water-
> melons, toted the stove wood, swept the yards,
> carried slops to the hogs, and gathered eggs." He
> also "rode mules and horses through the woods,
> jumped out of the barn loft into huge piles of oat
> straw, wrestled and fought, fished and swam,"
> trapped and hunted in the woods and swamps. His
> father's store in town sold products made on the
> farm, "syrup, side meat, lard, cured hams, loops of
> stuffed sausage." During field work he would get
> up at 4 A.M., "go to the barn and catch the mules
> by lantern light, put the plow stocks, seed, fer-
> tilizer and other supplies on the wagons and drive to
> the field." When older, he would plow, harrow with
> discs, or work in the blacksmith shop near the

barn. He learned to make soap and lard, how to
mill wheat and corn, used haywire to repair everything from sickles to wagons. The farm planted
corn in March, then cotton, then peanuts. [From
the time he was five, one of his jobs was to sell
boiled peanuts on the street in Plains.] In June,
grain was cut, shocked and thrashed, watermelons
were carted to town; later came the major harvest,
cotton picked by hand and peanuts pulled, corn
leaves tied and velvet beans gathered, peanut hay
baled. In winter, hogs were slaughtered, meat was
cured, sugar cane was converted into syrup.
They also produced honey, wool, goose feathers,
milk, pickled pigs feet, sold jams and jellies and
wine made from cherries, peaches and muscadines,
even sold homemade ketchup.

    It is a life of detailed husbandry, where the
esthetic of the life is found in each act; each detail
lives inside the detail that brought it forth. In that
way, it might be analogous to the life of a writer for
whom no passing experience is not worthy of observation. Of course, any similarity had to end there;
fantasy was an obscene indulgence to the farmer.
The passion of the farmer was to reduce the sum of
stuff he had to throw away. His art was to find a
use for waste. What a prodigy of organization and
what an abhorrence of useless waste must have developed in Carter during his boyhood; what a capacity to work!(1)

In looking over this account the reaction of many American
urbanites and suburbanites may be a sense of nostalgia for
pleasant memories or, more likely, a sense of romantic and
vicarious sharing of the memories of the "good life," with clean
air, wholesome food and rewarding work. It may be perhaps a
minor theme, but there is also a prominent painful memory for
some of the bruising and often painfully hard aspects of farm
work, and for not a few, the remembered feelings of hunger
with meals of restricted variety and often limited quantity.
    There are many ways in which the experiences that
Carter describes overlap with the life-style of villagers in
Eastern Europe before and immediately after the Second World
War. There were also, of course, important differences, in
particular economic foci, degree of subsistence production and
social-structure relationships, black workers, and the case of
peanuts and cotton as cash crops in the American context. In
the European context, above all, there is the role of centrally
planned and programmed communist modernization.
    In this chapter I want to focus on the recollections of a
woman, now in her late thirties, who came from a village in

central Serbia, studied to be a lawyer, and subsequently emigrated to the United States. I do not claim that her experiences were precisely shared by all other Eastern European villagers in the postwar period but rather, by relating directly some aspects of her experiences, it is possible to gain brief insights into the kinds of transformations which have taken place in Eastern Europe during the last generation. The fact that these are a woman's recollections is of heightened significance because while changes have been great for men, the possibilities and problems that recent societal evolution has opened up for women have been even greater.

Perhaps more than any other experience, expanded educational facilities provided by the socialist state have afforded the possibility for social mobility and "escape" from the village, a means of "shaking the village mud off our shoes and setting forth on the high road to town," as many have put it.

In 1951 I finished the four grades of elementary school in my village and since a second four years were not added to the local school until several years later I had to go five kilometers to the nearest town. So until I finished the fifth grade of high school (gymnasium) I had to go back and forth every day. It was very hard. I had to attend classes in the morning. They started at eight o'clock, which meant that I had to get up an hour earlier because I needed that much time to walk. But my father used to wake me earlier because I had to take my sheep and cow out to graze. Thus it always meant that I had to wake up at least two hours before school started, that would be five-thirty or six o'clock. Then I would go out with the animals.

Since I didn't have a watch my mother would call me when she thought it was time for me to go to school. I would then come home, take a sandwich in my hands and walk to school. My food was a piece of bread with some cheese, or sometimes it was a piece of meat left from supper. There were lots of girls and boys from my village going to school but since my house is at the end of the village and near the Belgrade-Skopje highway I was lucky to get quickly to the main road. I wanted to get out of the mud because when it rains it is very muddy. Usually I would walk alone. Many times it would rain or snow and it was very hard. I would come to school absolutely wet, shaking all over, sometimes frozen. My teacher would put me next to the stove. I would lose time from my classes by drying myself. They felt I should not sit in class for I might get sick. I would read a book until I was dry enough and then I would attend the rest of the day's classes. My parents never had enough money to afford an apartment in town during the winter. It was particularly hard because I was very small and weak although not ill. The wind was sometimes so strong that as I would walk one meter forward the wind would blow me two meters backwards. I would struggle. Sometimes I came to school an hour late because it took me two hours on the road. I would be absolutely frozen and my teachers felt terrible about it. I could have stayed home for that day but my parents wanted me to go to school. They would tell me, "I don't want your teacher to talk to me about your absence."

When I came back from school, it was usually two or three o'clock. I would eat my lunch, throw my books aside and then, depending on the season, go join my parents in the fields. Or, if the animals were hungry, I would take them out again. Actually I never really had time for study during the day. The only chance I had to study was at night, but my parents were against my studying at night. So when they were asleep, I would put the light on [The village had been electrified in 1949.] and read my books and write my homework, especially in math and physics the subjects in which I had a lot to do. For these five years it was very hard. There were even many times when our teachers asked us to come back in the afternoon, as in the third year of high school, when I had to go back to the laboratory to do my physics. This meant I would go home eat my lunch and go back because my parents did not know and I had to tell them. This made four hours of walking and coming home in the evening. Sometimes my father would wait for me on the road outside the village, but sometimes he didn't have the time for he was at the flour mill or someplace else.

It was very scary. Lots of dogs were let loose in the evening and were wandering around the road. I was attacked many times and I still have scars on my leg where I was bitten. For five years it went on like this.

There were many more boys than girls who went to school then, some finished although many dropped out. Among those girls who finished, one is a nurse, now married and working in Belgrade, another completed law and is now working in our town. One boy became an engineer, another a doctor. These two were from very poor families. Some of those who dropped out got factory jobs.

Against this background of social, spatial and occupational mobility for some of the village youth there were also changes taking place within the village itself. One of the most important of these changes was the introduction (in the mid-fifties) of an eight-year elementary school which meant that some of the sufferings of the previous pupils could not be avoided.

Not all the innovations in the village seemed to have met felt needs so well:

> In 1952-53, they built our Cooperative Building
> (Zadruzni Dom). They finished it, put the roof on
> and then didn't do anything more. This building is
> still sitting there unfinished. In the course of ten
> years they finished just three offices. Now this
> enormous building is just sitting there, starting to
> slowly sink. Sitting there right in the middle of the
> village, unused. I don't see the purpose of it.

Originally these large structures were supposed to serve as village "command posts" for the collectivization of agriculture. When policies changed and the majority of land was permitted to remain in private hands, the local organizations lost some of their intended functions. In many villages these buildings were used for administrative offices, for the agricultural cooperative store, or as a clinic. Sometimes auditoriums were built where movies could be shown but they might end up being used for grain storage. Many have remained underutilized, a kind of monument to earlier policies.

A much more important development was the initial land reform in which the state took over all landholdings of more than ten hectares of arable land and then, by exchanging parcels, used this land as the basis for the creation of consolidated estates. These socially owned agricultural enterprises were intended to be the forerunner of the eventual socialization of all land. This policy of the eventual elimination of private farming remains a future objective but no time limit has been set. These state farms came into being after the policy of collectivization of agriculture was abandoned in the early 1950s. The villagers initially saw such farms as a threat and were understandably hostile to them.

> You know that in Yugoslavia land is not all in
> one place, there are many different parcels that an
> individual owns. But this is land which belonged to
> your great-great-grandfather, then your great-
> grandfather, your grandfather and your father. Now
> it is yours. How would you feel if somebody comes
> and takes a piece of this land and you cannot go
> there. You cannot plow this land. You cannot do
> anything on it. This was very bad. It was hard to

make people believe that they had lost their lands.
They couldn't believe that they took all those pieces,
not just the land in one place. A big tractor would
come and plow these parcels. You plow with your
oxen on the land that remains yours and you see
this tractor plowing the field that used to be yours.
It was very, very bad. Nobody would work for the
State Farm.

They brought people from the hills. There are
nearby villages where the land is very poor. The
people who live there have only sheep and little
land.

The State Farm just wasted the land. They
didn't know what to start planting there. They
started with watermelons, which is nonsense. The
land is very good for corn and wheat. I don't know
why they did this. Then they put clover all around
and so it is now clover fields. They couldn't hire
enough people to work. For example, for harvesting
they couldn't get enough workers even from those
hill villages. They couldn't get them to come and
work on the farm at the right time. The workers
were mostly women. They brought these people in a
cart pulled by a big tractor. They brought them
back home every evening but these people had to
bring their own lunch. Every day they would travel
25 kilometers back and forth to their hill village.
The land in our village was rich because it was
located on a flat plain near a river, although it used
to sometimes flood. They would sometimes work from
eight or nine in the morning until eight in the
evening. They weren't paid very well.

After they put in the clover, they planted
corn. After that they put in wheat. They would
have had good results if they had done their work
correctly and on time. But at harvest time they
sometimes couldn't get enough people. If you don't
harvest wheat in time, in three days it can get
overripe and everything can go to seed. This is
also true of corn. And so they failed and put in
clover again. They make a profit grazing animals
but still this is wasting good land. Before, people
had put in corn and wheat and always had good
income from this land.

One of the reasons it was hard to recruit labor for the State
Farm was that other employment opportunities were available.
Some of these opportunities were traditional. Certain villagers
would go to work seasonally on the rich wheat plains of the
Vojvodina, across the Danube, just as poorer hill villagers

would come and work in this relatively more prosperous low-
land. In addition there was also a tradition of masons and
construction workers from this area going out to seek temporary work.

> People often go out of the village to work
> during the harvest season. They usually go to the
> Vojvodina to the State Farms. Or the builders
> (zidari), leave when they hear that something new is
> being built, like the new university in Nis. They
> may work from six months or a year before they
> come back. Sometimes they go and work on building
> a new railroad. While these zidari are away their
> wives and children work on the land and go to
> market and carry on their everyday lives. These
> men usually don't have much land. But they don't
> use their earnings to buy more land. I believe this
> is because they are not home to work the land.
> Their wives would have to put in a great amount of
> work if they had more land, or they would have to
> pay someone to work the land. Now they just live
> very comfortably with their garden and small vine-
> yard. But they do buy things for the house. I
> remember that a zidari family was the first household
> in our village to have nice beds and mattresses, nice
> soft beds. They threw out the old hard beds. This
> was in about 1953 soon after we received electricity.
> They also bought a radio. They always eat meat.
> They eat more than other people in the village when
> they are at home.

More important then the temporary migration of traditional
village craftsmen and seasonal work in more prosperous agricultural areas has been the large number of jobs which initially
opened up in this region due to the construction of large
factories in the nearby town as a result of planned industrialization.

> Peasants even though they think that by hard
> work they are going to achieve more, never really
> know because it all depends on the weather. There
> might be hail, or a big storm or flood. Young
> people who work elsewhere think that by hard work
> they are going to achieve more. These young people
> from my village started working at the factory when
> there were three shifts. Some people worked on two
> shifts and didn't get much sleep. The factory paid
> them double for night work. They volunteered.
> When they earn more money they usually plan in ad-
> vance what they are going to buy with this money.

> They carry on until they achieve this and after that
> they might work a bit less.   There is a tendency to
> think that whoever works harder gets more.   Today
> being a rich man can mean one who has a big family
> with many sons working in the factory and bringing
> cash into the house.

Because of the limitations on private landholdings extra income
is usually not used to buy land but more commonly for personal consumption and a better standard of living.   These new
opportunities for employment not only create enhanced possibilities they also give rise to a variety of tensions within
households.

> Probably before it was more often the case that
> sons remained home and listened to their fathers and
> married the girls their fathers asked them to.   My
> father, for example, who is 63 now, always referred
> to the fact that he had to listen to and obey his
> father and mother, especially his father.   Today
> when a man has a son and the son goes to school,
> the father doesn't ask him to remain in the village
> because he knows the son is not going to listen.
> But he begs his son, when he finishes school or
> learns a skill, to at least remain in the nearby town
> and find work there.   Of course, many like to leave
> the village and go far away but some sons do come
> back and work in a town nearby.   They then come
> and see their parents.   Or a few live in the village
> with their father and mother and go to work by
> bicycle.   But now the relationship between father
> and son has really changed.   It is very different
> than it was even ten years ago.   Parents cannot
> speak in an absolute way to their son.   They cannot
> say, "Don't you see that working the land is better
> for you than going to school."   This is so because
> the son realizes that this is not true.   The son has
> worked on the land and he knows that is it hard
> work.   He also knows that going to school will give
> him better opportunities and that he can have money
> of his own and not have to ask his father.

The increased roles of the socialist state in providing greater
educational opportunities and through industrialization increasing jobs in industry have not been the only ways in which
state planning has made its personal impact on villagers.   Even
for older villagers there has been the possibility of free medical care and pensions.   Although opportunities for private
farmers have been more restricted than for workers in the
socialized sector they have existed.   This has meant dealing

with a complex bureaucracy which has also been amenable to ties of friendship and sometimes incidental graft, practices which recall earlier times.

Before the war my father worked seasonally in a local sugar mill at the same time that he was tilling his own land. During the fall when the beets were ready to be made into sugar there would be a three-month period when the factory needed a large number of people. He worked in this factory on and off for about ten years. Then when the war came he went into the army and was a prisoner-of-war in Germany for four years. Years later someone told him that he could get a pension. I remember that he was ready to laugh at this. But by accumulating his working time before the war and then adding his four years in Germany he would be eligible for some kind of pension. This would not be a full pension but what is called an "invalid's pension." But it was a hard process. He had to see lots of doctors. My father is not an invalid but he does have rheumatism. His heart and lungs are perfect but all the veins in his legs are swollen, and when the weather is bad he has difficulty moving about. So the doctors decided to give him treatments, free treatments, to cure his rheumatism. So they sent him to Belgrade and they gave him shots and cured his left leg. But the shots are painful and my father is such a coward, he always feels he will die any minute. He decided to leave Belgrade. He decided that he is, first, not going to look for a pension and second, not going to seek a cure for his legs.

Meanwhile, my mother thought that maybe he should still get a pension. She has a friend, a doctor, who was a good customer, to whom she took butter and cheese for many years. My mother went and talked to this doctor who happened to be President of the Commission to decide about pensions. So my father went there and was examined again. Somehow, it was decided that my father would get an invalid's pension. I think that this was after we gave the doctor two or three pigs. In the beginning this pension was very small but my father was very happy. But this pension increased during the years so now it is relatively good. Since my parents are old now it is enough to pay people to help them work the land. But still they have trouble finding people willing to work so now they must put in lots of clover. He just couldn't carry on with planting wheat and corn.

New ideas and revised practices have come into village life
since the war. Cultural patterns have changed but innovations have always been mediated through village social networks in which gossip has played an important role. New
material items must be assimilated into a preexisting structure
and their potentialities examined before they are accepted.

> As you know my father has rheumatism. When
> he returned home from Germany he built himself an
> outhouse with a seat. It was kept very clean and it
> was a good idea. It was practical for him to be able
> to sit. But this was regarded as a terrible idea in
> the village. People just began gossiping and saying
> how something was wrong with my father, that he
> was out of his mind. "Just look what he built, why
> don't you go there and see, go to his house and see
> the nice seat he has in his outhouse!" For days and
> days people didn't talk about anything else. But
> even though they gossiped all those who came and
> visited us found it was really comfortable, clean and
> much neater this way. Lots of people built their
> own. But my cousins resented it. Somehow because
> they are younger and one of them is working in
> town, they feel more educated. They resented the
> talk about their uncle. So they never built one.
> But they live next door to us and come into our
> yard.

New material comforts, new technologies, are adapted not only
by an individual, a family, a household, but by the village as
a social entity. All share in the pride of new acquisitions.
Such events can build social solidarity but they can also pro-
voke jealousies and may engender conflicts. In a village
community of this type there is no clear dividing line between
private and public matters.

> No matter what you have in your house it will
> be public immediately. Once, when I was away in
> Belgrade my parents bought everything new for
> their two bedrooms. They spent quite a bit of
> money. I came home on the train which stops in our
> village but I had to walk quite a way so that I
> passed more than a dozen houses. I reached the
> first house and a woman came out. She greeted me
> and said, "How are you? I haven't seen you for a
> long time! I have something to tell you. It's a
> surprise. But I wouldn't like to be the first to tell
> you."
> "Really, what is it?" I asked.

"Are you going to be surprised when you get
to your house!"
So I asked, "Why, what happened? Anybody
sick?" And I was really scared because she was
acting so mysterious.
She said, "Oh, no. When you get there you
will see. As a matter of fact I will tell you. Your
parents bought all new things, all new furniture,
new mattresses, and you will see it, it is beautiful.
We all went to look."
So, of course, in walking by another house the
woman came out and told me the same story and how
it was a secret and that there would be a surprise
for me. Finally I reached my house and I started
smiling and my sister said she wanted to surprise
me. She said "Come in," and I said, "I know."
And she was hurt because they really wanted to
surprise me, and they asked me how I knew. And I
told them that the whole neighborhood knows and
that I had passed many houses. That's what people
in the village do. It's very important to have something to talk about. So you can see how neighbors
and relatives, but particularly relatives, make things
public.

New technologies of mass communication can provide important
propaganda outlets, as well as new sources of information.
They can also create new patterns of use of leisure time and
restructure social interaction. But since items such as the
radio require learning a pattern of listening, or of least passive receptivity, they cannot immediately begin to function
primarily as channels of one-way communication. Evaluating
the content of what is communicated must relate to previous
knowledge and be diffused through existing patterns of social
interaction. It seems difficult to realize that listening alone to
a radio or phonograph is something we learn as children; it
does not come automatically when adults encounter the radio
for the first time. Initially, at least, it must fit into a familiar
social context. The radio can then serve to stimulate social
interaction. Understanding the precise content of what is
being communicated is often not directly relevant.

We were the first family in the village to get a
radio. My father got a radio in the fall. It was
muddy and rainy. First of all, children would come
every afternoon and adults every evening. Actually
it wasn't the first radio. There was a man who
worked for the factory, a technician or engineer,
and he built one for himself with earphones. But he
was never around the village so people didn't bother

him to go and listen. But we got our radio, a real
radio, in 1949, just a few months after we received
electricity in the village. The people started coming
and listening and looking every evening.

First, they drank a tremendous amount of wine.
They drank everything my father had that winter.
They also ate all our dried meat, everything. They
ate and they dirtied everything. It was almost impossible to live because we were never free. They
would come to listen to the Voice of America and
everything else. Lots of them would just be surprised to see a radio. I remember their remarks
like, "Look, a little box and there is a man inside,"
these were old people. There were lots of stories
about how it worked. They said that the man must
be on this little hill close to our village. They were
serious, I couldn't laugh. They would say, "I
know. I was born long before you, so I saw many
things and I'm telling you how it works. I'm not
fifty years old for nothing."

They would open the window so anyone within
three miles would hear the radio and come to the
house. There were always arguments about the program. In the evening there was news and they
would hear one word and cling to it. For example,
the announcer might say, "Thirteen years ago there
was war between...." And they would say, "Oooh
war!" And they wouldn't listen any more. They
would say, "I told you. I heard a rumor about this
war, of course." Then a discussion develops about
war. Some youngster would come and say, "While
you're talking why don't we listen to music?" And
they'd say, "No! Such important news, about war.
Get out of here! Women and children should not
listen to such things. That's very important. We're
in war and you're talking about music!" So there
would always be an argument.

This also happened in my family. My sister
and I would sometimes like to listen to music and my
father would say, "No." He would sit there with his
plum brandy and listen to the news but not really
hearing the news. When I would ask him what the
news was, what's new in the world, he would say,
for example, they are talking about some country in
Africa which is called Colombia and there were some
men who went to England who died. There were
things which had no connection with what the announcer had said. He had heard a piece here and a
piece there, which he made into a bit of news which
was unreal.

They also didn't like classical music. My
brother-in-law would sometimes put it on and my
father would say, "It's not music. They are making
noises like my wife in the kitchen." But folk music
is very popular as was a special program for farmers
which they began to have on Sunday morning, some
time after 1950. They would listen to this very
carefully, particularly the younger peasants. They
also had folk music between the farm news. Now almost everyone in the village has a radio.

Radio was introduced in a private social context. Television,
however, in part because of its high initial cost, was introduced in a public setting, at the village school. Like the
radio it was much more easily understood by the young.
Their greater adaptability to new technology and their superior
formal education helped to undercut and modify the former
pattern of respect for the older generation who had once been
the source of the accumulated wisdom of earlier generations.

Similar things happened when TV came to the
village. That was in about 1960. At that time they
got a set for the school. I took my aunt, who was
very old. She had never seen a movie. There was
a boxing match. It was very funny because she was
so scared and so excited. She thought it was such
an immoral thing that we were all sitting there
letting those people beat each other inside this little
box where they were so helpless. She was yelling
and everybody was laughing.
She didn't believe me when I told her that they
were not in the box. I said that there were waves
like radio that came through wires. And she said,
"People going through the wires? You're telling me
this!" She looked at me as if I were crazy. When
the program was finished she was furious. She
looked behind it, she looked inside it. People were
laughing and the youngsters wanted her to come
every evening to make fun. But she was so mad.
She didn't want to talk to me. "How could you
bring me to see such a thing? People are beating
each other there, young boys, nice boys, like my
sons! Those people were all looking and nobody
helps them!"

These initial moments in village history have passed and now
both radio and TV are common in rural homes and villagers
have become more sophisticated. It is necessary to see these
innovations in terms of not only what they have added to village life but what they have displaced. Before radio and TV

there were spinning bees, especially in the fall and winter when village women, girls and young men would get together. The formal purpose was to accomplish a domestic task, but these were times when there was a chance to sing together, tell stories and engage in informal courting. Perhaps even more important and certainly more frequent was the opportunity for children to hear folk tales and epic narratives from their parents and close relatives. Since this passing on of tradition was oral it had a directness and intimacy lacking in the mechanical affect of mass communications. Such contacts also helped reinforce the sense of the village as a social entity. All these activities required an active participation and not the passive receptivity of radio listening and television viewing. This is not to say that if one watches television or listens to radio actively it is not possible to be informed more directly about a wider world, but rather that the activity is essentially passive or supplementary, i.e., the radio is often listened to while performing some other task.

> Sedelka means to get together, to sit down and talk. It does not mean particularly to work a lot because this is the time when all harvesting is finished and people are free from work. Young girls and women now have a chance to knit. A fire is made from the waste after the flax is beaten. Young people usually gather and build the fire. It is out on the village street. Everybody comes, people bring chairs and something to drink and they stay there and sit around the fire, then older people come too. On these occasions stories are told; ghost stories, tales about personal experiences, and then people sing. Then there is betting and dares. "I'll bet you two liters of plum brandy that you wouldn't dare to go to the cemetery now!" Young people like this kind of joke. After a while the fires are put out and everyone goes home.

Learning a curing incantation from a traditional healer is also recalled:

> When I was a little girl I asked her to teach me those magic words to help people when they have headaches. She told me to bring a liter of plum brandy and come to her under a young plum tree giving fruit for the first time. We met there. She told me I should not ask questions, but that I should climb the tree and listen. She would sit under the tree and tell me. I should repeat what she said and not ask any questions. So I climbed the tree and she sat under the tree slowly sipping plum brandy.

> She started telling me a verse. Then she told me
> how to deal with the evil eye. So I sat there in the
> plum tree and then she told me, "that's enough for
> today." She liked me particularly because I was the
> only one among the young people who showed any
> interest. I told her that I really believed every-
> thing she said.

A basic problem of change concerns the nature of relationships
within the extended family which have altered in response to
the diverse pressures of modernization. The model we are
often given in viewing social life in rural Eastern Europe is
one of strict sexual division of labor, or patriarchal authority
and of large families. In the postwar period, with the onset
of industrialization it is frequently assumed that patriarchal
authority has declined and the nuclear family has replaced the
extended family. Such simplistic models have little analytical
utility because they mask a variety of interrelationships. I do
not intend to develop a model here but rather, by presenting
firsthand descriptive data, to suggest some of the complexities
which have always been present in village life.
    A characteristic form of household structure in Eastern
Europe has been the extended family. In the Balkans this
cultural prototype has been the zadruga. Patriarchal authority
and descent in the male line provides the context in which the
core of the coresident group, sharing a common economy, has
been a father and his married sons with their children. At
the basis of this organization has been the acceptance of
hierarchal authority relations among a father and his sons,
between a husband and wife and the working out of essentially
egalitarian relationships among sons- and daughters-in-law.
Crucial to the functioning of such a group has been the allocation of specialized tasks by the patriarchal household head
on the basis of sex and age. The basis for the continuation
of such extended family groups over time has been the continued residence of sons in the household and the inheritance
of property, principally land.

> My father lived in a zadruga. My grandfather
> had three sons and two daughters. The sons all
> married and lived together in the old house, which
> was later ours. My father was the youngest brother,
> and I had two uncles. One of my aunts eloped with
> a man who was already married. This was very bad
> for our family name. My grandfather chased her out
> with a gun. He wanted to find her and kill her.
> My father and uncles took part in the chase. Even
> today when his sister comes to visit, my father, who
> is the only surviving brother, is not completely
> delighted to see her. He acts indifferently toward
> her.

She has continued to live with that man, who
finally separated from his first wife. This aunt of
mine never received a dowry. When my other aunt
married the household gave her a dowry. This included a little land, a hectare, which was unfortunately next to the river. Because of frequent floods
and erosion only about 30 are of the original hectare
remained.

I don't remember my grandfather. They say
that he died suddenly, that he had an ulcer or
something. This happened just before my father got
married. When my mother, who came from a very
wealthy family, arrived she brought a large dowry.
This was not only the personal trousseau of things
she had made but also a hectare and a half of land
from her father. It was good vineyard land. But
my father and his middle brother never got along
very well. My father had always thought of separating, so right after their father's death was a
good time. My father asked his mother if she
would like to live with him in the old house, and the
two older brothers built houses right next to ours.
Even today my mother and the wife of my second
uncle are not on speaking terms. It's funny. They
are from the same family, the same village; they
lived only about three houses apart in that village,
but they stopped speaking the moment my mother
married into the family. My aunt said that it was
because of her that my mother married into the
family, but they still wouldn't speak. Years later
we children tried to get them on better terms, to
make peace, but we could not.

My grandfather had died suddenly and had left
no will or instructions. All three brothers got together and decided that they wanted to separate.
They first divided the best land, so everyone got a
little piece of this good land, even though they
broke it up into smaller parcels. This was in 1935.
The division was approximate. Now, for example,
you can see that my middle uncle has more land in
one place than the others. This was because they
measured with ropes. Then they divided the vineyards. This caused an argument because there are
two hills. One is near the village called Gilja but
this land is not as good as the one on a hill on the
way to town, known as George's Hill. Near the town
the vineyards are very good and produce a kind of
grape called Smederevka. What happened was that
my older uncle said that he wanted all his vineyard
land on George's Hill. My father and my middle

uncle said that no, it couldn't be done. So then he said, "Okay, I'll give you a piece of good land if you give me the good vineyard." He wanted to have all his vineyard in one place. Finally he did make an agreement with my middle uncle, giving him 50 ares of good wheat land, and in return he received that uncle's share of the vineyard. But my father didn't want to do this, so now the sons of my older uncle have a large vineyard while ours, next to it, is very small.

When they started to divide the household property it was assumed that everything belonged to their parents. But this raised problems because of what the brides had brought. How were they going to divide the things that the brides had brought? This led to arguments about the division. My father thought that certain items belonged to his mother, while one of his sisters-in-law maintained that they were hers. So things didn't get divided in quite the right way. But after they started having their own families, relationships improved. After they had separated nobody talked to anyone else. But they finally finished the dividing and they were separate.

We still have certain things which belonged to my grandparents. What they did was to bring everything into one room - all the forks, all the spoons and say, "One for you, one for you, one for you," dividing everything by three. Grandmother, who decided she was going to stay with my father, said that she was going to take certain things for herself rather than giving them to my uncles. Thus my father got, for example, his mother's wedding chest and sofre [a Turkish-style low kitchen table], while my uncles got little three-legged stools.

They had lots of sheep. It was very funny. My oldest uncle knew exactly which sheep were the best and gave the most milk, so they started the dividing with good ones for each. They did the same with the pigs. The funniest thing was the corn. The actual division took place in the fall, after the harvest. They actually divided by ears of corn, "One for you, one for you." So they sat there for two days until it was all divided.

There was one big house where they all lived while their father was alive but there was also a new house being built at the time he died. When they divided my middle uncle remained living in the old house while he built a house for himself with the help of his brothers. That was an odd situation because they were angry and not speaking to each other, yet all living together. Each had his property in his own room and the storehouse was divided into thirds with boards separating the corn. They also divided the sheep hutch in three parts. Then the children would go out to watch the sheep, my older sister with our sheep, and my cousin with his family's sheep. They didn't even agree that one child should watch all the sheep. But they did help each other with the house building. My father felt that he should do it because he wanted to get rid of them, to get them out of the house. As a matter of fact they didn't hire any masons. The three brothers did all the building themselves. One of these two houses still stands. The original house in which we lived was torn down when my father came home from Germany in 1944.

When we built our new house, one uncle was already dead, and the other was very ill, but his sons helped. Now, I have no uncles but I do have three cousins. The sons of my older uncle lived together in a sort of zadruga with their mother in one house until last year. One son is working in town as a store clerk and the other is working the land. They were happy until they got married. As soon as they married the new wives didn't get along at all. What they did was to build exactly the same kind of house on either side of their old house. They continued to live in the old house while the younger brother worked and brought home money from his job and the older brother farmed until the two new houses were finished.

I was there the day they divided and it was very sad. Everyone cried. They decided that they were ready to separate and it was now a question of where the mother would go. Finally she decided she was going to live with her younger son. The division occurred on the day of their slava [the feast day of the family's patron saint]. It was time to transfer the kolac [the ceremonial loaf]. The candles and the loaf had been set out and the mother sat there and began dividing things. She distributed everything, one to each of her sons, everybody sat there and cried. Finally they broke the kolac in half. Each brother took half and went into his own new house. Then they invited friends and each had a slava feast. First, the older brother invited the younger brother to come and have lunch, and for supper the younger brother invited the older brother to come to his house. My father was present during all of this and he gave them advice

because he is the only uncle and the oldest one in
the family. These two cousins still come and ask
him certain things, more like a father. Our houses
are so close together. They always continue to help
my mother and father. They also continue to help
each other.

The younger brother is very bright. He is
particularly concerned with educating his children
and also with the education of his brother's children. For example, when the daughter of his older
brother happened to have gotten a bad grade, the
older brother said, "You are not going to school any
more, you are stupid." Then the younger brother
started talking to his older brother saying that she
would improve and finally convincing him that he
should permit the girl to continue. She did improve
the following year and went on in school. The older
brother always did little things around his younger
brother's house while his brother was working in
town. He would always help his sister-in-law with
certain things such as pasturing their sheep with
his, for the younger brother has to work on the
land in addition to his job in town. What this
younger brother does is to let his wife work a
certain number of days for his older brother and, in
turn, the older brother and his wife work together
to help the younger brother finish his farm tasks.

An important perspective gained from an account such as this
is to help us understand that even when extended families
divide, their relationships continue, although they function in
quite a different way than when they were all under one roof
sharing a common economy. They continue to interact with
one another in an intensive way and to cooperate in ways
which are economically significant. An important conditioning
factor is geographic proximity, since they continue to live on
what was formerly common land and thus often end up as
neighbors. The case cited, where one brother remains a
farmer and the other brother commutes to a job in town shows
the ways in which they assist each other. The older brother
helps with the agricultural economy while the younger brother
takes an interest in the schooling of his older brother's children, presumably with a view to their eventual social mobility.
We can also see with these examples over two generations how
division was a natural event in the cycle of the extended
family, with the division of property and cooperative construction of new houses marking the fission. However, given
the new avenues of mobility for the third generation it seems
unlikely that this kind of division will be repeated. It is also
important to stress that the surviving parent, often the

mother, is taken care of by one of the sons and that this
assumption of responsibility is reflected in the way that the
property is divided. There is a tendency for the parent(s) to
remain with the youngest son and so there is an incipient
pattern of ultimogeniture.

The ideal pattern of the zadruga was one where authority
rested on a consenual basis with the eldest male usually being
the formal head. The common pattern has the key ties among
a father and his married sons as the basic social bonds. The
survival of the unit then rested on the working relationship of
a father and his sons, with the essential cooperative support
of the mother and the daughter-in-law. There were various
strains implicit in these relationships and they became increasingly more difficult to maintain as life span increased and
parents commonly survived to old age. Patriarchal authority
was no longer unquestioningly accepted. At the same time
expectations for personal consumption and individual achievement were raised, new economic opportunities developed, and
women were in the position to inherit property. The increasing tendency for women to have more formally egalitarian
roles created critical strains in this social unit.

In the zadruga the father was the head of the
household and controlled the economy of the whole
family. He paid the taxes, assigned the labor, controlled all the money, deciding on family expenditures, and went to town to sell the important things.
He demanded obedience from all members and his
word was final in all important decisions. Education
was not considered important and only a few people
went to school [beyond the fourth grade] and these
few were boys. The father was responsible for
finding wives and husbands for his children and he
made all the arrangements for the dowries and
weddings. Often the young people never saw each
other before they were married but they rarely
dared to complain. The main considerations for
finding a wife for a son were that a girl be of good
family, bring a good dowry and be strong so that
she could do hard physical labor. The father also
sought to find a young man of good family for his
daughter.

The obedience the father expected from his
children was even greater for his daughter-in-law.
The Serbs have a saying, "the daughter-in-law is
our right hand"; this is true because when she
arrives in the new household she is expected to help
everyone. She must particularly honor her parents-
in-law and has to pay more attention to pleasing
them then to pleasing her husband. The father-in-

law usually demanded a great deal of labor before he was satisfied. The daughter-in-law must be particularly careful with regard to her mother-in-law. She must act distant toward her husband because the mother often fears losing her son when he gets married. The daughter-in-law must do the household work; clean, sew and wash and even help a sister-in-law prepare her trousseau.

In this situation there were many strong hostilities, especially if the family was large and included several brothers and their wives, plus sisters, mother and father. The majority of the hostility was felt by the head of the house since he had the authority, or toward the mother-in-law since she had control over the daughters-in-law. But people rarely dared to tell openly of their complaints. Thus frequently aggressions were taken out on other members of the household. When daughters-in-law argued, the frequent cause was feelings toward the mother-in-law, which had to be directed elsewhere. If the mother-in-law seemed to favor one daughter-in-law, the second daughter-in-law would express her anger at the other young woman rather than at her mother-in-law.

Sons and daughters rarely dared to complain to their father. Wives frequently complained to their husbands and were a cause of quarrels between brothers. There were many things to argue about. When a large group of people living together in close quarters, each with different needs and wants and when all decisions depend upon one member it is very difficult for peace and a smooth life to follow. How smooth life was depended on the skill of the zadruga head.

The authority of the father was by no means absolute and if he abused his role he could cause the splitting up of the household.

An old man was the father of four married sons, all of whom had children. He was very strict but finally took to drinking a lot. The family had a lot of land but with the father drunk most of the time and making decisions when drunk, the economy of the zadruga declined greatly. In addition, when drunk he used to insult the other members of the family, beat his grown sons, and punish their wives. This brought shame on the family and finally the sons decided to break up the zadruga. They all separated. Nobody wanted the father to live with

them so the old man and his wife had to remain alone
in their house until he died.

There was another similar case when the father
began drinking a lot and spending the money which
his sons earned. This caused a great argument in
which the sons beat their father. The oldest son
then took control of the lands and became head of
the zadruga. The father, in this case, remained in
the house but his authority was gone.

Conflicts among men could occur due to the
division of labor. For example, if, in assigning
work, the head of the household told the older son
to take a scythe and mow all day and the younger
son to go tie up the vines in the vineyard, this
would not be a fair division of labor. Mowing is
extremely hard physical work. Or, if one man goes
all day carrying a vine spray on his back and another watches the sheep. These inequalities occur
often, and it is very hard to maintain an equal
division of labor. Brothers complain, not to their
father, but among themselves, and so factions develop within the family.

If the father is not tactful in his remarks, another type of conflict arises. The father may say to
one son, "You are not capable of living. You are
clumsy. You are like a girl. You are not strong
enough." This can lead to a real complex and to
this brother avoiding his other brothers and breaking up the relationship. My middle uncle, for example, fell from a horse when he was very young and
hurt his leg. He was a bit lame. He did go to war
and died in Germany but he had this defect. His
father was always telling him that he was not as
capable as his two other brothers. The father would
say, "When I divide, I am not going to give you the
same share as the others. You are lazy and weak."
Actually, that is why my middle uncle started all
sorts of fights when the time came to divide. He
always was very bitter. He always said to his
brothers, "You regard me as incapable, not just
Father, but you, too, feel this way."

But now people are more in touch with modern
life. They see that the sons of other men are free
to go to town to work or are free to tell off their
fathers. By seeing these examples many sons now
dare to tell their fathers that they don't want to
listen to their requests.

In one case the father started drinking and did
not give any money to the household. The oldest
son worked in a factory in town, and the younger

brother worked on the railroad. Both were married. One day the oldest son lost his temper when the father came home drunk and started yelling at his mother. He took a big stick and slammed the father over the head and pushed him into a little room in the barn. He kept him there all day until he came to his senses. The father then started saying that he would kill the son if he did not open the door. So finally the son said, "All right you are sober now, so I'll open the door." Then the father said, "Get out of the way! Get out of my house!" So the son rented a room in the village from an old woman who lived alone. He also got credit from the factory where he worked and started building a house, near his father's house. The father said, "All right! All right!" And then the father suddenly decided that he was going to help the youngest son build a house. He didn't like the younger son either but at least the younger son did not beat him. So both brothers began to build houses close to the father's old house.

Conflicts also arise among women. When a woman arrives as a mlada or bride if she is bright enough she can pretend that she doesn't know how to do certain things. She can say, "In my Father's house I never did this kind of work," or, "I really don't know how." The other wives will show her a few times but if she still doesn't do it right, usually the mother-in-law will get annoyed and tell her never to do it again. Then the other wives will get annoyed.

Dowry also plays a great role among wives. For example, a girl comes from a rich house, bringing 10 blankets, 20 shirts, and many socks for her husband. Jealousies start. The one from the poorer family feels ashamed and would always find something nasty to say about the other wife, "Oh, I know that her aunt made two of those blankets for her, she didn't do it herself." Thus factions start. Or they can feel the mother-in-law is unfair, that she doesn't control [her portion of] the money fairly, or doesn't let all the women have a turn going to market.

Children too have a role in breaking up relationships. When they play they sometimes hit each other. One might go back and complain. The parents talk it over and one woman tells another, "You'd better tell your child not to hit mine!" These complaints start women talking to their husbands.

Descriptions like these are all based on clearly definable sex roles. It is also important to bear in mind that in any culture, including a peasant society, there is a degree of variation in which there can be a reversal of roles.

I used to like to do boys' work. I just didn't like to sit all day with my sister and try to knit one sock. I thought somehow it was more interesting to go and plow with my father all day long or do some other hard thing which all girls cannot do but some girls can. I surprised my sister by working with a scythe when I was sixteen. Mowing is very hard, and it is not girl's work but my father taught me very early how to do it. As a matter of fact he bought a small scythe for me and then later I tried to use his scythe. It was very hard because you have to keep using your muscles and stand straight and know how to stack the hay. You have to keep the same distance all the time because you don't want to cut your legs. Of course, at first I did it with grass and when I was a little older I tried it in a clover field. One day my father let me mow for an hour in the wheat field, which is very difficult, because you have to cut the wheat all in the same direction. I also liked to go and plow all day by myself, if my father helped me to set the plow in the ground (which I couldn't do because it is so heavy). It is also heavy to take down from the cart. I was tired out of my mind when I came home but I did do it and I was very proud. In the evening my father would come and put the plow back on the cart and we would go home.

My cousin likes to do girls' work. He is older than I and when I was a baby he was about fifteen and he used to come in the morning to be the first to wash me and to put my clothes on. He used to stay with the girls to sew and knit. He also likes to draw, he has a very good eye. He also likes to iron, make beds and he helped his mother a great deal, like a daughter. She was very grateful for the help. Of course, his older brothers used to tease him, call him a girl but this didn't bother him. He married but his wife was lazy. He always wanted a daughter. So they had two daughters and a son. He likes to buy the daughters dresses and sometimes he makes them himself. He brings home a pattern or makes a model and gives it to someone to sew because he doesn't have the time. Of course, before he got married his brothers told him that he can never get married that there is something strange

about him. Now, after he married and started
working in a store people stopped talking. He also
does the work on the land, but he prefers women's
work.

One of the key aspects of traditional peasant society is the
nature of the individual entrepreneurship required to dispose
of agricultural products in the marketplace. It is also here
where the peasant interacts most directly on a regular basis
with the urban world. The feeling of being caught between
two worlds comes out most acutely in recollections of marketing, a role with which the informant was familiar but which
was incompatible with her self-image as a schoolgirl.

> One time I went with nuts. I first peeled
> them, taking off the green skin. My hands were
> absolutely brown, covered with brown, but I
> couldn't do anything about that. It was 10 days
> before school was to begin. I couldn't go to school
> with such hands. It was not allowed. I looked
> terrible. But I went to sell the nuts. I was deter-
> mined to sell them and take the money and buy
> certain books. Then along came my professor of
> German. She saw me selling the nuts and asked the
> price. I felt very ashamed to ask anything of her.
> So I took a huge big bag and I filled it up and I
> gave it to my professor saying, "They're nothing.
> They're really nothing. I really don't want to sell
> these nuts. We have lots of nuts." I said this
> although it wasn't true. "Why don't you take them?"
> All the time I kept my hand behind me. I was very
> embarrassed being there and asking her for money.
> I just couldn't, so I gave her the nuts. She was
> very surprised and said, "Are you sure your mother
> is not going to be angry?" She was pleased but she
> reminded me. "Oh no, they're mine. My mother has
> nothing to do with them. Really, I just came to
> market."
> After that I sold the few kilos which I had left.
> When I came home my mother asked me how it went.
> I said that it was nothing much and that I didn't
> have enough money to buy even one book.
> Another time I was selling grapes. A woman
> came by who made me very mad. She was from the
> town. She started picking over the grapes. All the
> grapes were very nice but she just picked and
> picked. She started messing things around in my
> basket. Finally I got the scale and measured the
> amount out very nicely. As a matter of fact it was
> more than she asked for. But she said it was not

exact and that I should put in a little more. I really was angry. So I said, "I won't sell you any!" She was very surprised and told me how badly brought up I was, and that I was a village idiot. I just told her to move from my basket or I was going to call the police. She was really terrible. She spoke very loud, "What's she thinking of to treat me like this?" I decided to wait for my mother. When she came back I said, "Please sell your grapes; I can't stay here." I never liked to sell in the market. I just didn't know how to ask for the right price. I always felt ashamed to ask, because I thought it would be too much.

The descriptive recollections in this chapter are not intended to give a comprehensive picture of Eastern European peasant life. They do provide insights into the nature of peasant society as seen by an observant, young and articulate person who grew up in that environment at a time when values and the economy were rapidly changing. In part, as we have indicated earlier, it relates to a broader experience of societal change, also shared in recent times by North Americans. Particularly regarding the role of the extended family, the semisubsistence nature of peasant agriculture, and the activist role of the state in the postwar period, the events described here are more characteristic of the East European experience.

Individual accounts are, of course, conditioned by the perceptions of the person doing the retelling, and the person receiving the account, but to understand the total process of rural change over the last generation in this or any other area we need to combine the perspectives provided by these first-hand, local accounts with those derived from overall socio-economic analyses on provincial, regional and national levels.

These examples were from Yugoslavia. The experiences in countries such as Poland, Hungry or Bulgaria will have differed in degree and in emphasis, but I feel confident in asserting that they share a common theme and are easily recognizable across national boundaries.

NOTE

(1) Norman Mailer, "The Search for Carter," New York Times Magazine, September 26, 1976, pp. 82-83.

11 Continuity and Change in Latin America's Rural Structure

Henry A. Landsberger

CHANGING PERSPECTIVES IN THE STUDY OF RURAL LATIN AMERICA

Writings about rural Latin America published in the 1970s are very different both in mood and intellectual approach from those which were produced 25 or 30 years ago.

It is, of course, easy to exaggerate that difference. Enthusiasm for new perspectives has sometimes led, at least in this case, to attribute unfairly to earlier scholars a narrowness of vision, a lack of sophistication, and a naive optimism which they either did not possess, or which given some of the facts as they then were, made earlier paradigms(1) at least very understandable. And who knows whether, 20 years from now, the gloomy and semiconspiratorial interpretations of today might not in turn be seen as largely a reflection of an equally transitory state of affairs. This author is, however, sufficiently time-bound to be skeptical of such extreme relativism. Today's gloom about the state of affairs of Latin America's rural sector (as compared with the mild optimism of 20 some years ago) appears justified if only because throughout most of recent history, agriculture and therefore those associated with it have been in a state of turmoil. Rural life has painfully declined in relative importance for centuries. That, indeed, is almost by definition the nature of industrialization. And the poor have borne the brunt of those vast changes as they always bear the brunt of all changes except, possibly in the early stages of one or another revolution, when higher classes suffer too. Whether and in what ways economic systems other than today's world capitalism would have made the life of the rural poor very different is far from clear. Either way, the rural picture in Latin America is bleak and is, in my opinion, likely to remain so for decades.

Let us leave aside, then, these somewhat puristic and philosophical warnings not to exaggerate the difference between the two epochs and the very different literatures to which they gave rise. For when all is said and done, the differences are substantial, and it is appropriate to be aware of them. Twenty-five years ago, for example, writers on rural social structure would have focused largely – not exclusively, if they were prescient, but largely – on the rural setting itself and no doubt on a specific locale at that. One of the classics of the period, and a classic still – Oscar Lewis' Life in a Mexican Village (2) – may serve as an example. It typifies both what was common at the time but also, precisely, how even then the germ of future approaches could be discerned.

As would be expected from a major anthropological study, half or more of the book's chapters focus on the family, on different stages of the life cycle, on friendship, neighborhood, and local politics, and on religion, personality and belief systems. But the book begins with a discussion of economic factors and in that sense is similar to more recent monographs. There are extensive discussions of land tenure, local industry, markets and trade, status distinctions due to differences in wealth and to levels of living. And as to basic perspectives (or "paradigm") Lewis stresses already in the introduction that:

> Tepoztlan is discussed from two points of view: first, as an entity in itself, with its internal organization which includes the family, the barrio...; and second, as part of the units larger than itself such as the municipio, the state, the nation, and the world.(3)

That quotation, and particularly the final reference to "the world," illustrates that at no time were great writers completely insensitive to the relationship between the tiny spot they studied and the larger system of which it was a part. Nor was Lewis – and others like him – a writer who was an undiluted optimist, or pessimist. True, he concluded that Redfield's vision was erroneous. Redfield had portrayed rural "folk" society as the quintessence of the morally good, integrated, satisfying society, and encroaching urbanism as socially and morally destructive.(4) Yet Lewis, though far less enamored of rural society, had no illusion whatever that "modernization" was necessarily an unalloyed blessing. The book ends, if anything on a bitter, though not hopeless note, with sharp references both to the "instability and chicanery of Mexican politics" in which the Mexican peasant was a mere pawn, and references to the presence in the countryside of "Coca-Cola, aspirin, radios...." "Can Western civilization offer them no more?" is the book's final sentence. True, Lewis' analysis also stresses - as some of today's writings might not - the ominous importance of resource scarcity, of a permanent land and water shortage in the face of an exploding rural population, as well as the continued inhibiting existence at the "psychocultural level" of "primitive beliefs and values," in other words "the culture of poverty." But it has yet to be proved, as distinct from asserted with vehemence, that these are obstacles to happiness only in the setting of today's capitalist system, and that they would disappear or cease to be major obstacles in other settings.

And yet, despite the reference to external factors, Lewis' study does have a flavor very different from what would be conveyed by studies in the modern style. Above all, while the impact of the external system is admitted and its potency recognized, there is no vision and no detailed analysis of an all-important and determining world capitalist system centered in the United States and Western Europe. Changes in that system, its concrete needs and all-consuming interests, are looked upon by many writers today as being the almost exclusive determinants of events in peripheral or semiperipheral countries such as Mexico, and down to the village level. And the urban centers of these semiperipheral and peripheral countries are in turn seen as imposing, in a more or less deliberate manner, their needs on a countryside now viewed as doubly "dependent."(5)

Lewis basically saw changes in Tepoztlan as being the result of a general, classic process of "acculturation" and "cultural diffusion." Change was brought about by the building of roads, the consequent growth of new forms of transportation, and thus more contact. He emphasized the importance, for good and evil, of the expansion of the school system. And Lewis was struck by the increase in wealth following the Mexican revolution and a subsequent reform in the system of land tenure, which he saw as substantially positive, even if its effects were limited.(6) On balance, Lewis saw recent changes as having resulted in more equality and not less, even though he was fully aware of the bitter tensions inherent in rural life, both before and after "modernization."

Lewis' assessment was, of course, contrary to what had been asserted by his predecessor, Robert Redfield. Redfield, a traditionalist, had viewed urbanization (a part of what would later be called "modernization") as an almost unmitigated, destructive evil. Lewis seemed, rather, to appeal to the powers-that-were to permit the benefits of modernization to spread to the countryside. And by assuming that this was within the realm of the possible, his posture was at variance with that of today's dependency theory.

The general tenets of that theory are applied to Latin America's rural setting as they are to all other aspects of Latin American society, and may be summarized according to the following points.

First, the most important changes and events in the "dependent" (i.e., less developed, peripheral, or semiperipheral countries) are determined by developments in the core or metropolitan countries of what is now a worldwide capitalist system. They are not determined by forces and policies within the dependent countries themselves. Hence, according to dependency theory, it is not fruitful to study rural social structure in isolation. For example, if one wishes to understand the increase during the last 30 years in the landless labor force as compared with the labor force resident on large estates, the best place to start is to study trends in world markets for agricultural products, the transfer of inappropriate high-level technology from metropolitan to peripheral countries and other macroprocesses.

Second, dependency theory maintains that in the not-even-very-long run, but certainly in the long run, most changes - especially in the rural sector of dependent societies - represent a deterioration in the relative and perhaps even in the absolute position of this sector vis-a-vis the metropolitan centers, i.e., the United States and Western Europe. It is probably even a deterioration vis-a-vis their own, more modernized urban sectors. This is one aspect of the manner in which the core countries inevitably expropriate the peripheral countries, especially their agricultural sectors.

Third, in the above sense, and in many others and for many other reasons, dependency theory maintains that "underdevelopment" develops out of being dependent on the metropolitan countries. It is the inevitable inverse of the positive development of the core countries, a dynamic which cannot be overcome while dependency continues. This is the thesis of "the development of underdevelopment" proposed by Andre Gunder Frank in the late 1960s.

Fourth, dependency theory further argues that dependency will in all likelihood not be broken without a revolution which will have some of the characteristics of a war of liberation (from the core countries). Postulating a need for a major social upheaval rests on the assumption that there exist in the peripheral countries a number of classes and interest groups with a great deal of power, whose interests are congruent with those of the core countries, and who are supported by these countries.

Fifth, according to dependency theory, the all-pervasive influence of the core countries extends beyond the economic and political sectors to the educational, cultural, religious and, indeed, all other societal sectors and activities.

Sixth, all the above, according to dependency theory, is brought about in large measure without deliberate planning. It is the work of the "hidden hand" of latter-day capitalism, or the "half-hidden hand" of multinational corporations, which are seen as playing a key (negative) role. However, when driven to the wall, i.e., threatened by the possibility of a profound change, the core countries and/or their allies in the dependent countries will manipulate the system deliberately, including the protection of their interests by force. This proposition is supported by United States intervention in Guatemala in 1954 where, incidentally, the threat of specifically agrarian changes was certainly one element provoking the mobilization of American interests. The military take-overs in Brazil (1964) and Chile (1973) and the swing to the right of the Peruvian military after 1975 are also seen as supportive evidence by <u>dependista</u> theorists. For in all three countries, important commercial interests were beginning to be threatened and, from the point of view of this chapter, the fact that agrarian unrest was on the rise in these countries is of special relevance. The United States and other Western countries, or at least the sectors representing the corporate capitalist interests of the core countries, were pleased with, and sometimes actively supported, the elimination of elements moving toward "independence." This, of course, provides further grist to the mill of dependency theory.

Finally, in the agricultural sector as in the urban, the primary focus of analysis no matter what the specific issue, should be on the control of economic resources - land and water - and on the control of the forces of coercion. Other institutions - religion, community, family, education - are secondary, relatively speaking.

This is obviously not the place for a detailed evaluation of "dependency theory" or its predecessors. The Marxist version goes back to the writings of Karl Marx himself: references to the worldwide spread of capitalism are to be found in the <u>Communist Manifesto</u>. Non-Marxist Latin American economists were grappling with these phenomena since shortly after World War II. Their analysis was initiated by Dr. Raul Prebisch, the first director of the Economic Commission for Latin America (ECLA-CEPAL). My aim here is simply to describe the kind of change in perspective which the literature on the rural structure of Latin America has undergone in the last decade or two. The reader should bear this change in mind when reading a particular monograph or article, asking himself: When was it published? and, of course, Who wrote it? But more immediately, for purposes of this chapter, I would like to link the following discussion of some of the major characteristics of Latin American rural social structure with these changed perspectives. Hence, it was necessary to describe briefly the recent substitution of "paradigms." The note of skeptical ennui which occasionally creeps into this chapter when touching on what appear to be excessive claims to novelty on the part of dependency theorists, is now shared publicly by at least one of its originators, Brazilian social scientist Fernando Enrique Cardozo. The title of an article by him - "The Consumption of Dependency Theory in the United States" - is sufficient to indicate its flavor.(7)

SOCIAL STRUCTURE AT THE LOCAL LEVEL: FROM "CORPORATE" VERSUS "OPEN" COMMUNITIES TO "THE TRIANGLE WITHOUT A BASE"

Writings in the 1950s and the early 1960s described a bewildering variety of kinds of rural social structure: settlement patterns, types and sizes of landholdings, relations to the market, prestige and power hierarchies in villages and cultural and personality orientations. They had to do so if they were to be true to the facts.

One unusual and now classic essay by Richard N. Adams(8) focused exclusively on the great variety of landless labor, and the many different forms it took. Such labor would usually be found on large estates, which authors customarily divided (at the least) between traditional haciendas used for prestige purposes, underutilized and undercapitalized, and more commercially oriented, more efficient plantations. Landless labor might be resident or nonresident on the hacienda and plantation; if not resident on the estate, it might be resident locally or it might be purely migrant. Its rewards might be in the form of cash or in kind or in land; or it might pay for rented land in variable "shares" or in a fixed cash rent. And, of course, the same person might play several of these roles, and the estate use several different kinds of labor.

But more usual were analyses which focused on landowning peasants. Such analyses would contrast relatively intact Indian comunidades, in which Indian culture patterns of language and dress, as well as indigenous systems of local government and Indian communal landholding patterns predominated, with more "modernized" villages. In the latter, mestizos or cholos (those who had adopted "Spanish" culture) would be described as constituting a local middle class, dominating and exploiting the remaining, but declining, Indian population. The seminal essays in this genre were those of Eric Wolf,(9) written in the mid-1950s. Wolf's essays are particularly interesting because the contrast between the two types of villages is already cast in economic and market - deliberately not in cultural - terms, i.e., Indian versus non-Indian. Wolf's typology contrasts "closed" communities which seek to insulate themselves from external, but also very much from internal, sources of instability (such as population pressure and internal stratification) with "open" communities which are much more integrated into a cash market, and much more stratified.   Yet the market for cash crops is not otherwise further analyzed by Wolf: there is no reference to its ultimately being the last link in the chain of a world capitalist system.   A decade and a half later, Wolf would posit "North Atlantic capitalism" very explicitly as the prime mover of events in the countryside and as the cause of peasant revolutions.(10)

But regardless of whether or not an author emphasizes these ultimate origins of the differences between one type of rural community and another, the literature has continued the distinction between culturally more traditional and economically more isolated communities on the one hand, and on the other those which are more integrated into the national economy and more mestizo.   An early, well-known example was Charles Wagley's essay, "The Peasant," contrasting two villages in Guatemala and Brazil.(11)   A more recent example, focusing on Peru to contrast Indian communities and areas which are more "modernized" is to be found in Howard Handelman's Struggle in the Andes.(12)   Both, of course, see the semi-isolated village as being under pressure and in decline.   Wagley, an anthropologist, and writing earlier, stresses the destructive role of insidious, unplanned diffusion.   Handelman, a political scientist and writing after the rural turmoil of the 1960s, puts more emphasis on the deliberate efforts of government and their hostility toward Indian communities.

But the combination of the slow disappearance of the typical "anthropological" community on the one hand (i.e., changes in the realm of reality) and on the other, the upsurge of the paradigm of dependence in the realm of intellectual approach has had the dual effects of: 1) lessening interest in the isolated traditional village, and 2) reconceptualizing it as perhaps at bottom not so different, after all, from the more modern village, or from rural labor.   From stressing variety, and attempting to account for it, the emphasis today is on the basic similarity underlying all these different peasant statuses.

The change in perspective is just that: it does not deny the facts previously established, nor does it really adduce anything startlingly new by way of fact.   It simply regards the manner in which facts had previously been analyzed as less worthy of attention.

What has been emphasized recently is that all the lower strata of rural Latin American society are both isolated and at the same time integrated, regardless of detail.   Instead of looking upon Indian communities as a dual society next to the hacienda or plantation, it is now pointed out that the so-called "isolated" Indian community in fact served as a reservoir of labor for the hacienda; that it enabled the hacienda to pay low wages because many of its laborers could supplement their income by subsistence farming in the communal sector; and that depression in the world market could be weathered as peasants withdrew from the market to subsistence farming, thus relieving the state and the property-owning classes of responsibility for them. The latter point had been made by Eric Wolf in one of his earlier essays in which, however, the stress was still on the desire of the village to control its internal affairs, not its external relations.(13)

If even the "isolated" Indian community could be seen as playing a critical role in the survival of the market-oriented plantation or hacienda, what importance could such minor differences as those between migrant and resident labor have, except, perhaps, in affecting peasant militance and causing divisions within the peasantry?

If, in one sense, all kinds of peasants and rural labor were integrated into the commercial, basically export-oriented economy of the dependent country, there was however another sense in which all were isolated. For none had direct, unmediated access to economic resources, to markets, to political power centers, or to those cultural resources such as education which ultimately conveyed or at least supported power. The lower rural strata always depended on some kind of patron or intermediary. If that intermediary was not the hacendado, then, as in the case of seemingly "independent" Indian communities, it was the official and the politician of the nearest administrative center.

The concept of the patron and his clients had been used originally in the 1950s, as a descriptive term in a variety of contexts - economic, political, cultural. It obviously had a critical connotation and indicated recognition on the part of its user of a larger national system. But a decade or two ago, the system itself was not a focus of attention or concern.

Some ten years ago, however, the fact that the Latin American peasantry always and in all respects was dependent on a broker, became systematized in the image of "the triangle without a base."(14) There was no line between points at the base of the triangle, i.e., there was no base, since one peasant did not relate to another but only upwards to a focal point. The hacendado, or the town official, in the case of Indian communities, saw to it that peasants did not combine. And they also saw to it, as long as they could, that all contact with the outside regional and national system remained in their hands. Thus, something which students had taken for granted 20 years ago - that most poor people, but especially most poor rural dwellers, have little contact both with each other and with the outside - was now reinterpreted in a broader, more system-serving and even deliberately conspiratorial manner.

As is always the case when a sociopolitical situation is portrayed in the form of a simple, graphic image, careful empirical research shows the real situation to be more complex. Thus Gitlitz's recent study of Peru (where, after all, the image of the "open triangle" originated) indicates that peasants did to some extent manage to combine even in the "bad old days."(15) They managed to resist the demands of the powers-that-be if they became too onerous, and especially if these demands exceeded what was customary and traditional, and constituted a threat to survival.(16)   Peasants had more options than a picture of uniform extreme oppression and coercion would lead one to believe.   Apart from resisting in unison as they sometimes did, many peasants availed themselves of the chance to migrate (but to what fate?) and a few have always used the possibility of rising above their fellows.

But these worthwhile corrections of an oversimplified picture should not obscure the fact that no student of Latin American rural society questions that the lot of the majority, of all but a few owners, and of a very small and heterogeneous rural middle sector, has been miserable and is often getting worse rather than better; that outright coercion, reinforced by coercion through the manipulation of vital resources, has been endemic;(17) and that with rare exception, Latin American governments until the 1960s had not even pretended that they were doing anything about this state of affairs.

PEASANT REACTION:
FROM APATHY TO REVOLUTIONARY HERO

The reaction of peasants to their deprived condition has been, of course, a topic of considerable concern to students of Latin American rural society.   And here, too, interesting changes in interpretation have occurred.

The late 1950s and early 1960s were dominated (though never totally preempted) by portrayals of the peasant as enveloped in a "culture of poverty" which made all resistance impossible, and for the most part not even desired by him. Apathetic and fearful, suspicious even - or especially - of those in a position similar to his own, oriented only to the welfare of his family, afraid that the betterment of others could be achieved only at his expense (Foster's image of "the limited good"(18)), such a peasant was an unlikely participant in a revolutionary upheaval.   At most, he might ridicule his class antagonist and cultural enemy in stylized indirect form at annual festivals, or convert his rage into somatic symptoms.(19)   And given the events of the 1940s and 1950s - or better, the absence of any large series of dramatic events during these two decades - this picture was quite realistic.

But once again, certain historical occurrences since that
time, but even more a definite change in the mood of intellectuals studying these occurrences, led to the portrayal of a
very different picture in the late 1960s, and the early 1970s.
Based on an early, and mistaken, interpretation of the Cuban
revolution as essentially a successful peasant revolt,(20) a
picture began to be portrayed of a Latin American peasantry
on the brink of revolution.   The new image of the peasantry
was reinforced by an equally exaggerated perception of the
extent of peasant support for the rurally located guerrilla
activities of groups of university students in Guatemala, Peru,
Venezuela, and Colombia in the mid-1960s.(21) The Chinese
and the Vietnamese revolutions, in which peasants did indeed
play critical, albeit only supportive, roles, appeared to support the prediction that peasants might spearhead the overthrow of institutions for which, as many saw it, Latin America
was more than ripe.   Indeed, as much as the above ambiguous
facts, it was probably the mood of a new generation of Latin
American, European and North American social scientists which
accounted for the reformulation of what the typical and the
likely peasant reaction was, and had been historically, to
deprivation and oppression.   A new generation of young
scholars was personally outraged at the conditions they found
in rural Latin America, and elsewhere; hostile to the classes
and systems they regarded as responsible for those conditions;
desirous to see dramatic change; and both hopeful that it
could and would soon occur, and fearful that it might not.

There is no question that outbreaks of peasant unrest
have been much more frequent in Latin America than anyone
had thought - and more frequent than the kind of peasant
mentality portrayed by Foster would have led one to believe
was possible.   That fact was soon established by the new,
committed scholarship and it deserves to be highlighted. In
Peru, for example, peasant unrest did not suddenly crystallize
in the early 1960s with the rent strike in the La Convencion
Valley. (22) It was frequent from at least the 1870s onward.(23)   And well before the 1960s, peasants had played
significant roles in two of Latin America's few major revolutions, the Mexican (1910-1917), and the Bolivian (1952).(24)

Both the Mexican and the Bolivian revolutions were, in
retrospect, essentially classic middle-class revolutions with a
not unusual tinge of nationalism.   In both countries, foreign
economic influence, especially American, but also British, was
considerable and was resented by many where it was present.
In both countries, wealth was extraordinarily concentrated and
the concentration probably had been increasing, not diminishing.   It thus threatened not only the poorest but also some
middle-class sectors, including middle-level landowners.   But
in addition to purely economic middle sectors, discontent was
also rife among professional and intellectual groups.   These

had been growing in size and self-confidence, but had found insufficient rewards in what was - at least in Mexico - substantial if very unequally distributed economic growth. Disaffected professionals and intellectuals contributed to the revolutionary climate as they had done in other revolutionary situations such as in Russia prior to 1917.

In both countries, the urban middle-class sectors who were the backbone of the revolution did not, of course, act primarily for the benefit of the rural poor. Far from it. A very few idealists may have acted on behalf of the peasantry, or the even smaller urban working class, and soon came to appreciate the support they could gain there. But for the most part, rural "platforms" were incorporated into revolutionary ideology only late, only partially, with reservations and with opposition, as in the case of Mexico. And the rural sector, in both Mexico and in Bolivia, rose up - to the extent that it did rise at all - after the proclamation of the urban revolt, not before it or even simultaneously with it.

With tremendous variations, and at very different times and over very different time periods, processes which were yet in some respects quite similar to those of Mexico and Bolivia took place in other Latin American countries. They, too, have had some kind of "middle-class revolution." The beginning of the decline of Chile's traditional elites is generally traced to the 1920 election of President Arturo Alessandri. A further and more substantial spurt forward occurred in 1938, with the election of the Popular Front government.(25) Neither of these periods may have been of much objective benefit to the rural sector (measurement is very difficult), but it was enough of a tremor to weaken the mold of traditional relationships. But major attention was indeed paid to the rural sector from the mid-1960s onward. By this time, the concept of agrarian reform was a political issue in all Latin American countries, partly at the instigation of the United States, which incorporated it into the declaration of Punta del Este (1961) initiating the Alliance for Progress. The Alliance for Progress, as a whole, and agrarian reform in particular, were of course motivated not only by humanitarian concerns, but very much by the desires to blunt the appeal of the Cuban revolution, including its appeal in the countryside.

In the period 1965-1973, Chile's peasantry underwent a change as substantial or almost as substantial as had that of Bolivia after 1952 and that of Mexico between 1910 and 1917 or, better, under the presidency of Lazaro Cardenas, between 1934 and 1940, when agrarian reform became truly effective in Mexico. In Peru, the period of "agitation" fell between 1962 and 1968, with dramatic reform following the military revolution of 1968. In Venezuela, land reform followed the ouster of dictator Perez Jimenez in 1957 and the ascent to power of the Accion Democratica.(26)

In all these countries, the creation of peasant movements preceded or accompanied the process of structural change. But the word "movement" can easily mislead, for it covers everything from widespread, but uncoordinated, essentially local, unrest and protest, to the establishment - perhaps at a later stage - of more structured organizations on a regional or even national level. It obscures differences in membership - as varied as the peasantry and rural labor itself - and of goals - from raising wages to the recovery of communal lands, from reformist to radical. It hides differences in leadership and sponsorship - from those, usually local groups, in which peasants themselves may play key roles, although rarely exclusively so, to those helped, and perhaps dependent on, local intellectuals and middle-class supporters, to those essentially sponsored by outside entities, whether political parties, the Catholic church, or government agencies. And any specific movement may embody several of these characteristics. It may be government sponsored and yet harbor groups at the local level which are peasant led, sometimes heavily influenced by urban intellectuals.(27)   It may espouse several goals and be internally in conflict over them.   Periods of change and fluidity - such as marked the late 1960s and early 1970s in Latin America - support a kaleidoscope of groups, each itself composed of different elements.

But in a series of other Latin American countries, the stage of agitation was never followed by one of concrete reform.   With greater or lesser degree of violence, and with greater or lesser degree of explicit intervention by the military, the process of structural reform in the countryside was halted in these countries, or never allowed to begin.   In Brazil, the intervention of the military was overt and dramatic: a government was ousted partly because it had permitted widespread organization in the countryside.(28)   In Ecuador and Colombia, the reform process simply never got underway because it was very deliberately stymied by bureaucratic lethargy and recourse to legalisms.   And in other countries where massive reform did get thoroughly underway - in Chile, above all - the process came to an abrupt halt, and has been in part reversed.   Peru, too, should be included here although there has been little dramatic violence.   Indeed, so should Mexico be included under this rubric.   In both Mexico and Peru, the extension of the reformed "sector" is not being seriously, as distinct from rhetorically, discussed by those in power.   The issue is, rather, that of consolidating and reorganizing that which now exists - "limiting the damage" done by reform, or "internally strengthening the reform sector" according to the mood of - and the facts - confronting these and other increasingly conservative, often military, governments.

WHERE IS THE PEASANTRY NOW?

An accurate overall evaluation of what - and how much, if anything - peasants have gained as a result of such changes as have taken place is necessarily very difficult and would in any case be quite misleading. Differences between countries are, obviously, monumental. And so are the abrupt changes which can occur both upward and downward even in one country in as short a historical period as a mere five years. Beyond these difficulties facing anyone who wishes to generalize are such problems of measurement as whether subjective feelings (e.g., "feeling free"), or the objective facts of continuing poverty ought to be the criteria. And if the latter, whether comparison with the past, with today's urban dweller, or some imaginary might-have-been situation should be the measure of improvement. Are we to evaluate the peasant organizations which now exist in so many countries as positive avenues of peasant expression and participation or as pseudo-organizations, explicitly or at least de facto used by governments to defuse genuine independent peasant pressure groups? These are some of the difficulties facing anyone wishing to evaluate the status of Latin America's peasantry today.

There are, nevertheless, some broad generalizations which can be made. First, at the level of individuals and their happiness, it is generally accepted that where massive land reform has taken place, and whatever the objective facts of the situation, peasants prefer the new situation to the old one, especially if they were previously dependent on a hacienda. Freedom from personal restraint and domination is deeply appreciated. The new, more complex, but still continuing dependence, now on a variety of "brokers" - local politicians, buyers, lenders, lawyers - is to the peasant preferable to subjugation to one individual. There is also no question that in most Latin American countries, the rural population has greater access to education than it had before (in terms of absolute numbers even if sometimes not in percent terms) and that it highly values that access. So much for the positive.

Second, in none of the countries in which massive land reform was tried has it resulted in a buoyant, healthy, smallholding peasant economy, and/or a healthy rural cooperative economy. The reformed sector is generally a deeply troubled one. Productivity does not increase as fast as in the remaining, and often once again growing, private sector; the individual peasant is probably deeply in debt to the public lending institutions which are usually set up by the state as part of the overall reform package; and certainly the growing labor force is not substantially absorbed by the reformed sector. (Nor, of course, is it absorbed in other sectors and

least of all in the private agricultural sector.) To what extent
this economic malaise is due to unbenign neglect - resource
starvation - on the part of governments which may have cooled
on agrarian reform, or to what extent it is due to the fact
that neither small-scale nor cooperative farming are socially
and economically viable, particularly in a setting of rapid
population growth and of limited land and water resources is a
much disputed question. But few observers deny that the
reformed sector is generally not a healthy one.

Finally, at the level of politics, of political "culture" and
political dependency, the picture is a complex one with perhaps many shadows as well as highlights. After reform, and
the "middle-class revolution" and political liberalization of
which it was a part, peasant organizations have generally
operated with greater freedom and effectiveness than they did
under the old regime, if, indeed, they were even allowed to
exist before. Nevertheless, most students of these movements
and organizations would question the extent to which they are
or ever could be effective in representing the peasants' interests. And there is certainly a question about the extent to
which they are run by peasants.

In some countries, such as Mexico, the peasant confed-
eration is little more than the downward extension of an essentially bourgeois-dominated, quite authoritarian, one-party
state. The Confederacion Nacional Campesina (CNC) is not a
grass roots-upward organization and at best serves to solve
individual grievances much as the old city machines did in the
United States - and similarly, in exchange for votes. The
kind of "bossism" and "clientelism" to which this gives rise is
surely an improvement over the absolute dependence which
existed previously, but it is not genuine autonomy. In other
countries, peasant movements are divided and thereby weakened on an ideological basis, as are urban trade unions, each
guided more by ideologically and politically committed leaders,
often middle class and intellectual, than by peasants pursuing
their interest as they themselves define them. And, of
course, these organizations are weakened by economic conflicts
within the peasantry itself.(29) The mood of disappointment
which generally assails those observing the supposedly improved state of affairs is well illustrated in a recent survey by
Singlemann.(30) And once again, the question is: to what
extent is the continuing political powerlessness of the peasantry due to the deliberate institutional action of other classes
hostile to its interest? And to what extent is that powerlessness due to divisions within the peasantry itself and indeed, due to lingering cultural traits of apathy, suspicious-
ness, and fatalism?

However that may be, the continuing economic and political malaise of the peasantry even after a middle-class revolution or after middle class-sponsored change has been graph-

ically described by recent authors, many of whom write from a neo-Marxist dependency or world-system point of view. In other words, the implication is that but for a bourgeoise-capitalist system, whether local or worldwide, the situation of Latin America's peasantry would be better.

PERMANENT CONSTRAINTS ON THE PEASANTRY

My purpose in this final section is not to either agree with or challenge what is, in any case, an unprovable assertion since it concerns itself with might-have-beens. It is, rather, to point to certain facts and conditions which are likely to leave the peasantry in a far from enviable situation regardless of the sociopolitical system under which they live - or, at least, are in practice likely to live.

Primary among these constraints are two economic ones. First, no matter what the system, a nation's gross national product is limited in any one year. Even if one assumes that it is higher under a socialist than a capitalist system (and Cuba's economic performance gives one pause) it will still be limited. That product will have to be apportioned, if not between rich and poor (these differences will surely be lessened in a socialist society), then certainly between urban dwellers and those of interest here, those living in the countryside. All governments manipulate this distribution, whether by taxation and transferring income from one sector to another, or by manipulating relative prices, that is, by raising the prices of agricultural products relative to industrial ones, or doing the opposite. The decision of which sector to disappoint, and which to gratify - whether to cheapen food for the urban sector, or whether to permit high real incomes in the agricultural sector through fixing high prices for agricultural products - is a tough decision which all governments have to make.

There is no reason to think that any system of government other than a capitalist one is more likely to favor farmers and antagonize urban sectors than is a capitalist government. There is certainly no a priori reason to think a socialist government would tilt the scales a bit more in the direction of the rural sector. Indeed, there is some reason at the level of ideology to think that it would not. Socialism is more an urban than a rural ideology, keener on industrialization than on agrarianism. Whether the recent drastic "return to the land" policies instituted in Cambodia, and to a lesser extent in Vietnam, are harbingers of a change in ideology and policy is difficult to say. In any case, no one claims that they have benefited peasants as distinct from hurting urban sectors.

But if a socialist regime were to favor agriculture, the resources available to do so for both consumption and investment purposes would still necessarily be very limited. However self-evident, that fact is rarely made explicit. And the shortage is not alone one of material goods for consumption and investment, it is also one of human resources, of personnel skilled in giving technical assistance, in helping to organize production and marketing, and in management in general.

The second economic constraint is that of the rapid rise in population in the countryside and elsewhere. In a socialist society, the hope is that general egalitarian policies such as opening the world of work to women, as well as positive social policies such as providing women and everyone else with better health care and information about health, will lead to a reduction in the birth rate and thereby lessen the problem in the agricultural sector created by a rapidly increasing population. But even if there were no gap between such hopes and reality,(31) relieving the pressure of population on resources is still a matter of time. And during the transition, economic improvements for the peasantry are likely to be severely limited.

The second major constraint on the peasantry is political. It is clear that even quite progressive bourgeoise governments - such as the Venezuelan or the Chilean governments between 1965 and 1973 - have sought to channel, to manipulate and, ultimately, even to limit peasant political activity. That outright totalitarian governments of the Right, such as those of Brazil, Honduras, and Chile since 1973, have done so hardly need to be said. And those countries in some kind of a "middle" in-between - the Mexican, the Colombian, and latterly, the Peruvian - have also obviously intervened in peasant politics. In short, no one leaves the peasantry politically free and autonomous.

The real question is whether any government, no matter what the nature of the regime, is likely to restrain itself from intervening when the stakes, both positive and negative, are so high. Almost by definition, an autonomous class or interest group implies a group which will pursue and pressure for the implementation of some policy different from that foreseen by other groups, including governments representing "society as a whole." Why should any government care for such a scenario, especially a government that believes that it has worked out an economic and social policy which is to the best interest of everyone - and well may be so. But above all, such a government is likely to believe that the policies pursued by any one sector are selfish, antisocial, perhaps even inspired by old-fashioned bourgeoise and counterrevolutionary ideas and elements. The history of how the Soviet regime dealt with the "workers' opposition" in Russia in the 1920s is

certainly not reassuring. And since there is some reason to
believe, and this author is one who subscribes to the belief,
that peasants prefer to work for themselves, i.e., incline
toward a capitalist type of agriculture regardless of whether or
not it is the most beneficial for them materially, there is
indeed some merit to the fear that they are inclined to be
"counterrevolutionaries." Under these circumstances, are
unregulated, autonomous peasant organizations likely? Even on
a purely administrative basis (leaving aside differences over
substantive policy), what government known to man or woman
really wants to see the policies it has decided upon, and their
implementation held up, discussed, and altered? If it can
prevent such delay, it probably will.

Finally, if a utopian picture of the Latin American peasantry depicts the peasantry as being not only equal to other
groups in society, but also egalitarian and relatively unified
within itself, there is simply the age-old question: Are
equality and harmony so much part of the human makeup that
stripping away the distorting influence of capitalism will make
them flourish? Many students, including the author, would
consider continued stratification and even conflict within Latin
America's peasantry as inevitable, regardless of regime. (I
would consider such conflict inevitable, too, within industrial
labor, bureaucracies and intellectual groups.) There are
simply too many structurally built-in conflicts of interest -
zero-sum situations in a world of limited goods - for social
equality and harmony to be a likely state of affairs. And
there is, too, such a wide range of personality types in any
Latin American rural community - from hard-bitten materialistic
individualists to comtemplative humanists - that this alone
would produce a tendency toward inequality. Stratification
and conflict might lessen somewhat under other systems; they
would certainly take other forms, and they might be in part
obscured, but neither phenomenon will come close to disappearing.

NOTES

(1) To use the currently popular term. The term was
    coined by Thomas S. Kuhn in his The Structure of
    Scientific Revolution (Chicago: University of Chicago
    Press, 1962) in which he argues that major advances in
    science occur not through continuous quantitative ac-
    cretions to knowledge, but through sudden total re-
    visualizations of what the world is all about. That par-
    adigm of how science advances did not sweep the social
    sciences until the last few years!

(2)   Oscar Lewis, Life in a Mexican Village (Urbana, Ill.: University of Illinois Press, 1954).
(3)   Ibid., p. xx.
(4)   Robert Redfield, "The Folk Society," American Journal of Sociology 52 (January 1947): 292-308; and Tepoztlan - A Mexican Village (Chicago: University of Chicago Press, 1930).
(5)   For a vigorous statement of the theory as applied to Latin America, see Ronald H. Chilcote and Joel C. Edelstein, eds., Latin America: The Struggle with Dependency and Beyond (New York: John Wiley and Sons, Halstead Press, 1974). To obtain something of the flavor of the theory in all its variety and with all its internal differences, browsing through Latin American Perspectives, a journal sponsored by radical social scientists of both North and South America, may be best. Some authors wish to speak of imperialism, not dependency; some believe that there is a feudal stage in Latin America, others heatedly deny it. A balanced discussion of "dependency theory" and its predecessors, as well as a basic bibliography, is to be found in Alejandro Portes, "On the Sociology of National Development: Theories and Issues," American Journal of Sociology 82 (July 1976): 55-85.
(6)   Lewis, Life in a Mexican Village, p. 446.
(7)   Fernando Enrique Cardozo, "The Consumption of Dependency Theory in the United States," Latin American Research Review 12 (1977): 7-24.
(8)   Richard N. Adams, "Rural Labor," in Continuity and Change in Latin America, ed. John J. Jackson (Stanford, Calif.: Stanford University Press, 1964), pp. 49-78.
(9)   See, for example, Eric R. Wolf, "Types of Latin American Peasantry: A Preliminary Discussion," American Anthropologist 57 (1955): 452-71.
(10) Eric R. Wolf, Peasant Wars of the Twentieth Century (New York: Harper and Row, 1969). See especially "Conclusions."
(11) Charles A. Wagley, "The Peasant," in Continuity and Change, ed. Johnson, pp. 21-48.
(12) Howard Handelman, Struggle in the Andes, Latin American Monograph, no. 35, (Austin: University of Texas Press, 1975).
(13) Eric Wolf, "Aspects of Group Relations in a Complex Society: Mexico," American Anthropologist 58 (1956): 1065-078.
(14) The term became well known through Julio Cotler's, "The Mechanics of Internal Domination and Social Change in Peru," Studies in Comparative International Development 3 (1967-68).

(15) John S. Gitlitz, "Hacienda, Comunidad and Peasant
      Protest in Northern Peru" (Ph.D. diss., University of
      North Carolina, Chapel Hill, N.C., 1975.)
(16) The theory that peasants will tolerate being exploited in
      return, but only in return, for a guarantee of basic
      subsistence, has been elegantly argued by James C.
      Scott, The Moral Economy of the Peasant: Rebellion and
      Subsistence in South East Asia (New Haven, Conn.: Yale
      University Press, 1976).
(17) A graphic description is to be found in Ernest Feder,
      The Rape of the Peasantry: Latin America's Landholding
      System (Garden City, N. Y.: Doubleday, 1971).
(18) George N. Foster, "Peasant Society in the Image of
      Limited Good," American Anthropologist 67 (April 1965):
      296-303.
(19) Seven years before the publication of Foster's article,
      the ever-provocative Edward C. Banfield had already
      painted a very similar picture of the southern Italian
      peasant in The Moral Basis of a Backward Society (Glen-
      coe, Ill.: Free Press, 1958). Both authors were soon
      subjected to vigorous attack.
(20) The error was pointed out by Gil Carl Alroy, "The
      Peasantry in the Cuban Revolution," The Review of
      Politics 29 (January 1967): 87-99.
(21) See for example, Gerritt Huizer, The Revolutionary
      Potential of the Peasantry in Latin America (Lexington,
      Mass.: D. C. Heath, Lexington Books, 1972).
(22) Wesley W. Craig, Jr., "Peru: The Peasant Movement of
      La Convencion," in Latin American Peasant Movement, ed.
      Henry A. Landsberger (Ithaca, N. Y.: Cornell University
      Press, 1969), pp. 274-295.
(23) Edward Dew, Politics in the Altiplano (Austin: University
      of Texas Press, 1969).
(24) No comprehensive, integrated analysis exists of the role
      of the peasantry in the Mexican revolution. This is no
      doubt due, at least in part, to the fact that the revolu-
      tion was a regionalized and long drawn-out series of
      events, difficult even to date with precision. Hence
      synthesis is not easy, and the literature consists mostly
      of a series of regional studies. John Womack, Jr., Zapata
      and the Mexican Revolution (New York: Random House,
      1968), is the best known of these. For Bolivia, see
      Gerrit Huizer, The Revolutionary Potential of the Peasant-
      ry.
(25) For a history of Chile's peasantry, see Brian Loveman,
      Struggle in the Countryside: Politics and Rural Labor in
      Chile - 1919-1973 (Bloomfield: University of Indiana
      Press, 1976).
(26) See John D. Powell, Political Mobilization of the Venezu-
      elan Peasant (Cambridge, Mass.: Harvard University

288 THE PROCESS OF RURAL TRANSFORMATION

Press, 1971). For various case studies see both the
volume by Landsberger, ed., Latin American Peasant
Movement; and Rodolfo Stavenhagen, ed., Agrarian Problems and Peasant Movements in Latin America (Garden
City, N. Y.: Doubleday-Anchor, 1970).

(27) This was the case in Chile, for example, especially
during the period 1970-1973. See Loveman, Struggle in
the Countryside.

(28) An excellent study of all aspects of the status of the
peasantry in Brazil (cultural, social, political, economic,
both past and present) is Shepard Forman's The Brazilian
Peasantry (New York: Columbia University Press, 1975).

(29) Henry A. Landsberger and Cynthia N. Hewitt de Al-
cantara, "Ten Sources of Weakness in Latin American
Peasant Movements," in Agrarian Problems and Peasant
Movements, ed. Stavenhagen.

(30) Peter Singlemann, "The Closing Triangle: Critical Notes
on a Model for Peasant Mobilization in Latin America,"
Comparative Studies in Society and History 17 (October
1975): 389-409.

(31) Seventeen years after the revolution, Cuban women still
have a long way to go both in the occupational structure,
and in terms of attitudinal response by men. See
Marjorie King, "Cuba's Attack on Women's Second Shift,
1974-1976," Latin American Perspective 4 (Winter and
Spring 1977): 106-19.

12 Politics, Modernization, and the Yugoslav Peasantry*
M. George Zaninovich and Douglas A. Brown

SOME THEORETICAL ISSUES

Research on the values and attitudes of various sectors of a
given population must take into account the fact that these
population sectors within a developing society will hold different perspectives on basic societal questions. This quality of
variance among population sectors is dictated by a range of
historical, social, and economic factors. It is also possible to
conceive of particular sectors of a population as occupying
different positions along a continuum representing the processes of modernization. One sector may be highly modernized
(and modernizing), another may be found to hold a difficult
transitional position verging on modernization, while yet
another may be considerably less modernized than other
sectors of the population. We may assume that in most cases,
the peasant sector in a developing society will be the least
modernized. On the basis of this assumption, and through the
use of survey research data, this chapter attempts to assess
where the peasants of Yugoslavia stood as of 1967-68 by
comparison with other sectors of the population as regards
their values and attitudes.

For the peasant in a traditionalistic society, the small
world of the village is his universe. If his needs cannot be
met within the context of that microsociety, then they cannot
be met at all. When things are good in the village, when the

---

*The authors wish to express their appreciation to Alan
Woolfolk and Joseph Kremers, graduate students in political
science at the University of Oregon, for their assistance in
preparing these data for analysis and interpretation.

conditions of land tenure, employment, taxation and prices are bearable, then life is bearable and even good. When these conditions become unbearable, for whatever reason, the peasant strikes out not at the larger world around him, but at those aspects of his own immediate universe which he feels he can influence.(1)   As these traditionalistic societies give way to modernization and change, this parochial universe of the peasant is forcibly expanded against his will.   Forces beyond his own small world begin to affect his day-to-day activity and his life-style, and the peasant's response to these forces bears serious consequences for modernizing societies.   The peasant plays a crucial role in rapidly changing societies such as Yugoslavia, and the way in which he relates to the political system can determine the course of political development.

Since the peasant world and society are small and isolated, the peasants in any given village or area tend to be very much alike.   Life is lived out within a small sphere of friends, family and clan.   Since he communicates with relatively few people, the peasant comes to feel that what he knows and believes is what all men know and believe, or at least should believe.   Behavior must conform to certain standards, and as a result becomes highly structured and conventional.   Things are done in a certain way not because somebody has decided that they should be, but because they have always been done that way and are a part of the nature of things.

The economic structure of peasant society tends to be communal.   Where people are bound by ties of tradition and kinship, there is no place for the private entrepreneur who "gets ahead" at the expense of others.   Thus, there is little incentive for the motive of commercial gain.   Work becomes not a way of advancing economically in relation to others, but an ethic in its own right.   The peasant works, saves and prospers not because of any economic incentive, but for the social recognition which it brings.   The peasant's activity remains a basic function of life-style rather than a matter of expediency or calculated profit taking.   Traditional ways of doing things become not only habits for the peasant, but mores as well.   They may also take on a symbolic and sacred connotation.   Accustomed at an early age to certain ways of doing things, it becomes psychologically, even morally, difficult for the peasant to contemplate the idea of change.(2)

For these reasons, the peasantry has often been held to be an extremely conservative force, resistant to change, loyal to church and to throne, hostile toward the city, involved with family and village, and suspicious of any person or concept which represents change.   Since modernization has become the issue in many of the so-called traditionalistic societies, this image of the conservative peasantry has been challenged.   One observer, Samuel P. Huntington, sees the peasant as a force for change, even revolution:

Each of the major revolutions in Western, as well as non-Western societies, was in large part a peasant revolution. This was true in France and in Russia as it was in China. In all three countries, the peasants more or less spontaneously acted to overthrow the old agrarian political and social structure, to seize the land, and to establish a new political and social system in the countryside. Without this peasant action, not one of these revolutions would have constituted a revolution.(3)

Even in the throes of revolution, however, the peasant has always viewed the city and its inhabitants in a suspicious manner. Attempts by urban intellectuals to rouse the peasant to revolution have generally failed. In almost all cases, peasants revolt when the social and economic conditions of life in the village provide them with concrete motives for such action. Urban groups, including intellectuals, students, industrial workers, and professionals may be able to ally themselves with peasants who are rebelling, but they cannot make the peasant into a revolutionary.(4) Only unbearable conditions of life in the village can induce the peasant to overcome his psychological and moral apprehension regarding change. To again quote Huntington, "Peasant action in all the great revolutions was directed primarily to the prompt, direct, and, if necessary, violent rectification of the immediate material conditions which had become unbearable."(5)

The attitude of the peasant toward the existing political and social structure, then, may be determined in large measure by the extent to which those structures tend to meet his immediate material needs. Although the peasant may not perceive a political structure in the society as a whole as responsible for adversity and unbearable conditions, he will surely rebel against the local agents of that structure to which he is able to ascribe responsibility. A contented peasant who feels things in the village are as they should be is not a threat to the political system. If his life situation becomes unbearable, he can become an agent of revolution, regardless of what the good intentions of the existing political structure may be.

HISTORICAL PARAMETERS - THE PEASANT CONTEXT

A historical consideration of the Yugoslav peoples is important when attempting to understand why any given sector of the population, such as the peasants, relate as they do to aspects of modernization. The word "Yugoslav," meaning "South Slav," has been applied to a group of some six Slavic-speaking peoples enjoying common historical roots. A long process of repeated migration, foreign conquest, and religious conversion has resulted in the original Slavic inhabitants of the area that is now Yugoslavia being deeply divided along linguistic, cultural, religious, and political lines. The first Slavic settlers appeared in the region in the sixth century. Geographic isolation was influential in the emergence of three basic linguistic groups (Serbo-Croatian or Croato-Serbian, Slovenian, amd Macedo-Bulgarian or Macedonian Slav) and five nationalities (Serbs, Croats, Slovenes, Macedonians, and Montenegrins). A sixth group is the Slavic-speaking Moslem population centered mainly in Bosnia-Herzegovina, who, while of Slavic extraction, tend to identify themselves as "Muslimani" or simply as undeclared Yugoslav peoples.

It has not only been the Islamic faith which has introduced a factor of cleavage among Slavic speakers in the Balkans. The overriding difference between Serb and Croat nationalities is based in the Croatian adherence to the Roman Catholic faith and the Serbian allegiance to the Orthodox faith. The presence at one time or another of Austrian, Hungarian, and Turkish overlords has given the Yugoslav peasant wide experience with political subjugation and cultural adaptation. Furthermore, the various divisive factors mentioned above have operated to give peasants in one region a greater similarity and affinity for their overlords than, it would seem, for their culturally alien but linguistically related cousins in other regions of the south Slavic area.

As mentioned above, the village is the point of identification for traditional peasant peoples, and this was as true of the south Slavic peasant as any other. South Slavic peasant families were gathered in kinship groups called zadruga, which were extended family associations oriented to communal production. These have been described as "a household composed of two or more biological or small families closely related by blood or adoption, owning its means of production communally, producing and consuming its means of livelihood jointly, and regulating the control of its property, labor and livelihood communally."(6) These often included as many as 200 persons.

Yugoslavia's complex history of migration and conquest is reflected in the village, with the type of architecture, the dress and customs of the people, the food and drink, even the music, reflecting the history of the particular area. Thus, the peasant of each area has a stamp of local identity in his cultural makeup that distinguishes him from his counterpart in other parts of the country that may be as different as Istanbul is from Venice, or Rome from Moscow. The emergence of a single Yugoslav state from this mosaic of peoples, cultures, and faiths is a noteworthy achievement, and has been made possible in part by the impact of modernization on the strongly held traditions and mores of the peasantry.

The political realities of present-day Yugoslavia can be traced to the division of the early Slavs into two politico-religious groups. To quote from George Hoffman and Fred Neal: "Those that went South - the modern Serbs and Macedonians - came under the influence of Byzantium, from which they accepted Christianity. They thus became Orthodox Catholics. The tribes that went westward - primarily the modern Croats and Slovenes - early came under Germanic and Hungarian influences, and through them became Roman Catholics."(7) In Slovenia, the overlords were primarily German as well as being Roman Catholic. The peasants retained the use of the Slovenian language, and thus were quite distinct from the upper German-speaking classes, and alienated from the political structure. The relatively good economic conditions in their area, however, made of the Slovene peasants rather satisfied and docile subjects. In Croatia, a national consciousness emerged early, in the tenth and twelfth centuries. But in return for the right to maintain their institutions and a separate national identity, the Croats had to submit first to Hungarian, and later to Austro-Hungarian rule. Here too, an alien class of Austro-Hungarian overlords ruled over the Slavic peasants, replacing the old Croatian aristocracy, though not to as great an extent as in Slovenia, where a native aristocracy had never emerged. Croatia, thus, although able to maintain a rather tenuous "legalistic" nationhood, had in fact to submit to foreign influence and occupation. Serbia, although ethnically and linguistically of common stock with the Croatians, was Orthodox in faith, and Serbian culture was largely a product of Byzantium. The Great Serbian Empire, a power in its own right by the early twelfth century, was destroyed by the Turks in 1389, although Serbian nationalism remained strong throughout 500 years of Turkish domination.

Despite the destruction of the Serbian state and its aristocracy, the peasants retained most of their traditional culture. In fact, as national institutions were destroyed and the larger towns occupied by Turks, the Serbian village became the receptacle and storehouse of Serbian culture. Those few members of the aristocracy who had survived merged with the peasantry. This leveling effect of the Turkish occupation made of Serbia a very nearly classless society, separated by a great gulf from their Turkish con-querors. To a lesser extent, this was true of those areas under Austro-Hungarian rule as well. While the aristocracy adopted Austro-Hungarian mannerisms and, to some degree, loyalties, the peasant village remained a repository of more traditional Slavic culture.

In Croatia, the rise of nationalism was accompanied by the emergence of the peasantry as a political force. The earliest uprisings against non-Slavic overlords occurred in the thirteenth century, and were led by subvassals and town dwellers, notably in the areas around Zagreb and Split. The first major peasant rebellion occurred in 1573 under the leadership of Matija Gubec, in an attempt to free Croatia of an increasingly abusive system of feudalism. The peasants met with quick and decisive defeat as the rebellion was crushed and as many as 6,000 peasants put to the sword, including Gubec himself. Despite his dismal failure in the initial revolt, the memory of Gubec became the chief motivating factor uniting the peasants of Croatia against their overlords, and rebellions continued to sputter across the countryside until the abolition of serfdom in the nineteenth century.(8)

Turkish rule was harsh, though often not as efficient and brutal as that of the Austro-Hungarian Empire. Thus, peasants were able to rebel more succcessfully in the Turkish areas. For three centuries, Balkan Slavic peasant groups known as hajduci were able to harass the Turks with a type of guerrilla warfare, attacking military outposts, cutting the lines of communication and transportation, even occupying towns for short periods. The Serbian revolts of 1804 and 1815 marked the demise of Turkish domination in Serbia. The first of these revolts, led by the peasant chieftan Karadjordje, was initially successful in clearing the Turks from the countryside and small towns, but the early withdrawal of Russian assistance doomed the Serbians to defeat. After suffering several years of Turkish reprisals, the peasants rose again in 1815, this time under Milos Obrenovic, who was able to conclude a peace treaty with the Turks which recognized him as Prince of Serbia. Under increasing pressure from Slavic Russia, Turkish overlords and troops gradually withdraw, allowing the Serbians to assume control of their own affairs.

As the growing preeminence of the peasant village as the repository of traditional Slavic culture became manifest, a glorification of peasant culture by nationalist elements also emerged. Second only to the peasant rebellions in its influence on Yugoslav nationalist sentiment was the emergence of movements characterizing the peasant language and culture as the embodiment of south Slavic history and traditions. The nineteenth century scholar, Vuk Karadzic, brought to Serbians a new awareness of their west Serbian peasant dialect and folkways in Herzegovina, through which were expressed the epic ballads commemorating the heroic deeds of historical figures. Karadzic's work did much to advance this west Serbian dialect as the literary language of Serbia, although the eastern influence of old "church" Slavonic remained strong. The Illyrian movement in Croatia was a similar linguistic-political phenomenon. Its leader, Ljudevit Gaj, had been challenged by the work of Karadzic, and was able to gain wide acceptance in Croatia of a Croato-Serbian dialect similar to that promoted by Karadzic. Together, these two movements did

much to bring the Serbs and Croatians closer together linguistically, and to give them an appreciation of common ethnic
and historic roots. Already, the concept of a unified South
Slavic people, bound together by a common peasant culture,
was beginning to develop.(9)

With independence and the assumption of state power
by peasant leaders in Serbia, the passing of traditional
Yugoslav peasant society also began. The zadruga basis of
peasant communal agriculture began to dissolve. Land which
had been under Turkish ownership was returned to the
peasants as individual and private holdings. The population
began to expand, and surplus land was exhausted, forcing
excess population to flow toward the cities, seeking employment
in emerging industrial centers. In keeping with this process,
a new factor emerged on the political scene with the appearance of peasant political parties. In Serbia, a Union of
Peasants was founded in 1919, based on radical, agricultural
socialism. The party leadership early became divided between
"liberal" and "reactionary" wings, and as a result, the party
failed to develop as a significant factor in Serbian politics. A
Slovenian Peoples Party, maintaining strong ties to the Roman
Catholic church, also had its main strength in the peasant
villages. It was able to develop an impressive cooperative
movement in Slovenia, but while it accomplished a great deal
for the social and economic well-being of the peasantry, it was
never able to attract a mass following.

The strongest peasant movement to emerge, and perhaps
the most interesting, was the Croatian Peasant Party, founded
in 1905 by Stjepan and Antun Radic. This party attempted to
mobilize the peasant majority in Croatia as a counterweight to
existing bourgeois parties. Although it gained a small following
in the pre-World War I years, it was to become significant in
the postwar kingdom of Serbs, Croats, and Slovenes. Its
ideology glorified the peasant, maintaining that the Croatian
peasantry was the embodiment of the Croatian nation, being
the repository of a true Slavic language and culture, and that
the interests of the peasantry took precedence over all others.
The party was strongly pan-Yugoslav and, because of the
sociopolitical hold of the church over the peasantry, anti-
clerical. Even so, the party had serious defects. Its
nationalism and glorification of the peasant, as expressed in its
rhetoric of "soil" and "country" was highly romantic, and it
failed to develop any viable economic program based upon its
ideology. Stjepan Radic was both anticapitalist and antisocialist, although he is said at first to have been much
impressed with the Bolshevik experiments in Russia. The
party tended to oppose the one thing offering the best solution
to peasant overpopulation - the transformation of large
numbers of peasants into industrial workers - because it
feared the effects on the peasant culture and ethos.(10)

Despite the emergence of these peasant-based parties, it was worsening social conditions and World War I itself which effectively mobilized the peasantry throughout the region. The basic cause of peasant dissatisfaction was the situation found in the village. In Bosnia and Herzegovina, populated by both Serbs and Croats, serfdom was still common. In Croatia and Serbia, population pressures on the land were growing, while national divisions and foreign domination restrained the movement of landless peasants to industrial centers in other regions. The creation of a unified south Slavic state after World War I, embracing the Serbs, Croats, and Slovenes, presented the people of the area with an entirely new political and economic situation. Foreign overlords were gone, national boundaries no longer restricted movement, serfdom was abolished, and agricultural and economic policies could now be equalized throughout the constituent states.

The interwar period was characterized by dictatorship and army control of a weak monarchy on the one side, and by a confusing and competing array of ineffective political parties which constituted no effective opposition parties, and there was some attempt on the part of Slovene and Serbian political leaders to strengthen their peasant ties in emulation of the Croatian Peasant Party. All parties, however, were bound to their own particular past, blinded by ethnic loyalties, unable to view issues in a pan-Yugoslav context, and committed to protection of their own constituencies. For the government, economic and social issues were secondary to the maintenance of political power.(11)

The ones who suffered most from this political and economic impasse were the peasants. Because of the ineffectiveness of the parties representing them in government, the peasants were unable to influence policy on their own behalf. They were subjected to police oppression, social abuse, and economic exploitation, and were excluded from political participation, even though they constituted better than three-fourths of the population of the country. This situation, as much as anything, contributed to the complete disintegration of the Yugoslav state in the face of fascist aggression at the beginning of World War II. The peasantry simply felt that the state in its present form was not worth preserving as its policies overlooked the needs of those who tilled the land. The liberation of Yugoslavia from this state of near total collapse, and from the occupying fascist armies of Germany, Italy and Hungary, fell to the Communist Partisans led by Tito, and the peasant supporters so prominent in his ranks. As in other times and in other places, the rhetoric and ideology of the revolution were left to the party leaders and intellectuals. The peasant was involved in the revolution because conditions in the countryside were unbearable, and

because of his historically nurtured antipathy to foreign
overlords. As a result, the Partisans became an effective,
peasant-based and pan-Yugoslav movement, able to generate a
"Yugoslav nationalism" as opposed to the narrower Serbian
nationalism prevalent in the interwar period.(12) By the sheer
weight of numbers, the peasant masses were able to exert a
certain influence on the communist party organization in the
war years and the period immediately following. That peasant
influence on party and state structures has declined since is
not surprising, and Yugoslavia today is far from being a
peasant state. This fact has been reflected by the decline in
numbers (from about 50 percent to 7 percent) of party
members who count themselves as peasants.

    As anticipated by the ideology of the Croatian Peasant
Party in the interwar period, the advent of modernization
accompanied by the transformation of large numbers of
peasants into industrial and agricultural workers presupposes
the destruction of traditional peasant culture and mores.
Since the primary focus of communist societies has involved
rapid moderization and industrialization, it is not possible for
peasants as such to maintain a leading role in society. In
becoming modernized, in accepting industrialization and
mechanization, the peasant is expected to forego his traditionalistic identity, and become a part of either the industrial
or an "agricultural proletariat." There is every indication that
this is now happening in Yugoslavia, however unsystematically,
and that the attitudes and value orientations of the Yugoslav
peasantry reflect this process.

                DATA SOURCE AND METHODOLOGY

The data presented in this investigation were obtained from
survey research completed in Yugoslavia in the course of
1967-68.(13) The sample of 1,186 respondents was structured
in such a way as to reflect three key features of the country,
these being the cultural region, the level of modernization of
the area, and the occupation of the respondent. The defining
variables of this particular investigation of peasant attitudes
and values are limited, first to the occupation of the respondent, and second, to whether the respondent is from the
northern or southern part of the country. Nine cultural
regions were considered in all. The number of interviews
obtained from each region, and the percentage of the total
Yugoslav population which that region represents, is shown in
table 12.1.

Table 12.1. Distribution of Population and
Respondent Sample by Cultural Region

Yugoslav Cultural Region	Total Population N	%	Total Sample %	N
Serbia Proper	4,823,276	26.0	21.3	251
Croatia-Slavonia	4,159,696*	22.4*	16.8	203
Adriatic Coast			11.6	138
Slovenia	1,591,507	8.6	12.9	153
Bosnia-Herzegovina	3,277,935	17.7	12.4	146
Macedonia	1,406,003	7.6	12.5	148
Montenegro	471,894	2.5	3.9	46
Vojvodina	1,854,965	10.0	4.3	50
Kosmet	963,988	5.2	4.3	51
Totals	18,549,264	100.0	100.0	1,186

*For census purposes, the Croatia-Slavonia and Adriatic Coast populations are combined.

Source: Population figures taken from Popis Stanovnistva, vol. VI, 1961.

Respondents were selected from 24 different communes distributed across the country in such a way as to reflect varied levels of modernization within each cultural region.(14) This was necessary, since in absolute terms, the level of modernization in Yugoslavia follows regional-ethnic lines very closely, with the Catholic Slovenes of the north being more highly modernized as a result of long and close association with Austria, with the Orthodox Macedonians of the south being much less so as a result of long years of stagnation under Turkish rule. In order not to confuse the effect of these regional-ethnic aspects with those of modernization, it was necessary to control for the two types of variables in the research design.

The distribution of respondents for each commune was structured in terms of occupational category. In all 24 communes, an attempt was made to interview a specific number of individuals from each of several representative occupational groupings: the political leadership (federal and republican delegates, commune representatives and administrators, directors of enterprises), the professionals (educators, journalists, lawyers, doctors, students, priests), the workers (industrial workers, members of workers councils), and the peasants (private farmers, agricultural workers).

This structuring of the occupational categories for each commune means that occupation as a variable has been controlled in the research design in relation to both level of modernization and cultural region, and all three variables can be considered as constant in relation to one another. The purpose of this investigation and the analysis which follows is to compare the differential attitudinal and value orientations of the peasant group against those of the political leadership, professional and worker groups. Before doing so, however, a few additional comments on the sample are in order.(15)

The selection of respondents based upon structured occupational groupings tends to produce a sample skewed somewhat toward the higher status population sectors. In a situation involving such a structured sample, it is necessary to use extreme caution making generalizations regarding attitudinal and value orientations. For example, one should not characterize the sample on which this investigation is based as representing the attitudes and values of the Yugoslav population as a whole. Since the sample was designed to reflect specific structural features of the population, one can only make assertions about the individual sectors of the overall sample with any degree of confidence. And, since the sample is skewed to the higher status group, generalizations concerning the peasant sample are on the whole acceptable, while generalizations regarding the attitudes and values of the higher status groups will be biased by the overrepresentation of those groups in the sample.

A factor analysis of 38 items selected from a wide range of attitudinal and value responses elicited by the survey instrument was performed for the 1,186 cases in the sample. This was done in order to determine which value items would tend to group themselves in such a way as to reveal underlying dimensions to which a concept could be applied. Twelve usable factors were generated by orthogonal and oblique rotations, from which a set of six were selected for further analysis. In selecting the six factors and the 31 items to be retained, both the explanatory strength of the factor and its substantive relevance were considered.(16) Each of the six derived factors was then given a label which was determined from the nature of the value items which had grouped themselves under that factor. This makes it possible to speak in terms of a value dimension which characterizes a specific grouping of survey items. The derived factors, and the factor loading for each survey item grouped under them, are reported in table 12.2. For purposes of analysis, the selected value items are treated as separate dependent variables, but with a shared or common dimension revealed by factor analysis. The assumption is that variation in responses to

Table 12.2. Factor Loadings for Value Items
Grouped under Each of Six Retained Factors

Factor	Value Item	Loading
Anxiety-Pessimistic	1. "If you don't keep all four eyes open, people will exploit and deceive you."	.617
	2. "Human nature is such that there will always be war and conflict."	.615
	3. "The world always changes for the better."	-.401
	4. "A man can have faith in a majority of the people."	-.758
Parochial-Traditional	1. "It is not necessary to talk with individuals whose thoughts are in opposition to ours."	.563
	2. "In order to fulfill their personal goals and desires, individuals must compete with and subdue one another."	.561
	3. "The world is governed by supernatural forces which predetermine the course of events."	.561
	4. "The children of great people are endowed with the qualities of their parents."	.437
	5. "The most important thing for children is that they learn to obey parents."	.433
	6. "Nationality is important in our country."	.393
	7. "It is important for a man to speak his own dialect."	.301

(continued)

Table 12.2.   (Continued)

Factor		Value Item	Loading
Egalitarian-Allocative	1.	"There is no need to correct any kind of excessive increase in differences in personal incomes."	-.707
	2.	"Individuals must be rewarded above all on the basis of the results of their work."	-.612
	3.	"Individuals must be rewarded above all in accordance with the social significance of the work they may perform."	-.585
	4.	"Individuals must be rewarded above all according to their qualifications and educational preparation."	-.510
	5.	"For our society, it is important that people from the villages have the opportunity to transfer to city occupations and improve themselves."	-.499
	6.	"A man must settle in another region of Yugoslavia if he finds better work there."	-.498
	7.	"Productive work must be rewarded the very most."	-.493
	8.	"Since all individuals have the same needs, differences in rewards should be minimal."	*
Socialist-Patriotic	1.	"The memory of the national liberation struggle lives today among our people."	.843
	2.	"State celebrations are important for me."	.502

(continued)

Table 12.2. (Continued)

Factor		Value Item	Loading
	3.	"The initiative for social and economic progress must originate in the commune."	.358
	4.	"Voters' meetings contribute to fulfilling the will of the working people."	.316
Statist-Rationalist	1.	"Better to change society by rapid, planned means than by a gradual, natural path."	.797
	2.	"A rapid pace of economic development depends heavily on a strong centralized authority."	*
	3.	"It is both necessary and beneficial that the state regulate the economy."	*
Competitive-Decentralist	1.	"A rapid pace of economic development depends heavily on a strong centralized authority."	-.770
	2.	"It is both necessary and beneficial that the state regulate the economy."	-.707
	3.	"Since all individuals have the same needs, differences in rewards should be minimal."	-.498
	4.	"Individuals must be rewarded according to qualifications and educational preparation."	-.481

(continued)

Table 12.2.   (Continued)

Factor	Value Item	Loading
	5. "In large cities the family faces a crisis situation."	-.427

*Loadings are reported only for value items that generated a factor score higher than 0.300. These items were included here because of their substantive relevance to the given dimension, although they did not demonstrate high enough factor scores for inclusion under a strictly statistical criterion.

these value items can be attributed to an individual's life situation, i.e. whether he is a peasant, or a member of one of the higher status population sectors.(17) The association between life situation and value response is determined by viewing occupational categories and the level of agreement with value items as two ordinal scales which can be compared statistically.(18)

The general hypotheses guiding this investigation are: 1) that peasants tend to hold values and attitudes that differ considerably from those of the higher population groups; and 2) that the values and attitudes held by peasant groups will vary depending upon whether the individuals interviewed live in the nothern or southern part of the country. It is expected that these variations will be explainable in terms of the community context, i.e., nationality, religion, socioeconomic level of the commune, as well as other attributes which vary geographically across Yugoslavia. That is to say, it is posited that the peasant will reflect the culture and traditions of the geographic area in which he lives more so than other population groups simply because his traditionalistic attitudes and values have been less exposed to the influence of modernization. The attitudes and values of the more modernized population sectors can also be expected to be more homogeneous.(19)

THE PEASANT PROFILE

A few generalizations about the peasant in the Yugoslavia of today will serve to introduce a more extensive discussion. In contrast to the other, higher status sectors of the population, the peasantry is less educated (95 percent of the peasant sample had finished primary school or less), highly religious (more than 80 percent identify themselves as religious), and relatively less likely to belong to the Communist Party (only 7 percent of the peasant sample are party members, compared to 45 percent for the higher status groups). Peasants tend to have less income than other population groups (75 percent of peasant families in the sample earn less than $65 per month), and have a low level of participation in sociopolitical functions (60 percent of the peasant sample reported no significant participation). The peasant emerges as traditionalistic, less educated, and relatively nonparticipant as compared to the higher status groups in Yugoslav society.

It is noteworthy that as compared to the other groups in the population, proportionately commensurate numbers of peasants served with the Partisan forces during World War II. The fact that peasants do not appear in the Communist Party of Yugoslavia in numbers proportionate to other sectors of the population testifies to the decline in political significance of the peasantry in Yugoslavia since the war years, even though the political leadership of the country has been drawn in large measure from former Partisan fighters.

The impression regarding the "traditionalistic" orientation of the Yugoslav peasant can be elaborated by examining the gamma correlations generated by statistical comparison of value responses for the peasant and nonpeasant groups. These correlations are presented in table 12.3.

Table 12.3. Gamma Correlations between
Population Sectors and Value Dimensions

Value Item	Peasant/Nonpeasant Correlations (Gamma)
Anxiety-Pessimistic	
People will exploit	.43
Always be war and conflict	.30
World changes for better	-.01
Faith in majority of people	-.07
Parochial-Traditional	
Not necessary to speak with opposition	.40
Individuals must compete	.32
World governed by supernatural forces	.56
Children have qualities of parents	.29
Children must obey parents	.54
Nationality is important	.31
Speaking own dialect important	.37

(continued)

Table 12.3.   (Continued)

Value Item	Peasant/Nonpeasant Correlations (Gamma)
Egalitarian-Allocative	
Income differences acceptable	-.18
Reward on results of work	.12
Reward on social significance of work	.13
Reward according to education	.06
Opportunity to transfer to city	.34
Settle in another region for work	.08
Reward productive work	.33
Minimize reward differentials	.26
Socialist-Patriotic	
National liberation struggle lives	.12
State celebrations important	-.09
Progress originates in commune	.03
Voters' meetings important	.16
Statist-Rationalist	
Planned rapid change	-.11
Strong centralized authority	.34
State regulates economy	.28
Competitive-Decentralist	
Strong centralized authority	.34
State regulates economy	.28
Minimize reward differentials	.26
Reward according to education	.06
Family crisis in large cities	.07

In the first value dimension, that of anxiety-pessimism, we find a fairly <u>strong</u> conviction on the part of the peasantry that exploitation is inevitable (gamma =.45), and that war and conflict are unavoidable and even necessary (gamma =.30). Apparently, the peasant's long history of exploitation and victimization in war has left its mark on his psychological makeup. In regard to hope for the future and faith in mankind, the last two items in the anxiety-pessimism dimension, there is no substantial attitudinal difference between the peasant and nonpeasant groups. These data suggest that the peasantry is somewhat more pessimistic and anxious about human nature and the world than are the nonpeasant respondents.

The value responses for the parochial-traditional dimension show the peasants to be consistently more traditionalistic and particularistic than the nonpeasant sample. The conviction that the world is governed by supernatural forces was not only the strongest value response within this dimension (gamma =.56), but also the strongest value response for all items retained in the analysis. This was followed in regard to strength of association with being a peasant, again for both this dimension and the investigation as a whole, by the conviction that children must learn to obey their parents (gamma =.54). The peasants also seem to be more attached to their own particular ethnic background than are other groups in the population (the importance of nationality resulted in a gamma =.31, and speaking one's own dialect a gamma =.37), and rather narrow in their acceptance of the viewpoints of others (gamma =.40 for the lack of need to speak with those who hold opposing viewpoints). Peasants accept heredity as a determining factor in an individual's character (gamma =.29 for children having the same qualities as their parents). There is also a relatively strong disagreement among peasants and nonpeasants on the need for individual competition (gamma =.32), the peasants favoring this more strongly. The effect is to suggest that peasants are considerably more traditionalistic and parochial in their general orientation than are the nonpeasant sectors of Yugoslav society.

In regard to the socialist-patriotic dimension, there seems to be no apparent difference to speak of between peasant and nonpeasant value orientations (reflected in consistently low gamma scores). The memory of the national liberation struggle and the importance of state celebrations are the first two values in this dimension, and the broad agreement among all sectors is apparent and understandable. The trauma of the fascist occupation and the participation of most sectors of society in the liberation movement led by Tito's Partisans has led to a high degree of attachment to patriotic values in Yugoslavia. Since the devastation and the turmoil caused by the fascist occupation was greater in some regions of the country than in others (Croatia, for example), one might expect some regional variation on patriotic values, but not as between occupational categories. The last two values in this dimension relate to the importance of local voter meetings and the idea that progress originates in the commune. They were included as an indicator of attachment to participatory values as expressions of official ideology. The expectation would be that the nonpeasant sectors would perhaps have a stronger attachment to participatory values as a result of their more sophisticated urban experience. The results show, however, that there is broad agreement among all occupational groups in their orientation to the participatory values summarized by this dimension.

On the statist-rationalist dimension, there seems to be considerable disagreement between peasants and nonpeasants on the need for a strong centralized authority (gamma =.34) and on state regulation of the economy (gamma =.28). Members of the peasant sector would seem more disposed to look to centralized authority and to favor a regulated economy for meeting their needs than the nonpeasant population sector. As a result, it would appear that it is the uneducated rural peasant who adopts the view that centralized political authority offers a remedy to his problems. The competitive-decentralist dimension similarly indicates that peasants disagree with nonpeasants as regards strong centralization and state control, as in the statist-rationalist dimension, but are in basic agreement with nonpeasants on rewarding individuals according to education and on the existence of family crisis in the cities. There is also considerable disagreement on the need for equalization of reward-differentials (gamma =.26), a course the peasants seem to favor over the nonpeasantry. In short, the peasant is relatively more egalitarian regarding reward differentials, and may see centralized economic and state management as the means of achieving his goals. Stated in terms of factor dimensions, the peasantry would seem to be more statist-rationalist and less competitive-decentralist than the nonpeasant sectors of Yugoslav society.

The egalitarian-allocative dimension has been left until last because it, perhaps more than the other dimensions, reflects the impact of modernization on the peasant as well as some value inconsistency. This can be seen in the absence of any identifiable pattern of response to the value items composing this dimension. The peasantry tends toward agreement with the nonpeasant sectors on such items as the need for rewarding socially significant work, rewarding on the basis of results of work and educational qualifications, and desirability of sociogeographic mobility. But significant differences still arise on rewarding simply for quantity or productivity of work (gamma =.33), minimizing income differentials (gamma =.26), and favoring the opportunity to move to the city (gamma =.34). Peasants face a value conflict in that they, on the one hand, agree generally with the higher status, more modernized sectors of the population on the need to reward on the basis of skill and merit in a technological society, on the relevance of education, and on the importance of mobility. On the other hand, they still hold to basic egalitarian concepts which justify reward in their own life situation, i.e., equal distribution of rewards for productive labor in general, as well as their insistence that income differentials be at a minimum. Finally, like peasants in every situation where modernization is taking place, they equate moving to the city with an improved life situation. As a result, the pattern on the egalitarian-allocative dimension for the peasant reveals an ambivalence,

namely, he honors some inegalitarian principles (e.g., reward
for socially significant work) necessary to modernization, yet
still holds to his "naturalistic" egalitarian impulses (e.g.,
minimum income differences). In short, the peasantry seems
to be caught in the midst of a value transformation process
endemic to transitional societies everywhere.

In summary, then, a number of contradictions regarding
the peasant attitudinal profile seem to emerge from this
investigation, but contradictions consistent with what we know
of traditionalistic man when faced with the onset of modernization. The Yugoslav peasant is more pessimistic regarding
exploitation and conflict, he is more traditionalistic and family
oriented, and somewhat more distrustful of others, than are
other sectors of the population in Yugoslav society. Regarding commitment to Yugoslav society, the peasant feels deeply
that the national liberation struggle was significant, and that
state celebrations are important, attitudes he shares with the
nonpeasant Yugoslav populace. The peasant also holds to
egalitarian concepts in regard to productivity and income
distribution, yet recognizes the need for taking quality of
work, social importance of work, and educational preparation
into consideration in determining income. Significantly, the
peasant is rather more favorably disposed than are other
groups in the society to centralized political authority and
state control of the economy, perhaps feeling that this
represents his best protection against exploitation by others.
Consistent with this societal commitment, he is also supportive
of participatory values (e.g., voters meetings), a feature
which is shared equally by the nonpeasantry.

Ironically, the peasant seems to be anxious to move to the
very place where traditionalistic values would help him the
least and where they perish soonest - the city. This he
believes despite the fact that he recognizes the existence of a
family crisis in the cities, and hence in one sense fears
mobility and change. In fact, the profile we have just
described is not really so much that of a traditionalistic
peasant, as it is that of a somewhat unsure "transitional man"
involved in and cognizant of the onset of an ambiguous
modernizing process.

REGIONAL VARIATION IN PEASANT ATTITUDES

Our analysis up to this point has centered on the "vertical"
attitudinal and value cleavages within the Yugoslav population,
i.e., those cleavages which seperate the peasant sector of the
population from the higher status sectors. This part of the
investigation will focus on the "horizontal" cleavages related to
geographic location which divide peasants living in the north-

ern part of the country from those living in the south. This
analysis is rooted theoretically in the historic division of the
Yugoslav peoples into two politico-religious areas: the Roman
Catholic north, Austro-Hungarian in its historical affiliation;
and the Orthodox south, dominated first by Byzantine culture,
and later by the Turkish Ottomans.

Table 12.4. Gamma Correlations for Peasant
Population Controlling for Region

Value Items	South/North Correlations (Gamma)
Anxiety-Pessimistic	
People will exploit	.30
Always be war and conflict	-.09
World changes for better	.40
Faith in majority of people	.05
Parochial-Traditional	
Not necessary to speak with opposition	.21
Individuals must compete	.16
World governed by supernatural forces	.12
Children have qualities of parents	-.03
Children must obey parents	.30
Nationality is important	-.05
Speaking own dialect important	-.07
Egalitarian-Allocative	
Income differences acceptable	-.22
Reward on results of work	.23
Reward on social significance of work	.22
Reward according to education	.07
Opportunity to transfer to city	.00
Settle in another region for work	.34
Reward productive work	.31
Minimize reward differentials	.04
Socialist-Patriotic	
National liberation struggle lives	.22
State celebrations important	.21
Progress originates in commune	.06
Voters' meetings important	.32

(continued)

Table 12.4.   (Continued)

Value Items	South/North Correlations (Gamma)
Statist-Rationalist	
Planned rapid change	.19
Strong centralized authority	.30
State regulates economy	.27
Competitive-Decentralist	
Strong centralized authority	.30
State regulates economy	.27
Minimize reward differentials	.04
Reward according to education	.07
Family crisis in large cities	-.27

Examination of the gamma correlations presented in table 12.4 reveals some interesting contrasts between the two geographic areas. These correlations contrast value responses among peasants on the basis of geographic region, with positive correlations indicating a stronger agreement with the item among southern peasants, and negative correlation indicating a stronger agreement with the item among peasants living in the north.

Looking at the anxiety-pessimism dimension, southern peasants tend to be more anxious than those in the north, but not necessarily more pessimistic. Interestingly enough, southern peasants couple their fear of exploitation and deception (gamma =.30) with an expectation that the world changes for the better (gamma =.40). This can be substantiated by recourse to a value item not included in the original analysis, an assertion that the world continuously changes. Southern peasants agreed with that assertion (gamma =.34) to a greater extent than the northern peasants. Thus, the southern peasant emerges as more suspicious and fearful of exploitation and deception, but still convinced that the world can and will change for the better. That conviction is not nearly so strong among the northern peasants, who seem to be more pessimistic about constructive improvements in their world.

Similarly, the southern peasant is shown to be somewhat more traditional than his northern counterpart, but not necessarily parochial. The parochial-traditional dimension shows southern peasants recording noticeably more strength regarding the need for strong parental authority (gamma

=.30), and somewhat more close-minded in their refusal to listen to opposing points of view (gamma =.21). However, on items relating to the importance of nationality and speaking one's own dialect, almost no difference was registered between north and south. If close-mindedness and parental authority can be taken as indicators of traditionalism, then there is indeed a stronger expression of traditionalistic values in the south, but perhaps a stronger expression of provincialism in the north. This pattern of value response should also be related to the fact that southern Yuguslavia is less developed economically.

In discussing the egalitarian-allocative dimension earlier, we noted an apparent contradiction in peasant values regarding income distribution and the bases on which work is rewarded. It was seen that peasants, more than other sectors of society, see the need for an equal distribution of income, but also agree on the need to recognize skill, education, and the social importance of work performed in rewarding people for the job they do. We now see that the southern peasant reflects these very same contradictions, and to a greater extent than northern Yugoslav peasants. The negative correlation reported under the egalitarian-allocative dimension indicates that northern peasants tend to reject the need for income redistribution (i.e., income differences acceptable) more strongly than do the southern peasants (gamma =-.22), while those items which show stronger support among southern peasants include income distribution on the basis of work and productivity (gammas =.23 and .31) and social significance of work (gamma =.22). The southern peasant is also shown to be more willing to relocate to a new region if necessary to find work and employment (gamma =.34). The overall effect is to suggest that the southern peasants (Macedonians and Serbs) are somewhat more concerned with values relating to reward and income allocation than are the northern populations. The northern peasantry, living in a more highly developed area, tends to disvalue income redistribution and egalitarian distributional principles, since any regional reallocation of resources and revenues may work to their disadvantage.

Also, in our earlier discussion of patriotic-solialist dimension values, we found all sectors of Yugoslav society supportive of patriotic values, with peasants relatively more supportive of values relating to communal participatory aspects of that dimension. It was suggested in that discussion that differences in patriotic values might be found on the basis of region, since the impact of the war and the subsequent national liberation struggle was more pronounced in the north. While there are regional differences on patriotic values, it is in fact the southern peasants that support those values to a greater extent, relative to the north. These southern peasants attach greater importance to the memory of the national liberation struggle (gamma =.22) and are also more favorably inclined towards "Yugoslav" state celebrations (gamma =.21). The Serb and Macedonian peasants, then, are those who seem to cherish symbols of Yugoslav "federal" patriotism more than northern Croats and Slovenes. It is interesting to note, however, that while peasants generally see local voters' meetings as important, particularly southern peasants (gamma =.32), the peasant sector is the least likely of all population sectors to be found at such meetings, or to be involved in any important sociopolitical functions. There is a suggestion here of a sense of lack of political efficacy, particularly expressed among the Serbs and the Macedonians, despite the fact that these southern peasants seem to value voters' meetings more than do their northern Croat and Slovene counterparts.

The statist-rationalist dimension is found to be relatively stronger among the southern Yugoslav peasants, as reflected in basic values regarding strong centralized authority (gamma =.30) and state regulation of the economy (gamma =.27), as well as in support of planned rapid change (gamma =.19). There is a strong northern peasant bias in favor of the notion that a family crisis exists in the cities (gamma =-.27), although the northern peasantry is apparently far more skeptical regarding the virtues of centralized state power, both reflected in items under the competitive-decentralist dimension. In summary, the southern peasants support centralized economic control for purposes of advancing modernization and economic development, while the northern peasants are more likely to be aware of the social problems brought on by modernization (i.e., urban pressures on the family), and are desirous of regional or localized, rather than centralized, economic and political control. Again referring to items not included in the original analysis, southern peasants place a much greater emphasis on the importance of the family (gamma =.35) and on knowledge of one's own family history (gamma =.32), confirming the suggestion of greater traditionalism among southern peasants. If we conclude that the southern peasant is relatively more supportive of centralized political power and a regulated economy (i.e., statist-rationalist), then we need also to observe that the northern peasant is generally more supportive of competitive-decentralist values, and hence the notion of a decentralized political and economic system. Such a conclusion easily comports with the recent attitudes and behavior publically expressed by the Croats as compared to the Serbs.

With a few minor exceptions, then, the southern peasant reveals himself as stronger than the northern peasant in response to those value orientations which set the peasant apart from the general population (e.g., traditionalism and state centralization). The northerner seems to be less "peasant" in his values and attitudes than his southern counter-part, having more value orientations compatible with modern-ization, urbanization, and economic development (e.g., not being as disturbed by income differences). As a result, the value profile of the northern peasant (Slovenes and Croats), living in the more industrialized regions of the country, is inclined to be relatively more consistent with the expressed modernizing values and perspectives of the Yugoslav elite.

MODERNIZATION AND THE YUGOSLAV PEASANT

On the basis of this investigation of Yugoslav peasant values and attitudes, we can see that with respect to the level of modernization, Yugoslav society varies along two continuums, one defined by the socioeconomic status parameters usually associated with the modernization process and the other by simple geographic location. By viewing Yugoslav society as being split both horizontally and vertically along these two continuums, we can see that four population sectors can be identified: nonpeasant northern, peasant northern, nonpeasant southern and peasant southern. This is diagrammed in figure 12.1.

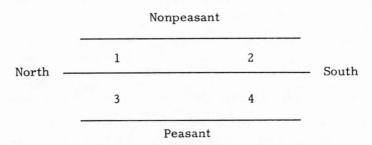

Fig. 12.1. Socioeconomic and Geographic
Cleavages in the Yugoslav Population

The numbers represent a rank ordering of the four population categories in terms of the degree to which the values that are held are conducive to the modernizing process. The most modernized sectors of the population fall in the upper range of both continuums (i.e., nonpeasant and northern) with the least modernized sectors falling in the lower range (i.e., peasant and southern). Accordingly, we would ideally expect to find southern peasants more traditionalistic, family oriented, pessimistic, suspicious and close-minded, attaching a greater importance to ethnic and linguistic considerations, rooted to the soil, less competitive and more collectivist and less willing to change. As we move up both continuums, we should expect to find individuals more open-minded, less traditionalistic and family oriented, more optimistic, more favorable to individual competition and laissez-faire economics, less rooted to the soil, generally more willing to change. These are of course "ideal-typical" constructs derived from the data analysis, which means that departures from these expectations specific to problems of modernization in Yugoslavia do and will continue to occur. Nonetheless, these data-based idealized value constructs do, we feel, convey a reasonably accurate picture of the cross-regional and cross-social structural value patterns found in Yugoslavia. In general, these data have shown that the northern peasantry has more in common (as regards basic values) with the Yugoslav higher status populations, particularly the political elite charged with the task of modernization, than do the peasants from the Yugoslav south.

We have found that compared to the higher status sectors of the Yugoslav population, the peasant is more anxious and pessimistic; he expects to be exploited and deceived, he expects there to be war and conflict, and he has relatively less faith in people and the future. If the impact of modernization conforms to our expectations, then these peasant value orientations would be expected to be weaker in the more modernized areas of the country. And, we do find this generally to be the case; namely, such values are more apparent in industrialized Croatia and Slovenia than they are in less developed Macedonia and Serbia. There is, however, one important exception to this. The peasants in the less developed southern regions express greater hope for the future; they are convinced to a greater degree than their northern counterparts that the world can and does change for the better. This seems to be in conflict with basic assumptions and expectations about the effects of modernization found in the general literature. For example, Daniel Lerner has found that modernizing peoples are happier and more optimistic regarding the future than are traditionalistic peoples.(21) In the Yugoslav case, apparently, peasants with the greatest exposure to modernization and industrialization (e.g., Croats and Slovenes) are the more somber about the kind of future which change might produce, they seem to have developed a rather cynical view about change. In all fairness, it must be noted that a peasant who has experienced some measure of modernization is not necessarily a modernizing individual, such as those to which Lerner refers. Still, there is an observable and important geographic effect manifest in regard to optimism about the future which corresponds to the relative level of modernization. This somewhat greater optimism among the southern peasants (Serbs and Macedonians)

might be explained by two factors: first, the sense that the
"federal" center is controlled by southern nationalities,
especially Serbs, and hence benefits are forthcoming; and
second, that the response set here was largely an expression
of hope relating to development, an important aspect given
their relatively backward economic situation. It should also be
noted that regional variations in the level of economic development in Yugoslavia have always been one of the major
political issues within the system.

It may be argued that the modernization of Yugoslavia, as
well as its viability as a state, rests on the ability of the
system to generate a "Yugoslav" patriotism and consciousness
supportive of federal institutions, as opposed to the various
regional nationalisms. Thus, it is important that symbols
common to all Yugoslavs be incorporated in the socialization
process. Our findings suggest, however, that as the process
of modernization advances, patriotic symbols of a pan-Yugoslav
nature tend to lose value. Peasants place more emphasis on
the memory of the national liberation struggle and various
state celebrations than do the higher status groups, and
southern peasants place more emphasis on these symbolic
experiences than do the northern peasants of the more industrialized Yugoslav regions. This apparent decline of
patriotic symbols as the process of modernization continues has
also been accompanied by a reemergence of intense regional
nationalism in recent years. It would seem that the memory of
the common struggle against German aggression and occupation
can only be maintained for so long, and is now in apparent
decline.

A peasant's attachment to the land presents obvious
difficulties for the modernization process. Needless to say, a
certain level of population mobility is necessary in meeting the
labor requirements of the industrializing areas, and it is
exceedingly difficult to distribute the benefits and mechanisms
of industrialization evenly enough to overcome the need for
relocating labor. As would be expected, peasants in Yugoslavia are less willing to relocate in other regions of the
country than are the higher status population groups.
Interestingly enough, northern peasants, the Croats and
Slovenes, who have been more exposed to modernization, are
less willing to move than are the southern Serbs and
Macedonians. Unless population sectors are willing to relocate
when necessary, it will of course be difficult to develop an
integrated, nationwide economic structure, or a sense of
transregional commitment, in Yugoslavia. Each region will
continue its tendency to develop on its own, and in relation to
its own, immediate and parochial center, a tendency which will
significantly reduce economies of scale in the Yugoslav industrialization process. It is not enough that Serbs be willing
to move to Beograd, or Croats to Zagreb. Each nationality

must be willing to relocate in areas dominated by other nationalities, and be constructively and positively accepted there, a situation which does not exist at present. An integrated economic strategy that seeks to maximize the benefits of modernization across all regions requires that the population be mobile enough to meet basic development priorities.

In a society which has depended upon centralized authority and state management of economy, the attitudes toward centralization and state planning are indicative of future trends. Again, it is the more modernized population sectors, nonpeasant and northern (i.e., Slovene and Croat elites), who seem least favorable to centralized, as compared to decentralized, economic management, and to collectivist, as compared to individualized, notions of work compensation and income distribution. This is not surprising, although it is disturbing in terms of future prospects and possibilities for the modernization and integration process in Yugoslavia. State policy in Yugoslavia in the past has sought consciously to tax the more developed regions more heavily, and to invest comparatively more in less developed regions so as to equalize the modernization process as much as possible. Social policy has also favored lower income groups at the expense of higher status groups. Furthermore, it is to be expected that southern peasants (the Serbs and Macedonians) would be the most favorably disposed to this practice, and as a result, more supportive of centralized authority. But should continued modernization be accompanied by increasing opposition to this redistributive allocation of economic and social resources on the part of northerners, the practice may become nonviable and counterproductive from a practical point of view long before the need for it has been eliminated in a social and economic sense.

So, while presenting a somewhat contradictory and inconsistent attitudinal profile, Yugoslav peasants seem to be much like those in other so-called traditional societies. They are, in short, rather pessimistic, parochial and close-minded, and committed to the traditionalistic values of family, religion, nationality, and soil. It might be concluded that it is the failure of the modernization process in Yugoslavia uniformly to change these orientations which bodes ill for the future of Yugoslav modernization, as well as for the unity and survival of Yugoslavia itself.

COMMUNIST IDEOLOGY AND INSTITUTIONAL EXPRESSION

This chapter has focused on the value and attitudinal differences which separate the mainstream of Yugoslav society from the most tradition-bound of its social groups - the peas-

antry. In one sense, however, the problems faced in integrating this backward segment of the population into the
mainstream differ very little from the other issues of unifica-
tion which face Yugoslavia. The primary goal continues to be
one of adapting and refining the Yugoslav ideological version
of societal reality such that diverse, and sometimes opposing,
groups can find a common meeting ground that will eventually
result in the creation of an enduring society and state institutions. In fact, moving the peasant toward modernity may
well be paradigmatic for overcoming the most seriously divisive
problems. Traditional conflicts often fade with the onset of
shared modernizing concerns, even though modernization often
creates new conflicts and problems.

The formation of a unifying ideology, especially in Yugoslavia, derives not so much from the articulation of interests
(as Marx would have us believe), but from the recognition that
modernization creates societal strains which appear on the level
of the individual personality. Ideology in this respect may be
viewed as a sort of "patterned response." It is not merely
an elaborate emotional reaction to some diffuse disturbance,
but provides a model for interpreting and dealing with social
reality where traditional social and cultural guidelines have
crumbled. For this reason, it is important that the ideology,
as well as public policy, reflect existing social conditions as
directly and as accurately as possible precisely in those
situations where the malintegration of society seems to be the
greatest.(22) In Yugoslavia, of course, this has been occurring among the peasantry.

A strictly materialistic conception of consciousness, such
as put forth by Marx, would suggest that it is not possible for
ideology to close the gap of historical consciousness, in this
case the disparity between peasant attitudes and the rest of
Yugoslav society. Since consciousness is a mere epiphenom-
enon of social conditions, it is entirely secondary to social
reality, becoming less dependent on those conditions only as
history progresses from "the kingdom of necessity" to the
"kingdom of freedom." Obviously, the peasant belongs with
the "kingdom of necessity" in this regard, so according to a
rigidly materialistic interpretation, he must remain bound to
the determinism of history. Yet, Yugoslavia, like all modernizing countries in the socialist bloc, cannot afford to take Marx
quite so literally. Instead, they must presume that ideological
commitment can make up for a lack of historical development,
and that it can break the bonds of the determinism of history.

The responsibility of ideology then is to provide a
"patterned response" to "patterned strain" while recognizing
that a historically limited awareness restricts men in their
ability to conceive of a qualitatively different social arrangement. The limitations on the peasantry becoming a true
revolutionary force can be seen in their deterministic and

pessimistic approach to life. They can react to unbearable conditions in a violent manner, but they tend, on the whole, to resist change. In addition, the tendency to define the personality in local terms (i.e., regional nationalism) imposes further restrictions on the nature and extent of ideological appeals aimed at improving solidarity and loyalty to a Yugoslav state ethic. Even so, these restraining views do not necessarily decrease susceptibility to ideological pleas; they merely condition the form it must take. Material incentives and goods are a necessary consideration, but they cannot erase the fact that the peasant is the focus of tensions associated with modernization, tensions which predispose the peasant to ideological commitments.

Yugoslav social ideology has sought to capitalize on these contradictions and tensions by promoting a maximum degree of decentralization in the institutional structure. The recognition of local interests entailed in this responds to the need for a regional identity while simultaneously working toward peasant recruitment into the more modernized sectors of the industrial and agricultural proletariat. It affords the peasant the opportunity to rationalize his fluctuating loyalty between a dying traditionalistic culture and a strongly attractive modernizing society.

This ideological pragmatism will only be outgrown when the legitimacy of Yugoslav society is secured in stable patterns of institutional participation. The 1963 constitutional reforms were aimed explicitly at increasing the role of the peasantry in significant social and political functions so as to accomplish just this goal. Biases which existed under the former system of representation favored the proletariat at the expense of the peasantry; these have now been corrected at least in the formal legal structure. This, in conjunction with an increased emphasis on mass participation in general, has upgraded the significance of the peasant masses. We must reiterate, however, that the peasant as such will play an increasingly less significant role in society as the process of modernization continues, since industrialization and economic development by their very nature change traditionalistic peoples into transitional, and eventually, modern peoples; a conversion of agricultural peasants into industrial and agricultural workers would be expected. The Yugoslav case is somewhat unique in that is has attempted to maintain, and even enforce, peasant representation and participation as long as the peasantry remains a significant sector within the Yugoslav population.

NOTES

(1) For a discussion of the material bases of peasant political behavior, see Samuel P. Huntington, Political Order in Changing Societies (New Haven, Conn.: Yale University Press, 1968), p. 375.
(2) The characteristics of peasant or "folk" society presented here are those identified by Robert Redfield, "The Folk Society," American Journal of Sociology 52 (January 1947): 293-308.
(3) Huntington, Political Order in Changing Societies, p. 293.
(4) The nineteenth-century Russian narodniki movement reflects this frustration with attempting to stimulate the revolutionary zeal of the peasantry. Gustav A. Wetter, Dialectial Materialism (New York: Praeger, 1958), pp. 63-64. Karl Marx, as a leftist revolutionary intellectual, was himself, of course, very cynical about any possible revolutionary role for the peasantry.
(5) Huntington, Political Order in Changing Societies, p. 374.
(6) Philip E. Mosely, "The Peasant Family: the Zadruga, or Communal Joint-Family in the Balkans and its Recent Evolution," in The Cultural Approach to History, ed. Caroline F. Ware (New York: Columbia University Press, 1940), p. 95. Also, see Robert F. Byrnes, ed., Communal Families in the Balkans: The Zadruga (London: University of Notre Dame Press, 1976).
(7) George W. Hoffman and Fred Warner Neal, Yugoslavia and the New Communism (New York: Twentieth Century Fund, 1962), p. 46.
(8) This brief account of the rebellion of 1573 in Croatia is drawn from Jozo Tomasevich, Peasants, Politics, and Economic Change in Yugoslavia (Stanford, Calif.: Stanford University Press, 1955), pp. 66-68.
(9) Robert Lee Wolff, The Balkans in Our Time (New York: W. W. Norton, 1967), p. 76.
(10) For a fuller discussion of peasant party movements, see Tomasevich, Peasants, Politics, and Economic Change in Yugoslavia, pp. 252-260; and, Wolff, The Balkans in Our Time, pp. 103-08.
(11) Tomasevich, Peasants, Politics, and Economic Change in Yugoslavia, p. 261.
(12) Regarding the communist mobilization of peasants in Yugoslavia during World War II, see Chalmers Johnson, "Peasant Mobilization in Wartime Yugoslavia," in Peasant Nationalism and Communist Power (Stanford, Calif.: Stanford University Press, 1962), pp. 156-75; also, see M. George Zaninovich, The Development of Socialist Yugoslavia (Baltimore: Johns Hopkins Press, 1968), pp. 44-50.

(13) The survey data employed in this investigation were
obtained in cooperation with the Public Opinion Section of
the Yugoslav Institute of Social Sciences in Belgrade.
The authors wish to acknowledge this cooperation and
express their appreciation to the staff of the institute.

(14) The commune in Yugoslavia is defined as a territorially
delineated community of citizens in which direct participation in self-government in all aspects of social,
economic, and political life can be widely practiced. For
a discussion of this institution, see Jovan Djordjevic and
Najdan Pasic, "The Communal Self-Government System in
Yugoslavia," International Social Science Journal 13 (July
1961): 389-407; and Anton Vratusa, "The Commune in
Yugoslavia," Socialist Thought and Practice (1965): 99-
116.

(15) A structured sample was used for this research in order
to assure that all elements of the population were represented from each commune so that individuals could be
compared across regions. A purely random sample would
not have allowed this, since in the less developed peasant
communes, the chances of randomly selecting a member of
the professional or political leadership group would have
been considerably reduced.

(16) Elaborations of factor analysis as a technique can be
found in Benjamin Fruchter, Introduction to Factor
Analysis (Princeton, N. J.: Van Nostrand, 1954); and
R. J. Rummel, Applied Factor Analysis (Evanston, Ill.:
Northwestern University Press, 1970).

(17) Three related terms will be used that require elabora-
tion: "value dimension" refers to the six groupings of
survey items generated by factor analysis, each of which
has been given a label; "value item" refers to any item
from the survey instrument which is included under any
of the six value dimensions; and "value response" is used
where the pattern or distribution of responses is
stressed.

(18) The statistic used is the Goodman and Kruskal Co-
efficient of Ordinal Association, or gamma, which requires
ordinal data. The gamma statistic is used because it
yields a measure of both degree and direction of association between two variables, yet requires only that
ordinal assumptions be met, rather than the more difficult
assumptions of more powerful parametric statistics. In
comparing peasant and nonpeasant groups, a positive
correlation indicates stronger peasant approval of an
item, a negative correlation a stronger nonpeasant approval. Correlations which fall nearer to zero indicate a
wider degree of agreement between groups. See Linton
C. Freeman, Elementary Applied Statistics (New York:
John Wiley, 1965), pp. 79-87, 162-75.

(19)   Rather than use the generated factor scores, which in effect collapse the range of specific value items, factor analysis was used here only to group those value items that were substantively similar. This avoided the inevitable loss of information usually associated with factor analysis. Specific value items were dropped if they were deemed inappropriate to the modal dimension implied by the majority of value items within a factor category in terms of what is already known about Yugoslav society, or were left in for the same reasons even though they generated a low factor score.

(20)   For a more complete analysis of regional differences in value orientations in Yugoslavia, see M. George Zaninovich, "On Comparing East European Political Systems: The Case of Yugoslavia," Studies in Comparative Communism 4 (April 1971): 58-70; and Gary K. Bertsch and M. George Zaninovich, "A Factor-Analytic Method of Identifying Different Political Cultures," Comparative Politics 6, (January 1974): 219-44.

(21)   See Daniel Lerner, The Passing of Traditional Society (New York: Free Press, 1958), particularly the section entitled "The Model of Transition," pp. 69-75.

(22)   See Clifford Geertz, "Ideology as a Cultural System" in Ideology and Discontent, ed. David E. Apter (New York: Free Press, 1964), p. 54.

V
Conclusion

Conclusion

13 Patterns in Rural Transformation: A Concluding Overview

Richard E. Lonsdale
and William P. Avery

This volume has focused on the various elements of change in nonurban life in three geographical settings - Eastern Europe, Latin America, and Australia. Persons from several academic disciplines have examined various aspects of rural transformation in an effort to identify and analyze some of the problems associated with changes in the rural sphere. However, with the increasing urbanization of societies around the world, one might appropriately ask: Why study the countryside? Is not the countryside of diminishing significance in a rapidly urbanizing world, and does it really merit special attention? It is of course true that worldwide more and more people are becoming urban dwellers, but that in itself has highly significant implications for the surrounding countryside. The out-migration of young people seeking a better life in the city is but one universal example. Land hunger, the lack of sufficient employment opportunities in rural areas, rural depopulation, and the overcrowding of cities almost inevitably have important social, economic, and political consequences.

In this concluding chapter, we identify those elements of the rural transformation process most frequently stressed in the preceding chapters. While it is difficult to place these elements in discrete categories because of interconnectivity and many cases of circular causation, the procedure does permit the formulation of some generalizations about the rural transformation process. It is important to bear in mind that we are generalizing at a broad, macrolevel about a complex process for a variety of nations possessing contrasting geographic, social, political, and economic environments. Unfortunately, the process of rural transformation is relatively little understood, and there are no established guidelines or norms against which we can compare our observations. Only three regions of the world are here investigated and no doubt rural regions in other parts of the world might reveal different sets of rural change characteristics. Despite these reservations, however, eight generalizations are presented which provide a basis for organizing our thoughts on rural transformation.

RURAL TRANSFORMATION IS AN
ONGOING INTERNATIONAL PROCESS

The universal character of rural transformation as a process seems abundantly evident from the chapters in this volume. Similarities in experiences among nations appear easily to outnumber dissimilarities, and this assists us in the search for underlying order. The process is generated and strongly conditioned by the ongoing forces of modernization which to one degree or another are present everywhere.(1)   Certain principles seem to hold which transcend such obvious and important differences as those in political systems and levels of economic development. To name but a few: increased agricultural productivity displaces workers; rural job opportunities are more limited in scope than urban ones; urban areas are the centers of most political power and innovation; and conditions of physical geography and distance place some rural areas at a disadvantage.

While rural transformation is an international process, this is not to say there are not important distinctions and variations conditioned by local attitudes, objectives, and technical abilities. Indeed, many such distinctions and variations exist, each presumably explainable in terms of local conditions past and present, but this does not negate the fact that as a process at the macrolevel of analysis, rural transformation knows no national boundaries.

It is also an ongoing process, knowing no time parameters.   To be sure, many elements of rural change have a discrete beginning and/or end, but overall change is ever present - more often imperceptible than dramatic.   Perhaps we are too accustomed to working with economic cycles and models of development, both suggesting starting and finishing points. In the case of Australia and the United States it is indeed customary to think of rural development, or transformation of the rural sector, as commencing with European settlement, but in both instances native peoples occupied rural space prior to the Europeans' arrival.

MODERNIZATION PROVIDES THE BASIC FORCES
GENERATING RURAL TRANSFORMATION

Societies are always undergoing change, and it is perhaps the most characteristic feature of the contemporary period that change has been more pervasive and rapid than in any other time in history. As Black describes it, "the process of change in the modern era is of the same order of magnitude as that from prehuman to human life and from primitive to civilized societies; it is the most dynamic of the great revolutionary transformations in the conduct of human affairs."(2) Rural change is created and molded by the diversity of forces associated with the process of modernization, a process that touches on seemingly every aspect of rural life and activity.

Modernization generates change in rural areas through transformations in communication and transportation, bringing greater awareness of outside events, easier movement of goods and ideas across space, and more rapid adoption of new ideas and knowledge. Traditional agriculture is transformed through mechanization, the introduction of fertilizers, chemicals, and seed varieties, all of which increase yields and alter traditional land/labor ratios. Urbanization also accompanies modernization, furnishing a pull in out-migration as well as critical "origin points" for diffusion of modernization.(3) Modernization affects rural politics with the introduction of new and sometimes unsettling ideologies. Medical and health services are transformed, reducing death rates and setting into motion the classic demographic cycle. Industrialization supplies modern goods for rural areas and alters consumer tastes for material products. It also provides nonagricultural employment opportunities and suggests a managerial-organizational model for agriculture to emulate. Education, which accelerates the modernization process, requires often difficult social adaptation as traditional social relationships are modified and old attitudes, aspirations, and material comforts change. It is amost a truism to say that rural transformation and modernization are inextricably linked.

THE RATE AND DIRECTION OF RURAL
CHANGE ARE VARIABLE

What is doubtlessly universal about the process of rural change is the scope of that process, a scope that affects gradually the whole of rural life in all its dimensions, economic, social, spatial, and political. The temporal rate of transformation, however, is highly variable. As a process it can be stalled, accelerated, or decelerated. New exogenous changes may occur which have the direction and strength necessary to redirect the process.(4)

Halpern (chapter 10) suggests that for some rural areas there may have been more change in the past 40 years than in the previous 2,000 years. The daily lives of some American farmers, especially those in the United States South in the 1930s, involved work procedures and techniques relatively unchanged since the time of Christ. A modernization wave engulfed the South after World War II, and the subsequent rural transformation there has been remarkable.

The three regions examined in this book illustrate well the variability of change. The pace of rural change in Eastern Europe was slow for several centuries, as Volgyes documents in chapter 5, but after World War II, according to Hoffman (chapter 2), "few countries in the world have experienced such far-reaching basic structural changes in their cultural, economic and political life." In much of rural Latin America modernization has been spotty, and progress in overcoming what are frequently severe conditions of under-development has been largely disappointing. In Australia, on the other hand, the "good life" has already been achieved, thanks in part to the large land mass and small population. With relatively little incentive for major change, McKnight (chapter 3) observes that "the geography of rural Australia in the mid-1970s differs little from the geography of rural Australia in the 1950s." As a generalization this would seem to be reasonably valid, but changes brought by mining, new irrigation projects, and urban-initiated "hobby farms" all contribute to a continuing process of rural transformation.

RURAL REGIONS UNDERGO DIFFICULT DEMOGRAPHIC ADJUSTMENTS WITH MODERNIZATION

The impact of advanced societies (e.g. colonial powers) on the demographic structure of traditional societies is well known. It is a case of exporting certain facets of modernization, in particular modern medicine and public health practices. The same process operates when urban centers of an industrializing nation "export" their goods and ideas to that nation's rural areas. As in colonial lands, rural areas experience the benefits of modern health care, but generally without the presence of new job-generating industry. Death rates fall, but birth rates decline much more slowly than in urban areas. The resultant increase in population, frequently combined with a declining need for farm labor (also a product of modern-ization), sets into motion a difficult and burdensome process of demographic adjustment.(5)

The demographic problems which most rural areas experience at one stage or another include 1) a growing population combined with declining employment opportunities; 2) continued high fertility rates; 3) large-scale out-migration, especially of younger people; 4) a changing age structure of the population, with a higher percentage of older persons; and 5) many rural communities experiencing population loss, economic stagnation, and loss of many central-place functions. Rural regions within less developed nations are likely to experience the first three or four problems, while rural sections of advanced societies are more likely to experience the latter three.

In most areas of Latin America, as Thiesenhusen observes in chapter 6, population growth is high, and although there are some signs of declining birth rates, they are not very rapid. Mechanization has released people from employment in agriculture, but alternate job opportunities in rural areas are very limited. The resulting exodus to the burgeoning cities and the emergence of shantytowns adjacent to them is one of the great tragedies and failings of Latin American development.

Australia provides a sharp contrast. The nation was settled in the nineteenth century by Europeans who had already passed through a part of the demographic cycle. In a sense, rural Australia was "born modern"; birth rates were never very high and rural population densities were always low. It has, nonetheless, experienced the usual problems of out-migration, aging of the population, and the stagnation and demise of many country towns. However, rural Australia would now seem to be approaching demographic stability, and it may soon follow the United States pattern wherein rural areas experience modest population growth.

In Eastern Europe, the establishment of socialism and collectivized agriculture (subsequently modified in Poland and Yugoslavia) had dramatic demographic impacts. Forced industrialization and the rapid mechanization of agriculture brought a large-scale shift of labor from rural to urban areas. Modern medical care and changing social attitudes (e.g., a sharply higher female labor force participation rate as well as increased desires and opportunities for the material elements of the "good life") brought a pronounced drop in both birth and death rates, and overall population growth rates declined. In some nations there is now a problem of labor shortages in both urban and rural areas. Perhaps, as in Australia but in sharp contrast to Latin America, rural Eastern Europe is reaching a point of demographic stability, despite a much different history in arriving at this point.

REGIONAL INEQUITY AND RURAL POVERTY
ARE PERSISTENT PROBLEMS

In the developing countries of the world, more than 80 percent of the poor are estimated to live in rural areas.(6) And although most governments are willing to experiment with rural development projects, many are not successful or at best only modestly so. One important reason for this lack of success is that economic policies at the macrolevel are often inconsistent with rural development and agricultural needs. Pricing policies, for example, favor urban-based manufacturing industries and are usually aimed at keeping food prices low in urban areas. Financial institutions often view rural investment as a higher risk proposition. Further, national fiscal policies discriminate against the rural sector, with public spending heavily concentrated in the urban sector. Thus, national economic policies frequently work against rural areas and many of the goals of rural development.

A prominent theory among economists posits that as a nation moves from underdevelopment to more advanced industrial development, the nation passes through a cycle of regional inequity in income levels. Prior to large-scale industrialization, most people are engaged in agriculture and in traditional forms of trade and cottage industry. With industrialization and the concomitant centralization of production, regional inequity is intensified.(7) But with industrial maturity, the diseconomics of overcentralization become increasingly evident and there is a tendency for regional inequities to diminish as a result of labor and capital migration, interregional linkages, and government policy.(8) There is a long history in most nations of policies for economic development of underdeveloped regions within their borders.(9) However, the historical experience of almost all developed countries is that regional inequity and instances of rural poverty stubbornly persist.

Experiences in Latin America, Eastern Europe, and Australia generally support the idea of a cycle of regional inequity. Of the three areas, rural Latin America has quite clearly made the least progress through the cycle. In chapter 6, Thiesenhusen emphasizes that regional income patterns are becoming ever more unequal. Gains in income are largely associated with the growing urban-industrial centers while the peasantry is increasingly pauperized. Most rural people are poor, and the bottom 60 percent are relatively worse off than 20 years ago. In most Latin American nations there is scant evidence of forces building up to reduce regional inequity. Furthermore, there seems to be little concern with the problem on the part of urban-based national decision-making structures.

Regional inequities within East European nations have diminished dramatically since about 1960. Farm incomes are higher and opportunities for rural residents to engage in nonfarm occupations have greatly expanded. This is in sharp contrast to the earlier post-World War II period when the rural sector suffered great deprivation while growing urban-industrial centers received the bulk of investment capital. Eastern Europe has progressed through much of the regional inequity cycle with remarkable rapidity, as Volgyes observes in chapter 5. However, instances of rural poverty are still to be found in spite of serious attempts by the communist governments, specifically in such backward rural areas as Bosnia-Herzegovina, Moldavia, and many parts of Bulgaria.

In Australia regional differences in income levels have not been dramatic, thanks to fairly uniform national wage policies and strong labor unions. Ironically, this measure of regional income equity discourages industrial decentralization, and rural Australia does suffer from inadequate employment opportunities and limited social services.(10) Rural poverty has persisted in some areas (e.g., the dairy belt of coastal New South Wales) despite government price supports and other forms of assistance.

PRESSURE FOR LAND REFORM IS A RECURRENT THEME

All three regions examined in this book, despite sometimes dramatic contrasts in conditions and outcomes, provide much evidence to support the generalization that land tenure is a recurrent issue in rural life. The desire for land and a sense of injustice where there is gross inequity in land distribution are among the most basic instincts of rural mankind. Where the number of people available for farming exceeds the available land and where ownership is concentrated in a small but powerful land-based elite, there is pressure for change. Land reform is also the focal point where a desire exists to reorganize agriculture to further general economic development.(11) Programs include the reparceling of existing land, resettlement schemes, and the creation of new farm lands.

Land reform appears to be most pressing as a political issue in those countries with high inequality in land ownership patterns and a large percentage of the labor force engaged in agriculture.(12) Thus, in much of the modernizing world, the land question is a major and often explosive political issue. In 1950, Bolivia had what was certainly one of the world's most inequitable land tenure structures, an economy with more than 60 percent of the work force involved in agriculture, and at least 20 percent of total farms in tenancy. In 1952, Bolivia experienced an agrarian revolution. The land ownership patterns in Iraq were also severely unequal and the rural labor force high at the time a modernizing military junta took power in 1958 and launched a program of land reforms. Numerous other examples could be cited, but the central point is clear. In countries where the importance of agriculture is relatively high (as evidenced by a large agricultural component of the work force) and the land ownership patterns highly unequal, land reform is likely to be a particularly salient issue.

Given these conditions, how does land reform become a reality? In attempting to answer this question, analysts have distinguished between elite-based reform ("reform from above") and massed-based reform ("reform from below").(13) Huntington maintains, however, that "successful land reform involves action from both directions. The efficacy of land reform by revolution, of course, is that it does involve both elements: the rapid centralization of power in the revolutionary elite and the rapid mobilization into politics of the peasantry."(14) Again citing the Bolivian experience, the peasants first seized the land, after which the new revolutionary elite confirmed their actions through the enactment of land reform laws.

An important part of the history of Eastern Europe is associated with changes in land tenure, and this has been particularly true since World War II. As is well known, and as Hoffman and Volgyes describe in this volume, collectivization greatly transformed the rural landscape of Eastern Europe. Small farms and fragmented field patterns gave way to large collective and state farms with large fields suitable for mechanization; fences, hedgerows, and dispersed farmsteads were virtually eliminated.(15) Only in Poland and Yugoslavia has collectivization subsequently been relaxed, but there too more equitable individual ownership patterns have been created. The question remains: Is pressure for land reform still a force to be reckoned with? In Poland and Yugoslavia there are those who doubt the wisdom of present "liberal" policies; in the other countries there is abundant evidence that many peasants remain disenchanted with collectivization. Pressure for reform is subdued in an authoritarian environment, but the basic roots of change are present nonetheless.

We should emphasize, however, that there is growing evidence that peasant attitudes toward collectivization and land ownership are changing in Eastern Europe. There are some peasants who no longer desire to work even on their household plots, who do not wish to own land, and who opt for fixed hours of work, leisure time, and vacations. The determinant of this changed attitude seems to be the profitability of working on the collective land. In areas where the good collectives offer a great deal of positive remuneration adequate for the demands of the rural population, as in parts of Hungary, attitudes toward land ownership seem to have been altered.

In Australia, the mid-nineteenth century saw much of the land taken over by "squatters" engaged in extensive grazing, but from the 1850s on the colonies enacted a series of land reform measures designed to break up the large properties and promote closer agricultural settlement. The "dream of Australian plains filled with a sturdy and independent yeomanry"(16) was impractical, however, because of the arid and semi-arid nature of much of the land, limited domestic markets, etc. Land legislation often led to the creation of farms and grazing properties too small to be economically viable. Of particular note in more recent years have been several major irrigation development schemes, described by McKnight in chapter 3, but their high cost has made them politically controversial and the number of new farms created has been rather small. While land legislation was a major issue in Australia's formative period, it has waned in importance as Australia developed into a modern, highly urban, technologically advanced society.

It is difficult to generalize on the experience of Latin American nations, but by and large the forces of traditions have prevailed with most of the prime farm land still in the hands of a relatively small number of landholders. Thiesenhusen (chapter 6) observes that "perhaps the most telling indicator of transformation there would be the extent to which countries have [not] instituted agrarian reforms." There has been some land reform, but, except in Cuba, no major transformation has occurred. For the most part, land reform laws are written by landholding elites who have relatively little concern for the plight of landless peasants. As one observer notes, "the willingness of landowners to lose their property through land reforms short of revolution varies directly with the extent to which the only alternative appears to be to lose it through revolution."(17) Expensive programs for the colonization of marginal, frontier areas have been widely publicized, but their main effect has been to divert public attention from the more fundamental land tenure issues.

AGRARIAN-POPULIST POLITICAL MOVEMENTS DEVELOP IN RESPONSE TO MODERNIZATION

The role of the countryside in the politics of modernization is crucial. It has been said that "he who controls the countryside controls the country."(18) In traditional societies, both the urban and rural sectors are dominated by a rural landowning oligarchy. As these societies undergo modernization,

the middle sectors and new urban groups emerge to challenge
the traditional elite.   Their success, however, depends upon
their ability to win support from rural elements.   Similarly, in
order for the existing government to survive, it too must
enlist the support of peasants.   Thus, the focus of politics is
on the countryside, with the governmental elite competing with
urban groups (usually including a revolutionary intelligentsia)
for rural allies.   And mass-based populist appeals soon come to
characterize   peasant-oriented   politics.   In   instances   where
political participation is restricted, though, it may be enough
for the government to have the support of the landowning
traditional elite.   But the peasantry is the key group where
participation and political awareness is expanding.   In short,
"if the peasantry acquiesces in and identifies with the existing
system, it furnishes that system with a stable foundation.   If
it   actively   opposes   the   system,   it   becomes   the   carrier   of
revolution."(19)
      In chapter 9, Powell sees a striking commonality in the
origins   of   agrarian-populist   movements   (e.g.,   those   which
appeared in Central and Eastern Europe in the interwar
period).   These movements gained momentum in rural areas
suffering from the impact of international and domestic market
forces during the early phases of economic modernization.
Powell argues that the emergence of these movements was a
defensive response to the changes wrought in rural societies
by the emerging dominance of modern urban-based economic
systems.   As political movements or parties, they displayed
strong   attachments   to   traditional   values   and   pushed   for
protection from foreign competition, programs of social insurance, agrarian reform, maintenance of the "rural way of
life," and government aid to cushion the impact of modernization and its many ramifications on rural life.
      Australia never had a peasantry or the scale of rural
poverty experienced by many other societies, but rural dissatisfaction with urban-based political and economic institutions
did lead to political action.   Rural areas felt cheated of their
rightful heritage as farm populations dwindled, rural towns
stagnated,   and   economic   growth   was   concentrated   in   a   few
large coastal cities.   As a defensive response, the Country
Party was founded toward the end of World War I, and it has
played an effective role in national politics as the voice of
rural interests.
      Agrarian-populist movements in Eastern Europe have
developed in response to the exploitation of the cities and have
been frequently centered around demands for land.   In some
of the countries of the region, these movements were led by
intellectuals who idealized the peasantry and sought equity for
them.   These movements, however, have all been destroyed by
the   communist   governments   which   were   only   interested   in
changing the land ownership structure.   Current agrarian-

populist ideas can only concentrate therefore on transforming
other - nonownership - attributes of rural life and hence this
aspect of rural transformation concentrates on improvements of
outward amenities.

In Latin America, the peasants' overriding desire for land
predisposes them to support political parties and organizations
that advocate land reform. Possession of land represents for
the peasant a means of providing for his family and an important, age-old form of physical and psychological security.
Peasants have thus formed a mass support for various populist
parties, including Venezuela's Accion Democratica and Christian
Democratic (COPEI) parties, the Partido Revolucionario In-
stitucional (PRI) in Mexico since the mid-1930s, and the
National Revolutionary Movement (MNR) in Bolivia from 1952
through 1964. It should be emphasized, however, that once
the peasant has received his plot of land, he has reached his
ultimate goal and becomes politically apathetic. For him, the
"revolution" is over.(20)

RURAL SOCIETY IS CONSTANTLY IN A STATE OF
"CATCHING UP" WITH THE SOCIAL ATTITUDES
AND LIFE-STYLES OF URBAN SOCIETY

Modernization generally has its origins in urban areas where
social change is not only assimilated rather quickly, but is
indeed fostered by urbanization itself. Rural areas, on the
other hand, are the eventual recipients of this urban-
generated modernization and all its social impacts. It places a
more or less constant "burden of change" on rural areas (i.e.,
they must adjust to urban-generated standards). It would
seem, therefore, that the lot of rural areas is always one of
"catching up" with urban areas, i.e., adjusting to and
adopting urban life-styles, attitudes, aspirations, and the like,
which come to be treated as the national norm. Modern communication and transportation have accelerated the process of
adjustment and the demands of the rural population for urban
amenities, but an urban-rural gap still persists, even though
to a much lesser extent in more advanced industrial
nations.(21)

Many rural areas have a rich heritage of social attitudes
and values molded through centuries of experience with their
environment. These attitudes and values are not easily
modified or abandoned under the impact of modernization, and
change is often slower than urban dwellers would like.(22)
City people almost everywhere have traditionallly tended to
disparage rural folk for their "backward" attitudes and adherence to "old-fashioned" practices.

Nowhere is the stress and strain of adjustment more evident than within rural family units themselves where the younger people have embraced the new urban-based life style while the older folks cling to the older ways. In chapter 10, Halpern provides some marvelously poignant insights to this situation in Eastern Europe, an area where the forced and rapid social transformation of rural society has been a paramount state policy.

In Latin America, where most rural people live in a separate world from urban society, traditional attitudes and life-styles are more prevalent. But the "catching-up" process is nonetheless still operative, however wide the urban-rural gap. The pressure for social change is partially mitigated by conservative urban-based regimes who themselves are uneasy about rapid social change. Social mobility is much more restricted here than in more advanced industrial societies.

Rural Australians emulate urban mass society in their attitudes and life-styles in much the same manner as rural Americans. There are, of course, distinct rural life-styles, especially in more remote "Outback" areas, but attitudes, values, and aspirations are not particularly distinctive. There is easy social mobility between rural and urban environments, helped by the lack of major differences in economic and educational levels.

POSTSCRIPT

This concluding chapter has identified some common themes in the preceding chapters and set a foundation for examining the process of rural transformation in a cross-national context. It is hoped that readers have found the comparative approach useful in better understanding what must be regarded as a general and international process. It is also hoped that this book will stimulate more research on a topic where there are unusually abundant opportunities for further empirical observation and hypothesis formulation.

NOTES

(1)   Among the vast literature on modernization, the following are of particular value: C. E. Black, The Dynamics of Modernization (New York: Harper and Row, 1966); Seymour Martin Lipset, The First New Nation (New York: Basic Books, 1963); S. N. Eisenstadt, Modernization: Protest and Change (Englewood Cliffs, N.J.: Prentice-Hall, 1966); Dankwart A. Rustow, A World of Nations

(Washington, D. C.: Brookings Institution, 1967); Samuel P. Huntington, Political Order in Changing Societies (New Haven, Conn.: Yale University Press, 1969); Daniel Lerner, The Passing of Traditional Society (Glencoe, Ill.: Free Press, 1958); Lucian W. Pye, Aspects of Political Development (Boston: Little, Brown, 1966); and Leonard Binder et al., Crises and Sequences in Political Development (Princeton, N. J.: Princeton University Press, 1971). Some specific discussions of modernization and the peasantry are: Guy Hunter, Modernizing Peasant Societies (New York: Oxford University Press, 1969); and Barrington Moore, Jr., Social Origins of Dictatorship and Democracy (Boston: Beacon, 1967).

(2) Black, The Dynamics of Modernization, p. 4.

(3) The notion that modernization and change originate just in large urban centers is effectively questioned by E. A. J. Johnson, The Organization of Space in Developing Countries (Cambridge, Mass.: Harvard University Press, 1970), pp. 28–71.

(4) Gunnar Myrdal, Economic Theory and Underdeveloped Regions (London: Methuen, 1965), pp. 80–81. For an excellent discussion of modernization and political deceleration or decay, see Samuel Huntington's famous article, "Political Development and Political Decay," World Politics 17 (April 1965).

(5) See Erich H. Jacoby (in collaboration with Charlotte Jacoby), Man and Land (New York: Alfred A. Knopf, 1971); Kingsley Davis, World Urbanization 1950–1970, vol. II (Berkeley: University of California, Population Monograph Series, 1972); and Joginder Kumar, Population and Land in World Agriculture (Berkeley: University of California, Population Monograph Series, 1973).

(6) Rural Development (Washington, D. C.: World Bank, 1975), p. 5.

(7) Benjamin Chinitz, "The Effect of Transportation Forms on Regional Economic Growth," Traffic Quarterly 14 (April 1960): 130–33.

(8) Jeffrey G. Williamson, "Regional Inequality and the Process of National Development: A Description of the Patterns," Economic Development and Cultural Change 13, part 2 (July 1965): 8–9.

(9) Myrdal, Economic Theory and Underdeveloped Regions, p. 43.

(10) Richard E. Lonsdale, "Manufacturing Decentralization: The Discouraging Record in Australia," Land Economics 48 (November 1972): 321–38.

(11) Erich H. Jacoby, "Agrarian Reform: Planning, Implementation, and Evaluation," in Rural Development in a Changing World ed. Raanan Weitz (Cambridge, Mass.: Massachusetts Institute of Technology Press, 1971), p. 269.

338   THE PROCESS OF RURAL TRANSFORMATION

(12) Huntington, Political Order in Changing Societies, pp. 381-84. See also: Bruce Russett, "Inequality and Instability: The Relation of Land Tenure to Politics," World Politics 16 (1964).
(13) For an excellent analysis of these types of revolution, see Moore, Social Origins of Dictatorship and Democracy.
(14) Huntington, Political Order in Changing Societies, pp. 384-85.
(15) Dean S. Rugg, "Aspects of Change in the Landscape of East-Central and Southeast Europe," in Eastern Europe: Essays in Geographical Problems, ed. George W. Hoffman (New York: Praeger, 1971), pp. 83-122.
(16) O. H. K. Spate, Australia (New York: Praeger, 1968), p. 45.
(17) Huntington, Political Order in Changing Societies, p. 385.
(18) Ibid., p. 292.
(19) Ibid., p. 293.
(20) Anibal Quijano Obregon, "Contemporary Peasant Movements," in Elites in Latin America, ed. Seymour M. Lipset and Aldo Solari, (New York: Oxford University Press, 1967), pp. 301-40.
(21) S. Groenman, "Social Aspects of Backwardness in Developed Countries," in Backward Areas in Advanced Countries, ed. E. A. G. Robinson (New York: St. Martin's Press, 1969), pp. 29-34. For a discussion of the political effects of the urban-rural gap, see Huntington, Political Order in Changing Societies, pp. 433-38.
(22) Jack M. Potter, "Modernization Processes and Rural Development in Developing Countries: An Anthropological View," in Rural Development in a Changing World, ed. Raanan Weitz (Cambridge, Mass.: Massachusetts Institute of Technology Press, 1971), p. 356.

Index

Aborigines, 47
Adams, Richard N., 274
Agrarian reform, 10, 21-22, 25-26, 73-74, 97-103, 106, 108-111, 116-117, 135-137, 143, 198, 209-210, 213-214, 217, 219, 221, 247, 271, 279-281, 331-333
Agro-industrial complexes, 26, 28, 111, 116
Albania, 21-22, 31-32, 92, 110
Allende, Salvador, 218-221
Anthropologists, 7, 10, 270, 275
Argentina, 130-132, 136
Arid frontiers, 60-62, 68, 71-82
Aughey, Samuel, 72, 82
Austria, 100, 102, 292-294

Berger, Suzanne, 216
Bessey, Charles, 77
Bicanic, Rudolf, 22
Black, Cyril, E., 8, 327
Bolivia, 128, 130-131, 136, 229, 278-279, 331-332, 335
Brazil, 130, 134-136, 273, 275, 284
Brigalow Development Program, 62-63
Brown, James, E., 78
Brown, Ralph, 70

Bulgaria, 21-22, 26-29, 31-33, 36, 92, 96, 100-103, 109-112, 116, 205, 207, 215, 331
Burks, R. V., 214-215
Burton, Sir Richard, 71

Campesinos, 136, 138
Capital, 22, 94, 100, 141, 152-157, 167-169, 224, 274
Capitalism, 93, 99, 176, 206, 211-212, 217, 225, 269, 272-273, 275, 283, 285
Carter, Jimmy, 243-244
Chile, 130, 136, 195, 198-199, 211-212, 216, 218-221, 225, 229, 273, 279-280, 284
Christaller, Walter, 9
Collective farms, 7-8, 23, 25-27, 30, 106-111, 121, 175, 332
Collectivization, 24-26, 34, 107-112, 114, 116, 121, 180, 247, 332
Colombia, 130, 133, 226, 229-230, 278, 280, 284
Communication facilities, 5, 48, 100, 163, 177, 179, 253-256, 327, 335
Communist Party, 29, 107-108, 110, 175-176, 180-181, 196, 202, 211, 213-220, 222, 229, 296-297, 304

339

Mackay, D. F., 71
Magsaysay, Ramon, 199
Mailer, Norman, 243
Malnutrition, 134-135, 137
Mantoux Thesis, 97
Marxism
  development model, 12, 35, 218
  ideology, 25, 93, 106, 180, 218, 273, 317
Mechanization of agriculture, 24, 28, 30, 34, 89, 101, 106, 108, 112, 114, 116, 118-119, 121, 137, 144, 152, 156, 167, 224, 248, 327
Meinig, Donald W., 78, 81
Mexico, 130-133, 136, 270-271, 278-280, 282, 284
Mining, 49-53, 63-64, 328
Models of rural transformation, 12
Modernization, 3, 4, 6, 23, 89, 242-243, 289, 292, 297-298, 307, 313-316, 318, 326-329, 333, 335
Multinational corporations, 130, 273
Myrdal, Gunnar, 129

Natural environment.
  See physical environment
Natural resources, 49-51, 57-60, 131, 135, 141, 144, 156, 165-166, 205, 273
New South Wales, 50, 54-55, 57-58, 141-143, 145-146, 162-170, 331
News media, 130, 137, 230, 253-256
Nordlinger, Eric A., 195
Northern Territory, 56, 62, 142, 145
Norway, 195, 205

Olmsted, Frederick, 77
Ord River scheme, 62
Orthodox Church, 92-93, 292-293, 298, 309

Pakistan, 198, 201-202

Paraguay, 130-131, 136
Peasant workers, 9, 30, 32-34, 36, 100-101
Peasants, 4, 10, 12, 21-23, 26, 36, 44, 89-103, 107-112, 116, 121, 176, 183, 194, 197-232, 242, 245-268, 270, 274-285, 289-318, 332-335
  attitudes and values, 3, 5-7, 10, 106, 136-137, 182-183, 205-206, 212-213, 242-268, 277-278, 289-318
  attributes, 90-91, 100-101, 289-291
  defined, 90
  landless, 21-22, 25, 99, 114, 135, 194, 210, 213, 272, 274, 296, 333
Peru, 133, 136, 198-199, 273, 275, 278, 280, 284
Petras, James, 218
Philippines, 199, 226, 228
Physical environment, 42, 44, 68, 71-82, 135, 163, 181-182, 326
Pioneer settlement, 68-70, 143, 333
Plow theory, 70-76, 78-79, 81-82
Poland, 11, 21-23, 26-27, 30-33, 95, 97, 99, 102-103, 109, 111-112, 114, 116, 121, 205, 209, 211, 213-215, 329, 332
Policy makers, 12, 23, 92-93, 95, 103, 106-110, 129, 136, 147, 188, 198, 199-200, 202, 206, 209, 223, 227, 231, 284, 296, 330
Political processes, 3, 10, 12-13, 23-24, 35, 48, 54, 73-74, 78-79, 101-102, 107-111, 121, 136-140, 143-145, 179-181, 187, 194-232, 270, 277, 280-285, 290-297, 316-318, 327-328, 331-334
Political scientists, 7, 10, 193
Population
  birth rates, 3, 102, 183, 284, 328-329

characteristics, 30-35, 47-48, 103, 113, 137, 140, 183-184, 329
density, 42, 152, 222
migration, 30-34, 51, 96, 101, 112, 121, 150, 152, 179-180, 230, 327, 329
trends, 9, 51-52, 96, 102-103, 112, 129-131, 137, 178-179, 205, 284, 325, 327-329
Poverty, 23, 99, 129, 135-136, 138, 147, 152, 271, 281, 331
Private farming, 23, 25-27, 30, 34, 109, 111, 121, 140-170, 175-189, 205, 381, 285, 295, 332
Puerto Rico, 132-133, 203

Queensland, 46, 53, 55, 57-58 62-63, 141-142, 145

Redfield, Robert, 270-271
Regional studies, 10-11
Revolution and rebellion, 94, 129, 271-272, 278-279, 290-291, 294, 296, 332-333, 335
Rokkan, Stein, 193-195
Roman Catholic Church, 92-93, 102, 205, 280, 292-293, 295, 298, 309
Romania, 11, 21-22, 27, 31-32, 37, 92, 96, 99, 102-103, 106, 110-112, 209
Romany, Pal, 187-188
Rostow, W. W., 9
Rural life styles, 5, 35, 95, 122, 152, 166-170, 175, 177, 179-183, 206, 242-268, 270, 289-318, 336
Rural sociologists, 9
Rurality, 4-6, 43
Rural-urban distinctions, 4-5, 24-25, 28, 34-36, 101, 193, 195, 281, 291, 305-306, 335-336
Russia. See USSR.

Schomburgk, Richard, 77
Settlement
expansion, 54-57, 60-64, 70, 73-75, 82, 137, 143, 333
patterns, 42, 44-45, 52, 54, 79, 143-144, 146, 151, 175-189, 274
structure, 9, 10, 25, 29, 44-45
Serfdom, 21, 94, 97, 294, 296
Sertel, Ayse K., 200
Service facilities, 5, 30, 116, 137-138, 152, 163, 177, 179, 188, 227, 231
Silverman, Sydel, 223-224
Snow, Frank H., 72
Social change, 9, 10, 23-26, 34-35, 89, 94, 101, 106, 121, 129, 179, 183, 185, 194, 200, 205-207, 217-221, 226, 230, 244-268, 270, 281, 285, 290, 292, 295, 297-298, 307, 318, 327-329, 332, 334-336
Social mobility, 129, 226, 245, 275, 301, 307, 336
Socialism, 23-25, 29, 34, 106-122, 176, 180, 215-216, 218-220, 242, 245, 247, 283-284, 329
Sociologists, 9, 10
Sorokin, Pitrim, 9
South Australia, 54-57, 60-61 68, 72, 74-76, 78-79, 81-82, 142
Stamboliiski, Aleksandur, 207, 209
State farms, 26-27, 30, 107, 109, 111, 175, 247-249, 332
Subsistence farming, 23, 99, 135, 179, 199, 225, 276

Tanyas, 175-189
Tarrow, Sidney, 200, 217
Tasmania, 43, 58, 141-142
Taxation, 93, 100, 108, 160-162, 188, 283, 290
Tomasevich, Jozo, 21
Towns, 5, 29, 44-45, 52-53, 63-64, 92, 96, 163, 176-177, 180, 186, 205, 245-268, 329

About the
Contributors

IVAN VOLGYES is Professor of Political Science and Director of the Project on Comparative Rural Transformation, University of Nebraska, Lincoln. Among his various publications are Politics in Hungary (with Peter A. Toma) and Comparative Political Socialization: Eastern Europe. He is currently conducting studies on the transformation of Hungarian peasants while on leave in Hungary as a Fulbright-Hays Scholar.

RICHARD E. LONSDALE is Professor of Geography at the University of Nebraska, Lincoln, and a member of the Council of the Association of American Geographers. His major interests are in industrial decentralization and the economic base of small towns, and he has researched these topics in the U.S., Australia, and the U.S.S.R. He is co-editor of Nonmetropolitan Industrialization and editor of An Economic Atlas of Nebraska.

WILLIAM P. AVERY is Associate Professor and Vice Chairperson of the Department of Political Science, University of Nebraska, Lincoln. His published articles have appeared in the American Journal of Political Science, Foro Internacional, International Organization, International Studies Quarterly, Journal of Common Market Studies, and Mondes en Developpement. His current research concerns the role of the state in Latin American rural society.

DOUGLAS A. BROWN is Assistant Professor of Political Science at Western Arizona College. He is author of "Administration and Dependence in the Third World" and has served for two years as a field officer with the U.S. Agency for International Development.

MARTHA JEAN WILLIAMS FERRILL is an instructor in the Division of Continuing Education and a Ph.D. candidate in Geography at the University of Nebraska, Lincoln. She received her A.B. at Southern Illinois University and the M.A. at Nebraska. Her major interest is in the perception and comparative studies of frontier settlement, specializing in the grasslands of North America and Australia.

JOEL M. HALPERN is Professor of Anthropology at the University of Massachusetts, Amherst. He has traveled and conducted research in the Balkans and Yugoslavia, as well as in mainland Southeast Asia. Among his numerous publications are A Serbian Village; The Changing Village Community; and The Changing Peasantry of Eastern Europe. His current interests include historical demography, rural-to-urban migration, and socio-cultural change.

GEORGE W. HOFFMAN is Professor and Chairman, Department of Geography, University of Texas, Austin. His primary interests are in the economic development of Southeastern Europe, and energy resources of Eastern Europe and the Soviet Union. His books include A Geography of Europe; Regional Development Strategy in Southeast Europe; and The Balkans in Transition.

HENRY A. LANDSBERGER is Professor of Sociology at the University of North Carolina, Chapel Hill. A well-known authority on the urban and rural masses in Latin America, he served as president of the Latin American Studies Association during 1973. He is author or editor of a number of publications including Latin American Peasant Movements.

TOM L. McKNIGHT is Professor and Chairman, Department of Geography, U.C.L.A. His long-term research and teaching interests focus on Australia, in particular economic development, pastoralism, and zoogeography. Based on research during four lengthly visits, he has published one textbook, two monographs, and many articles on Australia.

JOHN DUNCAN POWELL is a member of the Political Science faculty at Tufts University. He has published widely on the peasantry and agrarian reform in Venezuela and on the politics of clientelism. He is author of Political Mobilization of the Venezuelan Peasant.

ROBERT H.T. SMITH is Professor and Head of the Department of Geography, University of British Columbia, Vancouver. He is a former Guggenheim Fellow and has served on the staffs of Monash, Queens, and Wisconsin Universities. He received his A.B. and Ph.D. degrees in Australia, and during his appointment at Monash he chaired a panel of the Institute of Australian Geographers which prepared a brief on the distribution of Australia's population for the National Population Inquiry.

WILLIAM C. THIESENHUSEN is Professor of Agricultural Economics and Agricultural Journalism and past director of the Land Tenure Center, University of Wisconsin, Madison. He has traveled extensively in Latin America and written widely on the subject of agriculture and agrarian reform in the region. Author of Chile's Experiments in Agrarian Reform, his current research deals with the rural poor and appropriate technology in developing countries.

NANCY A. VOLGYES is a graduate student in Geography at the University of Nebraska, Lincoln. She has a special interest in rural settlement systems and government policy affecting them. She has spent three years in Hungary doing research and mastering the language.

M. GEORGE ZANINOVICH is Professor of Political Science at the University of Oregon, and has been a visiting professor at Columbia University. He has made more than ten visits to Yugoslavia, where he conducted a major survey of Yugoslav attitudes. His publications include The Development of Socialist Yugoslavia; and Comparative Communist Leadership (co-author).